COMPANION TO
THE SONG BOOK

OF

THE SALVATION ARMY

COMPANION TO
THE SONG BOOK
OF THE
SALVATION ARMY

compiled by

GORDON AVERY

SALVATIONIST PUBLISHING AND SUPPLIES, LTD.,
JUDD STREET : KING'S CROSS : LONDON, W.C.1H 9NN

© THE SALVATION ARMY 1961
First published . . . 1961
Second edition . . . 1962
Third edition . . . 1968
Fourth edition . . . 1970

SBN   85412   068   8

MADE AND PRINTED IN
GREAT BRITAIN BY THE
CAMPFIELD PRESS,
ST. ALBANS

CONTENTS

FOREWORD BY THE GENERAL

IN *The Song Book of The Salvation Army* are to be found expressions of the Christian faith drawn from men and women of diverse personality, owing allegiance to varying denominational creeds, yet finding common ground in a belief in, and love for, the Saviour of the world. Much is to be gained by some knowledge of the authorship of songs, many of which are an expression of the writer's own Christian testimony and experience.

The Salvation Army has had in its ranks over the years many gifted writers whose songs have gone far beyond the boundaries of their own lands, for when their words have been translated, as many have been into scores of different languages, and sung by Salvationists and others all over the world, the influence of their ministry has been immeasurable.

Following repeated demands from many lands for a record of the origin and history of songs used in Salvation Army meetings, the author offers the results of a life-time study of the subject. Though quite naturally stories of verses written by Salvationists are of fascinating interest in the Movement, brief notes concerning those taken over from other organizations have also been given, though most of these publish their own ' Companions ', where further details could be found.

Much of the information in this volume appears in print for the first time, and will enable leaders of meetings and other students of song to make the message of the gospel ring out with an even more convincing sound.

One could sometimes wish that it were possible to know more of the spiritual agonies in which many songs were born. More than one aspect of Army history is to be found in the songs written by Salvationists. In point of time the earlier years of our Movement saw the birth of many of our well-known songs of experience and testimony, the days of persecution saw the creation of our typically Army ' war songs ', the years that saw the stress and hunger for holy living were evidenced in the birth of songs having a depth unsurpassed in spiritual longing.

Salvationist writers are human and many of their songs came to birth when their eyes were dimmed with tears, and others in moments of great rapture, while still others were written for some special occasion, to comfort a sorrowing heart, or give courage to the soldier of Christ in his battles. Many writers were of humble birth, but God,

vii

through His Spirit, gave the power to fathom unspeakable mysteries—there was the treasure of their divine inspiration though found indeed in earthen vessels. The message demanded expression and they had courage to give it.

If the publication of such brief histories of the writers and their messages, as this limited volume can give, will help the reader to enter more fully into the longings and desires of these authors and share with them these expressions of their experiences, then such knowledge as the book imparts will not be without its everlasting gain.

Wilfred Kitching

TABLE OF SALVATION ARMY SONG AND MUSIC BOOKS

In addition to *The Christian Mission Hymn Book* (Ch.M.H.B.) and the 1878 (a revision with additions), 1899 and 1930 Salvation Army song books, the following are referred to:

Hallelujah Hymn Book, used by The Christian Mission.

Revival Music, 1876, compiled by William Booth for the use of The Christian Mission.

Salvation Army Music, 1880, a reprint of *Revival Music* with a few additions.

Salvation Music, Vol. 2, 1883, a collection of favourite songs.

Favourite Songs Supplement, 1885, a series of original Army songs which had become popular through their use by the Training Home Singing Brigade under the authority of Herbert Booth.

The Musical Salvationist, a monthly magazine of original songs first published in July, 1886.

Songs of Peace and War, a collection of the songs of Herbert and Cornelie Booth published in connection with their marriage in September, 1890.

Army Bells, 1904, a collection of songs for young people.

*   *   *

The references at the head of each set of notes concern the earliest known appearance of the song, the first Salvation Army publication to contain it and the issue of the Salvation Army song book first to include it.

THE SONG BOOK OF THE
SALVATION ARMY

*

I. All creatures of our God and King (Francis of Assisi; *translated by* William H. Draper)

Written in 1225; translated for the use of the school children for a Whitsuntide festival at Adel, Yorkshire; *School Worship* (London), 1926; *The Musical Salvationist*, September, 1939.

Francis (1182–1226), founder of the Franciscan Order, a Christian troubadour and evangelist, was one of the most extraordinary men of his age. Born in Assisi, Italy, he was the son of a wealthy Italian cloth merchant, whilst his mother has been described as ' a gentle and modest lady of noble stock '. His early life was marked by gaiety, idleness and self-indulgence, but after a severe illness when he was twenty-five years of age he devoted himself to the service of God and to suffering humanity, embracing ' poverty ' as his partner in life.

He built himself a small cell outside the city and gathered around him a few like-minded men who gave away all their personal belongings and depended for their sustenance entirely upon alms. So popular did the movement become that within ten years of its inception 5,000 men are said to have been wearing the rough brown cowl and cloak and rope girdle of the order.

Francis is also remembered for his friendship with the animals and birds.

Francis wrote these words as a sick man, prematurely aged by his service and fastings; he had suffered a real disappointment by the failure of his mission to the Sultan and to the Holy Land, which he had hoped would have been instrumental in bringing the Crusades to an end. Further, he had been warned that he was going to lose his sight. He lay, unable to endure any light on his eyes and plagued by field mice which probably had their home in the straw walls of his hut, and dictated to one of his followers. The friars learnt the words by heart and repeated them every day until the joy Francis had lost returned.

Rev. William Henry Draper, M.A. (1855–1933), was born at Kenilworth, educated at Cheltenham College and Keble College,

Oxford, and ordained in 1880. Mr. Draper wrote over sixty hymns and edited and compiled several collections.

He was Rector of Adel, Yorkshire (1899–1919); Master of the Temple, London (1920–30); then Vicar of Axbridge, Somerset.

2. All people that on earth do dwell (William Kethe)

Fourscore and Seven Psalms of David, Geneva, 1561; *Daye's Psalter* of the same year; *Scottish Psalter* of 1564; 1899 S.A. song book.

An exile, probably from Scotland, to Frankfurt (1555) and Geneva (1557), William Kethe became interested in the metrical translation of the Psalms and contributed twenty-five to the Psalter of his day. In 1561 he became Rector of Childe Okeford in Dorset, where he remained for a number of years. He died about 1593. 'All people that on earth do dwell' is a paraphrase of Psalm 100.

3. Before Jehovah's aweful throne (Isaac Watts; *altered by* John Wesley)

A paraphrase of Psalm 100 and published in the author's *Psalms of David*, 1719; John Wesley's *Charlestown Collection*, 1737; Ch.M.H.B.

Dr. Watts (1674–1748), aptly named 'The Father of Modern Hymns', was born at Southampton, the eldest of a family of nine. His father was a schoolmaster and a Dissenter who had suffered imprisonment twice on account of his religious convictions. He was in prison when Isaac was born.

After being taught Greek, Latin and Hebrew, Watts was offered a university education, but declined when he learned that this would involve his renouncing Nonconformity.

Returning home with his father one Sunday morning from the Above Bar Congregational Church, he expressed his feelings about the uninteresting singing. 'Then give us something better,' was the father's reply. Isaac determined he would, and the next Sunday took his first hymn to church where it was sung during the service. He provided a new hymn every Sunday for the next two years. Much of his *Hymns and Spiritual Songs*, published in 1707–09, was written during this period and was sung from manuscript at the Independent (later Congregational) Chapel.

In 1702 he became the pastor of Mark Lane Chapel, London. Failing health, however, caused him to retire in 1712 and he became the guest of Sir Thomas Abney at Theobald's Park, Herts., and later at Stoke Newington. The invitation for a week extended to thirty-six years, until his death.

He was buried at Bunhill Fields Burial Ground. A memorial bust stands in the south choir aisle of Westminster Abbey, and a statue in

Abney Park, Stoke Newington, on the site of the house in which Watts spent such happy years.

John Wesley (1703-91), founder of the Methodist Church, was born at Epworth and, impelled by missionary zeal, went with his brother Charles, in 1735, on an unsuccessful mission to Georgia to preach to the settlers and the Indians. In 1738 John Wesley experienced a great change of heart that ' confirmed his faith and determined his future ', and in 1739 began an apostolic life during which he travelled 250,000 miles, crossed the Irish Sea forty-two times and preached over 40,000 sermons. He died in London and was buried in the graveyard behind the City Road Methodist Church, in front of which a monument stands to his memory.

4. Fill Thou my life, O Lord my God (Horatius Bonar)

The author's *Hymns of Faith and Hope*, 3rd Series, 1866; 1930 S.A. song book.

Horatius Bonar (1808-89), son of a solicitor of excise, and said to have written about six hundred hymns, was born in Edinburgh and educated at the High School before going to the university in the same city where he received his degree of B.A. in 1832. Licensed to preach, he became the assistant minister of St. James's, Leith. Here, finding that the children of his parish disliked singing the solemn Psalms in metre, he wrote a number of hymns set to popular tunes and published them on leaflets.

Bonar was ordained minister of the North Parish Church, Kelso, in 1837; in 1853 the University of Aberdeen conferred on him the Doctorate of Divinity and he was chosen Moderator of the General Assembly of the Free Church of Scotland in 1883.

For twenty-five years he was the editor of the *Quarterly Journal of Prophecy*, publishing one of his hymns in each issue.

The secret and charm in Bonar's hymns are revealed in his words to a friend: ' I try to fill my hymns with the love and light of Christ.'

5. God of my life, through all my days (Philip Doddridge)

Written just before the author's death (see verse 3) in 1751; published by Job Orton in *Hymns founded on various texts of the Holy Scripture* in 1755 and based on Psalm 146: 2; No. 1 in *The Christian Mission Hymn Book*.

Born in London on June 26, 1702, Philip Doddridge was the twentieth child of an oilman; his mother was the daughter of an exiled Bohemian clergyman who was master of the Free School at Kingston-on-Thames. Most of the family died young; even Philip at birth was laid aside as being already dead. Orphaned at an early age, he was educated at Kingston Grammar School and at St. Albans. Later the

Duchess of Bedford offered to maintain him at Cambridge on condition that he became a member of the Established Church, but Doddridge threw in his lot with the Dissenters and concluded his studies at the Academy at Kibworth, Leicestershire. In 1723 he became the Congregational pastor at Kibworth. At the age of twenty-seven, largely persuaded by his friend Dr. Isaac Watts, he opened an academy for the training of young men for the ministry. He moved to Northampton in 1730, where he continued his theological college until he died of consumption in Lisbon on October 26, 1751.

His hymns were written to present in a brief and striking manner the principal points of his sermons and designed to be sung at the close of his services.

6. Jehovah is our strength (Samuel Barnard)

Spiritual Songs of Zion's Travellers, a collection of hymns including many by Samuel Barnard, a minister in Sheffield in 1803; 1930 S.A. song book.

7. Now thank we all our God (Martin Rinkart; *translated by* Catherine Winkworth)

Cruger's *Praxis Pietatis Melica* (1648) and probably included in the author's *Jesu Herz-Büchlein* (1636); based on Ecclesiasticus 50: 22, 23: 'Now therefore bless ye the God of all, which only doeth wondrous things everywhere, which exalteth our days from the womb, and dealeth with us according to His mercy. He grant us joyfulness of heart, and that peace may be in our days in Israel for ever.'

Miss Winkworth's translation appeared in her *Lyra Germanica* (2nd Series, 1858) and later in her *Chorale Book for England* (1863); *The Musical Salvationist*, December, 1919; 1930 S.A. song book.

Dr. Moffatt suggests that the first two verses were intended as a grace after meat to be sung by the author's household, while the last verse is a doxology.

The hymn very soon became so popular in Germany that it was used on all national occasions of thanksgiving. It was used at St. Paul's Cathedral when peace was declared after the Boer War, and at a world conference of the Women's Temperance Association held at Hastings in 1950 was sung unitedly by all the delegates using the words in their own tongue.

Martin Rinkart (1586–1649), son of a cooper, was born at Eilenburg, Saxony. Educated at the University of Leipzig, where he supported himself by his musical skill, he became Archdeacon in his native town in 1617 and remained there for the rest of his life.

During the Thirty Years' War all the clergy of the town died except Rinkart. War and plague caused so many deaths that often he had to conduct as many as fifty funerals a day. He buried about 4,480 people, including his own wife. It was during this period that his hymns were written. When peace was proclaimed in 1648 Rinkart was a prematurely aged man, worn out by overwork and terrible sufferings.

Miss Winkworth (1827–78) was born in Holborn, London, but spent most of her life in Manchester and Clifton, Bristol. She died suddenly of heart disease at Monnetier, Savoy.

8.   O Lord, I will delight in Thee (John Ryland)

Included in Dr. Rippon's *Selection* (1787); Ch.M.H.B. Written on December 3, 1777, and based on Psalm 37: 4.

Dr. John Ryland (1753–1825), son of the Rev. Collett Ryland, a Baptist pastor, was born at Warwick. The family removed to Northampton in 1759. John was converted at the age of fourteen and began to publish verse when but sixteen. In 1781 he became co-pastor with his father and five years later took sole responsibility.

Ryland was associated with Carey in organizing the Baptist Missionary Society at Kettering in 1792. Two years afterward he was appointed to the Presidency of the Baptist College, Bristol, and the pastorate of Broadmead Chapel, which duties he discharged until his death.

9.   O worship the King, all glorious above (Robert Grant)

Bickersteth's *Church Psalmody* (1833); based on Psalm 104.

Sir Robert Grant (1785–1838), born in Bengal, was the second son of Charles Grant, an eminent philanthropist and statesman. Educated at Magdalene College, Cambridge, Robert graduated B.A. in 1806 and was called to the Bar the following year. He became King's Serjeant in the Court of the Duchy of Lancaster and one of the Commissioners in bankruptcy. As a Member of Parliament he introduced a Bill granting rights to the Jews in favour of which Macaulay the historian made his maiden speech. After becoming a Privy Councillor (1831) and Judge Advocate General (1832), he received his knighthood upon the occasion of his appointment as Governor of Bombay in 1834. He died in Dapoorie, Western India.

10.   Praise God for what He's done for me! (Anonymous)

Ch.M.H.B.; *Revival Music*, where it is set to an adaptation of the secular tune 'The Mistletoe Bough' in 6–8 time, Iambic.

'An old Christian Missioner' writing in *The Bandsman and Songster*, September 12, 1908, recalled the song's being sung on the march by the

Notting Hill comrades in the early 1880s. The editor of *The War Cry* at that time was in the march and they were just singing

Once I was blind, but now I see . . .

when a dab of soft clay caught the editor in the eyes, thus nearly reversing his sentiments.

When, in April, 1931, *War Cry* readers were asked to name the song they would choose to be the last they would sing on earth, one reply contained the following:

' My last song I would choose is, " Praise God for what He's done for me! " For years I have been a terrible sufferer. Doctors have done what they can for me, and I have been given up to die more than once, yet, I still live. I cannot get about very much, but I can use my hands; I have good eyesight, so I can read. My hearing is good, so I can listen to others' troubles; I count my blessings one by one, and always try to send other comrades away with a smile. Praise God, He still helps me to sow seed for Him! '

II. Praise, my soul, the King of Heaven (Henry Francis Lyte)

A paraphrase of Psalm 103 and included in *The Spirit of the Psalter* (1834), a collection of 290 paraphrases of the Psalms in metrical verse; 1930 S.A. song book.

Henry Francis Lyte (1793–1847), author of 'Abide with me ', was born at Ednam, near Kelso. He entered Trinity College, Dublin, to study medicine, but abandoned this for theology. He received his B.A. degree in 1814 and took his first curacy, at Taghmon, near Wexford, the following year.

Owing to ill health he accepted another appointment, but before so doing passed through a remarkable spiritual experience recorded by Dr. John Appleyard of Brixham:

'A neighbouring clergyman was taken dangerously ill; Mr. Lyte visited him frequently. During these hallowed visits he was led to see the great importance of putting first things first, and whole-heartedly devoting himself to the work for which he had been solemnly set apart. . . . A higher sense of spiritual responsibility came to him, and he commenced to study the Bible more deliberately and systematically than ever before, and preach the gospel with greater zeal. From this time forth he served the Church with unabating diligence, and an ever-increasing love, demonstrating the value of rich and sincere godliness.'

In 1817 he settled in Marazion, near Penzance, and married Anne Maxwell, the only daughter of the Rev. W. Maxwell of Bath. Continued ill-health, however, necessitated further removing. In 1823 he accepted the charge of All Saints Church, Brixham. He visited the fishermen on their boats, providing Bibles for each vessel. He built up a regular attendance in his Sunday-schools of between seven and eight hundred children at a time when such activities were new in Devon. He was also an active worker in the anti-slavery campaign.

In search of health he set out for Italy in 1847 but died at Nice. On November 16, 1947, a tablet to his memory was unveiled in Westminster Abbey, close to those of Dr. Watts and the Wesleys.

12. Praise to the Holiest in the height (John Henry Newman)

Taken from the author's *Dream of Gerontius*, a poem representing his musings on the death of a dear friend. Mr. Newman was so dissatisfied with his efforts that he threw the manuscript into the wastepaper basket. Fortunately, it was discovered by someone who realized its worth. It appeared later in *Verses on Various Occasions* (1868). The repetition of the first verse at the end was made in order to turn it into a hymn. 1868 appendix of *Hymns, Ancient and Modern*; *The Musical Salvationist*, July, 1935.

John Henry Newman (1801–90), the author of ' Lead kindly Light ', was born in London into a home of marked spiritual influence and evangelical piety. While John was still a boy his father's banking business failed, but through careful economy he was sent to Trinity College, Oxford, where he graduated with honours in 1820. In 1828, four years after his ordination into the Church of England, he was appointed to St. Mary's, Oxford, and remained there for fifteen years, his distinguished preaching having a deep influence upon the University. In 1841 he wrote the famous Tract No. 90, in which he endeavoured to prove that the Articles of Religion of the Anglican Church conformed with Roman Catholic dogma. The tract caused a violent controversy and Newman was received into the Church of Rome in 1845, receiving the Cardinal's red hat in 1879. There is a statue of the Cardinal outside the Brompton Oratory, London, which he founded.

Mr. Gladstone considered it his favourite hymn next to ' Rock of Ages ', and General Gordon found comfort in the words when facing death at Khartoum.

13. Praise to the Lord, the Almighty, the King of creation
(Joachim Neander; *translated by* Catherine Winkworth (7))

Published in *Glaub und Liebesübung* (1680); based on Psalm 103 : 1–6 and Psalm 150; English translation in *Chorale Book for England* (1863); *The Musical Salvationist*, May–June, 1947.

The second verse of the song, omitted from our book, reads:

Praise to the Lord, who o'er all things so wondrously reigneth,
Shelters thee gently from harm, or when fainting sustaineth;
    Hast thou not seen
    How thy heart's wishes have been
    Granted in what He ordaineth?

Joachim Neander (1650–80), born at Bremen, as a pleasure-seeking student visited St. Martin's Church for amusement. The sermon spoke to his heart and led to his conversion, after which he associated himself with the Pietists and became a friend of Spener, the leader of the movement.

While headmaster of the Reformed Grammar School at Düsseldorf he sought, by preaching and private religious meetings, the spiritual good of his fellow citizens, but the authorities disapproved and he was suspended from office and obliged to leave the town. For some months he lived in a cave near Mettman on the Rhine and there composed some of his hymns. In 1679 he returned to Bremen as second preacher at St. Martin's Church but soon died of consumption.

14. Stand up and bless the Lord (James Montgomery)

Based on Nehemiah 9: 5 and written for the anniversary of Red Hill Wesleyan Sunday-school, Sheffield, held on March 15, 1824. The second line read 'Ye children of His choice' but Montgomery altered the line for his *Christian Psalmist*, 1825; Ch.M.H.B.

Described as the Cowper of the nineteenth century, James Montgomery (1771–1854) was born at Irvine, in Ayrshire, where his father was a Moravian minister. James commenced writing poetry in his tenth year. As editor of the Sheffield *Iris* he was twice imprisoned in York Castle for technical offences, but he used the time in producing the poems and hymns which he published in 1797 under the title *Prison Amusements*. Altogether he wrote more than four hundred hymns and metrical psalms. Although trained for the ministry it was not until his forty-third year that he made a public profession of his religion and became a member of the Moravian Church.

15. The people of God, Jehovah we praise (Charles Wesley)

Poetical Works of John and Charles Wesley, Vol. IX; 1930 S.A. song book.

Charles Wesley (1707–88), the youngest son and eighteenth child of Samuel and Susannah Wesley, was born at Epworth Rectory. Charles was taught the Lord's Prayer as soon as he could speak and on his fifth birthday Mrs. Wesley taught him the alphabet. After this he soon began to read simple passages from the Bible, and three years later entered Westminster School where his eldest brother Samuel was a teacher. Charles became, during the last of his ten years there, captain of the school. In his third year at Oxford a change took place in his spiritual experience. 'Diligence led me into serious thinking,' he wrote. 'I went to the weekly sacrament and persuaded two or three young students to accompany me and to observe the method of study prescribed by the statutes of the university. This gained me the harmless name of " Methodist ".'

In 1735, although he had intended to remain at Oxford as a tutor, he was persuaded to take Holy Orders and accompany his brother John as a missionary to Georgia.

During an illness after returning to England, Charles remembered the courage of some Moravians during a storm on the voyage and began to associate with their colleagues in London, and on Whit-Sunday, 1738, he was led to a true knowledge of Christ as his personal Saviour. He accepted a curacy in Islington, but he preached with such earnestness and insistence upon personal godliness that after nine months he was excluded from preaching in his own church. Despite the Archbishop of Canterbury's forbidding the clergy to allow either Charles or his brother John to use the churches because of their open-air preaching and similar activities, the two Wesleys continued in their God-given work throughout England, Wales and Ireland.

Charles Wesley wrote over 6,500 hymns. He was buried in Marylebone Churchyard, never having severed his connection with the Church of England.

In 1876 a monument was placed in Westminster Abbey to the memory of John and Charles Wesley.

While John Wesley was the Founder of Methodism, Charles was its hymn-writer.

16. Through all the changing scenes of life (Nahum Tate and Nicholas Brady)

Based on Psalm 34 and published in *A New Version of the Psalms of David, fitted to the Tunes used in Churches*, 1696; 1930 S.A. song book.

Nahum Tate (1652–1715), son of an Irish clergyman and born in Dublin, served as Poet Laureate under three British sovereigns. A man of intemperate habits and improvident living, he died hiding from his creditors.

Rev. Nicholas Brady (1659–1726), born at Brandon, Ireland, became Prebendary of Cork and later Chaplain to William III.

17. To God be the glory, great things He hath done! (Fanny Crosby)

Brightest and Best, 1875; *The Musical Salvationist*, September, 1928.

Frances Jane Crosby (1820–1915), a member of the Methodist Episcopal Church and writer of more than 6,000 hymns, was born at Southeast, Putnam County, New York. She became totally blind a few weeks after her birth when a doctor mistakenly applied hot poultices to her inflamed eyes.

In 1847 she became a teacher at The Institution for the Blind, New York City. Three years later she found salvation during a revival campaign while the congregation sang

> Here, Lord, I give myself away;
> 'Tis all that I can do.

In 1858 she married a blind musician, Alexander Van Alstyne.

Although Fanny Crosby did not begin her hymn-writing in earnest until she was turned forty years of age her output became so large that she used more than one *nom de plume*—' Charles Bruce ', ' Henrietta Elizabeth Blair ', ' Lizzie Edwards ' (see 758), ' Ryan Dykes ', ' Sally M. Smith '.

In February, 1913, the Cambridge (Mass.) Corps paid her a tribute. When the officer and bandsmen waited upon Dr. Campbell, with whom the author was staying, tears came to her eyes as she listened to some of her own compositions and expressed her thanks for ' this unmerited honour to a humble child of God '. During a lull in the playing she recited,

> And I shall see Him face to face,
> And tell the story, saved by grace.

Then the Salvationists marched to Dr. Campbell's church, with the doctor and Miss Crosby in a carriage, a police escort guided the procession through the crowds. At the service Miss Crosby recited a poem she had composed for the occasion.

18. What am I, O Thou glorious God (Charles Wesley (15))

Wesley's *Hymns and Sacred Poems*, 1749; Ch.M.H.B.
The original version has

> On me, the vilest reptile, me! (verse 1, line 4); and
> Which lifts poor dying worms to Heaven (verse 2, line 6).

19. What shall I render to my God (Charles Wesley (15))

The author's *Psalms and Hymns*, 1743; 1930 S.A. song book; based on the second half of Psalm 116.

20. Ye ransomed souls draw near (Charles Wesley (15))

Hymns and Sacred Poems, 1742; Ch.M.H.B.; where the verses commenced:

> Ye ransomed sinners, hear,
> The prisoners of the Lord . . .

A version almost the same as our present words appeared in *The Musical Salvationist*, December, 1903.

21. Ye servants of God, your Master proclaim (Charles Wesley (15))

Hymns for Times of Trouble and Persecution, 1744; 1930 S.A. song book.

England was at war with France and Spain. An invasion was expected daily to bring back the exiled representative of the House of Stuart and thus dethrone King George II.

The Wesleys were accused of being Papists in disguise and were brought before the magistrates for strict examination. Wesleyan preachers were the victims of false charges and persecutions, their meetings were often broken up by riots and many of their followers were pressed into military service.

An omitted verse makes special reference to those troublous days:

> Men, devils engage, the billows arise,
> And horribly rage, and threaten the skies;
> Their fury shall never our steadfastness shock,
> The weakest believer is built on a Rock.

22. All things bright and beautiful (Cecil Frances Alexander)

Hymns for Little Children, 1848, many of which were written with the purpose of making clear to children the meaning of the Apostle's Creed. More than a quarter of a million copies were sold in twenty years. This composition is based on 'I believe in God the Father Almighty, Maker of heaven and earth' and Genesis 1: 31. 1930 S.A. song book.

Miss Humphreys (1818–95), born in Co. Wicklow, Ireland, and married to the Rev. William Alexander (later Archbishop of Armagh) in 1850, began to write when she was nine but, belonging to a household where children were not allowed to assert themselves, she used to hide her poems under the carpet. Her father, hearing of her efforts, instituted a box for their reception, the contents of which she read aloud on Saturday evenings.

In Londonderry she was well known in the slums of the city. She visited the poor, took a keen interest in the Institute of District Nurses and daily attended the morning service in the cathedral. Her circle of friends included Dean Stanley, Matthew Arnold, Bishop Wilberforce and Bishop Wordsworth.

23. Begin, my tongue, some heavenly theme (Isaac Watts (3))

Hymns and Spiritual Songs, 1707; Ch.M.H.B.

24. For the beauty of the earth (Folliott Sandford Pierpoint)

Orby Shipley's *Lyra Eucharistica*, 1864; *Songs for the Home League*, 1949.

Mr. Pierpoint (1835–1917) was born at Bath and was for a time classics master at the Somersetshire College. Later he lived mainly at Babbacombe.

This hymn was originally intended to be sung at the celebration of Holy Communion, the fifth line of each verse reading, ' Christ, our God, to Thee we raise '.

25. God moves in a mysterious way (William Cowper)

Newton's *Twenty-six Letters on Religious Subjects; to which are added Hymns, &c., by Omicron*, 1774; *Olney Hymns*, 1779; Ch.M.H.B.

There is a popular tradition that William Cowper felt it was the will of God that he should offer his life as a sacrifice as Abraham was prepared to offer up his son Isaac. He ordered a post-chaise and instructed the driver to take him to a spot on the River Ouse. Owing to fog, however, the driver was unable to find the desired place and so had to take the poet back home, whereupon he composed these verses.

William Cowper (1731–1800), son of Dr. John Cowper, Chaplain to George II, was born at Berkhampsted, Herts. He was called to the Bar in 1754, obtained the office of Reading Clerk and Clerk of the Committees of the House of Lords, and in 1762 was appointed Clerk to the Journals. Unfortunately, his mind lost its balance and he was placed under the care of Dr. Nathaniel Cotton, who had a private asylum at St. Albans. While there he came into a personal relationship with the Saviour after casually picking up a Bible and reading Romans 3: 25.

Upon his recovery Cowper went to Huntingdon, and later to Olney, Bucks, at the invitation of the Rev. John Newton, with whom he collaborated in parochial and evangelistic work and in the production of what became known as the *Olney Hymns*. This collection included sixty-eight of Cowper's hymns and 280 of Newton's. Cowper died of dropsy at East Dereham.

The Rev. Arthur E. Gregory once remarked: ' Cowper is one of the great hymn-writers who ranks with the great poets. . . . Had Cowper never written a hymn he would have had fame sufficient as a poet; had he never written a poem he would still have lived through his immortal hymns.'

26. I'll praise my Maker while I've breath (Isaac Watts (3))

A version of Psalm 146 from *The Psalms of David*, 1719.

One of John Wesley's favourites; he used it in the last service he conducted at the City Road Chapel, on February 22, 1791. During the Tuesday night, before his death on the Wednesday, he was heard to repeat these words over and over again until, strength failing, he could but say, ' I'll praise—I'll praise— '.

27. Let us with a gladsome mind (John Milton)

Written in 1623, a paraphrase of Psalm 136, the words appeared in Milton's *Poems in English and Latin*, 1645; 1930 S.A. song book.

Milton (1608–74), author of *Paradise Lost* for which he received £18, was born in Bread Street, London, and educated at St. Paul's School and Cambridge. He commenced writing poetry at the age of ten. In 1648 he was appointed Latin Secretary of the Council of Foreign Affairs under the Commonwealth. He lost his sight four years later.

Milton was a staunch Puritan and became Britain's champion of liberty at a time when she was in danger of losing her freedom. 'The world's liberty owes as much to his mighty pen as to Cromwell's weighty sword.' He was one of our literary giants, being described as 'second only to Shakespeare in his mastery of the English tongue'. His one contribution to our song book, written whilst he was still a scholar at St. Paul's School, originally extended to twenty-four verses.

28. Come, let us all unite to sing (Howard Kingsbury)

Ch.M.H.B.

29. Eternal God, we look to Thee (James Merrick)

The author's *Poems on Sacred Subjects*, 1765; 1930 S.A. song book.

James Merrick (1720–69), born at Reading, was a Church of England minister who on account of his delicate health was unable to take a pastoral charge.

30. Father, whose everlasting love (Charles Wesley (15))

Hymns on God's Everlasting Love, 1741; 1930 S.A. song book.

Here is a relic of the controversy between the Wesleys and the Calvinists; it originally extended to twenty-seven verses. The Wesleys believed and preached the fact of God's 'all-embracing love'. Charles emphasized this same truth in his hymns. In this one he used the terms 'everlasting love', 'grace for all', 'the world to save', 'who died for all', 'Saviour of mankind', 'undistinguishing regard', 'sufficient, sovereign, saving grace'. It was one of their last onslaughts against those who would limit the grace of God. In the original, references to the teaching of salvation for all were printed in italics.

31. God gave His Son for me (Charles Fry)

Favourite Songs Supplement; 1930 S.A. song book.

Charles Fry, the Army's first Bandmaster, was born in Wiltshire on May 29, 1837. Both his father and grandfather were builders.

At an early age Charles and his brothers became very fond of music and each learned to play one or more instruments. The singing at the Wesleyan Chapel where the Frys worshipped was led by a small orchestra, and Charles was appointed conductor while also playing 1st cornet in the band of the local Volunteer Rifle Corps. ' Music was a passion and his cornet was his idol,' his son Fred wrote later, ' but the idol led him to the true God. At that chapel they always held a prayer meeting at the close of the ordinary service, but father never stayed to this meeting. One Sunday night, however, Mr. Arthur Mussell stopped father as he was leaving, held him in conversation and took hold of his cornet. After a little talk he persuaded him to stay to the after-meeting, in which he found salvation.' Charles was then seventeen years of age.

When The Christian Mission commenced work in Salisbury in March, 1878, Charles was a master builder and his three sons were in the business with him. He had taught them all to play instruments. The persecutions to which these early Missioners were subjected made an appeal to Charles Fry and he offered the services of his family to help in the outdoor meetings and on any special occasions.

The power of brass band music was apparent as they assisted the Founder in his campaigns. Early in 1880 they accompanied him to South Wales and to the Midlands and later assisted at the opening of the Marylebone Theatre in London.

The Founder then requested that they should assist him during the Whitsuntide season, but Charles said he would either have to give up his business career or cease to go on these tours. The Founder suggested he prayed about the matter; and Charles soon sold his business and offered the family for whole-time service in the Army.

They arrived in London on May 14, 1880, and immediately commenced their special duties, rendering faithful service themselves and inspiring their comrades to form bands all over the country. Bandmaster Fry's service was short for he died on August 24, 1882, at Park Hall, Polmont, where Mr. Livingstone Learmouth had made a home for Fry and his wife, and was buried in the Necropolis Cemetery, Glasgow.

Regarding Fry's song-writing Lieut.-Colonel Richard Slater wrote: ' His power of expression made his singing arrestive. It was the power of religion, the outcome of a personal fellowship with God, which gave him his emotional force as a vocalist. He was a song-writer and often set words to simple melodies. . . . He drew from personal experience the matter for his verses.'

32. God loved the world of sinners lost (Martha M. Stockton)

Hallelujah Hymn Book; Revival Music; 1878 S.A. song book.

Miss Martha Brustar (1821–85) married the Rev. W. G. Stockton of Ocean City, New Jersey. As a girl one hot afternoon in the west of

America she was alone in a farmhouse when a Red Indian squaw, with her papoose (baby) strapped on her back, called and asked for some bread and water. These were readily given and the visitor began to tell her story. Having lost her husband in some tribal fighting, she was on her way to her father's village in the far west. The Indian then spoke of a missionary from Canada who had visited her husband's village and told the people the story of God's love. The simple manner of the squaw led the girl to spend her life in making known the same good news, and in 1871 the memory of that experience and the words of the visitor were embodied in this song.

33. God's love to me is wonderful (Sidney E. Cox)

The Musical Salvationist, June, 1932; first sung by the author, together with Commissioner Damon and Lieut.-Colonel Fitton, in the Orlando Sanitorium, Florida, at the bedside of a veteran Army officer.

Born in Northampton on June 29, 1887, Sidney Cox moved to Canada in 1907. At the age of twenty-one he was converted in the Central Methodist Church, Calgary, Canada, and almost immediately joined the Army corps in that city. He entered the training college in 1909, and served as an officer in Canada for about ten years until he was transferred to the U.S.A. Southern Territory. There he laboured as Territorial Young People's Secretary, Education Secretary, Training Principal, and finally as Territorial Revivalist with the rank of Brigadier, until his resignation in 1944 to take up other evangelistic work.

His first song, ' You can tell out the sweet story ', was published in 1914, since when he has continued to write words and melodies which he himself describes as ' simple, singable and scriptural '.

34. O God, my God, in whom combine (*translated from the German by* John Wesley (3))

Hymns and Sacred Poems, 1739; 1930 S.A. song book.

35. The King of love my Shepherd is (Henry Williams Baker)

The appendix of *Hymns Ancient and Modern*, 1868; *The Musical Salvationist*, September, 1910.

Sir Henry W. Baker (1821–77), eldest son of Vice-Admiral Sir H. L. Baker, was born in London, and became Vicar of Monkland, near Leominster, in 1851. He was the chairman of the committee responsible for the production of *Hymns Ancient and Modern*. He quoted the words of verse three just before he died.

36. The Lord's my Shepherd, I'll not want

Scottish Psalter, 1650; *The Musical Salvationist*, February, 1904; 1930 S.A. song book. Cannot be attributed to any one person.

Marion Harvey, a servant girl of twenty, when on her way to execution at Edinburgh with Isabel Allison, for having attended the preaching of Donald Gasgill and for helping his escape, said, as they were being pestered by a curate with his prayers, 'Come Isabel, let's sing the 23rd Psalm.'

37. What shall I do my God to love (Charles Wesley (15))

Hymns and Sacred Poems, 1749; based on Ephesians 3: 17, 18, and originally commencing:

> Infinite, unexhausted Love!
> (Jesus and love are one:)
> If still to me Thy bowels move,
> They are restrained to none.

38. All hail the power of Jesus' name! (Edward Perronet; *altered by* John Rippon)

The first verse was published in *The Gospel Magazine*, November, 1779, where the following April the complete song appeared; Ch.M.H.B. The verses were suggested to the author's mind after the Coronation of King George III.

Edward Perronet (1726–92), son of a Church of England clergyman, came from a French family which had settled in England in 1680. He became associated with the Wesleys, to whom he was known by the familiar name of 'Ned', and later with the Countess of Huntingdon's movement. He died in Canterbury, where he was minister of an Independent Chapel, and was buried in the cloisters of the cathedral.

Dr. John Rippon (1751–1836) was born at Tiverton, Devon, and was for over sixty years minister of the Baptist congregation in Carter's Lane, Tooley Street (afterward New Park Street), London.

39. Christ is our corner-stone (*translated by* John Chandler)

A Latin hymn of the sixth or seventh century translated in *Hymns of the Primitive Church*, 1837; 1930 S.A. song book.

John Chandler (1806–76), son of a Church of England clergyman, was born at Witley, Godalming, Surrey. He took Holy Orders in 1831 and became Vicar of Witley in 1837.

40. Come, let us join our cheerful songs (Isaac Watts (3) (verses))

Hymns and Spiritual Songs, 1707; Ch.M.H.B.; based on Revelation 5: 11–13. Chorus: *The Juvenile Harmonist*, 1843.

41. How sweet the name of Jesus sounds (John Newton (verses))

Olney Hymns, Book 1, 1779; Ch.M.H.B.

Son of a sea-going Captain, John Newton (1725–1807) went to sea with his father at the age of eleven and soon became notorious for his wickedness. For a time he became an avowed atheist and took a delight in blaspheming the name of God. Once when he overstayed leave from his ship he was caught by the press gang, and later, after deserting his ship, was flogged. During a voyage home from West Africa he read Stanhope's *Thomas à Kempis*. That night a terrible storm arose and all feared the vessel would be overwhelmed. Newton's whole former life passed in review before him and he was awakened to his need of a Saviour. For the rest of his life Newton observed March 10th as a day of humiliation and thanksgiving for his ' great deliverance '. ' In evil long I took delight ' refers to his experience.

In February, 1750, he married Mary Catlett, whom he had loved for eight years. After his marriage he became captain of a slave ship, devoting his leisure to the study of religion and the Bible. Those serving under him felt the effect of his new way of life; swearing was repressed and two religious services were held on board every Sunday. Later he realized the horror of slavery and did his utmost to expose the cruelty of the trade. In 1764 he became curate of Olney, Buckinghamshire, where, during a fifteen years' ministry, he wrote a new hymn every week for the Tuesday night prayer meeting. For the remaining twenty-seven years of his life he was rector of St. Mary Woolnoth, Lombard Street, London.

When General and Mrs. Carpenter visited Egypt in 1946 and stood in the king's chamber of the largest of the pyramids, the guide revealed the acoustic properties of the room by shouting a word that echoed and re-echoed. Then he asked the visitors to sing and they replied with ' How sweet the name of Jesus sounds '.

42. I know Thee who Thou art (Albert Orsborn)

The War Cry, November 5, 1949.

Son of officers, General Albert Orsborn (1886–1967) became an officer from the Clapton Congress Hall in 1905. After serving as a corps, divisional and training officer he became Chief Secretary in New Zealand, Territorial Commander for Scotland and Ireland, and British Commissioner. In June, 1946, he became the General. His story is told in his autobiography, *The House of my Pilgrimage*.

It was at the first corps cadet camp, held at the Hadleigh Land and Industrial Colony, that Albert Orsborn made the consecration which involved the deliberate surrender of his life for service in the Army's ranks.

'I think it was a natural process,' writes the General regarding his song-writing. 'I had inherited, probably from my father, an instinct for the rhythm and music of poetry. The creative desire wakened in me whilst I was quite a boy. I wrote for the love of it, with no thought of an audience. Nothing serious was attempted until my early teens. I was a corps cadet at the time. *The War Cry* came out with a competition for young song-writers. The theme was to be something suitable for use in the open air; the tune to be one well known in The Salvation Army. The prize, one pound sterling, was a great attraction to the junior clerk, but the chase was even more attractive than the goal. My young heart longed to express itself in service, and especially in praise and song, and I set to work. After much labour I produced a song which I have long since forgotten. After a seemingly interminable delay, during which—as I afterward discovered—the then editor scoured the files and song books to discover if the young writer was guilty of plagiarism, I received the prize. And I was thereby well and truly launched on my song-writing career.

'The really serious part of my song-writing commenced in my training days. It was part of my consecration. Our Principal, Commissioner T. Henry Howard, knowing my proclivity to rhyming in the lighter and even satirical vein, one day talked seriously to me about my responsibilities to God, the result of which was the consecration of my talents and my promise that my poetry would be a practical expression of my consecration. Long, long since I came to understand how little I had to offer my Lord, but I praise His dear name that from my training garrison days until now I have been enabled to keep my promise, in the spirit of the words:

> I have not much to give Thee, Lord,
> But all I have is Thine.

From the time of my full consecration, when I gave my all, my Beloved Master has lent me the talent to be used in His service. The full flood-tide of opportunity came through the central holiness meetings at the old Congress Hall, Clapton, from 1912 onwards. Many songs and choruses of those days have passed into the currency of Salvation Army singing. But perhaps the deepest seal on the cadet's consecration was reserved for the officers' council days, when it was my privilege to offer my Lord the songs, "In the secret of Thy presence", and "Except I am moved with compassion", and some others.

'There is only one theme worth singing about and it is inexhaustible —" Worthy is the Lamb!"'

'"I know Thee who Thou art",' according to the author's own words, 'grew out of the ploughshare of suffering. Once the theme got started . . . I could not stop it flowing, though the third verse was born out of due time, for it came after the verse numbered four. . . . It is the song of which the last verse is my own favourite; I often sing it to myself as a private prayer.' This is the only song by General Orsborn in our song book to which he himself has provided the musical setting.

43. Jesus, I love Thy charming name (Philip Doddridge (5) (verses))

Ch.M.H.B.; based on 1 Peter 2: 7 and written on October 23, 1717. Chorus: *The Juvenile Harmonist*, 1843.

44. Jesus, the name high over all (Charles Wesley (15) (verses))

Wesley's *Hymns and Sacred Poems*, 1749; Ch.M.H.B. Originally twenty-two verses.

In 1744 Charles Wesley was preaching in Laneast in Cornwall, denouncing the drunken habits of the people and urging them to repentance, when a man began to blaspheme and to contradict the preacher. 'Who is this that pleads for the devil?' exclaimed Wesley. The blasphemer stood up and Wesley exposed the man's sin with such tremendous power that he was driven from the service—' and devils fear and fly '.

David Garrick, the famous actor, often went to hear George Whitefield preach. He said on one occasion, referring to the fourth verse, that he would give £100 if only he could say ' O ' like Mr. Whitefield.

Almost the last words which General Bramwell Booth uttered to his wife before lapsing into unconsciousness were: ' Darling, the name of Jesus—His beautiful name—a name to live by and a name to die by ' —a commentary upon the last verse.

45. Jesus, the very thought of Thee (*attributed* to Bernard of Clairvaux; *translated by* Edward Caswall)

Translation in Caswall's *Lyra Catholica*, 1849; Ch.M.H.B.

Bernard (1091-1153), born at Fontaines, near Dijon, France, of a knightly family, joined the Cistercian Monastery of Citeaux, Burgundy, at the age of twenty-two. Within three years Citeaux was full to overflowing and Bernard was appointed abbot of a new monastery called the Valley of Wormwood, in Champagne, but which was changed by Bernard to ' Clairvaux', meaning the ' Bright Valley '. All classes of people would flock from long distances to his quiet retreat to seek his counsel and hear him preach. It was Bernard's wonderful eloquence that inspired the second crusade in 1146, the complete failure of which left him a broken man. His dying counsel to his monks was ' to abound more and more in every good work '.

Edward Caswall (1814–78), born at Yateley Vicarage, in Hampshire, was educated at Oxford and took orders in the Church of England in 1838, but followed Newman into the Roman Catholic Church in 1850. For twenty-eight years he ministered to the sick and cared for the needy at Edgbaston, Birmingham.

46. Let earth and heaven agree (Charles Wesley (15))

Wesley's *Hymns on God's Everlasting Love*, 1741; Ch.M.H.B.

This, as No. 30, is one of Wesley's hymns written during the controversy with the Calvinists. Neither of the Wesleys could brook any doctrine that limited in any way the ' universal love ' of Christ.

When writing to his wife from Dublin in September, 1748, he said: 'At five I went forth to an innumerable multitude, and the Lord astonished me with the power He gave me. . . . For two hours I spoke with a trumpet voice and the hearts of all were bowed before the Lord.'

' With a trumpet voice '; but what was the subject-matter? Surely, we have a suggestion in the last two lines of this song!

47. O for a thousand tongues to sing (Charles Wesley (15))

Hymns and Sacred Poems, 1740; Ch.M.H.B.; written in 1739 to commemorate the first anniversary of the author's conversion. He had consulted Peter Böhler, the Moravian who had so much to do with leading both the Wesleys into their new-found experience, about praising Christ. Böhler had replied, ' Had I a thousand tongues I would praise Him with them all.'

Verse four (there were originally eighteen) was a favourite with William Booth. It was for the words of this verse that he personally introduced the tune ' Grimsby ' (*The Salvation Army Tune Book*, No. 66).

48. Of all in earth or Heaven (Nathan Aldersley)

The New Zealand *War Cry*, April 1, 1893; *The Musical Salvationist*, October, 1897; 1930 S.A. song book.

Nathan Atkinson Aldersley (1826–99) was converted before reaching the age of seventeen, and at eighteen was a Methodist local preacher. After joining the Army in Keighley, Yorkshire, he went to New Zealand in 1884 and became a soldier at Christchurch and later at Wellington.

For a number of years, crippled with rheumatism, he would be wheeled to the meetings in his bath chair. During this period and later when bedridden he wrote a number of songs which became extremely popular.

49. Take the name of Jesus with you (Lydia Baxter)

Pure Gold, 1871; 1878 S.A. song book.

Mrs. Baxter (1809-74), an American Baptist born at Petersburg, New York, was an invalid for many years. Her sick-room became a 'centre for gatherings of Christian workers who came to her for inspiration or advice'. She was a prolific writer and published a volume of her own in 1855.

Mrs. Lieut.-Colonel Thomas Bridson recalls a patient in an Army leper colony in Indonesia who had once been imprisoned but had since become a Salvationist.

'Gifted with a beautiful voice, he charmed us many times with his solos. One evening, when sickness prevented his attending meetings other than in the wards, he sang very feelingly a free translation of "Take the name of Jesus with you", then gave his testimony, saying he was glad he had become a leper as he would never have heard the name of Jesus in his own village.

'This made such an impression in that small meeting that two patients publicly dedicated themselves to God's service when he had finished speaking. The following Sunday a little company gathered round an open grave wherein his mutilated body was tenderly laid to rest whilst the words of his last solo were sung by his fellow-patients.'

50. The great Physician now is near (William Hunter)

Ch.M.H.B.; present version (with additional verses) in *Revival Music*,

Dr. Hunter (1811–77), born near Ballymoney, Northern Ireland, when six years of age emigrated to America with his parents. He became the editor of two religious journals, author of about 125 songs, Professor of Hebrew in Alleghany College, and subsequently minister of the Methodist Episcopal Church, in Alliance, Ohio.

A railway accident in which many persons were killed or injured provided the author with the theme of this song. Four or five medical men happened to be on the train and they, with their timely aid, were instrumental in saving the lives of many who would otherwise have died.

51. There is a name I love to hear (Frederick Whitfield (verses))

1855 in leaflet form; *Sacred Poems and Prose*, 1861; *The Musical Salvationist*, September, 1913; 1930 S.A. song book.

The author was born at Threapwood, Shropshire, in 1829 and wrote these words while being educated at Trinity College, Dublin. He commenced his ministry in the Church of England in 1859 as curate of Otley, Yorkshire, later serving at Kirby Ravensworth, Greenwich, Bexley and Hastings. He also filled the office of Association Secretary for the Irish Church Missions. He died at Croydon in 1904

52. There is beauty in the name of Jesus (Will. J. Brand)

The Musical Salvationist, January, 1945; written to music composed in August, 1944, by Colonel Bramwell Coles.

Born in Chatham in August, 1889, of Salvationist parents, Will. Brand spent his childhood in Dover where he became a chorister at Christ Church. Later he became a junior soldier and corps cadet before transferring to Folkestone and then to Gravesend. For a time he worked at International Headquarters. Later he turned to engineering and in 1924 qualified for the Diploma of the Institute of Cost and Works Accountants. At one time Will. Brand was Deputy Songster Leader of Catford Corps and is still a commissioned songster. He was a member of the Song Book Revision Council.

Referring to his song-writing he writes: 'I was launched into Army song-writing through the visit of Mrs. Vickery to our home. She was the wife of Songster Leader Vickery whose brigade was visiting our corps. Showing her some verses I had written for my own pleasure she counselled me to send them to her brother (then) Brigadier Alfred Gilliard, editor of *The War Cry,* who passed them to Brigadier (later Colonel) Bramwell Coles. Since then more than one hundred and forty songs have been passed for publication by the International Music Board.'

53. Thou hidden source of calm repose (Charles Wesley (15))

Hymns and Sacred Poems, 1749; Ch.M.H.B.

54. A light came out of darkness (William A. Hawley)

Written in Calgary, Canada, and first published in *The Musical Salvationist,* October, 1901; 1930 S.A. song book.

Envoy Hawley (1870–1929) was born at Bellville, Ontario, Canada, into a Christian home, and lived for many years at Campbellford, near Peterborough, Ontario. At the age of eleven he was taking his place at the organ in the local Methodist Church and at fifteen was leader of the choir. After studying medicine in Toronto he turned to music in Boston, where he stayed several years as a student, then as a teacher in one of the conservatories. Owing to an accident to the fourth finger of the left hand he had to forsake the organ and concentrate on piano tuning. Removing to Charlottetown, Prince Edward Island, 'Professor' Hawley (as he was familiarly called by his associates) found congenial employment and became organist and choir leader and commenced composing anthems for the choir. Every Sunday afternoon he sang to the patients in the County Hospital.

One day he attended an Army meeting attracted primarily by the clear musical voice of an officer, whose self-sacrifice led Hawley to become a Salvationist. His first Army song, ' From the General down to me ', was written in 1898 and was later included by Colonel Arthur Goldsmith in his selection, ' The Banner of Liberty '.

Moving to Winnipeg, Hawley interested himself in the social service side of the Rupert Avenue Corps. For two winters he assisted with meetings at the Coffee House on Logan Avenue, and in the Police Court. The last twelve years of his life were spent at Calgary.

55. Have you ever heard the story (Mrs. S. Z. Kaufman.)

1899 S.A. song book.

56. Jesus laid His glory by (John Lawley)

1899 S.A. song book; written when travelling with William Booth in Holland.

John Lawley (1859–1922), born in the village of Foulden, Norfolk, was the fourth child of a farm labourer who earned nine shillings a week. To eke out those scanty earnings members of the family would, as soon as they could walk, help by hunting for mushrooms and assisting with the fruit and potato harvests. At eight years of age John became a member of a threshing-machine party and later moved with the family to Bradford, where there was to be had abundant work and better wages.

With more money at her disposal Mrs. Lawley sent John to school, but he had no liking for lessons and once more went to work, first with a spinning firm and then as an engine cleaner in a mill where he ultimately had charge of the engine.

One drizzling night a man wearing oilskins offered John a handbill in Westgate, Bradford, and said: ' God bless you, my boy. Tomorrow night in Pullan's Theatre there'll be a casting out of devils by the power of the Holy Ghost. You come.' The man was James Dowdle of The Christian Mission and in that meeting John was converted. Nine months later he was appointed the fortieth evangelist of The Christian Mission. As A.D.C. to both the Founder and General Bramwell Booth he will ever be remembered. With them he travelled the world, leading their prayer-meetings, singing solos and pleading with sinners and guiding them into the Kingdom.

' He had no musical education or training,' wrote Lieut.-Colonel Richard Slater, ' but sang as naturally as do the lark and blackbird. He had those inborn gifts which go to make a successful singer, both as soloist and as a leader of singing in congregations. He was always more or less employed in working out a song, using notebooks or odd pieces of paper for preserving lines, verses and forms of a chorus for a song on a subject which had fixed his attention. He would turn the subject over and over until he found the particular word to move the heart, for he considered it more important to kindle the feeling than to convey knowledge or rouse interest by an intellectual presentation of religious truths.'

57. Jesus, Thy far-extended fame (Charles Wesley (15))

Hymns and Sacred Poems, 1749; 1930 S.A. song book, where the first verse began 'Jesus, Thy great and glorious fame'; based on Hebrews 13: 8. Originally there were twelve verses.

58. Our sufferings, Lord, to Thee are known (Charles Wesley (15))

Hymns and Sacred Poems, 1740; 1899 S.A. song book; written amidst the stress of temptation. Originally there were twenty verses.

59. Tell me the old, old story (Katherine Hankey)

Published in full in 1867 by William Macintosh; *Revival Music;* 1899 S.A. song book.

Miss Hankey (1834–1911), born in Clapham, London, was the daughter of a banker and member of the group of Evangelicals known as 'The Clapham Sect'. While still a girl Kate, with her sister, commenced teaching in a Sunday-school at Croydon, and at eighteen started a Bible class in London for the girl assistants in some of the large shops in the West End. Her influence was lasting, and five of those girls met at her funeral fifty years after the class had ceased. A visit to South Africa to nurse and bring back home an invalid brother, at a time when travel up-country could be accomplished only in a bullock-wagon, inspired her with an interest in foreign missions, to which she devoted the proceeds of her writings. She published a volume of Bible class teachings, a booklet on confirmation, and a collection of her hymns under the title of *The Old, Old, Story and Other Verses* (1879). Her later years were spent in hospital visitation and other good works.

Of ' Tell me the old, old story ', originally a fifty-five-verse poem of four lines each, Miss Hankey wrote: ' I wrote Part 1 toward the end of January, 1866. I was just recovering from a severe illness and the second verse really indicated my state of health, for I was literally " weak and weary ". When I had written the first part, which consisted of eight verses, I laid it aside and it was not until the following November that I completed the whole hymn.' The first part was entitled ' The story wanted ', the second part, ' The story told '.

Dr. William Doane, who wrote the melody, was attending a Y.M.C.A. convention in Montreal when an English general named Russell read the words from a paper. As he proceeded tears rolled down his cheeks. The words and the manner of their delivery made a profound impression upon Mr. Doane, who obtained a copy and later, when travelling in a stage coach in the White Mountains, composed the music.

When the Winnipeg Citadel Band visited Ottawa in 1938 the Prime Minister of Canada, the Right Hon. W. L. Mackenzie King, asked for 'Tell me the old, old story' because it was his mother's favourite hymn.

60. Tell me the story of Jesus (Fanny Crosby (17))

Sankey's *Sacred Songs and Solos*; *The Musical Salvationist*, June, 1916.

61. Thou art the Way: to Thee alone (George Washington Doane)

The author's *Songs by the Way*, 1824; 1930 S.A. song book; based on John 14: 6.

Bishop Doane (1799–1859) was born in Trenton, New Jersey, U.S.A., graduated at Union College, Schenectady, was ordained in 1821 and became assistant minister of Trinity Church, New York. From 1824 to 1828 he was Professor of Belles Lettres in Trinity College, Hartford, Conn., and in 1828 became rector of Trinity Episcopal Church, Boston, a pulpit later occupied by Phillips Brooks. At the age of thirty-three Doane was appointed Bishop of New Jersey. One of his most famous contributions, 'Fling Out the Banner!' was written in 1848 when students of a girls' school asked him to prepare some verses appropriate for a flag-raising ceremony.

62. Who is He in yonder stall (Benjamin R. Hanby)

The Dove, a Collection of Music for Day and Sunday Schools, Chicago, 1866; *Sacred Songs and Solos*; *The Musical Salvationist*, December, 1939.

Benjamin Hanby (1833–67), an American minister, was born in the state of Ohio, U.S.A., and for some years wrote vocal music for the firm of Root and Cadby in Chicago. His most popular number was probably the words of 'Darling Nellie Gray', for which his sister wrote the music (No. 359 in *The Salvation Army Tune Book*).

63. Alas! and did my Saviour bleed (Isaac Watts (3) (verses); Asa Hull (chorus))

Hymns and Spiritual Songs, 1707; Ch.M.H.B.

Asa Hull was an American author who composed the tune 'Remember me'.

In November, 1850, Fanny Crosby was converted in New York. She had been anxious about her spiritual condition and, referring to the singing of 'Here, Lord, I give myself away' (a line from this song), she wrote, 'My very soul was flooded with celestial light; I sprang to my feet shouting "Hallelujah!" and then for the first time realized that I had been trying to hold the world in one hand and the Lord with the other.'

The Rev. Edward Payson Hammond, author of No. 257, was converted during the singing of these words.

64. All ye that pass by (Charles Wesley (15))

Wesley's *Pocket Hymn Book for the Use of Christians of All Denominations*; *Hymns and Sacred Poems*, 1748; Ch.M.H.B.

65. Arise, my soul, arise (Charles Wesley (15))

Hymns and Sacred Poems, 1742; Ch.M.H.B.

66. Behold! behold the Lamb of God (Joseph Hoskins)

Ch.M.H.B.

For ten years Joseph Hoskins (1745–88) was Congregational minister at Castle Green, Bristol, and during the last three years of his life wrote nearly four hundred hymns.

67. Behold Him now on yonder tree (George S. Smith)

Written in 1887 and published in *The Musical Salvationist*, June, 1891; 1930 S.A. song book.

Bandmaster Smith, a foreman shoemaker, of Kingswood Corps, Bristol, formed a band in 1881 when instruments were difficult to obtain and suitable music very limited. His first song appeared in the first volume of *The Musical Salvationist*, and during the next few years he contributed such numbers as 'Thou art a mighty Saviour' and 'Now I am trusting in Jesus'.

Following those days George Smith was for many years a lay missioner of the London Wesleyan Mission.

68. Behold the Saviour of mankind (Samuel Wesley)

John Wesley's *Psalms and Hymns*, Charlestown, South Carolina, 1736–7; Ch.M.H.B.

Samuel Wesley (1662–1735), father of John and Charles Wesley and for thirty-six years Rector of Epworth, was born at Whitchurch, near Blandford, Dorset, and educated at Dorchester, Newington Green, London, and Exeter College, Oxford. He was ordained in 1689 and married Susanna, daughter of the Rev. Dr. Samuel Annesley, the following year. After a short period as chaplain on board a man-of-war, he entered, in 1693, the living of South Ormsby, Lincs.

On the night of February 9, 1709, there were sleeping in one room of the Epworth Rectory, John Wesley (then five years of age), three of his sisters, and Charles and his nurse, when the place caught fire. The nurse, picking up the baby, fled from the room, calling upon the other children to follow. They all did so but John, who was fast asleep. When he awoke he found the ordinary means of escape cut off and went to the window. His father made two attempts to reach him by the stairs, but was beaten by the flames. As there was no time to bring a ladder one man stood on the shoulders of others and was just able to reach the trapped boy a few moments before the house collapsed. 'Come, neighbours,' cried the Rector, as he clasped John in his arms, 'let us thank God; He has given me all my children; let the house go, I am rich enough.'

Next day there was discovered in the grounds a scrap of paper, charred but still decipherable, bearing the words of ' Behold the Saviour of mankind '. It had, apparently, been laid on a table near a window and been blown out during the fire.

There were two more verses in the original.

69. Dark was the hour, Gethsemane (— Gatham)

Song Life for Sunday Schools by Philip Phillips (The Sunday School Union, London, 1872); *Revival Music*; 1878 S.A. song book.

70. Hail, Thou once despisèd Jesus (John Bakewell)

Poetical Tracts (1757–74); Ch.M.H.B.

Born at Brailsford, Derbyshire, John Bakewell (1721–1819), great-grandfather of Dr. William Moulton, became an ardent evangelist at the age of eighteen and one of Wesley's preachers ten years later. For some time he was the master of the Greenwich Royal Park Academy.

The author's tombstone in the City Road Chapel burial ground, in London, states that he ' adorned the doctrine of God our Saviour 80 years and preached His glorious gospel about 70 '.

71. Hark, my soul! it is the Lord (William Cowper (25))

Maxfield's *New Appendix*, 1768; Ch.M.H.B.; based on John 21: 16.

72. In the Cross of Christ I glory (John Bowring)

The author's *Hymns*, 1825; based on Galatians 6: 14.

Sir John Bowring (1792–1872) was born at Exeter, and educated at the Grammar School, Moretonhampstead, Devonshire, before entering his father's woollen goods manufacturing business. Before he was sixteen John was able to speak and write in Spanish, Italian, Portuguese, French and German, and later to translate from twenty-five languages. He published *Specimens of Russian Poets* and *Danish and Norwegian Literature*, and translations from the Bohemian, Bulgarian, Slavonic, Servian and Polish. He introduced the florin into British currency, became editor of *The Westminster Review* when only thirty-three years of age and in 1835 became M.P. for Kilmarnock, Scotland, and was able to make a notable contribution to the cause of prison reform. He served his country in capacities as various as Commissioner to France, Consul at Canton, Governor of Hong Kong and Minister Pleni-potentiary to China, received his LL.D. degree from Groningen University, Holland, and was knighted in 1854.

Bowring is thought to have been inspired to pen his popular hymn while travelling down the coast of China to Macao, where several centuries earlier Catholic missionaries and Chinese Christians had erected a stately cathedral on a high point overlooking the sea. Many years before the author's visit, however, a hurricane had destroyed the sacred building though the tower had withstood the tempest. This tower was surmounted by a triumphant cross which silhouetted against the sky far above the wreckage strewn on the shore below. The cross appeared to defy destruction. To Bowring, as he gazed upward from the vessel on which he was sailing, that cross seemed to bear witness to the victorious and eternal nature of all those things symbolized by the Cross of Christ.

73. It is the Blood that washes white (William Pearson)

The War Cry, February 23, 1881; 1899 S.A. song book.

Colonel Pearson (1832–92), who was born in Derby, became a Christian Mission evangelist in 1874, at the time the Founder was concerned about the needless discussions taking place in the leaders' meetings and allowing the less spiritually minded to frustrate the planning of the evangelist of the Mission station. Pearson learned how to manage these awkward people, and Bramwell Booth wrote of him: ' The best of our evangelists to manage these meetings was Pearson. He would get his leaders and elders together and have a red-hot prayer-meeting. . . . Then when he had screwed them up to the highest pitch, and made them in love and faith ready for anything, he would tell them that he had a little business to go through before they separated. It was really wonderful how he succeeded in getting his resolutions passed! '

Typical of his work was his report in *The Christian Mission Maga-zine*, June, 1875, from the Shoreditch Station: ' Scarcely had we begun our open-air meeting, when a band of roughs succeeded in bringing two men who played a harp and hurdy-gurdy. For more than an hour they were playing, and the roughs and others were dancing.

This for a time arrested the attention of the people, but by persevering we succeeded in turning the tide. The devil missed his mark and did us a good turn against his will. The opposition caused an extra stir and created sympathy and drew a great crowd—bringing hundreds to hear the word of eternal life. Blest with a good voice, I was enabled nearly to drown the sound of the instruments and big tears ran down many cheeks, but our opponents, seeing their attempts were fruitless, quitted the field, leaving us masters of the position.'

William Pearson was the publisher of the first *War Cry* (December 27, 1879) and author of ' Come, join our Army '—one of the first songs specially written for the Army's own use. His story is told in *He Conquered the Foe*.

74. Jesus came down my ransom to be (Emmanuel Rolfe)

The Musical Salvationist, July, 1894—a special number entitled ' Songs from Many Lands '. This entry represented Jamaica where the author was then stationed. 1899 S.A. song book.

Brigadier Rolfe, whose son Victor became a Lieut.-Commissioner, was born in Berwick St. James, Wiltshire, and entered the Army work from North Ormesby, Middlesbrough, in 1879. In July, 1882, from the Congress Hall he farewelled with Mrs. Rolfe for Australia, where he assisted the pioneer officers, Captain and Mrs. Sutherland. As Mrs. Catherine Booth, who was conducting the meeting, presented new colours to be taken to Australia, she charged ' Captain and Lieutenant Rolfe ' to be faithful. After service in New Zealand and Jamaica, Emmanuel Rolfe returned to his homeland. He was promoted to Glory on February 15, 1914.

75. Jesus, keep me near the Cross (Fanny Crosby (17))

Bright Jewels for the Sunday School, 1869, an American publication edited by the Rev. Robert Lowry; *Hallelujah Hymn Book*; *Revival Music*; 1878 S.A. song book.

76. Jesus, Thou all-redeeming Lord (Charles Wesley (15))

Hymns and Sacred Poems, 1749; Ch.M.H.B. Originally there were eighteen verses.

77. Jesus, Thy blood and righteousness (Nicolaus L. von Zinzendorf; *translated by* John Wesley (3))

The original German words were composed by Zinzendorf in 1739 on the Island of St. Eustatius on his return from visiting the Moravian missionaries in the West Indies, the translation by John Wesley being made in 1740; Ch.M.H.B.

Count Zinzendorf (1700–60) was born in Dresden; his pious father, who held an important position under the Elector of Saxony, died when the boy was only six weeks old. He was brought up under the spiritual influences of his maternal grandmother and educated at the Paedagogium, Halle, where he formed his companions into a religious order, binding them with mottoes and insignia to devote themselves to the service of Jesus Christ.

About 1722, the time of his marriage, he heard of the sufferings of the Moravians under the Austrian Government and expressed his willingness to receive the persecuted refugees on his estate, where he erected a settlement named 'Herrnhut'—'The Lord's Shelter'. Nine years later he resigned all his public work in order to be able to devote himself entirely to spiritual operations. He became the President of 'Herrnhut' and laboured incessantly on behalf of its spiritual welfare. He commenced to write hymns as a child and his literary accomplishments numbered over a hundred published works.

78. Man of Sorrows! what a name (Philip P. Bliss)

The International Lessons Monthly, 1875; 1930 S.A. song book. Soon after the composition of this song Mr. Bliss sang it in the State prison at Jackson, Michigan, after having given an address on 'The Man of Sorrows'. Many of the prisoners were so greatly affected that they yielded to Christ.

Philip P. Bliss (1838–76) was born in Clearfield County, Pennsylvania, U.S.A. As a boy of seven he made musical instruments from the reeds which grew near his father's house, and from other crude materials. When ten years of age he helped to increase the meagre income of his family by trudging along the village streets selling vegetables which he carried in a basket on his arm. Whilst thus engaged he heard his first piano. Drawn by the sound of music coming to him through the open door of a house, he entered the room where a lady was playing a piano accompaniment to the song she was singing. Entranced, Philip stood listening, his soul in a sea of delight; such music he had never heard. The lady at last turned and saw him. Indignantly she ordered him out of the house. 'Get out of here', she cried, 'with your great bare feet!'

In 1864 Mr. Bliss went to Chicago to work for Dr. George F. Root, the musician, conducting musical institutes and composing Sunday-school melodies. He possessed a voice of remarkably wide range. First a Baptist, then a Methodist, in 1871 he became a choir-man of the First Congregational Church, Chicago, and the Superintendent of its Sunday-school. In 1874 he joined D. W. Whittle in evangelistic work, to which cause he gave the royalties from his *Gospel Songs* worth some £6,000. Two years later he was travelling in a railway train in Ashtabula, Ohio, U.S.A., when a bridge gave way and the carriage in which he and his wife were travelling crashed from a height of some sixty feet. Mr. Bliss escaped, but lost his life in trying to save his wife from the blazing wreckage.

The author provided the music for most of his songs.

79. Not all the blood of beasts (Isaac Watts (3))

The author's *Psalms, Hymns and Spiritual Songs*, 1709; Ch.M.H.B.

Dr. Watts thought out the first draft of these words in Smithfield Market, London, as he stood looking at the newly slain animals. He instinctively recalled the countless number of animals sacrificed in accordance with the Mosaic ritual.

80. O come and look awhile on Him (Frederick W. Faber)

The author's *Jesus and Mary*, 1849 (in its original form); 1899 S.A. song book.

Of Huguenot stock, Dr. Faber (1814–63) was born at Calverley, Yorks., and educated at Shrewsbury, Harrow and Oxford. He graduated in 1836 and became a Fellow of University College, Oxford, in 1837, taking Holy Orders the same year.

About this time he became a great admirer of John Henry Newman and threw himself enthusiastically into the Tractarian Movement. Although in 1843 he became Rector of Elton, Huntingdonshire, he was received into the Church of Rome two years later. In 1849 he established the Brotherhood of the London Oratorians in King William Street, Strand, London. The Oratory moved to Brompton in 1854 and Dr. Faber laboured there until his death.

Dr. Faber took as models for the writing of his own hymns the *Olney Hymns* of Newton, because of their simplicity and intense fervour.

81. O sacred Head now wounded (Paulus Gerhardt, from Bernard of Clairvaux (45); *translated by* James W. Alexander)

Gerhardt's translation from Bernard's original in Crüger's *Praxis*, 1656; translation from the German in *The Sacred Lyre*, 1830; *The Musical Salvationist*, February, 1932.

Paulus Gerhardt (1607–76) was born at Gräfenhäynichen, in Saxony, son of the burgomaster. His first pastorate was at Mittenwalde in 1651, and six years later he was called to St. Nicholas Church, Berlin, where he remained for nine years until he was deposed from his office owing to his uncompromising adherence to the Lutheran doctrine.

The following year he was reinstated but, learning that he would be expected to believe and to preach contrary to the dictates of his conscience, he again took a firm stand and was superseded. Leaving

Berlin he decided to return to his native land of Saxony. Depending upon the alms of friends to save him from starvation, and journeying on foot, Gerhardt bore up bravely. It was during this journey that he was inspired to write, ' Commit thou all thy griefs ' (No. 746). Altogether he wrote 123 hymns.

In 1669 he was appointed Archdeacon of Lubben and remained in office until his death. His portrait hangs in the church there and bears the inscription, 'A divine sifted in Satan's sieve '.

Dr. James Alexander (1804–59) was born at Hopewell, Louisa, Virginia, and educated at Princeton College, where he was twice a professor. He was also Pastor of the Fifth Avenue Presbyterian Church, New York.

82. On a hill far away stood an old rugged Cross (George Bennard)

The Musical Salvationist, May, 1924.

'At the youthful age of sixteen George Bennard (1870–1958) desperately needed a lasting support of strength to help him meet the family responsibilities that had suddenly been thrust upon his inexperienced shoulders at the death of his father,' wrote Bertha Blanchard in *The War Cry*, U.S.A. Southern edition. ' He found this sustaining force in The Salvation Army. Joining this group, he worked with them for some time, constantly seeing the struggles of humanity and knowing its need for something to cling to—something to help the people over the rough road they daily travelled. The inspiration for the writing of " The old rugged Cross " thus came to George Bennard as a result of his work in The Salvation Army.'

Commissioner John J. Allan was at one time Lieutenant to Captain George Bennard, who after a number of years became a minister of the Methodist Episcopal Church.

In a radio poll taken in the U.S.A. about twenty years after this song was written, ' The old rugged Cross ' headed the poll by receiving over 6,000 more votes than its nearest competitor—' Nearer, my God, to Thee '.

' The words of the finished hymn were put into my heart in answer to my own need,' wrote George Bennard. ' In fact, they were born out of a real soul struggle.' ' I'll be true to the Cross of Jesus,' he prayed at the end of the battle; ' I will cling to it, please God, all my life.'

The author was conducting meetings in Albion, Michigan, U.S.A., for a fellow minister who lived at Pokagon Parsonage. ' The Bostwicks were musical people, so after supper we went to the piano, I was anxious to show them my hymn. I sang it to them, then nervously asked what they thought of it. " So much ", they answered, " that we must have it printed. . . . Leave it to us; we will look after

32

the cost." ' Its first public appearance was at an interdenominational convention at the Chicago Evangelistic Institute, introduced by a group of trained singers. ' Soon that large audience was singing it, with eyes wet and lips trembling, pouring into it their very souls in a new, exalted consecration, carried away in the glory and inspiration of a gospel song that few moments before they had not even heard.'

Homer Rodeheaver bought the copyright of the song from the author and made contracts with various gramophone companies for its reproduction.

83. On Calvary's brow my Saviour died (William Darwood (verses); William Fairhurst (chorus))

Written by an American minister; *Sacred Songs and Solos*; 1899 S.A. song book; chorus by the grandfather of Commissioner William Cooper.

The original chorus, now detached from the verses, was:

> O Calvary! dark Calvary,
> Where Jesus shed His Blood for me;
> O Calvary! dark Calvary!
> Speak to my heart from Calvary.

84. On the Cross of Calvary (Sarah Graham)

The Musical Salvationist, July, 1886; 1899 S.A. song book.

Miss Graham, who used to write songs before her conversion, listened one Sunday to two Salvationists of the Lindsay Corps, Ontario, Canada, singing one of her songs as a duet. During the singing she made her way to the Penitent-form. Afterward she became a soldier of the corps. ' Life's morn will soon be waning ', another of her contributions, was penned under tragic circumstances. She was engaged to be married when her fiancé was stricken with galloping consumption and died. Miss Graham never really recovered from the shock and died about 1889 when thirty-five years of age.

85. There is a fountain filled with Blood (William Cowper (25) (verses))

Written when William Cowper was forty years old and published in Dr. Conyer's *Collection of Psalms and Hymns*, 1772; *Olney Hymns*, 1779; Ch.M.H.B.; chorus: Philip Phillips's *Hallowed Songs*, 1873.

' We had just closed the meeting last Sunday night at West Bromwich,' wrote Adjutant Theodore Kitching (father of General Wilfred Kitching) in *The War Cry*, July 11, 1891, ' a meeting in which we had had four precious souls seeking salvation, when a man, partly under the influence of drink, burst into the barracks and asked us to go at once with him and pray with his poor old mother who lay dying.

' We went and found a poor old soul, more than one hundred and two years of age, almost ready to pass from time into eternity, and unsaved!

'Our first business was to pray. This we did each in turn; while one or other of us in turn dealt faithfully with her soul. Then we sang " There is a fountain filled with Blood " with the chorus, which we sang over and over again. As we were doing so the fifth or sixth time she raised her hand and, looking up, shouted, " Glory! He does set me free! I do believe! " '

86. There is a green hill far away (Cecil Frances Alexander (22))

Hymns for Little Children, 1848; 1899 S.A. song book.

In the middle of the nineteenth century some Irish boys were complaining that the Church Catechism which they had to learn was dull and dreary. Their godmother heard of their complaint and wrote verses week by week which would make the meaning of the Catechism plain, until the subject became full of interest.

'Do no sinful action' was written to explain the promise to 'renounce the devil and all his works'; 'All things bright and beautiful' expanded the truth ' I believe in God the Father Almighty, Maker of Heaven and earth '; ' Once in royal David's city ' and ' There is a green hill far away ' explained the birth and death of Jesus, the latter being composed by the bedside of a sick girl whom the author visited a number of times.

Charles Gounod, during the Franco-German War of 1870, sought refuge in England, residing with his family in Blackheath. His daughter Jeanne went to school and was taught the words of ' There is a green hill far away '. Jeanne recited it to her father, who was immediately attracted by its truth and beauty and set to work to write a melody worthy of the message. In his estimation he thought it to be the most perfect hymn in the English language. The Rev. Leslie Weatherhead in *His Life and Ours* speaks of it as ' a hymn which is the most profound commentary on the Atonement I have ever seen '.

87. We worship Thee, O Crucified! (Albert Orsborn (42))

The Beauty of Jesus; written for a ' Good Friday ' series of meetings held at the Congress Hall, Clapton, in 1914.

88. When I survey the wondrous Cross (Isaac Watts (3))

Hymns and Spiritual Songs, 1707, intended for use with the Sacrament of the Lord's Supper; Ch.M.H.B.; based on Galatians 6: 14.

Watts originally wrote, ' Where the young Prince of Glory died ' (verse 1, line 2), but later changed it to the present form.

Matthew Arnold, the great poet and literary critic, thought we had no greater hymn. He sang it in church during his last Sunday on earth

34

and was afterward overheard quoting part of it in his room the day he died.

In his *Yale Lectures* Silvester Horne said : ' The whole gospel is contained in that beautiful verse commencing " Were the whole realm of nature mine ". That is to say that my soul is bigger and greater than the whole realm of nature. . . . It affirms that the soul in every forced labourer on the Amazon is of more value than all the mines of Johannesburg, all the diamonds of Kimberley and all the millions of all the magnates of America. It affirms that in God's sight all the suns and stars are of inferior worth to one human spirit dwelling, it may be, in the degraded gutter population of a great city, who has descended to his doom by means of the multiplied temptations which our so-called society environs him. It is a romantic creed, but if it is not true Christianity itself is false.'

89. When Jesus was born in the manger (John Lawley (56) (verses 4 and 5))

The Officer, May, 1893; *The Musical Salvationist*, June, 1893; 1899 S.A. song book.

On another page of *The Officer* in which these words first appeared the following notes were given: ' " To save a poor sinner ", our " Song of the Month ", was composed in America by a soldier and first sung by the late Mrs. Major Dale. It was introduced in England by Major Aspinall and taken up by Colonel Lawley, who has moved thousands in the General's recent meetings while singing it over and over again.'

Mrs. General Carpenter, in her life of Commissioner Lawley, wrote: ' The Founder much liked the first verse and chorus of this song but not the other verses (in the original); he told Lawley to write new ones. The Founder and his staff were travelling in Queensland, Australia, when a hot axle caused the train to pull up at a remote spot. Lawley slipped out of his carriage, and going along to the General's compartment repeated [the] verses . . . which he had just completed. He received the General's twinkle, " Those will do ".'

The Founder considered this to be his favourite Christmas carol, and when he was very near the end of life remarked: ' Oh, if I could only hear again dear old Lawley sing, " To save a poor sinner like me ", and oh, if I could only hear him say, " General, there's a poor drunkard coming right from the back of the hall—He's coming to Jesus ", that would be the sweetest music I could hear.'

90. While passing a garden, I lingered to hear (George Hun Nobbs)

Revival Music; 1878 S.A. song book; *The Musical Salvationist*, January, 1904, with the music still associated with the words.

The following account appeared in *Heirs of Exile* (The Story of Pitcairn Island) by Alta Hilliard Christensen, published in the U.S.A. in 1955.

In 1828, at the age of twenty-nine, George Hun Nobbs arrived on Pitcairn Island and became teacher and pastor of the people there, but in 1856, with nearly two hundred residents, he left for Norfolk Island. As guide and leader he was honoured and respected. He died in 1884, leaving sons to carry on his work.

The poem ' Gethsemane ', written by Mr. Nobbs and still sung by the Norfolk Islanders to music composed by Driver Christian, who for many years was the local choir-master, begins

> While nature was sinking in stillness to rest,
> The last beams of daylight shone dim in the west,
> O'er fields pale by moonlight, I wandered abroad,
> In deep meditation I thought of my Lord.
>
> While passing a garden I paused to hear
> A voice faint and plaintive from One that was near;
> The voice of a Sufferer affected my heart,
> While pleading in anguish the poor sinner's part.

Then follow the verses as in our song book with slight alterations to some of the words.

91. Within my heart, O Lord, fulfil (Herbert H. Booth)

Songs of the Nations, International Congress, 1886; 1899 S.A. song book. Originally the song included the following chorus:

> Take my sins and purge their stain,
> Take my heart and o'er it reign;
> Lord, I only want to live and die for Thee;
> Take my heart and wash it white,
> Take my life and keep it right,
> Take my all, and in Thy might I will faithful be.

Fifth child and third son of the Founder and Mrs. Booth, Herbert was born in Penzance, Cornwall, on August 26, 1862. He married Cornelie Schoch (see song 140) on September 18, 1890.

The outstanding song-writer and composer in a remarkable family, Herbert Booth has thirty songs and eighteen choruses in our song book to his credit—more than any other Salvationist contributor. He usually provided the musical setting for his own words. Even after eighty years few corps during a week-end fail to use some verse, chorus or tune written by Herbert Booth.

We are indebted to Herbert Booth for the arrangements he made for the establishing of the Army's Music Department, and this when he was only twenty-one years of age; also for his ability to foresee the suitability and usefulness of many of the music-hall tunes of his day and for the way in which he adapted them so skilfully that their secular associations are now almost entirely forgotten. At the time of their marriage Herbert and Cornelie published a collection of their own songs under the title *Songs of Peace and War*.

He lived a busy life. For four years until 1888 he trained men cadets in London; he organized great demonstrations in one of which he conducted a brass band of five thousand men; he commanded Army work in Canada for four years, then in the Australasian Territory from 1896 to 1901.

After Herbert and his wife left the Army in 1902 he continued in active Christian work in America, Australia and New Zealand, in the latter country founding The Christian Confederacy in 1915. Cornelie died in 1919, in England, while her husband was in New Zealand. Four years later he married Annie Ethel Lane, an Australian. They settled in America, where Herbert died on September 25, 1926.

92. Wonderful story of love! (J. M. Driver)

The Musical Salvationist, September, 1924; 1930 S.A. song book.
J. M. Driver was an American minister.

93. Would Jesus have the sinner die? (Charles Wesley (15))

Hymns on God's Everlasting Love, 1741; Ch.M.H.B.

Whilst the verses, originally twenty-eight in number, emphasize the world-embracing love of Christ (see No. 30), they are the breathings of a heart that has been moved to the depths by the evidence of that love as revealed on Calvary.

General Bramwell Booth acclaimed this as one of his favourite songs. Writing in a supplement to *John O'London's* in 1925, he said: ' In my personal experience Charles Wesley's glorious poem beginning, " Would Jesus have the sinner die? " maintains its influence and charm after sixty years. Surely in one verse " deep calls unto deep " in the heart of every true disciple of Jesus Christ: " O let Thy love my heart constrain . . . ".'

94. Crown Him with many crowns (Matthew Bridges and Godfrey Thring)

Bridges' *Hymns of the Heart*, 1851 (verses 1 and 3), and Thring's *Collection*, 1880; *The Musical Salvationist*, July, 1920.

Matthew Bridges (1800–94) was born at Maldon, Essex, and published his earliest verses in 1825. He was influenced by the Oxford Movement and left the Church of England to enter the Roman Catholic communion in 1848. He died in Quebec, Canada.

Godfrey Thring (1823–1903), fourth son of the Rector of Alford, Somerset, was educated at Shrewsbury, and Balliol College, Oxford.

Ordained in 1846, he became Prebendary of Wells Cathedral in 1876 and died at Plonck's Hill, Shamleigh Green, Guildford.

95. Glorious things of thee are spoken (John Newton (41))

Olney Hymns, 1779; 1930 S.A. song book; based on Isaiah 33: 20, 21. Two verses have been omitted from the original.

96. God is with us, God is with us (Walter J. Mathams)

Written at the request of the National Council of Evangelical Free Churches for the Congress held in Nottingham in 1896, and published in the *Christian Endeavour Hymnal* the same year.

Born in London, the Rev. Walter J. Mathams (1853–1931) entered the Baptist College, Regents Park, in 1874. Known for his early adventures in the Arctic and his joining in the rush to the Alaska gold mines, he had a remarkable influence over men. After he had written *Jack's Almanac*, a book of sea proverbs, Lord Roberts asked him to write something similar for soldiers. Thus after serving as an army chaplain amongst the Seaforth Highlanders in Egypt he produced his *Soldier's Maxim Shot Note-book*. As a hymn writer it is said that ' lines flowed through his mind like waves, when the mood was on him '. After being the Baptist minister at Preston, Falkirk and Birmingham, in 1900 he entered the Established Church and became a Chaplain to the Forces. In 1905 he entered the Church of Scotland from which he retired in 1919.

97. Jesus comes! Let all adore Him! (Thomas Kelly)

An altered version from Josiah Conder's *Congregational Hymn Book: a Supplement to Dr. Watts's Psalms and Hymns*, 1836.

Son of an Irish Judge, Thomas Kelly (1769–1854) was born at Kellyville, Athy, and was educated at Trinity College, Dublin.

Destined for the bar, he entered the Temple, London, but, having undergone a very marked spiritual change and coming under strong evangelical influences, he decided to devote his life to religious work and was ordained in 1792. His earnest evangelical preaching led to his being inhibited by Archbishop Fowler and his founding a new sect. In addition to being skilled in the Oriental tongues and admired as a biblical scholar, he possessed some musical talent. In all he composed and published, over a period of fifty-one years, 765 hymns, many of which are still in use today. He is the composer of No. 136 in *The Salvation Army Tune Book*, ' On our way to God '.

98. Jesus shall reign where'er the sun (Isaac Watts (3))

Watts's *Psalms, Hymns and Spiritual Songs*, 1719; Ch.M.H.B.; part two of the author's version of Psalm 72. The original first verse ended, 'Till moons shall wax and wane no more'.

The inhabitants of the South Seas island of Tonga sent a message by canoe to Fiji, saying they would like to hear about the white man's religion. In response to this appeal a missionary was sent over, resulting, in due course, in a mass movement of the Tongans toward the Cross. This was led by the Tongan monarch, King George, an ancestor of Queen Salote. Surrounded by his chiefs and warriors, many of whom had been cannibals, together with natives from Fiji and Samoa, he held a great open-air service on Whit-Sunday, 1862, and in thanksgiving and praise to God declared his island kingdom to be Christian in faith and practice. Then as a dramatic climax the vast congregation joined in singing the Tongan translation of these words of Isaac Watts.

99. Lo! He comes with clouds descending (Charles Wesley (15))

Charles Wesley's *Hymns of Intercession for All Mankind*, 1758; Ch.M.H.B.; originally part two of a three-part hymn entitled 'Thy Kingdom come', written at a time when nearly all Europe was at war.

Wesley's small collection of forty hymns was suited to the circumstances of the country, for it included hymns of intercession for the fleet and the army, for prisoners and for enemies, as well as for the King and those in authority.

100. Rejoice, the Lord is King! (Charles Wesley (15))

Wesley's *Sacred and Moral Poems*, 1744; *The Musical Salvationist*, November, 1922.

The song is one of the three Wesley hymns to which Handel set music, the tune for this being 'Gopsal' (*The Salvation Army Tune Book*, No. 601).

101. See how great a flame aspires (Charles Wesley (15))

Written in November, 1746, and published in *Hymns and Sacred Poems*, 1749, where it is the last of four songs entitled, 'After preaching to the Newcastle colliers'; Ch.M.H.B. 'Perhaps the imagery was suggested by the large fires connected with the collieries, which illuminate the whole of that part of the country in the darkest nights.' The final verse is based upon Elijah's experience on Carmel (1 Kings 18: 44, 45).

102. Sing we the King who is coming to reign (Charles Silvester Horne)

Son of a Congregational minister, Charles Silvester Horne (1865–1914), was born at Cuckfield, Sussex. He was educated at the Newport

Grammar School and Glasgow University, and was one of the first students to enter Mansfield College, Oxford, which opened in 1886. He was minister of the Allen Street Church, Kensington, from 1889 to 1903, when he removed to Whitefield's Tabernacle in Tottenham Court Road. He was elected President of the Congregational Union in 1909, M.P. for Ipswich in 1910 and President of the National Brotherhood Movement in 1914. Returning by steamer from a trip to the Niagara Falls, he fell dead at his wife's feet as they were entering Toronto. His wife was the daughter of Lord Justice Cozens-Hardy, Master of the Rolls.

The author is said to have written these words especially for the tune 'The glory song', because he desired words more suitable than the original for his congregation at Whitefield's.

103. Ten thousand times ten thousand (Henry Alford)

The author's *Year of Praise*, 1867; written as a processional song for use on saints' days; *The Musical Salvationist*, April, 1912.

Son of the Rector of Aston Sandford, Bucks, Henry Alford (1810–71) was born in Bedford Row, London. He was educated at Ilmington Grammar School and at Trinity College, Cambridge, where he took his B.A. degree in 1832. In 1833 he became Curate of Ampton and two years later Vicar of Wymeswold, Leicestershire, retaining this appointment until 1853 when he became Incumbent of Quebec Chapel, Marylebone, London. In 1857 he was made Dean of Canterbury by Lord Palmerston and continued here until his death.

He is described as being ' one of the most variously accomplished churchmen of his day—poet, preacher, lecturer, painter, musician, Bible scholar, critic and philologist. A man who could do anything and do it well—build an organ and play on it—whose artistic faculty would have made him a great landscape painter, had he not, either from preference or necessity, become a great Greek scholar and a Dean '. His chief literary work was his four-volume edition of the Greek Testament, an achievement which cost him twenty years' labour. For some time he was the editor of *The Contemporary Review*.

104. The head that once was crowned with thorns (Thomas Kelly (97))

1820 edition of Kelly's *Hymns* and based on Hebrews 2: 9, 10.

105. There is coming on a great day of rejoicing (Richard Slater)

Written in July, 1887, for the special song book used in connection with the Army's twenty-second anniversary held at the Alexandra

Palace, *The Musical Salvationist*, December, 1887; 1899 S.A. song book.

Now affectionately referred to as 'The Father of Salvation Army Music', Richard Slater was, at the time of his conversion, a professional musician, a widely read man, especially of scientific and philosophical books, a lecturer on infidelity and for some time a phrenologist. Born on June 7, 1854, just off Farringdon Road, London (Mount Pleasant Post Office now covers the site), son of an engineer who was also a very capable musician, Richard lost his father when five years of age. The son's most prized possession was his father's violin which had been used by his grandfather. At the death of her husband the widow, and her two sons, moved into one room in Cromer Street (off Judd Street), where young Richard slept on two chairs. Richard became a flute player in a mission drum and fife band and in time became a professional violinist, a teacher of music and a member of the Royal Albert Hall Orchestra Society, playing first violin under such conductors as Sir Arthur Sullivan, Sir Julius Benedict and Sir George Mount.

Although brought up to attend Sunday-school regularly and in time becoming a Sunday-school teacher, he astonished everyone when he was twenty-one years of age by standing up and publicly announcing that he had finished with Christianity: there was nothing in it.

He then took to lecturing on rationalism at London clubs and in open-air meetings. But in spite of his infidelity to which his reasoning had led him he had to confess that his spiritual and moral needs were disquietening. He still read the Gospels for the character of Jesus appealed to him—Jesus was the perfect Model for man to seek to imitate.

He was led to attend the Army, going first out of curiosity, but also because the meetings afforded opportunity for the study of character when under the emotional stress of religion.

He first attended some meetings at Chalk Farm, but in July, 1882, he walked from King's Cross to Hampstead and there, attracted by the sound of a drum, found himself in a converted dancing saloon listening to an Army meeting. With his inevitable notebook and pencil he sat ready to take notes of anything of more than ordinary interest. When the time for testimonies came a servant-girl jumped up and said: 'My missus says she believes I am saved because I sweep beneath the mats, and I didn't before I was saved.' 'This testimony came as a flash of divine lightning that struck my soul,' he afterward wrote. He had no peace of soul and began to attend the meetings in earnest to find something his soul was seeking.

At the Rink (Regent Hall) on Friday, September 22nd, at the conclusion of a holiness meeting he made the surrender. Speaking of the occasion he wrote: 'A resolve was formed within me to give myself entirely to God.' Soon he was taking his place with his violin in the corps, but was faced with a very serious problem: all his lecturing fees had ceased and a good deal of his musical work had also to be abandoned. For over twelve months a very hard time was his lot. Then came an interview with William Booth, the result of which was that on October 22, 1883, at the weekly wage of twenty-five shillings, he commenced work at the Army Headquarters. Together with F. W. Fry and Bandmaster Henry Hill, he assisted in the laying of the foundations and maturing the scheme for the managing of the Army's Music Department and of establishing the 'Praying, Speaking and Singing Brigade' (the first Headquarters musical combination).

One of the first tasks which he performed was to produce in 1884 the first band tune book—a collection of eighty-eight tunes—and two years later he commenced *The Musical Salvationist* for songster brigades. During his life-time he published 294 of his own songs with words and music, 127 sets of words to others' music and 166 tunes to other people's words.

He wrote the Army's first brass band march, an arrangement from the opera 'Lucia di Lammermoor', using the chorus as a bass solo and giving a trumpeting accompaniment to the cornets. This was an innovation that caused some heart-burning to the Founder for he was not sure that it was the right thing to do. Slater also provided us with our first band selection, entitled 'Old song memories'. His profound admiration for the works of the Masters also helped him to see that Army bands and songsters had opportunities to dispense this type of music. Richard Wagner was the 'star' of his musical world and he claimed that he had made an analytical study of every bar of Wagner's music.

On the occasion of Richard Slater's receiving his promotion to the rank of Lieut.-Colonel a 'band' was quickly mustered to play music of congratulation in the form of 'O the crowning day is coming, Hallelujah!' Slater appreciated the gesture and then turned to his leader, Commissioner Richard Wilson, and exclaimed, 'I think this is a time for prayer.' He was promoted to Glory in November, 1939, from Margate.

106. There's a golden day (Herbert H. Booth (91))

Written for the marriage, in the old Exeter Hall, of Commissioner George Scott Railton and Sergeant Marianne Parkyn, on January 17, 1884, 'There's a golden day' appeared on a leaflet in the spring of 1885; *Favourite Songs Supplement*; 1899 S.A. song book.

The text has been revised for the present song book in order to bring its rhythm more into keeping with the tune to which it is set.

107. Yet once again, by God's abundant mercy (Albert Orsborn (42))

Published in booklets used in connection with officers' meetings and in *The Beauty of Jesus*, and 'inspired by international occasion, merging into contemplation of the Saviour's final victory'. It first appeared in connection with the International Congress, 1914.

108. All the guilty past is washed away (Richard Slater (105))

The Musical Salvationist, April, 1888; and written in March for music by Colonel Thomas Emerson, who claimed to have been the first commissioned Bandmaster in The Salvation Army. 1899 S.A. song book.

109. Breathe on me, Breath of God (Edwin Hatch)

Published in a small collection printed privately in 1878; Allon's *Congregational Psalmist Hymnal*, 1886; *The Officer*, January, 1919; 1930 S.A. song book.

Born in Derby, Edwin Hatch (1835–89) was educated at King Edward's School, Birmingham, and Pembroke College, Oxford, where he was closely associated with Burne Jones, William Morris and Swinburne. His parents were nonconformists but he took orders in the Church of England and for a time worked in an East End parish in London. In 1859 he accepted an appointment as Professor of Classics in Trinity College, Quebec, later taking the position of rector of the Quebec High School. In 1867 he returned to England and held various appointments until he became Hibbert Lecturer in 1888. He won European reputation for his work in historical research.

110. Come, gracious Spirit, heavenly Dove (Simon Browne)

The author's *Hymns and Spiritual Songs, in Three Books, Designed as a Supplement to Dr. Watts's*, 1720; 1930 S.A. song book.

Simon Browne (1680–1732) was born at Shepton Mallet, Somerset. After studying at the Academy of Mr. Moore, Bridgwater, he became an Independent minister at Portsmouth, and in 1716 pastor of the congregation in Old Jewry, London.

Seven years later when on a journey, he and a friend were stopped by a highwayman, who presented his pistols and demanded their money. Mr. Browne, being a strong man, seized the robber, flung him down and disarmed him while his friend went for assistance. But the grasp upon the man's throat choked him and when assistance came the thief was dead. This had a most distressing effect upon Mr. Browne's mind. Frequently he was tormented with a desire to destroy himself, and he always maintained that his mental powers had been taken from him, a condition which was aggravated, no doubt, by the fact that he lost his wife and only son the same year.

While in this state he wrote some twenty-three separate works, including one on the Trinity, a dictionary and an exposition on the First Epistle to the Corinthians for Matthew Henry's commentary. He also wrote 266 hymns yet cherished his delusion to the last that he had lost his power to think. He died in the town of his birth.

III. Come, Thou everlasting Spirit (Charles Wesley (15))

Hymns on the Lord's Supper, 1745; 1899 S.A. song book.

112. Holy Spirit, truth divine (Samuel Longfellow)

Vespers, 1859; *Hymns of the Spirit*, 1864; 1930 S.A. song book.

Born at Portland, Maine, U.S.A., Samuel Longfellow (1819–92), a Unitarian clergyman, was a brother of Henry Wadsworth Longfellow, the poet. Samuel was educated at Harvard University and at the Divinity School in Cambridge, Mass. While a student of divinity he enjoyed the companionship of Samuel Johnson, and with Johnson took a very keen interest in the hymnody of their denomination. In 1846 he was co-editor of *A Book of Hymns for Public and Private Devotion* which was revised and enlarged two years later. In 1848 he became pastor at Fall River, Massachusetts, in 1853 minister of the Second Unitarian Church, Brooklyn, and later of the Unitarian Church, Germantown, Pa. In 1883 he retired in order to devote his time to literary work.

113. Jesus is glorified (Charles Wesley (15))

Hymns of Petition and Thanksgiving for the Promise of the Father, with a sub-title 'Hymns for Whitsuntide', 1746; 1930 S.A. song book.

114. Near Thy Cross assembled, Master (John Lawley (56))

All the World, June, 1895, with a final verse beginning, 'In the upper room beseeching, Faith the promise seized'; 1899 S.A. song book.

Commissioner Lawley wrote this song after hearing William Booth preach on the 'Baptism of the Holy Ghost'. He had referred to an early period in his ministry when he had become very dissatisfied with the visible results of his preaching—only two or three people seeking salvation at the close of the meeting.

A very successful preacher, the Rev. Richard Poole, the Founder recalled, visited the circuit and spoke from the text, 'Said I not unto thee, that, if thou wouldest believe, thou shouldest see the glory of God?' (John 11: 40). Observing the results, William Booth went to his own room and resolved, regardless of men's opinions and his own gain and position, that he would ever seek the one thing, and there came to him a fresh realization of the greatness of the opportunity before him of leading men and women out of their misery and sin.

From that night he was a different man and during a Sunday soon afterward twenty-four people sought salvation, including the daughter of the professor under whom he had studied.

115. O Thou who camest from above (Charles Wesley (15))

Short Hymns on Select Passages of Scripture, 1762; Ch.M.H.B.; based on Leviticus 6: 13. The last line of verse 3 is reminiscent of 2 Timothy 1: 6.

Both Charles and John Wesley claimed these verses as their own Christian experience.

116. Our blest Redeemer, ere He breathed (Harriet Auber)

The author's *Spirit of the Psalms*, 1829; 1930 S.A. song book.

Miss Auber (1773–1862), daughter of the Rector of Tring, whose grandfather came to England in 1685 as a Huguenot refugee, was born in London. During the greater part of her quiet life she resided at Broxbourne and Hoddesdon, Herts, and was buried in the churchyard of the latter place.

The story is widely accepted that Miss Auber wrote the verses on a window-pane in her home at Hoddesdon during a time of illness. She was lying on a couch meditating on the Whitsuntide sermon she had heard that morning. Having no writing materials at hand and fearful lest she should lose the sudden inspiration which came to her, she used her diamond ring to scratch the words on the glass.

117. Precious Saviour, we are coming (Thomas McKie (verses))

Written just before the Great Northern March, 1886, and printed in the song book used in that campaign; 1899 S.A. song book. The chorus is an older production and appeared in the Ch.M.H.B. with the song which commences:

> Saviour, visit Thy plantation,
> Send us now a gracious rain;
> All will come to desolation
> Unless Thou return again.

'An ordinary Tyneside lad, Thomas McKie was charmed into the service by the "Hallelujah lasses", who made such a commotion in the North of England during the latter part of the seventies in the last century. He at once displayed remarkable enthusiasm for the cause, and at one leap became the idol of the British Field as an evangelist Captain. He evangelized in the biggest halls in England, including the Bristol Circus, Hull Icehouse, the Grecian Theatre, City Road, London, and the Congress Hall. He is a whirlwind Salvationist! On a Sunday night his meetings would last for four or five hours. He would often lead them wearing a red guernsey, the sleeves of which would be rolled up. His preaching was of the old Methodist order. Like a flaming sword, metaphorically speaking, he would raise his voice to a loud key and describe mankind " rolling down in a lava or shame to the pit of hell, the smoke of whose torment ascendeth up now and for ever "; and bending over the rail, with perspiration standing like crystals on his forehead, he would cry, " Will you be there? Yes; I will tell you this: you may be taking your breakfast tomorrow morning amid the raging billows of the wrath of God! " Thousands and tens of thousands flocked to his meetings, and with one or two exceptions " Tom McKie " has probably won more converts to the Army than any officer in the Movement.' (A. M. Nicol in *General Booth and The Salvation Army*.)

His appointments also included those of Territorial Commander for Australia, Germany and Sweden. For a number of years he was the Training Commissioner in London. He had relinquished his officership some years when he died on August 26, 1937, at his home in Northumberland.

118. Spirit of God, that moved of old (Cecil Frances Alexander (22))

The Church Hymnal for the Christian Year, 1852; 1930 S.A. song book.

119. Thou Christ of burning, cleansing flame (William Booth)

The War Cry, April 14, 1894; 1899 S.A. song book.

William Booth was born at Nottingham on April 10, 1829, was converted in 1844 and married Catherine Mumford in 1855. He was ordained as a Methodist minister in 1858 but commenced an independent work in the East End of London on July 2, 1865, a work which ultimately developed into The Christian Mission and later, in 1878, into The Salvation Army. He was promoted to Glory on August 20, 1912. A fuller story can be found in *William Booth* (128 pp.) by Minnie Lindsay Carpenter.

He wrote only a few songs himself but he was ' a sure and quick judge of the fitness of songs for his people's use. . . . In all things he was practical, and in the use of music and song he sought immediate spiritual results. He was averse to dreamy meditation, to mere mystical emotion, to indulgence in contemplation that would put off action to meet the demands of spiritual duties to some future day. He lived in the present; here and now he sought for something definite to be done in the soul affairs of the people he had to influence '.

120. Blessèd Lamb of Calvary (Barbara Stoddart)

The War Cry, August 12, 1893; 1899 S.A. song book.

Mrs. Brigadier Stoddart (*née* Wilson) was born in the Fair Isle, one of the Shetlands, on September 16, 1865. Her parents moved to Kirkwall, in the Orkneys, where she became converted soon after the corps was opened. Barbara quickly became an active Salvationist and in 1886 became an officer.

She was a gifted platform woman and after her marriage assisted her husband in British corps and divisional appointments. After a prolonged illness she was promoted to Glory on January 28, 1915, from Middlesbrough, where the Brigadier was the Divisional Chancellor.

121. Come, Holy Ghost, all-quickening fire (Charles Wesley (15))

Hymns and Sacred Poems, 1739; Ch.M.H.B.

122. Come, Holy Ghost, all sacred fire! (Francis Bottome)

R. P. Smith's *Gospel Songs*, 1872; 1878 S.A. song book.

Born in Belper, Derbyshire, Francis Bottome (1823–94) entered the ministry of the Methodist Episcopalian Church in America in 1850. He received the degree of Doctor of Divinity from Dickinson College, Carlisle, Pa. He died in Tavistock, Devon.

123. Come, Thou all-inspiring Spirit (Charles Wesley (15))

Hymns for Use of Families, 1767; Ch.M.H.B.

124. Gracious Spirit, dwell with me (Thomas T. Lynch)

The author's collection, *The Rivulet—a Contribution to Sacred Song*, 1855; *The Musical Salvationist*, July, 1913; 1930 S.A. song book.

Son of a surgeon, Thomas Lynch (1818–71) was born at Great Dunmow, Essex. For some time he studied at Highbury Independent College and in 1847 he took charge of a church in Highgate. His last appointment was a minister of Mornington Church, Hampstead, where he continued for the last nine years of his life.

For many years Mr. Lynch was misrepresented and suffered severely from physical affliction, but possessed a wonderful personal graciousness and cheerfulness of spirit.

His 1855 publication was a supplement to Watts's hymns for use in his own congregation. Unfortunately, owing to certain doctrines included, this book caused a fierce controversy to break out in Congregationalism, even entering into the ranks of other Nonconformists, but has since taken its place amongst many other recognized Congregational hymn books. Typical of the man, when the storm was at its height he said: ' The air will be all the clearer for the storm. We must conquer our foes by suffering them to crucify us, rather than by threatening them with crucifixion.'

125. Holy Ghost, we bid Thee welcome (Mrs. C. H. Morris)

1930 S.A. song book.

Born in Ohio, U.S.A., in 1862 and converted at the age of ten, Mrs. Morris, a life-long Methodist, published nearly a thousand gospel songs, often composing the music as well. ' The Stranger of Galilee ' is among her best known. Most of her songs were written in the prime of life after she had become totally blind.

Mrs. Morris wrote also chorus No. 120, ' Sweet will of God ', and No. 238, ' Sweeter as the days go by '.

126. I want the gift of power within (Charles Wesley (15))

Hymns and Sacred Poems, 1740; Ch.M.H.B.

127. Lord, we believe to us and ours (Charles Wesley (15))

Hymns and Sacred Poems, 1742; 1899 S.A. song book.

128. Spirit divine, attend our prayers (Andrew Reed)

Written for a Good Friday gathering of Congregational ministers in and near London for prayer and intercession. *The Evangelical Magazine*, June, 1829; Dr. Reed's own hymn book, 1842; Ch.M.H.B.

Born in London, Dr. Reed (1787–1862), fourth son of a watch-maker of Cloth Fair, Smithfield, as a young man sold the tools of his craft and bought standard classical and theological books, studying first at home, then in a class conducted by the Rev. Matthew Wilks, minister of the Tabernacle, Moorfields. Mr. Wilks introduced Andrew to Hackney College in March, 1807, and four years later he became minister of New Road Church where he had once been a member.

In three years the number of communicants at his church was trebled, in seven years 354 had been added and by 1828 it was found necessary to erect more commodious buildings, where Dr. Reed remained until he celebrated the golden jubilee of his ministry.

In April, 1816, he was married to Elizabeth Holmes, who wrote song No. 168.

From a very early age he had been drawn toward London's orphan children and soon after beginning his ministry he began to devote much of his time to their interests. ' My mother was an orphan and she found a home,' he explained, ' and in turn, she gave a home to more than one. Being called to visit a dying man, whose great sorrow in death was leaving his motherless children, we gave him a promise to befriend them. This led me to contemplate the need of an institution for orphan children.' After starting in a small way in a private house Dr. Reed launched a scheme which resulted in the opening, on January 16, 1825, of the London Orphan Asylum—now the Clapton Congress Hall.

He was buried in Abney Park Cemetery.

129. Come, Thou almighty King (Anonymous)

George Whitefield's *Hymn Book*, 1757; Charles Wesley's halfpenny leaflet, 1757, but not in John Wesley's *Collection* of 1779. These words were first sung to the tune of ' God save the Queen '.

130. Father of peace, and God of love (Philip Doddridge (5))

The Scottish Paraphrases, 1781, and based on Hebrews 13: 20, 21.

131. Holy, holy, holy, Lord God Almighty! (Reginald Heber)

Hymns, Written and Adapted to the Weekly Church Services of the Year, 1827; *The Musical Salvationist*, February, 1934; a metrical version of Revelation 4: 8-11.

Son of the vicar, Dr. Reginald Heber (1783-1826) was born at Malpas, Cheshire, educated at Whitchurch Grammar School and Brasenose College, Oxford, where he won the Newdigate Prize for a poem entitled ' Palestine ' which is still considered to be the best poem ever to gain that honour. He was ordained in 1807 and presented with the living of Hodnet in Shropshire, became Prebendary of St. Asaph's Cathedral in 1812, and in 1823 was appointed Bishop of Calcutta, India. His diocese, which covered the whole of India, laid a heavy burden upon him and three years later he died of apoplexy in his bath at Trichinopoly. On the south side of the choir in St. Paul's Cathedral stands a fine statue to his memory. All his fifty-seven hymns were written at Hodnet. Two small exercise books with problems of Euclid on one side and his hymns in his own handwriting on the other are preserved in the British Museum.

132. O Father and Creator (Albert E. Chesham)

The Musical Salvationist, January–February, 1953.

Lieut.-Commissioner Chesham was born in Lincolnshire, England, spent his boyhood in western Canada, was trained as an accountant, converted at Spokane, Washington, in 1905, and commissioned as an officer in Chicago in 1907. Three years later he married Captain Julia Williams. He became Territorial Commander of U.S.A. Southern

Territory in 1947 and retired from active service in September, 1952.

This song was written on a train between Chicago and Indianapolis. The Commissioner had long felt we had insufficient songs about the Trinity.

133. Thou, whose almighty word (John Marriott)

Written about 1813, these verses were read at a meeting of the London Missionary Society on May 12, 1825, six weeks after the author's death. The audience being greatly impressed by them, they were printed in *The Evangelical Magazine* the following month; *The Musical Salvationist*, July, 1915.

Son of the rector, John Marriott (1780–1825) was born at Cottesbach, near Lutterworth, Leicestershire, and educated at Rugby School and Christ Church, Oxford. Before ordination he became a private tutor in the family of the Duke of Buccleuch and in 1808 the Duke presented him with the living of Church Lawford, near Rugby, which he held for the rest of his life. He died at Broadclyst, near Exeter.

134. Afar from Heaven thy feet have wandered (Richard Slater (105))

Written on November 9–10, 1885, as a duet for the composer and his wife to sing in the Great Western Hall, and published in *The Musical Salvationist*, April, 1887; 1930 S.A. song book.

135. Almost persuaded now to believe (Philip P. Bliss (78))

Hallelujah Hymn Book; Revival Music; 1878 S.A. song book.

Mr. Bliss wrote these verses after listening to the closing words of a sermon preached by the Rev. Mr. Brundage—'He who is almost persuaded is almost saved, but to be almost saved is to be entirely lost.'

136. Art thou weary, art thou languid (Stephen the Sabaite; translated by John Mason Neale)

Dr. Neale's first edition of his *Hymns of the Eastern Church*, 1862, but in the third edition of this work he confesses that his translation contains so little of the original hymn that he ought not to have included it in the volume. 1899 S.A. song book.

As a child of ten, Stephen the Sabaite (725–94) was taken by his uncle, John of Damascus, to the Monastery of Mar Saba, a building, situated some ten or twelve miles from Jerusalem, in a gorge, amidst a region of deep ravines and awe-inspiring precipices. Weird desolation and wild grandeur surround the building—' Made up of several buildings, constructed on the small area formed by the aid of massive buttresses and walls, built up from below, terrace above terrace, every possible spot where a foothold can be had being utilized. There are tiny gardens of fruit and flowers and high defensive walls. These latter are necessary, for the place has been repeatedly plundered by robbers.' Stephen remained there for the rest of his days.

Dr. Neale (1818–66), son of a minister of the Anglican Church, was born in London, educated at Sherborne (Dorset) Grammar School and Trinity College, Cambridge. He was ordained deacon in 1841 and preached his first sermon at Shepperton the week after. In 1843 he accepted the small living of Crawley in Sussex where, armed with a hatchet and the churchwarden's consent, he set himself to hack down the pews as representing worldly distinction in the house of God. After a period of sickness he was offered the Wardenship of Sackville College ' at the princely stipend of £24 a year ' and accepted it. The foundation, an almshouse for old people, situated in East Grinstead, attracted him because of its antiquity (it dated from 1608) and also because of the chance of quiet leisure. He spent the remainder of his comparatively short life here.

137. Behold Me standing at the door (Fanny Crosby (17))

Biglow and Main's *Christian Songs* (U.S.A.), 1872; 1899 S.A. song book.

138. Behold One standeth at the door (Felix Charity)

The Australian *War Cry*; *The Musical Salvationist*, July, 1895; 1930 S.A. song book.

Felix Charity was the pen-name of a soldier of the Richmond Corps, Melbourne, Australia.

139. Boundless as the mighty ocean (Josiah Henry Waller)

The War Cry, November 18, 1893, in connection with a ' Boundless Salvation ' campaign in the November and December of that year; 1899 S.A. song book.

' Bandsman Waller, International Trade Headquarters ', a proof reader in the printing works, was Edmonton's Corps Secretary and later the Band Sergeant whose name appeared with *War Cry* songs of the period and in *The Musical Salvationist*, December, 1892. He was born in East London in 1865. During the First World War he served with the Y.M.C.A. in France, and in his profession he travelled as far as India, Western Samoa and Fiji. Finally he settled in New Zealand, where he died at the age of seventy-four.

140. Bring to the Saviour thy burden of grief (Cornelie Booth)

Canadian *War Cry*, Christmas Number, 1893; *The Musical Salvationist*, April, 1894; 1930 S.A. song book.

Born on October 13, 1864, Mrs. Herbert Booth (Cornelie Ida Ernestine Schoch) was one of three talented sisters, the daughters of a Dutch military colonel who, on becoming a Salvationist, was given the same rank in The Salvation Army and was appointed to a responsible position in our work in Holland. The other daughters married Commissioner W. Elwin Oliphant and Lieut.-Colonel Fritz Malan.

A number of Cornelie's compositions, both words and music, appeared in *Songs of Peace and War*, which was produced on the occasion of her marriage in the Congress Hall to Herbert Booth. Amongst the best known of her contributions are 'A perfect trust' with its refrain, ' O for a deeper . . . O for a perfect trust in the Lord! ' and ' Holy Spirit, seal me I pray '. Mrs. Booth died in 1919.

141. Can a poor sinner come to Jesus? (Anonymous)

1878 S.A. song book.

142. Come, every soul by sin oppressed (John H. Stockton)

Songs of Joy and Gladness (U.S.A.); *Revival Music*; 1878 S.A. song book.

Born at New Hope, Pennsylvania, U.S.A., John Hart Stockton (1813–77) was brought up in a Presbyterian home but, being converted at the age of nineteen in a Methodist camp meeting, became a Methodist minister. He died suddenly, three years after his retirement, while talking to friends after morning service at Arch Street Church, Philadelphia.

When Lieut.-Colonel Francis Dare opened Army work in Tanganyika in 1933 he reported: ' Our first open-air meeting was held on Sunday, October 29th, in a little street called " First Street ". Taking our stand under a tree we sang, " Come, every soul by sin oppressed ", using the Swahili song book.'

143. Come, for the feast is spread (Henry Burton)

Sacred Songs and Solos; the author's *Songs of the Highway; The Musical Salvationist*, February, 1922; 1930 S.A. song book.

Dr. Burton (1840–1930) was born at Swannington, Leicestershire, in the house where his grandmother, Mrs. James Burton, founded the first Wesleyan Juvenile Missionary Association in 1818, a home of faith and prayer. Dr. Burton recalled an outbreak of cattle plague in which his father's entire herd of twenty-four milking cows was swept away: ' One morning, when things were at their worst, it seemed as if we heard a clear voice from heaven which bade us "fear not". We were gathered in the kitchen for our morning prayers and the family Bible was laid on the table. Was it chance, or was it something more, that the chapter of the morning lesson should be Habakkuk 3: 17? As he read "Although the fig tree shall not blossom, neither shall fruit be in the vines; the labour of the olive shall fail, and the fields shall yield no meat; the flock shall be cut off from the fold, and there shall be no herd in the stalls: yet I will rejoice in the Lord, I will joy in the God of my salvation"—my father's voice faltered, and some eyes, at least, were wet with tears; for if an angel had suddenly appeared in our sorrowing circle, his voice could scarcely have been more clear, or more sweet, than the voice of God's word to our hearts that day.'

Soon after that event the whole family migrated to America where Henry continued his education, but in 1865, having returned to England, he entered the Wesleyan Methodist Church, and for more than forty years travelled the leading circuits. He edited 'St. Luke's Gospel' in *The Expositor's Bible*. He married a sister of the Rev. Mark Guy Pearse and from 1904 until his death lived in retirement at West Kirby, Cheshire.

144. Come, O come with me where love is beaming
(Anonymous)

Children's Hosannas, a Very Choice and Original Collection of Anniversary Music, compiled by John Burnham, 1889; 1899 S.A. song book; ascribed variously to Mrs. E. Anderson and to J. Burnham.

The War Cry of October 20, 1888, reported a meeting at Ipswich in which Miss Eva Booth, with banjo in hand, sang:

> None can be too vile for love so beaming,
> None can be too dark for light so streaming

Before the echo had died away she was heard to say: ' That is what we believe in The Salvation Army; that is what we teach; that is the burden of our message.'

145. Come, sinners, to Jesus, no longer delay (William Jefferson)

Ch.M.H.B.; with the chorus, 'For the Lion of Judah shall break. . .'

During the 1840s the people of Leicester were deeply moved by the Chartist movement, and crowds of people marched the streets singing in honour of their leader:

> The Lion of Freedom is come from his den,
> We'll rally around him again and again;
> We'll crown him with laurel, our champion to be,
> O'Connor, the patriot, for sweet liberty.

William Jefferson, the Primitive Methodist minister, put to the melody words suitable for the Ranters to sing through the streets. Thus 'The Lion of Judah' came into competition with the 'Lion of Freedom'. Many of the principles for which O'Connor contended have long since been adopted.

146. Come, sinners, to the gospel feast (Charles Wesley (15))

Wesley's *Hymns for Those who Seek and Those who have Redemption in the Blood of Jesus Christ*, 1747; Ch.M.H.B.; based on Luke 14: 16-24.

147. Come to the royal feast (Albert Midlane)

The Gospel Hall Hymn Book, 1860; 1930 S.A. song book.

Albert Midlane (1825-1909), a Newport (I. of W.) ironmonger, ministered regularly to a congregation of the Strict Brethren. 'Remarks which fell from the lips of my Sunday-school teacher', he wrote, 'first prompted me to poetic effort, and marked the outline of my future career. Most of my hymns have been written during walks around the ancient and historic ruins of Carisbrooke Castle.' Of his more than three hundred hymns, probably the most popular is 'There's a Friend for little children'.

148. Come to the Saviour, come to the Saviour (Anonymous)

Ch.M.H.B.

The chorus appeared in *Hymns as Poetry* by Tom Ingram and Douglas Newton, taken from Ned Wright's Hymn Book, 1870.

149. Come, weary sinner, to the Cross (Ralph E. Hudson)

The Musical Salvationist, June, 1889; 1899 S.A. song book. In *All the World*, June, 1889, the claim is made that the chorus is by Commandant Herbert Booth.

Ralph E. Hudson (1843-1901) was an American gospel singer and an enthusiastic worker in the cause of prohibition.

150. Come, ye disconsolate, where'er ye languish (Thomas Moore)

Hastings' and Mason's Spiritual Songs for Social Worship, 1832, altered probably by Dr. Thomas Hastings himself; 1899 S.A. song book.

Best known by his Irish ballads, which include ' 'Tis the last rose of summer' and 'The minstrel boy to the war has gone', Thomas Moore (1779-1852), son of a Roman Catholic grocer, was born in

Aungier Street, Dublin. He studied at Dublin University, graduated in 1798, left his own country for England the next year and in 1803 was appointed Registrar of the Admiralty Court at Bermuda. The work did not prove too congenial so he appointed a deputy and, after spending some time in America, returned to England. The deputy, however, fled with the proceeds of a ship and cargo, leaving Moore personally answerable for £6,000. His pecuniary embarrassments seem to have cast dark clouds over his otherwise gay life, although he was a favourite in London, and in 1835 received a pension from the Crown. Three years before his death at Sloperton Cottage, Wiltshire, he was reduced to a sad state of mental infirmity and required the constant attention of his wife.

151. Come, ye sinners, poor and needy (Joseph Hart)

Hymns Composed on Various Subjects, with the Author's Experience, 1759; Ch.M.H.B.

Joseph Hart (1712–68) was born in London of pious parents, received a good education and became a teacher of languages. In 1739 he commenced preaching and hymn-writing, and soon after became minister of the Independent Chapel, Jewin Street, London. In 1757 he received a profound impression from contemplating the sufferings of Christ, and wrote: ' The week before Easter I had an amazing view of the agony of Christ in the Garden. I was lost in wonder and adoration and the impression was too deep, I believe, ever to be obliterated.' He was buried in Bunhill Fields, City Road, London.

152. Dark shadows were falling (Evangeline Booth)

The Musical Salvationist, March, 1895; 1899 S.A. song book.

Evangeline Cory Booth, seventh child of the Founder, was born in London on Christmas Day, 1865. Early in her career she was appointed Captain of the Great Western Hall (Marylebone), a centre of great opposition. Later she became Field Commissioner for Britain, often facing riots, then Principal of the International Training Garrison, followed by appointments which placed her in charge of the Army's work in Canada, and in the U.S.A. where she served for thirty years. On September 3, 1934, she was elected General of The Salvation Army, retiring from the position in October, 1939. She was promoted to Glory from Hartsdale, New York, on July 17, 1950.

General Evangeline Booth was the author of *Love is all*, *Toward a Better World*, *Woman* and *Songs of the Evangel*. She was awarded the Distinguished Service Medal (by President Wilson) in recognition of the Army's service during the First World War; Fairfax Medal for Eminent Patriotic Service (1928); Order of the Founder (1930); Vasa

Gold Medal (Swedish) (1933); Gold Medal of National Institute of Social Science (1933); LL.D., Columbia University (1939).

'Returning to my quarters late one November evening,' wrote Evangeline Booth, 'after battling with cold, sleet and misery, dressed in rags that I might get nearer to the hearts and lives of the poorest of those with whom I mingled in the slums of London, I vainly struggled to banish from my mind and pitying heart the awful scenes I had looked upon. Men, women and children with broken lives, broken hearts and broken characters; hopeless and helpless, trapped like wild animals at bay.

'One picture I could not banish. The beautiful face and golden head of the little fifteen-year-old mother, appearing in the filthy, dark, boxlike room as a jewel amid ruins; the fast and bitter tears falling on the human mite dead in her arms; the despair in the frightened blue eyes as she said, "Look, there is no place for the baby or for me in life or in death. Where can I hide the baby? Where can I hide myself?"

'At one o'clock the following morning I wrote this song'—the answer to the heart-cry of the child-mother:

> The wounds of Christ are open ...
> There for refuge flee.

153. Guilty, lost sinner, from God thou hast wandered
(William Green)

All the World, March, 1896; *The Musical Salvationist*, October, 1896; 1899 S.A. song book.

Brigadier William Henry Green gave thirty years' service as an officer, commanding seven divisions in Great Britain before being transferred to Canada. A converted minstrel, he could sing well and accompany himself on guitar, concertina or flutina. Bandmaster Bert Twitchin recalled the Brigadier (as a Captain) and his wife 'Sunshine' being appointed in 1895 to the Regent Hall where his singing was greatly appreciated. He was promoted to Glory in July, 1917.

Brigadier Green described the writing of the song thus:

'One Sunday night I had been talking on the text "This year thou shalt die" (Jeremiah 28: 16). A young man was convicted and I saw the change in his face. I knew that he was getting ready to run away, so I got the people on their knees, gave the meeting over to the Lieutenant, and went to the door, where I intercepted him. "Jack," I said, "this is a God-given chance, don't neglect it."

'"Oh, Captain," said he, "why do you bother about me?" and he went out.

'About twelve o'clock on the following Tuesday he fell from the scaffold where he was working, broke his neck and died on the spot. After the funeral, and while still thinking over the occurrence, I wondered what more I could do to win sinners to Jesus. I took up my guitar and composed the song, "Guilty lost sinner". I sang it during the next Sunday night meeting and a dozen or so people were converted.'

154. Hark, sinner! while God from on high doth entreat thee (H. G. Anstey)

Ch.M.H.B.

155. Hark! the gospel news is sounding (Hugh Bourne and William Sanders)

Published in 1829; Ch.M.H.B.

Hugh Bourne (1772–1852), one of the founders of the Primitive Methodist Society and the editor of its first hymn book, was born at Fordhays, Stoke-on-Trent. His father was a farmer, wheelwright and timber-dealer who was passionate, drunken and dissolute, but a stiff churchman and a derider of Methodism and Dissent. His mother taught him thrift, patience, endurance, the fear of God and the love of righteousness. By hard study he acquired a knowledge of Hebrew, Greek and Latin. He became a Methodist in 1799, and in the following year commenced a series of prayer-meetings at Mow Cop Colliery, near Burslem, which culminated in a great camp meeting on Mow Cop Mountain on Sunday, May 21, 1807. Similar meetings followed, but were condemned by the Wesleyan Conference. He was excommunicated by the quarterly meeting at Burslem on June 27, 1808. Subsequent acts of coolness led him to organize the Primitive Methodist Connexion.

Hugh Bourne's first effort in hymn-writing was a general collection of hymns and spiritual songs for camp meetings, published in 1809.

William Sanders, born in 1799, was one of the Primitive Methodist song-writers.

156. Hark! the Saviour's voice from Heaven (A. Noble)

Ch.M.H.B. (No. 152), where the first verse begins, ' Yes, dear soul, a voice from heaven '.

157. Hark! the voice of Jesus calling (Albert Midlane (147))

Written in August, 1860; *Ambassador's Hymn Book*, 1861; Ch.M.H.B.

158. Have you any room for Jesus (Daniel W. Whittle)

Sacred Songs and Solos; 1899 S.A. song book.

A close friend and colleague of Philip P. Bliss, Daniel Webster Whittle (1840–1901) was born at Chicopee Falls, Massachusetts,

U.S.A., and saw much service with the 72nd Illinois Infantry during the Civil War. After a severe engagement at Vicksburg, during which he lost his right arm, he was taken prisoner. It was at this time that he was led to see his need of a Saviour. 'Having a desire for something to read, he felt in his haversack and found the little Testament his mother had placed there on the morning of his departure for the war. He read right through the book several times. Every part was interesting. He understood the presentation of the truth in the Epistle to the Romans that God gave Jesus His Son to be our Substitute, and that whoever would confess their sins and accept Him should be saved. While in this state of mind he was awakened one night by an orderly calling, " There's a boy in the other end of the ward who is dying. He has been begging me to pray for him, but I'm a wicked man, I cannot pray." "Why," said Whittle, "I can't pray. I never prayed in my life. I am just as wicked as you are!" "You can't pray?" said the orderly. "Why, I thought sure from seeing you read the Testament that you were a praying man. I can't go back there alone. Won't you come with me and see the boy at any rate?" Moved by the appeal young Whittle went with the orderly to the far corner of the room. A fair-headed boy of seventeen or eighteen lay dying. There was a look of intense agony on his face as he cried, " Oh, pray for me! Pray for me! I am dying. I was a good boy at home in Maine and went to Sunday-school. But since I became a soldier I have learned to be wicked. Now I am dying and I am not fit to die. Oh, ask Christ to save me!" "I dropped on my knees", said Whittle, "and held the boy's hand in mine, as in a few words I confessed my sins and asked God for Christ's sake to pardon me. I then prayed earnestly for the boy. He became quiet and pressed my hand as I pleaded God's promises. When I arose from my knees he was dead. A look of peace was upon his face, and I can but believe that God, who used me to bring Him to the Saviour, also used him to bring me to Christ."'

Whittle, who held the military rank of major, became a keen gospel worker and a very prolific song-writer, using pen-names which included 'El Nathan'.

159. Have you seen the Crucified? (John Lawley (56))

1899 S.A. song book.

Written in the train on the homeward journey after the Founder had made an appeal in Holland for workers in the Dutch East Indies (Indonesia).

160. Ho, every one that thirsts, draw nigh! (Charles Wesley (15))

Written to accompany a sermon on the words of Isaiah 55: 1, preached at Bristol during September, 1739; *Hymns and Sacred Poems*, 1740; Ch.M.H.B.

161. Is there a heart o'erbound by sorrow? (Edward H. Joy)

Written one Saturday evening after reading the words, ' Casting all your anxiety upon Him ' (1 Peter 5: 7, R.V.). That same evening Colonel Joy used the song at the Thornton Heath Corps; *The Musical Salvationist*, December, 1929.

Born at Canterbury on November 16, 1871, Edward Joy became an officer from Folkestone on July 24, 1894, being appointed as Lieutenant to Tunstall to work an outpost at Golden Hill. Following this, his only corps appointment, he served on various British provincial and divisional headquarters until 1917 when he became an under-secretary in the Foreign Office at I.H.Q. Later he served in migration work in Canada, then as Editor-in-chief for Canada West Territory, and finally editor of the South African *War Cry*.

From his days as a bandsman at Folkestone, which story he told in *The Old Corps*, Edward Joy was a song-writer, his first being published in *The Musical Salvationist*, April, 1892. In days of retirement he wrote, in addition to *The Old Corps*, *Marvellous in our Eyes* and *Gentlemen from Canada*. At the time of his promotion to Glory (February 16, 1949) from Carshalton he was a member of the Song Book Revision Council appointed in connection with the preparation of the present song book.

162. Is there a heart that is waiting (Annie L. James (verses); May Agnew (chorus))

Songs of Victory; 1899 S.A. song book. In *The Free Church Mission Hymnal* (1900) the song appears in a four-line setting to the tune, ' There shall be showers of blessing ', with the refrain:

> Jesus, thy Saviour,
>   Jesus is passing this way,
> Waiting to give thee free pardon,
>   Longing to save thee today.

The chorus ('Jesus is looking for thee') was published in *The Musical Salvationist*, December, 1890.

Captain May Agnew was an early-day Canadian officer serving on the training home staff in New York. She also wrote chorus No. 212, ' Have faith in God, the sun will shine '.

163. Jesus is tenderly calling thee home (Fanny Crosby (17))

Sankey's *Sacred Songs and Solos*; *Alexander's Hymns*, No. 3.

George C. Stebbins, an American composer, wrote the music to these words after returning from an evangelistic tour with Moody through Scotland in 1883.

164. Joy, freedom, peace and ceaseless blessing (Herbert H. Booth (91))

Salvation Music, Vol. 2; 1899 S.A. song book. A few minor alterations have been made to the original text.

165. Listen to the invitation (Annie Harris)

The War Cry, September 22, 1883, where the chorus is:

> Come with all your sin and sorrow,
> Low unto the Saviour's feet,
> And He will be sure to save you
> If with all your heart you seek.

The Musical Salvationist, March, 1892, where the present chorus is used; 1899 S.A. song book.

The author was a soldier of the Pembroke Dock Corps, and a frequent contributor to *The War Cry* of the 1880s.

166. Love of love so wondrous (Herbert H. Booth (91))

The Salvation Songster, 1885; 1899 S.A. song book.

While this song was being sung during a prayer meeting at the Chalk Farm Corps a young man became converted; he later became Lieut.-Colonel Roy Gilks.

167. O boundless salvation! deep ocean of love (William Booth (119))

The War Cry, December 23, 1893; *The Musical Salvationist* (supplement), Vol. 8 (1893-94), page 165; 1899 S.A. song book.

Known throughout the world as the Founder's Song, the words found their inspiration in a 'Boundless Salvation' campaign held in Great Britain in the autumn of 1893, and which reached its climax in two days' 'Boundless Salvation' meetings in the Exeter Hall, London, conducted by William Booth.

The War Cry for November 18, 1893, in preparation for the meetings to be held in the Exeter Hall during the next week, contained a page of 'Boundless Salvation' songs, which included one by Commissioner Booth-Tucker commencing, 'Boundless the salvation Jesus offers at the Cross', and song No. 139, 'Boundless as the mighty ocean'. It is not surprising then that the Founder's heart and mind were also steeped in this theme.

Staff-Captain (later Commissioner) Theodore Kitching had been working all night with Mr. Bramwell Booth at International Headquarters and had returned to Hadley Wood (the Founder's home) at six o'clock in the morning. Much to his surprise he discovered that

William Booth had also been busy throughout the night, for he handed him several sheets of paper which contained the verses of this song. They were introduced at the Exeter Hall meetings, for which occasion the Founder added to his verses the chorus:

> The heavenly gales are blowing,
> The cleansing stream is flowing,
> Beneath its waves I'm going,
> Hallelujah! praise the Lord!

The War Cry report of these meetings read: '358 souls take a platform plunge into the vast ocean of fathomless love.'

On the occasion of the Founder's Eighty-third Birthday Celebrations on May 9, 1912, in the Royal Albert Hall, he wrote in his diary: 'The hall was gorged when we arrived. . . . Every seat was occupied, and some very inconveniently so.

'The reception I received when I entered was overwhelming, but alas, when I opened my mouth with the first song, "O boundless salvation!", I found to my astonishment that my voice was broken. The ring of it was wanting and I had to put out the fullest effort possible to fill the building.'

Despite the disappointment as he announced this his last public song, few failed to hear him.

A Salvationist British Serviceman was walking through a German town in 1945 and was astounded to hear the music of 'O boundless salvation!' being played on a violin. Pushing his way through the crowd, he found playing in the gutter an old man who could speak English. He had lived in the U.S.A. for many years and had been a member of the New York Staff Band. The corps in the German town had almost been obliterated but he, as the Sergeant-Major, continued to proclaim the salvation message by singing and playing in this way in the streets.

168. O do not let thy Lord depart (Elizabeth Reed)

Written in 1825 and commencing with 'O do not let the word depart', these verses appeared in the Ch.M.H.B.

Mrs. Reed (1794–1867), *née* Holmes, the daughter of a London merchant, was married to Dr. Andrew Reed, a Congregationalist minister (see song No. 128), in 1816. Her songs, twenty in all, were contributed to her husband's collection and published in 1872.

169. O have you not heard of the beautiful stream (Richard T. Torrey, Jnr.)

Ch.M.H.B.

170.   O turn ye, O turn ye, for why will ye die (Josiah Hopkins)

Christian Lyre, Vol. 1, 1830, by Dr. Leavitt, a Congregational minister, was specially prepared for use in Charles Finney's revival campaigns; Ch.M.H.B.

Dr. Hopkins (1786–1862) was born at Pittsford, Vermont, U.S.A., and joined the Congregational Church in that place in 1803. After graduation at Auburn Theological Seminary, he was ordained pastor in 1809 at New Haven, Vermont. In 1830 he became minister of the First Presbyterian Church of Auburn, New York. He died in Geneva, New York.

171.   O wanderer, knowing not the smile (Herbert H. Booth (91))

Written to the ballad tune 'Footsteps on the stairs', and published in *The War Cry*, December 23, 1882; 1899 S.A. song book.

172.   O what amazing words of grace (Samuel Medley)

First published in 1789; Ch.M.H.B.

Born at Cheshunt, Herts, Samuel Medley (1738–99) was apprenticed to an oilman in London but, not liking the business, he claimed the privilege granted in time of war of finishing his apprenticeship in the Navy. After being severely wounded in the leg he was removed to the house of his grandfather, Mr. Tonge, who had trained him as a child at Enfield.

Mr. Tonge was a pious man and one Sunday evening read a sermon to his grandson, who saw his sinful condition and cried out for God's mercy. On his recovery he joined Dr. Gifford's Church in Eagle Street, London, and opened a school near Seven Dials. In 1766 he began to preach, and the following year became pastor of the Baptist Church at Watford, Herts. After five years he moved to Liverpool where his former life at sea made him master of those maritime expressions which were especially pleasing and easy to be understood by his seafaring hearers.

173.   Only a step to Jesus! (Fanny Crosby (17))

Royal Diadem, 1873; 1899 S.A. song book.

174.   Return, O wanderer, return (William B. Collyer (verses))

The Evangelical Magazine, May, 1806; Ch.M.H.B.; based on Jeremiah 31: 18–20.

Dr. William Bengo Collyer (1782–1854) was born at Blackheath and educated at Homerton College where, when sixteen years of age, he was entered as a student for the ministry. Before reaching his twenty-first birthday he became pastor of a Congregational Church consisting of ten communicants. He was ordained in December, 1801. For fifty-three years he laboured at one church, one of the most popular dissenting ministers in London. Of amiable disposition, polished manners and Christian courtesy, he attracted even royal dukes to his crowded chapel.

175. Sing them over again to me (Philip P. Bliss (78))

Written at the request of the publisher for the introductory issue of a magazine entitled *Words of Life*, 1874 (Fleming H. Revell); *Sacred Songs and Solos*; 1930 S.A. song book.

176. Sinner, how thy heart is troubled! (Fanny Crosby (17))

Sankey's *Sacred Songs and Solos*; *The Musical Salvationist*, June, 1917; 1930 S.A. song book.

177. Sinner, see yon light (James C. Bateman)

The Musical Salvationist, November, 1886, set to the tune 'Lottie Lane'; 1899 S.A. song book.

Captain Bateman was born in Hull, son of a flax dresser who earned good money which he spent freely.

'James was like his father in many things, as in his love of fun,' wrote Richard Slater. 'He fell down some steps in one of his boyish pranks, hurting his back, the results of which he carried with him for many years and, as he was a weakly boy, this accident added to his early disadvantages. He grew up to love the music-hall and theatre, as well as the public house. His natural musical gifts made him an acceptable singer and a good banjo player, so with his music and his fun-creating ability he was much sought after and was always given a welcome in any gay company. Managers of sing-songs, those of the free-and-easy kind, soon saw his value in their line of business. He was able to entertain a crowd for an hour at a stretch. Free drinks and cigars were, of course, at his command.

' Being engaged at an oil-mill in the daytime, it was at night, after working hours, that Bateman entered the wild, gay world that he found open to him as a consequence of his musical gifts. After the close, at about 11 p.m., of the places he visited he often roamed the streets with a group of jolly companions singing in boisterous fashion under the influence of the drink that they had indulged in so freely. On one of these occasions he resented the interference of the policeman, and his unruly conduct led to his being locked up. He was charged, found guilty, and fined two pounds.

'After a Saturday night's spree and a Sunday spent much in the same way, he found himself in anything but a fit state to go to work on the Monday. He had to help steady a load that was to slide down a ladder, but his foot slipped and he fell. Very much hurt, he was taken to the infirmary. The doctor told him one of his legs would have to be amputated. To this Bateman objected, and the doctor had to do what was possible without taking such drastic measures. Bateman made a fair recovery, but until his death he was lame.

' He became acquainted with the Army by its open-air work in the town in which he lived, but he was not favourably impressed. On one occasion the Army started a meeting outside the public house in which he happened to be drinking. The sound of the singing arrested his attention. An idea came to him suddenly—he would go outside, catch up the words, tunes and the manners of the Salvationists, then return to his companions in the bar parlour and have fun out of a mock Salvation Army meeting, he to be the mock Captain. This plan was carried through but with a heart by this time sick of the ways of sin and the world, for he became the object of the Holy Spirit's workings. The result was that he one night went right from a public house to the Army hall, was convicted of sin and in true penitence went to the Penitent-form and found salvation. Later he became a soldier, then a welcome special visitor to a number of corps, his singing and playing proving very attractive. At length he was induced to offer himself for officership. Among his commands were corps at Cradley Heath, Leicester, Openshaw, Northampton, Hanley (where he married Sister Polly Kirk), Middlesbrough and Clapton Congress Hall.

' He could play several instruments, had a good voice, and could admirably accompany his own solos, as well as lead congregational singing. He was an enthusiast for Army music, and as a song-maker stands in the front line of Army writers. He worked chiefly in writing words to popular secular tunes of the time, but he was also able to compose melodies such as have won the favour of Salvationists everywhere. He died on June 5, 1888.'

178. Sinner, we are sent to bid you (Anonymous)

Ch.M.H.B.

179. Sinner, wheresoe'er thou art (Fanny Crosby (17))

Written on October 3, 1871, and published in *Royal Diadem*; *Revival Music*, where the first line commenced, ' Mourner, wheresoe'er thou art '; 1878 S.A. song book.

180. Sinners Jesus will receive (Erdmann Neumeister; *translated by* Emma Frances Bevan)

Written as a conclusion to one of Neumeister's sermons on Luke 15: 2; published in the author's *Evang. Nachklang*, 1718; the translation appeared in Mrs. Bevan's *Songs of the Eternal Life*, 1858; 1899 S.A. song book.

Son of the school-master and organist at Uechteritz, near Weissenfels, Erdmann Neumeister (1671–1756) was in 1704 called by Duke Johann Georg to Weissenfels to be tutor to his only daughter and eventually court preacher. In 1715 he accepted the appointment of pastor of St. James's Church, Hamburg, in which city he died.

He began to write hymns in his student days, producing altogether more than 650, and is considered to be the originator of the cantata, of which he wrote many for use in church.

Mrs. Bevan (1827–1909), daughter of the Rev. Philip Shuttleworth, Warden of New College, Oxford, and afterward Bishop of Chichester, was born at Oxford. Notwithstanding the strong ties that bound her to the Church of England she joined the Plymouth Brethren, later turning from them to study the German mystics. She died at Cannes and was buried at Cockfosters, near London.

The chorus is said to have been arranged by D. W. Whittle when the song was published in Sankey's *Sacred Songs and Solos*.

181. So near to the Kingdom! yet what dost thou lack?
(Fanny Crosby (17))

The song similar to this (1930 song book No. 51) was merely an adaptation of Fanny Crosby's words and published in *The War Cry*, June 2, 1881, over the initials ' H. P., Cardiff '.

182. Softly and tenderly Jesus is calling (Will L. Thompson)

Songs of Joy and Gladness by McDonald and Gill, Boston; *The Musical Salvationist*, August, 1935.

Will L. Thompson (1847–1909) was born in East Liverpool, Ohio, U.S.A. One of his earliest song successes was written while he was at the Boston Conservatory of Music and was a secular song, ' Gathering up the shells by the seashore '. Later, however, he entered the field of sacred music, composing a number of songs and editing several choral collections.

Shortly before Dwight L. Moody's death, Thompson was admitted to the sick-room. Reaching out a feeble hand, the great evangelist said: ' Will, I would rather have written " Softly and tenderly " than anything I have been able to do in my whole life.'

The author also provided the musical setting.

183. Souls of men! why will ye scatter (Frederick W. Faber (80))

The author's *Oratory Hymns*, 1854; there were thirteen verses, the whole combining to give a picture of the tenderness and love of our

Saviour for the sinner; *Joy in Sorrow* by Miriam Booth; 1930 S.A. song book.

184. Ten thousand thousand souls there are (Anonymous)

Ch.M.H.B.; from earliest use these words have been associated with the sentimental tune, 'Down in a green and shady bed a modest violet grows'.

185. The heart that once has Jesus known (Mildred Duff)

The War Cry, September 28, 1889; 1930 S.A. song book.

Born in 1860 amid culture and comfort, Commissioner Mildred Duff as quite a young woman went with her maid to a tea meeting and heard some sailors testify. 'They seemed so happy that I grew wretched,' she acknowledged later. In low spirits she returned to the home in which she was being entertained and her hostess, realizing something of the work of God's Spirit that was going on, took her into her own room. They talked and prayed together and Mildred sought God's forgiveness.

She came into contact with The Salvation Army, and became an officer from North Walsham in 1886. She shared in pioneering work in Sweden and then served on the International Training Garrison in London. After a time as the leader of the slum work in Great Britain she became the editor of *All the World*, then of *The Young Soldier*, *The Warrior* and *The International Company Orders*. She travelled extensively on Salvation Army service and was also the author of a number of popular books. She was promoted to Glory from North Walsham, where she lived after her retirement from active service, on December 8, 1932.

186. There is a better world, they say (John Lyth)

Written on April 30, 1845, at Stroud, Gloucestershire, for the anniversary of the infant school in nearby Randwick; *Home and School Hymn Book*; Ch.M.H.B.

Born at York, Dr. John Lyth (1821–86) became a Wesleyan minister in 1843 and in 1859 had the honour of being the first Wesleyan minister to be appointed to Germany, to Winnenden. He returned in 1865 to England where he continued his ministry until retirement in 1883.

187. There is a Mercy Seat revealed (Arthur R. Gibby)

The War Cry, April 23, 1921, first prize in a song competition; 1930 S.A. song book.

Arthur Robert Gibby was converted in 1883 at Pembroke Dock

where he served for eight years as the Corps Sergeant-Major, for nine years as the Young People's Sergeant-Major and for some time as the Young People's Treasurer and Corps Correspondent.

Brother Gibby claimed that when he first met the Army he was no scholar, indeed he could ' scarcely write his own name '. But he composed over five hundred songs, one of the most well known being ' His love can ne'er be told '.

For the last thirteen years of his life he suffered acutely and was unable to take an active part in Salvation Army work. He died early in 1933.

188. There is life for a look at the crucified One (Amelia M. Hull)

Written in 1860 and published in Miss H. W. Soltaus's *Pleasant Hymns for Boys and Girls*, 1860; Ch.M.H.B.

Daughter of a magistrate, Amelia Matilda Hull was born at Marpool Hall, Exmouth, and devoted much of her time to the cause of education and to works of religious usefulness. She wrote several books including a hymn book for children.

189. Though your sins be as scarlet (Fanny Crosby (17))

Sacred Songs and Solos; The Musical Salvationist, January, 1909; 1930 S.A. song book; based on Isaiah 1: 18; 55: 7; 43: 25.

The song lay dormant for a number of years after it was written, coming into circulation only after George C. Stebbins had popularized it as a solo.

190. We have a message, a message from Jesus (R. R. Couch)

Written by a soldier of New Brompton (now Gillingham) Corps and published in *The War Cry*, December 22, 1881; 1899 S.A. song book. The French version of these words constituted the first song used by The Salvation Army in the Belgian Congo, in 1934.

191. Weary souls that wander wide (Charles Wesley (15))

Wesley's *Hymns for Those who Seek and Those who have Redemption in the Blood of Jesus Christ*, 1747; Ch.M.H.B.

It was during the singing of the second verse in a small Methodist church that Mrs. Fry, mother of Charles Fry, the first Army Bandmaster, found ' on earth the life of Heaven '.

192. Weary wanderer, wilt thou listen (John Lawley (56))

1899 S.A. song book.

'At the time I composed it ', wrote the Commissioner, ' the

Founder was preaching from the text, " Behold, I stand at the door, and knock " (Revelation 3: 20). His sermon took such a hold upon me—I saw the humility of Jesus so clearly and the refusal of the people to open the door and admit Him into their hearts and lives, that I decided to write a song to second what the General was saying. As I composed the last verse the fountain of my soul burst and I could find relief only in tears.'

After singing it for the first time, at Norwich in 1889, Lawley felt the Founder's hand on his shoulder and heard William Booth's voice: ' Well done, Lawley, that song will go round the world.'

193. We're travelling home to Heaven above (Richard Jukes)

Philip Phillips's *Hallowed Songs*, 1873; Ch.M.H.B.

Born at Goathill, Salop, Richard Jukes (1804–67), a Primitive Methodist minister, was called ' The Bard of the Poor ' for they greatly prized his hymns.

The story is told of a street singer, clasping a handful of printed hymns he had been singing and selling, who said: ' Your Jukes has been a good friend to us street singers, I have sung lots of his hymns and made many a bright shilling thereby. I shall always think well of your Jukes.'

194. What could your Redeemer do (Charles Wesley (15))

Wesley's *Hymns on God's Everlasting Love*, 1741; Ch.M.H.B.; based on Ezekiel 18: 31.

Charles Wesley's teaching is that if man is ultimately lost it will be because he himself has resolved to die.

195. What is the love of Jesus to thee? (Richard Slater (105))

Written on March 24, 1898, and published in *The Musical Salvationist*, January, 1900; 1930 S.A. song book.

196. What means this eager, anxious throng (Etta Campbell)

Songs of Victory; Hallelujah Hymn Book; Revival Music; 1878 S.A. song book. Written during a revival period at Newark, New Jersey, U.S.A., where the author, a teacher in Morristown, New Jersey, heard an address on Luke 18: 37. The song became very popular during the Sankey and Moody evangelical tour of Great Britain in 1874–76.

197. Who comes to Me, the Saviour said (William Kitching)

Written during days of retirement by the father of Commissioner Theodore H. Kitching and grandfather of the Army's seventh General, and published in *The Musical Salvationist*, January, 1913, to an original tune by the General who was then Deputy Bandmaster of New Barnet Band; also 1930 S.A. song book.

William Kitching was born in Gainsborough, Lincolnshire, in June, 1837. He became a school-master at the Quakers' School at Sidcot, near Weston-super-Mare, where he met another teacher, Louisa Wilmot, whom he married in 1862.

He then secured a teaching post at Ackworth School, Yorkshire, which was dubbed by the scholars 'The Quaker Eton'. Here Theodore Hopkins Kitching (see song No. 529) was born in 1866. William Kitching remained at Ackworth until 1880.

Concerning his gifts as a poet it has been said that ' his most musical verses were written amid the heather and gorse of the Yorkshire moors, or under the influence of the grand sea and mountain '.

After resigning from Ackworth owing to a breakdown in health William Kitching settled at Southport, Lancashire, a place recommended for its hydropathic treatment, where he opened a private boarding and day school accommodating seventy boys, and in which Theodore became a member of the teaching staff.

When The Salvation Army invaded the fashionable seaside resort the Kitchings gave a warm welcome to the Salvationists.

On retiring from his profession William Kitching removed to Clevedon, Somerset, where he died in December, 1906.

A fuller story can be found in *T. H. K.* by Arch R. Wiggins.

198. Who'll be the next to follow Jesus? (Annie S. Hawks)

1899 S.A. song book.

Mrs. Annie Sherwood Hawks (1835–1918), the author of hundreds of gospel songs and a member of the Hanson Place Baptist Church in Brooklyn, was born in Horsick, New York, and died in Bennington, Vt.

199. Whosoever heareth! shout, shout the sound (Philip P. Bliss (78))

Hallelujah Hymn Book; Revival Music; 1878 S.A. song book.

Written during the winter of 1869–70 after twenty-eight-year-old Mr. Henry Moorhouse had preached a course of sermons on John 3 : 16 in Moody's Church in Chicago. The same sermons helped Moody himself to understand more fully the love of God for the worst sinner and ' to draw his sword full length, to fling away the scabbard and enter into the battle with a naked blade '.

200. Will your anchor hold in the storms of life (Priscilla J. Owens)

Sankey's *Sacred Songs and Solos.*

Miss Owens (1829–99), a Baltimore public school teacher of

Scottish and Welsh descent, was for fifty years actively engaged in Sunday-school work, for which her gospel songs were written.

201. With a sorrow for sin must repentance begin (Anonymous)

Ch.M.H.B.

Describing a march from Mile End Road to the Dancing Academy, New Road, Whitechapel, where Sunday services were held for seventeen months until February, 1867, William Booth wrote of the efficient company singing, ' We're bound for the land of the pure and the holy ', when ' the people ran from every direction. Drunkards came forth to hear and to see; some in mockery joined our ranks; some laughed and sneered; some were angry; the great majority looked on in wonder; some turned and accompanied us as on we went, changing our song to

> With a turning from sin let repentance begin,
> Then conversion itself will draw nigh;
> But till washed in the Blood of a crucified Lord,
> We shall never be ready to die.

' The hall was filled, the audience was of the right kind, many were awakened and several professed to find Jesus ' (*The History of The Salvation Army*, Vol. 1, p. 51).

202. Would you be free from your burden of sin? (L. E. Jones)

Alexander's *New Revival Hymns*; 1930 S.A. song book.

Born in Yates City, Illinois, U.S.A., Mr. Jones became a Y.M.C.A. worker at the age of twenty-six, receiving his training in Chicago in the same class as Billy Sunday, the evangelist. Mr. Jones died in Santa Barbara, California, in 1936.

203. A needy sinner at Thy feet (— Strong (verses); Emily E. S. Elliott (chorus))

The verses, by Captain Strong, an early-day officer, appeared in the 1899 S.A. song book and commenced, 'A weary sinner at Thy feet '. A few other alterations have been made. The chorus belongs to

> Thou didst leave Thy throne and Thy kingly crown,
> When Thou camest to earth for me . . .

which was printed privately for the use of the choir and school at St. Mark's Church, Brighton, of which Miss Elliott's father was rector, and later appeared in Sankey's *Sacred Songs and Solos*.

Miss Elliott (1836–97) came of a hymn-writing family; Charlotte Elliott (see No. 217) was her aunt, and her uncle, the Rev. Henry V.

Elliott, published in 1835 a collection of *Hymns for Public, Private and Social Worship*. Miss Elliott herself published two volumes of hymns and poems containing 141 hymns.

204. And can it be that I should gain (Charles Wesley (15))

Written in Little Britain, London, in May, 1738, immediately after the author's conversion, and published in *Psalms and Hymns* which appeared the same year; Ch.M.H.B.

' I began a hymn on my conversion, but was persuaded to break it off for fear of pride,' wrote Charles Wesley in his *Journal* for May 23, 1738. ' Mr Bray [a brazier with whom Charles was living] coming in, encouraged me to proceed in spite of Satan. I prayed to Christ to stand by me and I finished the hymn. Upon showing it to Mr. Bray the devil threw in a fiery dart, suggesting that it was wrong and that I had displeased God. My heart sank within me until I discerned that it was the device of the enemy to keep back glory from God, for it is not unusual for him to preach humility when speaking will endanger his kingdom and so honour Christ. Least of all would he have us tell what things God has done for our souls, so tenderly does he guard us from pride.'

205. Approach, my soul, the Mercy Seat (John Newton (41))

The Olney Hymns, 1779; 1930 S.A. song book.

206. As I am before Thy face (Herbert H. Booth (91))

The War Cry, November 18, 1893; 1899 S.A. song book.
These words were used as a solo in an all night of prayer as early as 1891.

207. By Thy birth and by Thy tears (Robert Grant (9))

The Christian Observer, 1815; *Congregational Hymn Book: A Supplement to Dr. Watts's Psalms and Hymns*, 1836; 1899 S.A. song book. Our present version is slightly altered.

208. Depth of mercy! Can there be (Charles Wesley (15))

Hymns and Sacred Poems, 1740; Ch.M.H.B., *Revival Music* with chorus:

> God is love, I know, I feel,
> Jesus weeps and loves me still.

209. Father, I dare believe (Charles Wesley (15))

Short Hymns on Selected Passages of Scripture, 1762; based on (verse 1) Psalm 130: 7, 8; (verse 2) Jeremiah 4: 1; (verse 3) Jeremiah 4: 14. 1930 S.A. song book.

210. I have heard of a Saviour's love (Philip Phillips)

Revival Music; 1878 S.A. song book.

Born on a farm near Jamestown, Chautanqua County, New York, Mr. Phillips (1834–95) first sang in public at the age of five and, although engaged in farming for a time, became a music teacher at nineteen. Two years later he became an itinerant music peddler, going from house to house playing his melodeon and endeavouring to sell his self-published songs. Once he was invited to sing before the United States Senate, President Lincoln enjoying his singing so much that he asked for a repetition. Encouraged, Philip Phillips decided to devote his full time to gospel singing, in which calling he became well known throughout America, England and Australia as ' The Singing Pilgrim '.

211. I have no claim on grace (Albert Orsborn (42))

The Beauty of Jesus, 1947.

During the winter of 1916 the author attended a meeting at the Custom House Corps, in East London. ' It was ', he writes, ' a real old-time " glory-shop ", a little hall crowded with hallelujah enthusiasts.' A Zeppelin raid was in progress as he made his way home on a bus, and shrapnel was spattering the almost deserted streets. These outward circumstances, however, were almost lost sight of because of an inward joy which flooded his soul as he recalled the glowing testimonies to which he had so recently listened. His spirit was moved and, the General continues, ' this song sang itself to me as I rode homeward. Having no pencil or paper with me, I had to hold on to the words until I reached home. Then, without taking off my overcoat, I sat down to pen these verses '.

212. Jesus, if still the same Thou art (Charles Wesley (15))

Hymns and Sacred Poems, 1740, and based on Matthew 5: 3, 4, 6; 1899 S.A. song book.

213. Jesus, if still Thou art today (Charles Wesley (15))

Hymns and Sacred Poems, 1740; 1899 S.A. song book.

214. Jesus, my Lord, to Thee I cry (Eliza Hamilton)

Songs of Joy and Gladness (U.S.A.); 1899 S.A. song book.

During revival meetings in Scotland a young girl inquired of her minister how she could be sure of salvation. The minister spoke to her and bade her go home and read the fifty-third chapter of Isaiah. Uneducated as she was, she cried, ' Oh, sir, I cannot read, I cannot pray!' and, throwing up her hands, exclaimed, 'Lord Jesus, take me as I am!' Eliza Hamilton heard of the girl's experience and wrote the words to which Mr. Sankey set the music.

215. Jesus, see me at Thy feet (Richard Slater (105))

The Musical Salvationist, November, 1887; 1899 S.A. song book.

Written on September 9, 1887, both words and music were inspired as a result of thinking of the great use made by the Army of the Rev. Robert Lowry's ' Nothing but the Blood of Jesus '. Said Lieut.-Colonel Slater: ' I wondered if I could be honoured in making a song on similar lines for Army use. Although not taking the American song as a model to imitate as to metre and melody I did seek to equal it in simplicity and clearness of presentation of the fact that salvation comes through the Blood of Jesus. My own soul was moved while at work on the song. On reaching home from the office I asked my wife to come to the piano that I might sing and play over to her my new composition, as was my custom, for I liked to have her judgment.

' The song made a deep impression immediately, and soon she joined me in the chorus. I noticed, too, that my elder daughter, then a child of three years of age, was also singing, and with much feeling, her eyes uplifted in a devotional mood.'

216. Jesus, Thou know'st my sinfulness (Charles Wesley (15))

Hymns and Sacred Poems, 1742; 1899 S.A. song book. The original version, 'Jesus, Thou knowest my simpleness', was based on the Prayer Book Version of Psalm 69: 5.

217. Just as I am, without one plea (Charlotte Elliott)

1836 edition of *Invalid's Hymn Book*; Ch.M.H.B.

Born in Clapham, Miss Elliott (1789–1871) moved to Brighton in 1823, where she lived with a married brother, a clergyman. One day in 1834 the rest of the family had gone to a church bazaar and Charlotte, by this time a helpless, incurable invalid, had been left lying on the sofa. Her ill health had been a sore trial but she felt her sorrows must be conquered in the grace of God. Taking pen and paper from the table, she deliberately set down in writing, for her own comfort, ' the formulae of her faith '. The memory of the advice of Dr. Caesar Malan, of Geneva, when visiting Charlotte's home at Clapham, in 1822, ' Cut the cable . . . you must come to Christ just as you are ', was the inspiration of the verses. He had found her trying to work out her own salvation and unwilling to trust entirely in Christ. When her sister-in-law returned home she found the verses lying on the table.

After the author's death more than one thousand letters bearing testimony to the power of 'Just as I am' were found among her private papers.

218. Lord, I hear of showers of blessing (Elizabeth Codner)

Written at Weston-super-Mare in the summer of 1860 and published the following year on a leaflet; Ch.M.H.B.

Mrs. Codner (1824–1919), daughter of Robert Harris, was born at Dartmouth and married the Rev. Daniel Codner, for some time curate of Peterborough. For many years she was associated with the Rev. W. and Mrs. Pennefather in their work at Mildmay Hall, London, and also edited a monthly missionary magazine, *Women's Work.*

A party of young people in whom Mrs. Codner was greatly interested, and about whose spiritual welfare she was anxious, had attended a meeting in which detailed reference had been made to the great spiritual awakening taking place in Ireland (1860). She appealed to them that they share in the blessings of which they had heard. On the following Sunday, but not being well enough to attend her class, she had an opportunity for a time of communion with the Lord. Without effort words took the form of 'Lord, I hear of showers of blessing', which she had no intention of sending beyond the limits of her own circle.

219. My God, my Father, dost Thou call (Edward H. Bickersteth)

Written for the London Church Mission in 1874 and published in 1876; 1930 S.A. song book.

Dr. Bickersteth (1825–1906) was born at Islington, London, son of the Rector of Watton, an eminent theological writer. Educated at Trinity College, Cambridge, and after serving as Curate of Banningham, Norfolk, and Tunbridge Wells, and as Rector of Hinton Martell, Dorset, and Christ Church, Hampstead, he was appointed Dean of Gloucester in 1885 and in the same year became Bishop of Exeter. He wrote several volumes of devotional poetry and edited the *Hymnal Companion to the Book of Common Prayer* in 1870.

220. My God, my God, to Thee I cry (Charles Wesley (15))

Hymns and Sacred Poems, 1740; Ch.M.H.B.

221. No, not despairingly (Horatius Bonar (4))

The author's *Hymns of Faith and Hope* (3rd Series), 1866; *The*

Musical Salvationist, November, 1911, in which setting an extra line, here retained, was added to the original; 1930 S.A. song book.

222. Not what these hands have done (Horatius Bonar (4))

The author's *Hymns of Faith and Hope* (2nd Series), 1861.

223. O Jesus, Thou art standing (William Walsham How)

Written, and published in Morrel and How's *Psalms and Hymns*, in 1867; 1930 S.A. song book.

Born at Shrewsbury, Dr. How (1823–97), the son of a solicitor, was educated at Shrewsbury School and Wadham College, Oxford. He took Holy Orders in 1846 and, after holding curacies at Kidderminster and Shrewsbury, became Rector of Whittington in 1851 where he remained for twenty-eight years. From 1879 to 1888 he was Rector of St. Andrew's Undershaft, London, and in 1888 accepted the Bishopric of Wakefield. ' Totally without ambition in the worldly sense, he declined the offer of the See of Manchester without even mentioning it to his wife, and later refused one of the most distinguished posts in the Anglican Church, the Bishopric of Durham, with an income more than double the one he then had.' He died at Leenane, County Mayo, Ireland.

A sermon in an English fishing village on the words, ' Behold, I stand at the door, and knock ', inspired Jean Ingelow to write a poem which came into the hands of William Walsham How. Of it he wrote: ' The pathos of the verses impressed me very forcibly at the time. I read them over and over again and finally, closing the book, I scribbled on an odd scrap of paper my first idea of the verses beginning, ' O Jesus, Thou art standing '.

224. O Love, Thou deep eternal tide (Anonymous)

1930 S.A. song book.

225. O Thou that hearest when I cry (Isaac Watts (3))

Part of a paraphrase of Psalm 51 and published in the author's *Psalms of David*, 1719. The Ch.M.H.B. contained five verses of Watts's original, the 1899 S.A. song book six and the 1930 edition eight in two songs—Nos. 182 and 183.

226. Pass me not, O loving Saviour (Fanny Crosby (17))

Philip Phillips' *Hallowed Songs*, 1873; *Revival Music*; 1878 S.A. song book.

In 1868 in the midst of her address to the criminals of an American

State prison Miss Crosby was interrupted by one of the inmates crying out in an agonized tone of voice, ' God, Lord, don't pass me by! ' The startling cry of the penitent man rang in her ears for days afterward, and under its wailing influence she wrote the verses of the song, ending with the refrain, ' Saviour, Saviour, hear my humble cry '.

227. Rock of ages, cleft for me (Augustus M. Toplady)

The Gospel Magazine, March, 1776; Ch.M.H.B.

Born at Farnham, Surrey, son of a major in the British Army who had died at the siege of Carthagena earlier in the year, Toplady (1740–78) was educated at Westminster School and at Trinity College, Dublin. He was converted in a barn in the village of Codymain, Ireland, when a youth of sixteen, after listening to a sermon preached by a Wesleyan Methodist named James Morris. In due course Toplady became a Calvinist and in 1762 was ordained in the Church of England, serving curacies at Blagdon, Somerset, and at New Ottery before becoming in 1768 the Vicar of Broadhembury, Devon. While minister of the French Calvinist Church, Orange Street, Leicester Square, London, he became the editor of *The Gospel Magazine*. During this period he wrote his controversial works which later were reissued in six volumes.

His mind was vigorous but his body was weak and he died of consumption at Knightsbridge, and was buried at Whitefield's Chapel in Tottenham Court Road, London.

There is a tradition that ' Rock of ages, cleft for me ' was written in 1762 whilst Toplady was sheltering from a thunderstorm near the village of Blagdon in a ' cleft rock ' in Burrington Combe in the Mendip Hills. Its first appearance, in *The Gospel Magazine*, was at the end of an article called: 'A remarkable calculation introduced here for the sake of the spiritual improvements subjoined. Questions and answers relating to the National Debt.' After pointing out that the National Debt was so large that the Government would never be able to pay it, he proceeded to calculate how many sins each human being was guilty of and that the debt could be paid only by the Blood of the Crucified.

228. Saviour, hear me while before Thy feet (Herbert H. Booth (91))

All the World, December, 1889; 1899 S.A. song book.

' The tune had been composed some eighteen months before, but put away as being unsuitable for Army use,' wrote Lieut.-Colonel Slater. 'I was present at the Founder's house, at Upper Clapton, where H. H. Booth was living at the time, on the occasion when the tune was composed, and took it down in shorthand fashion as its composer gave it from an organ at which he was sitting.

'"Ah, that's too classical for Army use," said H. H. B. when I spoke in warm fervour of the melody. "Put it in the waste-paper basket; it will be of no use." "No! no!" was my response, "I'll preserve it among your melodies for consideration at some future day."

' In the midst of great pressure of work in November, 1889, H. H. B. had an urgent request that he should supply a new song for the Christmas issue of *All the World*. Several efforts were made to meet that request, but without result. It had come to the last day that the printers could wait for copy, and yet no song was ready, although some sketches had been made. It fell to me to go to him to find what this last day's effort would bring forth.

' It was a dark, damp, gloomy November night when I went on my errand to Hadley Wood, where he was then living. He showed me some outlines of verses and told me his old tune, discarded eighteen months before, would come into his mind, and so the verse of a song might be constructed by its aid. But what about a chorus?

'As he paced his room, singing the air, to which he gave a new beautiful turn as a possible version for a chorus, he sang (I was at the piano keeping the music going so as to provide a sort of suitable atmosphere), " Grace there is my every debt to pay." That was committed to paper. A halt followed, and then the vague thoughts took definite shape once more in the line " Blood to wash my every sin away ". Again suspense, whilst I continued to keep the tune going as its composer murmured the words to the notes which rose and fell. Then with eager hand he wrote, " Power to keep me sinless day by day " (the word " spotless " was substituted later). But still the chorus was not complete, for there were four notes without words. Again and again words were tried; one combination and then another was put aside as unsatisfactory until, in an undertone, I said, " For me, For me! " " That will do! " broke out H. H. B., as in triumph he made his chorus complete.

' So this chorus went forth—an epitome of theology it may be called: *Grace* to deal with the past; *Blood* to make clean the present; *Power* to make the saintly life possible for the future. And for whom are all these blessings of salvation? " For me, for me! " '

An Army band and male voice chorus used this song at the author's funeral in Yonkers, U.S.A.

229. She only touched the hem of His garment (George F. Root)

Sankey's *Sacred Songs and Solos; All the World*, July, 1905; 1930 S.A. song book; and based on Matthew 9: 20-26.

Dr. Root (1820-95) was born in Sheffield, Massachusetts, U.S.A., and at the age of thirteen could play as many instruments as he was years old. Whilst still in his teens he moved to Chicago, studied music under Lowell Mason, and became an organist, choral director and teacher. Later he moved to New York City and taught in several schools, including the New York Institute for the Blind where Fanny Crosby was one of his pupils.

Dr. Root was a voluminous writer. He was a musician honourably recognized by the profession and was given the degree of Doctor of Music in 1873 by the Chicago University. Before devoting his talents to the writing of hymns and gospel songs, Dr. Root was America's foremost writer of war songs during the American Civil War. Amongst his popular tunes are 'Just before the battle, mother' and ' The vacant chair '.

He organized singing-schools in various States of the U.S.A. and was associated with the Chicago publishing firm of Root and Cady. He edited seventy-four song books, many cantatas and other music.

In *All the World* the words and music are introduced thus: ' This well-known song was much used during the General's memorable soul-saving campaigns of the early eighties, when thousands of people surrendered themselves to God.'

230. Weary of wandering from my God (Charles Wesley (15))

Hymns and Sacred Poems, 1749; 1899 S.A. song book; and based on 1 John 2: 1.

231. What can wash away my sin? (Robert Lowry)

Published in 1877; *Salvation Music*, Vol. 2.

Born in Philadelphia, Pennsylvania, U.S.A., Dr. Lowry (1826–99) was converted at the age of seventeen. After graduating from the Bucknell University he became Baptist minister at West Chester, Penn., later returning to his old university as Professor of Rhetoric. Although always fond of music, he did not undertake its serious study until after the age of forty. He became a musician of considerable ability and many of his songs are set to his own music. He edited several Sunday-school hymnals, one of which, *Pure Gold*, sold over a million copies. He died at Plainfield, New Jersey.

The influence of this song inspired Richard Slater to write No. 215.

232. When shall Thy love constrain (Charles Wesley (15))

The original setting contained twenty-two verses and was published in 1740; Ch.M.H.B.

Referring to the visit of David Greenbury to Nottingham when the Founder was a youth, Harold Begbie wrote in his *Life of William Booth*:

' This evangelist from Scarborough was the first man to realize the force and power of William Booth as a preacher. . . . He urged upon the young man that it was his duty to speak, that he owed it to God to conquer his timidity, which was a form of selfishness. One of Booth's favourite hymns came to his assistance. He was haunted by the verses:

> And can I yet delay . . .
> Nay, but I yield, I yield! . . .

' With the same sudden abandon that had characterized his surrender two years before to the urgence of conscience, he now not only threw himself into the work of street preaching, but became the recognized leader of the group.'

233. Why should I wait? I cannot flee (Philip P. Bliss (78))

Sankey's *Sacred Songs and Solos*; 1930 S.A. song book.

234. With all my sins and guilt (Charles Blake)

1930 S.A. song book.

Converted as a lad at Salisbury, Charles Blake (1866-1945) opened Child's Hill Corps, in London, in 1885, when he was a nineteen-year-old Captain. Later he became the Corps Sergeant-Major and served the corps for thirty-five years until his retirement. His promotion to Glory was announced in *The Musician*, October 27, 1945. He was interred at Salisbury.

' I had been away from home all day,' wrote the author, ' and with not a lot to do my thoughts had been full of the wonderful love of Jesus in dying on the Cross for all the wide world. The great tragedy of Calvary became very vivid to me. Upon returning home at night I was waiting on the railway station platform when the first lines of the song came into my mind, and while I was still waiting I wrote the first two verses; the third was written after I reached home.'

235. With broken heart and contrite sigh (Cornelius Elven)

Written in January, 1852, to be used with the revival sermons the author was then preaching to his own congregation, and published in *The Baptist Psalms and Hymns*, 1858; 1930 S.A. song book; based on Luke 18: 10-14.

During the fifty years' ministry of Mr. Elven (1797-1873) at the Baptist Church, Bury St. Edmunds, Suffolk, the membership increased from forty to six hundred.

236. A crown of peace to me is given (J. D. Allan)

The Musical Salvationist, January, 1887, with original music and chorus No. 274; 1930 S.A. song book.

Born in Scotland, J. D. Allan (1858–1946) met the Army in Paisley soon after his conversion.

When Herbert Booth planned the 1886 'Life Guards March' in which many cadets took part, J. D. Allan, though not a Salvationist, asked to be allowed to join in the three months' campaign from Newcastle to Birmingham. Early in the campaign Mr. Herbert's private secretary broke down and J. D. Allan offered to fill in the breach. When the march ended he continued to act in a secretarial capacity. About this time he wrote 'Come and be a soldier' which appeared in *The Musical Salvationist*, May, 1887, and he continued writing songs until the end of his life, often providing the music as well. He married Captain Grace Fooks. Becoming a Staff-Captain and A.D.C. to Herbert Booth he travelled on three continents. His last appointment, before becoming a Congregational minister, was as Divisional Officer for the Ipswich Division. In retirement he lived at Finchley, London.

When 'An Evening with the Songs of J. D. Allan' was arranged in the citadel at Highgate, the composer himself presided. Speaking of his early-day song-writing, he said: 'At that time I received a visitation of the Spirit that kindled and quickened me, like the fruit trees when they feel the power rising within them in spring-time.'

237. All that I was, my sin, my guilt (Horatius Bonar (4))

The author's *Hymns of Faith and Hope*, 1857; *The Musical Salvationist*, July, 1923; 1930 S.A. song book.

238. Before I found salvation (William Giles Collins)

The Musical Salvationist, June, 1887; 1899 S.A. song book.

Bro. Collins was Corps Sergeant-Major at Guildford; he also composed the music for these words. Born 1855; died 1931.

239. Begone, vain world! Thou hast no charms for me (Anonymous)

Ch.M.H.B.

240. Blessèd assurance, Jesus is mine (Fanny Crosby (17))

Published in 1873; 1930 S.A. song book.

'Here is a new hymn tune I have written,' said Mrs. Joseph Knapp to Fanny Crosby as they chatted one day in Miss Crosby's room; 'what does it suggest to you?'

While the blind hymn-writer listened Mrs. Knapp played her new tune over several times on the piano. 'Why,' exclaimed Fanny Crosby as her face suddenly lit up with inspiration, 'the music says,

" Blessèd assurance, Jesus is mine." ' And as she listened to the music words began to form into a song.

241. Come and rejoice with me (Elizabeth Rundle-Charles)

Written in 1846 and published in the author's *Poems*, 1868; 1930 S.A. song book.

The author of numerous works intended to popularize the history of early Christian life in Great Britain and other kindred subjects, Mrs. Rundle-Charles (1828–96) was born at Tavistock, Devon, the daughter of John Rundle, the local Member of Parliament. She was a convert of Caesar Malan, who brought Charlotte Elliott, the author of ' Just as I am ', to Christ. She married Andrew Paton Charles in 1851.

Dora Greenwell, the poetess, wrote of her: ' That woman always brings and leaves a sense of comfort. She talks away in a hurried and rather hesitating fashion, and with what Bunyan calls " a wonderfully innocent smile", and yet you feel she hits the mark. Tender and unassuming, and yet she has an unusually unfettered and even daring mind.'

The death of Mrs. Rundle-Charles was reported in *All the World*, August, 1896, thus: ' The Army has lost a warm friend and sympathizer. The last time we went to see her in the interests of *All the World* she gave us a poem for our pages called " Don't worry, try the sunlight ".'

242. Come, comrades dear, who love the Lord (Anonymous)

Ch.M.H.B., where the first line read, ' Come, brethren dear, that love the Lord '. The last line of the second verse was originally 'And yet we still are dry '.

243. Come, Thou Fount of every blessing (Robert Robinson (verses); Louise M. Rouse (chorus))

Probably written about 1758 during the author's ministry in Norfolk, and published in a book used by the church in Angel Lane, Bishopsgate, the following year; Ch.M.H.B. The chorus belongs to song No. 504.

Son of an exciseman, Robert Robinson (1735–90) was born at Swaffham, Norfolk. The early death of his father prevented Robert's training for the Church of England ministry and at fourteen he was apprenticed to a London hairdresser.

In his seventeenth year, in company with some of his companions, he joined in making an old fortune-teller intoxicated in order to make fun of his drunken predictions concerning themselves. In view of the fortune-teller's forecasts Robinson began to think about the responsibilities of life and went to hear George Whitefield preach. Robinson lived in fear as he pondered the sermon on 'The wrath to come', until he became converted two and a half years later.

In 1758 he was invited to take charge of a Calvinistic Methodist Chapel at Mildenhall, Suffolk, then as the minister of an Independent Church in Norwich. In 1759 he received adult baptism and shortly afterward became pastor of the Stone Yard Baptist Chapel, Cambridge. At one period he carried on business as a coal and corn merchant and regularly preached twice on Sundays besides engaging in evangelistic work during the week.

In 1790, shortly before he died, Robinson retired to Birmingham, where he lived with, and occasionally preached for, Dr. Priestly, a Unitarian.

'May I ask your attention to this hymn, and ask you to favour me with your opinion of it? Do you know it?' asked a lady as she handed a fellow coach traveller a book she had been reading; when he hesitated to reply she continued: 'That hymn has given me so much pleasure; its sentiments so touch me, indeed I cannot tell you how much good it has done me. Don't you think it very good?'

'Madam,' said the stranger, bursting into tears. 'I am the poor, unhappy man who wrote that hymn many years ago and I would give a thousand worlds, if I had them, to enjoy the feelings I then had.'

Wrote the Rev. S. W. Christophers: 'Poor Robinson! it was he, the victim of eccentricity, love of change, and self-conceit.'

Robert Hall said of the author: 'His mind was richly furnished with an inexhaustible variety of knowledge. His eloquence was the delight of every assembly, and his conversation the charm of every private circle. In him the erudition of the scholar, the discrimination of the historian, the boldness of the reformer, were united in an eminent degree with the virtues which adorn the man and Christian.'

244. Come, ye that love the Lord (Isaac Watts (3))

Hymns and Spiritual Songs, Book 2 (1707), where there were ten verses; Ch.M.H.B.

245. Comrades, I am on my journey (Anonymous)

Praises of Jesus, American Sacred Song, 1868; 1878 S.A. song book.

The first word has been changed from 'Christians' to 'Soldiers' and now to 'Comrades'.

246. Down at the Cross where my Saviour died (Elisha A. Hoffman)

Salvation Music, Vol. 2; 1899 S.A. song book.

Elisha Albright Hoffman, born at Orwigsburg, Pennsylvania, U.S.A., in 1839, was, like his father, a minister in the Evangelical

Association. More than two thousand hymns came from his pen, many of them being set to music by the author.

'We have been visiting some of the most affected areas where the Mau Mau have burnt down some of our schools and one of our halls,' wrote Lieut.-Colonel Francis Dare, General Secretary for East Africa during the time of the riots in 1954. 'As the sun was going down I visited this hall and prayed with the officers and some of the comrades. Shortly after I had left, and when darkness had descended, members of the Mau Mau surrounded the officers' quarters, calling upon the Captain to open the door. Instead of doing this he gathered his children around him, took hold of the drum and beat it with his might, as he and the children sang, " Down at the Cross where my Saviour died ". The Captain's wife gave out the African alarm cry. After a while the terrorists left the quarters, spared the officers, but burnt down the hall instead.'

247. Fade, fade each earthly joy (Jane C. Bonar)

Songs for the Wilderness, 1844; *Revival Music*.

Daughter of the Rev. Robert Lundie, minister of the parish of Kelso, Scotland, and sister to Mary Lundie Duncan, the author of 'Jesus, tender Shepherd, hear me' (No. 859), Jane Catherine Bonar (1821–84) was married in 1843 to Dr. H. Bonar (see No. 4).

248. God's anger now is turned away (Fred W. Fry)

Favourite Songs Supplement; 1899 S.A. song book.

Sons of Charles Fry, the Army's first Bandmaster, Fred and his two younger brothers made up the family band of four brass instruments which, in 1878, at Salisbury constituted the Army's first band. They assisted William Booth in his meetings in other parts of the country as well.

Fred W. Fry was a man of varied abilities. 'He played several instruments,' wrote Richard Slater; 'could sing and provide his own accompaniments in several ways; was a good shorthand writer; was well up in accounts, and had acquired a very varied knowledge of law in connection with municipal affairs on which he was employed in later years, and was an agreeable and welcome leader of religious meetings, while his kindly manner and readiness to help others in times of difficulty and trouble endeared him to a vast number of people both inside and outside the Army.'

After Fred Fry was appointed to Headquarters he endeavoured to meet the ever-growing needs of music for Army bands. Music was arranged and printed on stiff cards, No. 1 appearing in July, 1882.

In December, 1891, he was appointed Bandmaster of the Staff Band. In 1892 he took up a secretarial position in the Army in Canada under Herbert H. Booth. Returning to England, he was for thirty years in the Town Clerk's office at Gillingham and became a Methodist local preacher. He died in Gillingham, Kent, on June 24, 1939.

'We had to prepare a certain number of songs for each month,' wrote Fred Fry, 'and sometimes had great difficulty in making up the number required. On one occasion we were short of copy, so I said I would try and put something together to fill the gap. I tried for several days, but no inspiration came, until one night—I suppose the subject was very much on my mind—I awoke myself by singing the chorus, " My sins are under the Blood ". At once I struck a light and scribbled out the words and the air of the tune as it had occurred to me; having the chorus, it was not much trouble to fix up the words and music of the verses, of which there were seven.'

249. Gone are the days of wretchedness and sin (Herbert H. Booth (91))

The War Cry, December 9, 1882; 1899 S.A. song book.

250. Have you on the Lord believed? (Philip P. Bliss (78))

Gospel Songs, 1874; *The Christian Mission Magazine*, October, 1874; *Revival Music*; 1878 S.A. song book.

Written after hearing Mr. Moody relate the following story: 'A vast fortune was left in the hands of a minister for one of his poor parishioners. Fearing that it might be squandered if bestowed upon him too suddenly, the wise minister sent him a monthly allowance, with a note saying, " This is thine, use it wisely; there is more to follow." ' Mr. Moody after relating the story added, ' Brethren, that is just the way God gives to His children.'

251. How tasteless and tedious the hours (John Newton (41))

Olney Hymns, Book 1, 1779; Ch.M.H.B.

252. I am drinking at the fountain (Anonymous)

Songs of Joy and Gladness (U.S.A.); 1899 S.A. song book.

253. I am saved, blessèdly saved, by the Blood (Edwin Gay)

The Musical Salvationist, November, 1887; 1899 S.A. song book.

Born at Black Torrington, Devon, on April 11, 1860, Edwin Gay was converted on February 17, 1881, at Morice Town, Devonport, at which corps he became the first soldier to wear Army uniform, he and the Captain donning the cap and guernsey at the same time. Whilst at work one Saturday morning in 1883 he received a telegram from the Divisional Officer, Major Abram Davey, asking if he would go to

Barnstaple and take charge of the corps there because the officer, father of Lieut.-Colonel Alfred Narraway, had been taken ill. Two months later he went to the Training Home at Clapton. After eleven weeks' training he was appointed to open 'the new huge barracks' at Stratford, where in four and a half months 450 souls were won for God. Later in the year he was appointed to Truro, Cornwall, where he was soon in difficulties with the authorities because he, with his soldiers, knelt in the open-air ring, played a concertina and sang his songs. He was sentenced to a month's imprisonment, but the sentence was quashed.

'Are you willing for America? Wire reply,' was the message the Chief of the Staff, Mr. Bramwell Booth, sent Gay when he was stationed at Oxford. 'Anywhere with Jesus, nowhere without Him,' was Gay's reply; and later the same day orders were wired: 'Farewell Sunday. Exeter Hall Monday. Sail Tuesday.' Gay was placed in charge of the party of five, one of which was Joseph Pugmire, and given thirty shillings for expenses on arrival. By February, 1885, a building had been secured in Chicago and Captain Edwin Gay became the first Commanding Officer of the corps. After much pioneering in the Western States he returned a number of years later to England, where he served in divisional work and retired, in 1926, with the rank of Brigadier.

'Two or three things appealed to me when I first met the Army,' wrote Commissioner Brengle. 'One was their sacrificial spirit. Another was their virility. I shall never forget going down to the Number 1 Corps hall in Boston and seeing the officer in charge, Major Gay, come in blowing his trumpet, marching erect and with vigour, and preaching sermons with fire and bite in them. These Salvationists were so different from the theological students who were so soft and easy, so anaemic compared with men like Gay.'

'"Blessedly Saved" was inspired through the sneering remark of a man who entered a railway carriage in which I was travelling to visit a corps,' wrote the author of the time when he was Divisional Officer at Boston.

'Said the man: "I suppose you are *saved*."

'"Yes, sir, blessedly saved, saved by the Blood of the Lamb," was my rejoinder.'

Having previously set some words to the tune, 'There's a land, beautiful land, just beyond', he used the same tune, which was composed by Wm. J. Kirkpatrick, for a new song and based it upon the conversation which took place in the railway carriage.

The author was promoted to Glory from Portsmouth in May, 1952.

254. I am saved, I am saved (Anonymous)

Salvation Music, Vol. 2; 1899 S.A. song book.

255. I am so glad that our Father in Heaven (Philip P. Bliss (78))

Hallelujah Hymn Book; Revival Music; 1878 S.A. song book.

'I am so glad' was suggested to Mr. Bliss after hearing the chorus of the hymn, 'O how I love Jesus', repeated very frequently in a meeting which he attended in Chicago about June, 1870. After joining in the chorus a number of times the thought came to him, 'Have I not been singing about my poor love for Jesus, and shall I not rather sing of His great love for me?'

256. I could not do without Thee (Frances Ridley Havergal)

Written at Leamington on May 7, 1873, and published in *Home Words* the same year; 1930 S.A. song book.

Youngest of the six children of the Rev. W. H. Havergal, Frances (1836–79) was born at the Rectory, Astley, Worcestershire. At the age of eleven she lost her mother. The influence of life at the Rectory led her early to seek after the things of God but it was not until December, 1850, that she was able to write to her sister: 'Jesus has forgiven me, I know. He is my Saviour.' During a visit to Düsseldorf shortly afterward she found herself the only Christian among 110 girls there but became known for her Christian piety. In 1853 she was confirmed in Worcester Cathedral. Later she left Worcester and resided for different periods in Leamington and at Caswell Bay, Swansea.

In 1872 she read a book entitled *All for Jesus*; it spoke of the possibility and power of a holy life and made an instant appeal. Correspondence with the author brought further enlightenment so that Miss Havergal ultimately made a complete surrender to Christ and entered into the experience of full salvation. 'It was on Advent Sunday, December 2, 1873,' she wrote, 'I first saw clearly the blessedness of true consecration.'

Her knowledge of several languages included a sound acquaintance with Greek and Hebrew. She commenced writing verse at the age of seven, and over fifty of her hymns are still in use. In 1874 she caught typhoid fever and from then until her death at Caswell Bay she suffered almost continually.

257. I feel like singing all the time (Edward Payson Hammond)

The author's *Hymns of Salvation*; Ch.M.H.B.

An American evangelist born at Ellington, Connecticut, U.S.A., in 1831, the Rev. Edward Hammond ascribed his conversion in Southington, Conn., at the age of seventeen, to the singing of Isaac Watts's 'Alas! and did my Saviour bleed'.

Mr. Hammond was conducting a children's meeting and explaining the love of Christ as manifested by His death, when he noticed a girl burst into tears. In the after meeting he had the joy of pointing her to the Saviour. The next day she brought him a letter in which she had written, ' I think I have found the dear Jesus, and I do not see how I could have rejected Him so long. I think I can sing with the rest of those who have found Him, " Jesus is mine ". The first time I came to the meeting I cried, but now I feel like singing all the time.' The letter inspired the song.

258. I have found a great salvation (Thomas Plant)

1899 S.A. song book.

During the 1880s a furloughing officer conducted some meetings in Bicester, Oxon, and many people were converted. Tom Plant, who lived there and came from a Christian home, found himself captivated by the spirit of these meetings. When the officer returned to duty Tom continued the work, with two friends, until the Divisional Commander, the future Commissioner Rees, sent an officer and officially commenced the Army work there. The Plant family were all musical, employing their talent at sacred concerts, chapel soirées and private parties, Tom's part usually being to play the banjo. Soon Tom left Bicester and became shorthand-writer to the Divisional Commander in Reading and in 1888 became an officer. He served as one of the Founder's secretaries and accompanied him on some of his worldwide tours. He was also, for a considerable period, secretary and travelling companion to Commissioner Thomas McKie. For many years Tom Plant travelled the world giving his own musical programmes, using more than twenty instruments and singing his own songs. ' His subject-matter is racy,' stated a reporter. ' He imparts information about the customs in the lands he has visited and does not forget to tell about the position the Army occupies in them. He varies his programmes by exhibits. He moralizes and reads a portion of the Scriptures. He retains the sympathy of his audience in a spiritual strain and winds up well.' The diaries of Brigadier Tom Plant reveal that over 30,000 seekers were registered in these campaigns.

During the First World War he entertained the troops, being received at the conclusion by King George V at Buckingham Palace. During the Second World War, although retired, he served in a similar capacity again.

In 1906 he married Captain Florence Newell, who also was able to play several musical instruments and travelled with him to many of his appointments. After their retirement they settled at Pokesdown, Bournemouth, and the Brigadier was promoted to Glory on October 29, 1944, at the age of seventy-nine.

The Brigadier has many songs to his credit but most of them were written for his own use as solos in his campaigns. One of his choruses is No. 234.

259. I have glorious tidings of Jesus to tell (Richard Slater (105))

Written in November, 1885, and published in a Training Home report for that year, when the Music Editorial Department was in a room of the Clapton Congress Hall; *Favourite Songs Supplement*; 1899 S.A. song book.

260. I have seen His face in blessing (William McAlonan)

All the World, July, 1894; *The Musical Salvationist*, October, 1897, to the tune ' Mary of Argyle'; 1930 S.A. song book.

Commissioner McAlonan, born on June 12, 1863, became an officer from Ligoniel, Ireland, in 1882. During forty-three years he served in corps, divisional and national work, eventually becoming Territorial Commander of Sweden, Switzerland, Germany and Holland. Later, as International Secretary for Missionary Territories, he visited Japan, Korea, China, Canada, the U.S.A. and South Africa. His last appointment was as Managing Director of The Salvation Army Assurance Society. The Commissioner, who had married Captain Askew, in 1885, was promoted to Glory from London on May 1, 1925.

' The cause of the song's origin was my illness,' wrote Mrs. McAlonan. 'After nine weeks in hospital, and some months of still being unable to walk, I had the opinion from doctors that I would not get better. The Commissioner sat down and wrote out his heart's feelings in these verses.' Mrs. McAlonan recovered, but the depth of the Commissioner's spiritual struggle may best be seen in the verse not included in the present version of the song:

> I have stepped in waves of sorrow,
> Till my soul was covered o'er;
> I have dreaded oft the morrow,
> And the path which lay before.
> But when sinking in my sadness
> I have felt His helping hand,
> And ere day-dawn came His gladness
> With the courage to withstand.

261. I heard of a Saviour whose love was so great (Mrs. Read)

The War Cry, December 23, 1882; 1899 S.A. song book.

When Captain Annie Lockwood (later Mrs. Commissioner Richard Wilson) was stationed at Londonderry in 1882, Ireland was shaken by the murder in Phoenix Park, Dublin, of Lord Frederick Cavendish, the Irish Secretary.

' Nationalists and rebels were hunted across the country and given short shrift when captured.

'This situation affected the atmosphere of Annie's work in London-derry. She would lay abed at night . . . and often hear the clatter of horses' hoofs and the swift patter of running feet as yet another hunted man was chased by the police' (*The Yorkshire Lad*, by Bernard Watson).

'One day Mrs. Read, an earnest worker for souls, came to the quarters with some verses she had composed,' stated Mrs. Wilson, 'but which she could not arrange into proper order. The idea she desired to convey was the joy of a soul whose rebellion against God had been pardoned. I was able to help her with the needed sequence and rhyme. The song was sung by me—to a secular tune at that time popular in Ireland, "She grows more like him every day"—at the wedding of Mr. Bramwell Booth and Miss Soper in the Congress Hall, London, in 1882.'

262. I heard the voice of Jesus say (Horatius Bonar (4))

Written at Kelso and published in *Hymns Original and Selected*, 1846; Ch.M.H.B.

263. I left it all with Jesus long ago (Ellen H. Willis)

Gospel Songs by Bliss and Sankey; *Revival Music*; 1878 S.A. song book.

264. I once was very worldly (A. F. Knight)

The Musical Salvationist, November, 1887. The song has been considerably altered, the first verse and chorus being all that is left of the original song. 1899 S.A. song book.

The author spent his early life in the East End of London, finding his chief joys in bird-fancying, boxing, betting, drinking and public house sing-songs. Full of energy, enterprise and resource, he was a leader in his circle but with no concern for God or the future.

'We'll stop that!' he said to some of his companions as he set about forming a skeleton army in 1882 to oppose the activities of the Salva-tionists who had 'opened fire' in Clapton.

Everything seemed to be going in his favour, but he felt disturbed after hitting a Salvationist and hearing him say, 'God bless you, my brother!' He became a more and more determined opponent till one night he went into the Congress Hall himself and sat near the front. Before the meeting closed he knelt at the Penitent-form. He became a bandsman at the Congress Hall and soon developed into a song-writer.

It was the singing of the chorus of this song in an open-air meeting that first attracted Commissioner Adelaide Cox to The Salvation Army.

265. I will sing the wondrous story (Francis H. Rawley)

Sankey's *Sacred Songs and Solos.*

Born in Hilton, New York, in 1854, the Rev. Francis Rawley was educated at Rochester University, U.S.A., and became a minister of the Baptist Church in America, serving churches in Massachusetts, Pennsylvania and Illinois. He also became the President of the Massachusetts S.P.C.A. and of the American Humane Education Society.

'I was minister of the First Baptist Church of North Adams, Massachusetts, in 1886,' he wrote. 'The church and the community were experiencing a period of unusual interest in religious matters, and I was assisted by a remarkable young singer named Peter Bilhorn. One night after the close of the service he said, "Why don't you write a hymn for me to set to music?" During the night these verses came to me.' Bilhorn provided the music.

266. I'm a pilgrim and a stranger (Mary Maxwell)

Ch.M.H.B.

The author was born in 1814 and died in 1853.

267. I'm a soldier bound for Glory (Anonymous)

Ch.M.H.B., where the first verse began: 'I'm a pilgrim . . .'; sometimes attributed to Dr. Asahel Nettleton, a Connecticut (U.S.A.) Congregational minister, who compiled a collection of hymns which included these verses.

268. In evil long I took delight (John Newton (41))

Olney Hymns, 1779; Ch.M.H.B.; largely biographical in character and pictures the great spiritual change which took place in Newton's heart and life.

269. In golden hours of brightest joy (Herbert H. Booth (91))

The War Cry, June 8, 1882, 'To be sung at the Irish Anniversary Meetings'; 1930 S.A. song book. The third verse of the present version has replaced the author's original and was written by a member of the Song Book Revision Council specially for this edition.

270. I've a Friend, of friends the fairest (Ruth Tracy)

The Musical Salvationist, December, 1899; 1930 S.A. song book.

Brigadier Ruth Tracy was born at Wellington Street (now Almeida Street), Islington, London, on November 28, 1870, the seventh child of Plymouth Brethren parents. Her mother, who believed seven to be the perfect number, prayed that her seventh child might be specially dedicated to God's service. Ruth was given a good education at three different private schools in Enfield, Middlesex, where the family moved when she was seven years old. At the third school she did a little teaching as well and was, even at that time, especially interested in English grammar and languages.

In August, 1888, she went to stay with a cousin in Dorking, Surrey, taking with her a friend Kathleen Neal, who later became Mrs. Commissioner Frank Barrett. One day The Salvation Army—consisting of two lassie officers, a drum and fife band and a number of soldiers—marched by their window. The singing of ' Bright crowns ', ' O you must be a lover of the Lord ' and ' Will you go? ' evoked the inquiry as to where they met for their meetings.

On the fourth Sunday of the girls' holiday, coming away from the Methodist meeting rather early (they had decided to visit various places of worship in the town), they found the Army barracks and entered the prayer meeting. Two nights later, on September 3, 1888, they knelt on either side of the bed they were sharing and asked the Lord to save them the Army way. An open confession was made to Cousin Tom the next morning, and Ruth was soon reading her first Army book, *Orders and Regulations for Field Officers*.

After her return home she attended a number of meetings at Holloway Citadel where David Thomas (later Colonel) was the Commanding Officer. When she found she could walk from Enfield to Wood Green she would cover the four miles in time for seven o'clock knee drill, attend a full day's meetings and then walk the four miles home again.

After becoming a soldier she was advised by Lieutenant Kate Lee (later ' The Angel Adjutant ') to apply for a post at the Home Office, at International Headquarters, then at 149 Queen Victoria Street (close to Blackfriars Station). She was accepted and went to the Appointments Department then under Staff-Captain (later Commissioner) James Hay.

' Born with a strong sense of the charm of language, spelling and rhythm, I found rhyming coming to me naturally,' wrote the Brigadier. ' My first jingle—I was a small schoolgirl at the time—was about an elder brother's love affairs, fact and fiction interwoven. Many nonsense rhymes followed and one or two sentimental ones. Staff-Captain Hay saw one of my merry jingles—a take-off about departmental affairs—and called me into his office. Expecting a reprimand, I was relieved instead to hear an earnest suggestion that this gift should be turned to account for the Kingdom.

' " How? " I asked, bewildered.

' " Write a song for *The War Cry*," he said; and accepting it as a sort of command, I went away thinking quite seriously.

' Three crude verses resulted, but *The War Cry* printed them. The effort had definitely switched my mind on to more serious matters. The Bible, which I had only read by fits and starts, had been anxiously consulted, and I had sincerely prayed about that first song.'

Becoming an officer from Wood Green in 1890, Ruth Tracy was trained at the Walthamstow Garrison. Then for four years she served in corps appointments before being transferred to International Head-quarters in November, 1894, where until her retirement in 1931 she served in literary and editorial work. She wrote more than three hundred songs. She was promoted to Glory on September 17, 1960.

'This song was written', wrote the Brigadier many years later, ' when I was " Deborah Do-Better ", editing a weekly page of original songs for *The War Cry* and writing what were then called " Boomer's Notes ". I have read so many songs sent in by Salvation Army comrades that I sometimes wonder if an original thought or phrase would ever again emerge. Looking at my song now I recognize many phrases or thoughts of earlier writers, but at the time it was the true expression of my own joy in the friendship of the Lord Jesus. I wrote it, I think, to " Silver Threads ", and later Brigadier (later Commissioner) Robert Hoggard set an original tune to it.'

271. I've found a friend in Jesus, He's everything to me (Charles Fry (31))

Written at the house of a Mr. Wilkinson in Lincoln, in June, 1881, and first published in *The War Cry*, December 29, 1881; then with the music of the secular melody, ' The little old log cabin down the lane ', in *Salvation Music*, Vol. 2; 1899 S.A. song book. This song was among those adopted by Ira D. Sankey when on his evangelistic campaigns in this country and was included in *Sacred Songs and Solos*.

272. I've found a Friend, O such a Friend! (James G. Small)

The author's *Psalms and Sacred Songs*, 1866, and in Sankey's *Sacred Songs and Solos*, being set to the now popular tune by Geo. C. Stebbins; *The Musical Salvationist*, May, 1915; 1930 S.A. song book.

Born in Edinburgh and educated in that city at the high school and university, studying theology under Dr. Chalmers, the Rev. James G. Small (1817–88) threw in his lot with the Free Church of Scotland and in 1847 became the minister of the Free Church at Bervie, near Montrose. Owing to peculiarities of voice and manner he never made a real success of his preaching, but had the confidence of his brethren and was made clerk of the presbytery. He published several volumes of verse.

273. I've found the pearl of greatest price (John Mason)

The author's *Spiritual Songs*, 1683; Ch.M.H.B.; based on Matthew 13: 46.

Son of a dissenting minister, the Rev. John Mason (born about 1645) was brought up in Northamptonshire. He was educated at Strixton School in that county, and then at Clare Hall, Cambridge, where he received his B.A. degree. In 1668 he was appointed Vicar of Stantonbury, Bucks, and five years later Rector of Water Stratford, Bucks, where he exercised a useful ministry until his death in 1694.

Whilst at Water Stratford he published *Spiritual Songs*, a volume of sacred verse, probably amongst the first volumes of hymns, as distinct from the metrical psalms, to be used in the Church of England. The book passed through no fewer than twenty editions.

Wrote Richard Baxter: 'He was the glory of the Church of England . . . the frame of his spirit was so heavenly, his deportment so humble and obliging, his discourse of spiritual things, and little else could we hear from him, so weighty, with such apt words and delightful air, that it charmed all that had any spiritual relish.' Mason's sweetness and power in divine melody was found in his private devotions. Six times a day he went aside to wrestle with his Lord in prayer.

About a month before his death he had a vision of Christ wearing a glorious crown with a look of unutterable majesty on His face. Mason preached a sermon on this and proclaimed the near approach of Christ's Kingdom. Great excitement was caused in and around the village for Mason believed the Lord would appear in his glory at Water Stratford.

274. I've left the land of death and sin (Mrs. John T. Benson (verses); Edgar Page Stites (chorus))

Ch.M.H.B., with the original chorus, 'This world is not my home'; 1930 S.A. song book, with the present chorus.

Edgar Page Stites, the writer of the chorus, was born in 1837 and became a prominent business man in Cape May, New Jersey, U.S.A. Using the *nom de plume* of 'Edgar Page' he wrote more than a thousand songs.

'It was in 1876 that I wrote "Beulah Land",' Mr. Stites recalled. 'I could write only two verses and the chorus when I was overcome and fell on my face. I could only weep and could write no more. That was on Sunday. A week later I wrote the third verse and the fourth, and again I was so influenced by emotion that I could only pray and weep. The first time it was sung was at the regular Monday morning meeting of Methodist ministers at Arch Street, Philadelphia, when Bishop McCabe sang it to the assembled ministers.' The term 'Beulah Land' was taken from Isaiah 62: 1-4.

93

275. I've travelled the rough paths of life in my day (Benjamin Wilks)

The War Cry, June 23, 1883; *Favourite Songs Supplement*; 1899 S.A. song book.

Sergeant Wilks, of Swansea, South Wales, born at Woolwich in August, 1854, was converted through the instrumentality of Captain Kate Sheppard. Earlier he had been elected ' Mayor of the Sandfields ' on three occasions, a title bestowed annually upon the most prolific drunkard known in the district where Wilks lived. When the Captain paid her first visit to the convert's home the entire furnishings consisted of bricks and orange boxes, the proper furniture having been sold to obtain drink. A little later his new officers, knowing that Benjamin had been a singer in the public houses, suggested that he set about writing his own song. What better theme could he choose than that of his conversion, and what better tune could he use than that which he knew so well—' There's no one but Mother can cheer me today!' Over thirty years later, in 1917, during an 'Old Warriors' week-end at Swansea, Wilks sang it as a solo and recounted the story of its birth. He died in Swansea in May, 1929.

276. Jesus, and shall it ever be (Joseph Grigg)

Four Hymns on Divine Subjects, wherein the Patience and Love of our Divine Saviour is Displayed, 1765; Ch.M.H.B.

Born in humble circumstances between 1720 and 1728 and described as a labouring mechanic, Joseph Grigg became assistant pastor at Silver Street Presbyterian Church, London, in 1743. After four years he resigned, married a lady of considerable wealth and lived at St. Albans. He would preach occasionally and continued to write both prose and poetry, an art which he had commenced when ten years of age. He died at Walthamstow, London, in October, 1768.

277. Jesus came to save me (Sidney E. Cox (33))

The Musical Salvationist, March, 1939. Written while the author was an officer in The Salvation Army and first published in the U.S.A. in 1937.

278. Jesus is my Saviour, this I know (Richard Slater (105))

The Young Soldier, December 25, 1889, where verse 3, line 5, read, ' Children, come along then, let us go '; *The Musical Salvationist*, June, 1892; 1899 S.A. song book.

' For the Christmas issue of *The Young Soldier* for 1889, Herbert Booth was under a promise to provide a song,' wrote Richard Slater. ' But as no news of its having been written had reached the editor and the weeks were fleeting by, anxiety arose as to how the desire to have the song could be reconciled with the printer's urgent claims for copy, if the appointed date of issue was to be kept.

'Pressing requests were accordingly sent to Mr. Booth, but he had only a tune which might prove suitable. Efforts to write words to fit the tune were not successful, so once more he turned to me to help him out of his trouble.

'It was by no means helpful in verse-making to have to work under such conditions, but duty required an effort from me, so early in December I wrote the words to the tune supplied by Mr. Herbert Booth.'

279. Jesus saves me every day (Anonymous)

Hallelujah Hymn Book; Revival Music; 1878 S.A. song book.

280. Living in the fountain (Bramwell Booth)

Written on the morning of the author's twenty-first birthday as he prayed by the side of his bed, and published in *The Christian Mission Magazine,* February, 1878, under the title 'A good soldier's life'. At that time, and when published later in *The Musical Salvationist,* December, 1889, the song was written in five four-line verses but, that it might be sung to an eight-line tune, he added the first four lines of the last verse for the 1930 S.A. song book.

Eldest son of William and Catherine Booth, and second General of The Salvation Army (from 1912–29), William Bramwell Booth was born at Halifax on March 8, 1856. Giving himself up to the service of The Christian Mission in youth, he became an ardent worker, first as an evangelist and assistant to his father, then later a Chief of the Staff of The Salvation Army. In this position he was largely responsible for the Army's organization and extension. He was an outstanding exponent of the doctrine of holiness. His councils for young people, bandmasters and officers were of incalculable value in the teaching of the principles of our Movement. As General he gave a mighty impetus to missionary endeavour. He was also the author of a number of books as well as of numerous articles in Army periodicals. In 1929 he was appointed a Companion of Honour.

The General was promoted to Glory from his home at Hadley Wood on June 16, 1929, and was laid to rest in Abney Park Cemetery (London) on June 24th, a memorial service having been held in the Royal Albert Hall the previous evening.

281. Long in darkness and doubt did I wander from God (T. C. Marshall)

The Musical Salvationist, July, 1889; 1899 S.A. song book.

Regarding the author, who was born in London in 1854, Lieut.-Colonel Slater wrote: ' He was left motherless at two and a half years of age. His father was a very religious man, much occupied in mission work, and his venerable presence was a feature of the meetings at the Regent Hall, London, in the first few years after it was opened in 1882.

' The boy was converted at school, where his father, in conjunction with the master, held meetings of a revival character. At sixteen the boy entered his father's business, but not liking it was transferred to his grandfather to work on the land. In the small country town the lad learnt to smoke and drink, and his religion became only a memory.

' Still restless, he was sent out to a farmer at Kansas, U.S.A., in 1873. Later he went to China, and while there received copies of *The War Cry* sent to him by his father. These aroused his interest, so in 1882, on returning to England, he went to the Regent Hall on his first Sunday after landing. He was deeply impressed and after a period of delay in conviction of sin, on December 14th, he made a complete surrender at the Penitent-form. Not long afterward he was accepted as an officer and was able to put to use on *The War Cry* the journalistic experience he had gained in China.

' Later he became one of the Founder's scribes, and subsequently was transferred to the staff of the Training Home at Clapton. He was a ready writer, had verse-making capacity, wrote melodies as well as verses and added some good songs to the Army's store. He did not need to wait for what some people call inspiration. Anywhere and at any time he could write verses. Even amidst all the variety of sounds of an Army meeting he would ask for some tune to be named and then he would set to work to write, and later would sing his song in the meeting.'

Although he resigned his officership he remained a soldier at the Jersey City Corps, N.J., U.S.A., from whence he was promoted to Glory early in 1943. He contributed to the New York *War Cry* from 1891 to within a week of his death. He wrote nearly 450 songs and more than 200 poems.

According to his own testimony, ' Long in darkness ' was the only example in all his experience of direct inspiration without any previous prayer or intention of writing. He woke in the middle of the night with the strain of the music and the words in his mind and wrote them out as well as he could in imperfect tonic sol-fa. He was on holiday at Llanfairfechan, North Wales, and when he returned to London he took his song to Richard Slater who put it into shape.

The signatures at the end of a letter sent to William Booth from officers in the United States of America in connection with the fiftieth anniversary (1894) of his conversion, included: ' Thomas C. Marshall, Staff-Captain, Editor, " Conqueror ".' Elsewhere the author always signed himself ' T. C. Marshall '.

282. Lord, I was blind! I could not see (William Tidd Matson)

The author's *Christ, the Life of Men*; *The Musical Salvationist*, July, 1914; 1930 S.A. song book. A recounting of the tremendous change which came into the author's heart and life at the time of his real spiritual awakening.

Born at West Hackney, London, William Matson (1833–99) studied at St. John's, Cambridge, and then at the Agricultural and Chemical College, Kennington. He belonged to the Church of England until 1853, when he experienced a great spiritual awakening and felt led to join the Methodist New Connexion. At a later date, however, he became a minister of the Congregational Church. He wrote a number of poetical works and composed several hymns.

283. My Father is rich in houses and land (Hattie Buell)

The Northern Christian Advocate; Sankey's *Sacred Songs and Solos*; *Salvation Music*, Vol. 2; 1930 S.A. song book.

Mrs. Buell (1834–1910), born in Cazenovia, New York, wrote these words on her way home from a church service at Thousand Island Park, New York, in 1878 after meditating, during the sermon, on the joys to be had in being ' a child of the King '. A few months later she was attending a Sunday night service in the Methodist Church in Manlius, New York, when she was very much surprised to hear the soloist use her words. John B. Sumner had noticed them in *The Northern Christian Advocate* and had composed the musical setting without the author's knowledge.

284. My God, I am Thine (Charles Wesley (15) (verses only))

Hymns and Sacred Poems, 1749; Ch.M.H.B.

' It seemed to me unreasonable to suppose that I could be saved,' wrote Catherine Booth, ' and yet not know it. At any rate I could not permit myself to remain longer in doubt regarding the matter. If in the past I had acted up to the light I had received, it was evident that I was now getting new light, and unless I obeyed it I realized that my soul would fall into condemnation.

' I can never forget the agony I passed through. I used to pace my room till two o'clock in the morning; and when, utterly exhausted, I lay down at length to sleep, I would place my Bible and hymn book under my pillow, praying that I might wake up with the assurance of salvation. One morning, as I opened my hymn book, my eyes fell upon the words:

> My God, I am Thine;
> What a comfort divine,
> What a blessing to know that my Jesus is mine!

Scores of times I had read and sung these words, but now they came home to my innermost soul with a force and illumination they had never before possessed. It was as impossible for me to doubt as it had been for me to exercise faith. Previously, not all the promises in the Bible could persuade me to believe; now, not all the devils in Hell could persuade me to doubt. I no longer hoped that I was saved; I was certain of it. The assurances of my salvation seemed to flood and fill my soul.'

Throughout the years her confidence remained; and when members of her family and a group of leading officers were gathered round her death-bed the same verse was sung to bring her comfort.

285. My God, the spring of all my joys (Isaac Watts (3))

The author's *Hymns and Spiritual Songs*, 1707; Ch.M.H.B.; with the chorus:

> Fly away, fly away,
> While yet it's called today,
>   And we'll fly to Jesus' breast;
> And we'll soon fly up above,
> On the wings of eternal love,
>   And be forever blest.

Under the date May 14, 1847, Catherine Booth wrote in her diary: 'I entered into a fresh covenant with my Lord this morning, to be more fully given up to Him. Oh, to be a Christian indeed! To love Thee with all my heart is my desire. I do love Thee, but I want to love Thee more. If Thou smile upon me, I am infinitely happy, though deprived of earthly happiness more than usual. If Thou frown, it matters not what I have beside.

> Thou art the spring of all my joys,
>   The life of my delights,
> The glory of my brightest days,
>   And comfort of my nights.'

286. My heart is fixed, eternal God (Richard Jukes (193))

Ch.M.H.B., taken from among the Ranters' songs.

287. My Jesus, I love Thee, I know Thou art mine (Ralph Featherstone)

The London Hymn Book, 1864; Ch.M.H.B.; written when Ralph Featherstone (1842–70), who was born in or near Montreal, Canada, was sixteen years of age.

Here is an example of how by one song a brief life may become a source of holy influence upon masses of people. Regarding even the

last moments of Catherine Booth the Founder wrote to *The War Cry*:
'As well as she was able she joined us in singing the old song:

> I will love Thee in life, I will love Thee in death . . .

And then she kissed me and slipped away.'

288. My life flows on in endless song (Robert Lowry (231))

Bright Jewels, 1869; *Hallelujah Hymn Book*; *Revival Music*; 1878
S.A. song book.

289. My robes were once all stained with sin (Edwin O. Excell)

The Gospel in Song (U.S.A.); *The Musical Salvationist*, June, 1890;
1899 S.A. song book.

Mr. Excell (1851–1921) was born in Stark County, Ohio, served
his apprenticeship as a bricklayer and plasterer, and at twenty-two years
of age turned to the work of a musician. Keenly interested in young
people, many of his compositions were especially written for them.

As a singer he had few equals, possessing a voice of remarkable
sweetness and power, and was able to sway vast audiences with the
earnestness of his spirit and the choice rendering of his solos. He did
much to popularize the ' gospel song '. His last work was with Gipsy
Smith in Louisville, Kentucky; his last song, six months before he died,
was sung in the chapel of Wesley Hospital, Chicago, on Sunday
afternoon, January 16, 1921. Besides writing many songs he edited
over forty different hymnals.

290. My Saviour suffered on the tree (Hodgson Casson)

Ch.M.H.B.

Hodgson Casson, an old-time Methodist preacher, was converted
at the age of twenty-one, and having previously been possessed of a
strong will, gay and reckless in disposition, his whole capabilities and
energies were immediately consecrated to God and thrown into the
conflict against sin. Throughout the succeeding forty years of his
life he was a very eminent soul-winner. He used startling announce-
ments; he introduced secular melodies into his services, and made use
of a fiddle to attract and arouse the Christless and careless. On one
occasion he took a chair upon his shoulders and proclaimed at the top
of his voice through the streets of Kilmarnock: 'A roup! a roup!' (a
local term for ' a sale '). Crowds followed him. Upon reaching a
favourable spot he mounted the chair and began to speak on the words
' Wine and milk ' and how they were to be purchased without money
and without price. He was often misunderstood and maltreated, and

through a large part of his life he suffered from the consequences of a brutal attack.

Once when away from home on business he could not sleep because of a dance in another part of the tavern where he was staying. Unable to endure the noise any longer, he made his way to the dance saloon, took the fiddle from the astonished musician and, calling the dancers to halt, started singing to the tune to which they had been dancing:

> My Saviour suffered on the tree,
> Glory to the bleeding Lamb!

While the dancing with its constantly recurring tune had been going on, the words had formulated in his mind. He did not cease his singing and preaching until the dancers were on their knees.

291. My soul is now united to Christ, the living Vine (Hugh Bourne and William Sanders (155))

Ch.M.H.B. with the chorus:

> Hosanna, Hosanna, Hosanna,
> O come and help me sing!
> Hosanna, Hosanna, Hosanna,
> To our eternal King.

292. No home on earth have I (George Scott Railton)

The War Cry, March 31, 1881, and written to the tune 'A life on the ocean wave'; 1930 S.A. song book.

'The cablegram [from the Founder recalling Railton to London from the U.S.A.] was received in St. Louis on January 1, 1881, and was a queer New Year's gift for Railton, who, however, made no demur, although his heart was deeply mortified, but packed his small belongings and started for home. He was beset by anxiety for his American post, and it was while crossing the Mississippi on his journey back to London that he wrote this hymn:

> No home on earth have I . . .'

(*God's Soldier*, by St. John Ervine).

'Surely no writer has mirrored more completely in a single song his thought, feeling and ideals as Commissioner Railton has done in " No home on earth have I ",' wrote Richard Slater in *The Bandsman and Songster*, August 9, 1913. 'Here we have in a few short lines what may be called the scheme of life, the philosophy of personal religion, as understood and consistently applied by Commissioner Railton. It is the voice of personal triumph of a spirit that has risen to higher levels than are marked by time and space; it defines an altitude of religious experience where by a voluntary act the soul becomes absorbed in its God, and where there is elimination of all personal likes or preferences in such terms as here, now, loss, gain, pleasure, pain.'

Son of a Wesleyan missionary who was married in Antigua, but after six years' happy service had, on account of ill health, returned to Scotland, George Scott Railton, the Army's first Commissioner, was born in the Wesleyan Manse at Arbroath on July 6, 1849.

At the age of ten George was converted. He was brought under conviction of sin and of his need of a Saviour whilst suffering from an attack of influenza. He began to ponder on what he would do if he were called to meet God and, realizing his unpreparedness, he resolved that when the family went to the prayer meeting that evening he would earnestly seek salvation.

Thus he told the story: 'As soon as they had gone to the chapel service, I began to sing to myself that blessed song:

> Depth of mercy! Can there be
> Mercy still reserved for me?

The second verse:

> I have long withstood His grace,
> Long provoked Him to His face . . .

so precisely pictured my story, that as God gave me to see it all, my heart was filled with shame and grief. But I went to press upon myself those grand final lines:

> God is love, I know, I feel,
> Jesus lives and loves me still.

until their glorious message in all its fullness gladdened my heart.

' The joy of God made me for the moment free from the headache and pains that had burdened me all day. I marched round the little room singing and praising the Lord until I found out that joy did not entirely banish pain and weariness! Then I rested, until hearing my mother at the front door I rushed out to tell her the good news that I was born again.'

In 1872 he read the Founder's book, *How to Reach the Masses with the Gospel*, and as a result he offered himself unreservedly to William Booth for service. When he saw The Christian Mission at work, he was impressed by three things:

1. The poverty of the mission people.
2. The swing of the singing.
3. The arrangement of the Penitent-form in faith that sinners would come to it.

Whatever the noise and opposition indoors or out, he observed that the singing never flagged; the countless repetition and choruses arrested his attention. His heart and life were won for the Founder and the work he was doing for God. There was neither band, flag, uniform, nor many of the other things that we now accept as part of the Army, but the early singing, by its fierce fervour, repetition and soulful meaning, captivated Railton in such a way as to lead him to think that such singing, anywhere and everywhere, was almost all that the Army needed to gain its victories.

He did various kinds of work for the Founder, including writing, editing, speaking and surveying field operations and pioneering overseas. He also wrote a number of songs, mostly intended for congregational use. Some are Army versions of songs that were already popular in Sunday-school or revival movements. He put Army language into them and made them into war songs. He was an earnest, eager, impetuous, expeditious leader, and sought at all times to make Army singing of a like character. He died suddenly at the railway station at Cologne, Germany, in July, 1913. It is to the Commissioner's son, the Rev. David Railton, that the world is indebted for the idea of 'The Unknown Warrior's Grave'.

293. None the love of Christ can measure (Richard Slater (105))

Written on July 12, 1887, and published in *The Musical Salvationist*, October, 1887; 1930 S.A. song book.

294. Now I have found a Friend (Henry J. McCracken Hope)

Written about 1852; Ch.M.H.B.

Son of James Hope, a Dublin bookbinder, and himself of the same trade, Mr. Hope (1809–72) was born near Belfast and died at Shanemagowston, Dunadry, County Antrim.

295. Now, in a song of grateful praise (Samuel Medley (172) (verses))

The Gospel Magazine, June, 1776; Ch.M.H.B.; *Revival Music* where it is set to the tune 'Ring the bell, watchman', with the chorus, 'And above the rest this note shall swell' (S.B. 901), added to complete the tune—a rather unhappy blend of words and music; based on Mark 7: 37.

296. O bliss of the purified, bliss of the free! (Francis Bottome (122))

Written in 1869; *Hallelujah Hymn Book*; *Revival Music*; 1878 S.A. song book.

297. O happy day that fixed my choice (Philip Doddridge (5) (verses))

Originally appeared in 1755; Ch.M.H.B.; based on 2 Chronicles 15: 15.

Queen Victoria selected this song to be sung during the Confirmation Service of one of her children. Verse 3, ' 'Tis done, the great transaction's done!...' was sung by General and Mrs. Carpenter and the members of the High Council at their reception by the Lord Mayor of London, in the Mansion House on May 6, 1946. His Worship was so delighted with it that he especially requested it to be played by the International Staff Band which was in attendance at another function later in the year.

The chorus appeared in the *Wesleyan Sacred Harp* (Boston, U.S.A., 1854), being associated with John Cennick's hymn ' Jesus, my all, to Heaven has gone '.

298. O happy, happy day (John Lawley (56))

1899 S.A. song book; as with a number of the Commissioner's songs, this is thought to have been written when he was travelling with the Founder on one of the European railways.

299. O how happy are they who the Saviour obey (Charles Wesley (15) (verses))

The verses are from the first part of a sixteen-verse setting written in a slightly different rhythm; *Hymns and Sacred Poems*, 1749; Ch.M.H.B.

An omitted verse reveals the original metre:

> I rode on the sky
> (Freely justified I),
> Nor envied Elijah his seat;
> My soul mounted higher
> In a chariot of fire,
> And the moon it was under my feet.

The present arrangement has been adapted to fit the American Civil War tune, ' Tramp, tramp, tramp, the boys are marching '.

300. O Jesus, O Jesus, how vast Thy love to me! (Anonymous)

Ch.M.H.B.

301. O my heart is full of music and of gladness (Emma Booth-Tucker)

The War Cry, August 10, 1895; *The Musical Salvationist*, October, 1896; 1899 S.A. song book.

Fourth child of William and Catherine Booth, Emma Moss was born on January 8, 1860, at Gateshead, where her father was then the superintendent minister of the Methodist New Connexion. Her early years were spent amidst the stirring revivals which her parents conducted in various parts of the country, and then in London from 1865. In 1880 the Founder established training homes to fit men and women for officership in the Army, and Emma was installed as 'Training Home Mother', or Principal of the Training Home for Women. On April 10, 1888, she married Frederick St. George de Lautour Tucker in the Congress Hall, Clapton, some five thousand people being present at the ceremony. Known as the Consul, she shared her husband's appointments in India, Ceylon and the United States of America. On October 28, 1903, she was involved in a fatal railway accident at Dean Lake, near Marceline, Missouri.

'I had just come from our International Headquarters in London, and told her', wrote Commissioner Booth-Tucker of his wife, 'that as I was going up the steps of an omnibus a tune had come to me, which I thought might catch on, only the time was irregular and it would be difficult to find suitable words. On hearing the air she said at once, "You must have special words, something to suit your going up the bus steps." She then and there composed the words, "O my heart is full of music . . .".'

One Sunday evening in 1959 a verse and chorus of this typically Army song were included in a television feature in England, 'Meeting Point', to illustrate the various forms of Christian hymns. The Founder's reference to the devil and the best tunes was also quoted.

302. O my Jesus, my Jesus, how charming is Thy name!
(Anonymous)

Ch.M.H.B.

303. O tell me no more (John Gambold (verses))

Evangelical Echoes, by Fullerton and Smith; Ch.M.H.B. where followed the old refrain:

> I'll drink when I'm dry,
> I'll drink a supply;
> I'll drink at the Fountain that never runs dry.

Born at Puncheston, Pembrokeshire, where his father was vicar, John Gambold (1711–71) was educated at Christ Church, Oxford, and graduated M.A. in 1734. He became Vicar of Stanton Harcourt, Oxfordshire, about 1739, but resigned in 1742 to join the Moravians, who chose him as one of their bishops in 1754. About twenty-six translations and eighteen original hymns in the Moravian book are assigned to him. He died at Haverfordwest.

304. O Thou God of my salvation (Thomas Olivers)

Written at Chester; 1899 S.A. song book.

Born at Tregynon, Montgomeryshire, Thomas Olivers (1725–99), losing both father and mother when four years of age, was brought up by a farmer, a distant relative of the family, at Forden, in the same county. At school Thomas proved a more apt scholar in vice than in virtue. At the age of eighteen he was apprenticed to a shoemaker but his wickedness caused him to fly from the scene in order to escape public indignation. He went to Shrewsbury, then to Wrexham, and then to Bristol. Reduced to a state of extreme wretchedness of both mind and body he went to hear Whitefield preach at Bristol. The text of the preacher that day was, ' Is not this brand plucked out of the fire? ' ' No words ', wrote Thomas, ' can set forth the joy, the rapture, the awe and reverence I felt.' He became a new man. ' So earnest was I ', he continued, ' that I used by the hour to wrestle with all my might of body and soul till I almost expected to die on the spot.' Immediately after his conversion he returned to Montgomeryshire to settle all the outstanding debts he had incurred during his days of sinfulness.

Olivers became a local preacher of Wesley's Society at Bradford, Wilts, and was called by John Wesley to join him in Cornwall. ' On the morning of October 24, 1753,' wrote the Rev. S. W. Christophers (1866), ' a somewhat remarkable figure was seen walking out from the town of Bradford in Wiltshire. He had on a long heavy great-coat covering a dress of dark blue of primitive cut, rather after the style of the ordinary dress of the modern bishop. He wore heavy riding-boots, however, and had saddlebags filled with books and linen slung across his shoulders. His face would arrest attention; the open, well-formed manly features and the ever-kindling eye giving expression to a rare combination of acute perception and deep thoughtfulness, logical power, happy temper, quiet humour and bold imagination. It was one of Mr. Wesley's itinerant preachers, on his way to Cornwall, afoot. After many curious adventures on the road, he entered on his work among the then rude masses of the extreme west.'

At Tiverton Olivers bought a colt for five pounds and during the next twenty-five years travelled over a hundred thousand miles up and down Great Britain and Ireland in the service of the Master, often meeting with much opposition and violence. For about twelve years he had charge of printing the Arminian Magazine. For long a great sufferer, he died suddenly in London, and was buried in John Wesley's own tomb in the City Road Chapel burial ground.

Thomas Olivers was also the author of ' The God of Abraham praise ', concerning which James Montgomery declared: ' There is not in our language a lyric of more majestic style, more elevated thought, or more glorious imagery.'

305. O what battles I've been in (Herbert H. Booth (91))

Salvation Music, Vol. 2; set to the minstrel song tune 'Old Uncle Ned'; 1899 S.A. song book.

306. O what has Jesus done for me? (John Maffitt)

Ch.M.H.B.; Congreve's *Gems of Song with Music* (1871).

307. O what shall I do my Saviour to praise (Charles Wesley (15))

Hymns and Sacred Songs, 1742; Ch.M.H.B

308. Once I heard a sound at my heart's dark door (S. Dryden Phelps (verses); Robert Lowry (231) (chorus))

John Burnham's *Song Evangel*, a collection of songs for use in the Metropolitan Tabernacle, London, and published about 1886; 1899 S.A. song book.

Born at Suffield, Connecticut, U.S.A., Dr. Phelps (1816–95) graduated at Brown University in 1844 and became pastor of the First Baptist Church, New Haven, Conn., in 1846, and later of Jefferson Street Church, Providence, R.I. He received his Doctor of Divinity degree from Madison University in 1854, and for a time was editor of *The Christian Secretary*, published at Hartford, Conn.

309. Once I was far in sin (James C. Bateman (177) (verses); R. Kelso Carter (chorus))

Anniversary Hymns (Scotland), 1883; 1899 S.A. song book.

The author of the chorus was a professor in the Pennsylvania Military Academy. While there he was licensed as a Methodist lay preacher. Later he studied medicine and became a physician. The chorus is part of a song commencing: 'Rest to the weary soul.'

310. Once I was lost, on the breakers tossed (William Giles Collins (238))

The Musical Salvationist, August, 1887; 1899 S.A. song book.

This song soon gained popularity and by 1891 the Melbourne *War Cry* carried the rather humorous report regarding a musical festival in the Melbourne Town Hall: 'Colonel Taylor and Brigadier Rothwell were called upon to step forward. After a little coughing they sailed in courageously with

> Once I was lost, on the breakers tossed,
> And far away from shore . . .

This was as far as they went. The words were too appropriate, the duettists were completely at sea and, if I may be allowed to judge, were a trifle sea-sick into the bargain.'

311. One there is above all others (Marianne Nunn)

Written to adapt John Newton's hymn ' One there is above all others, Well deserves the name of Friend ' to the Welsh air, 'Ar hyd y nôs', and first published in the Rev. John Nunn's *Psalms and Hymns from the most approved Authors* in 1817; *The Christian Lyre* (U.S.A.), 1831, which was compiled by the Rev. Joshua Leavett and aroused much opposition from the more formal churches because it contained a number of arrangements of popular secular tunes; Ch.M.H.B.

Sister of the Rev. John Nunn, Rector of Thorndon, Miss Nunn (1778–1847) was born in Colchester.

312. Pleasures sought, dearly bought (Agnes Heathcote)

The Musical Salvationist, January, 1887; 1930 S.A. song book.

The gramophone record made by the Congress Hall Songster Brigade was used for some time in the daily half-hour religious morning services broadcast by the Army over an Australian radio network.

Agnes McDouall's father was a minister at Banff, in the north of Scotland. ' Her quiet, cultured, somewhat secluded life was brought under new shaping influences when the Army established a corps in that town,' wrote Richard Slater. ' Her father approved of the work done by the Army and spoke from its platform; her brothers were saved at its Penitent-form, and she attended a few meetings herself, but the crowded hall and some of the doings of the Salvationists left disagreeable impressions upon her mind. She could claim in truth that she loved God, but service, consecrated labour for Him, full surrender to His command—the Army made her feel that she came far short in those things. Restless and unhappy in consequence.

' In a Monday afternoon holiness meeting she went sobbing to the Army's Penitent-form that things might be put right. Several others followed her, and on raising her eyes she found that the one kneeling next to her was the family's washerwoman. But the surrender had taken away her pride, and she felt no humiliation in these unlooked-for circumstances.

' The next night she went to the meeting and right to the platform to take her place among the people who now she felt must be her people and fellow-workers for the Kingdom of God. She took up "Junior Work"; went visiting; took to selling *The War Cry*, rising from six copies till she could dispose of dozens.'

Her soulful singing as a cadet led Richard Slater to believe she had poetic gifts. At his suggestion she began to write verse. Training completed, she was appointed to the then new form of Salvation Army activity known as ' The Cellar, Gutter and Garret Work ', until she was transferred to the Training Home Singing Brigade, doing good work both in singing and in speaking on a lengthy tour. Service among children, in midnight rescue work, and as a Captain on the Training Home followed until, in 1888, she was married to Staff-Captain Wyndham Heathcote, who had resigned a curacy to become an officer.

313. Saints of God, lift up your voices (Anonymous)

Ch.M.H.B.

314. Salvation! O the joyful sound! (Isaac Watts (3) (verses 1 and 2); Walter Shirley (verse 3); W. T. Giffe (chorus))

Verses one and two in Watts's *Hymns and Spiritual Songs*, 1707; third verse in Wesley's 1780 hymn book; all verses and a different chorus in the Ch.M.H.B. The chorus is from a song entitled ' The banner of love ' in Ogden's *Silver Songs* and (with verses) in 1899 S.A. song book (No. 313).

Grandson of the Earl of Ferrers, the Hon. Walter Shirley (1725-86) was a friend of Whitefield and Wesley and the cousin of the Countess of Huntingdon, in whose chapel he often preached. He accepted the living of Loughrea, Galway, and although he was opposed because of his devotion to evangelical doctrines and his sympathy with the Methodist movement, he remained undeterred. When illness prevented him leaving home he would preach, seated in his chair in the drawing-room, to many who gladly assembled to hear him. About 1774 the Countess of Huntingdon appointed him to revise her collection of hymns.

W. T. Giffe was an American who lived toward the end of the nineteenth century.

315. So that He for me might die (Richard Slater (105))

Written in May, 1886, it formed one of a group of new songs by various writers prepared as the English contribution to the Army's first International Congress held in London in that year, where it was used by the author as a solo. *The Musical Salvationist*, June, 1887; 1899 S.A. song book.

316. Tell out the wonderful story (Sidney E. Cox (33))

The Musical Salvationist, June, 1915, the author's first song to be published.

'It was written on a Saturday evening just prior to an open-air meeting at which I anticipated the opportunity of " telling out the story ",' recalls the author, ' and it was while thinking of the privilege that the Army affords to everyone, and in which I shared, that the phrase " You can tell out the sweet story " found its expression. It took only a few minutes to work the phrase into a song.'

An order once reached London for a copy of *Revival Songs* (which includes this song) to be forwarded to Spain, a land with no Army work. The customer was the leader of a mission and he wanted to introduce ' You can tell out the sweet story ' at his next Christmas service.

317. The glorious gospel word declares (Thomas B. Stephenson)

Inspired by a Brighton convention and published in the 1878 S.A. song book. Considerable changes have been made in the first verse, which originally began: ' This is the glorious gospel word.'

Son of the Rev. John Stephenson, Thomas (1839–1912) was born at Newcastle and educated at Wesley College, Sheffield, and London University. He entered the Wesleyan Ministry in 1860 and laboured in Norwich, Manchester, Bolton and London. He founded the world-famous National Children's Home at Victoria Park, London. He was President of the Wesleyan Conference, 1891, and was appointed Warden of the Wesley Deaconess Institute in 1903.

318. The Saviour sought and found me (Sidney E. Cox (33))

The Musical Salvationist, December, 1935.

319. There is sunshine in my soul today (Eliza Edmunds Hewitt)

The Christian Choir, published by Ira D. Sankey and James McGranahan.

A personal friend of Fanny Crosby, Miss Hewitt was born in Philadelphia in 1851. For some time she was a school teacher but later she was confined to bed for many years. Whilst thus afflicted she turned her heart and mind to writing, producing hundreds of hymns. Eventually her physical infirmities were overcome and she spent the latter part of her life in active Sunday-school work.

320. Though I wandered far from Jesus (James C. Bateman (177))

The Musical Salvationist, April, 1888; 1899 S.A. song book. The author also gave the musical setting.

321. 'Tis the promise of God full salvation to give (Philip P. Bliss (78))

In compiling *Gospel Songs* in 1874, Mr. Bliss wished to include a well-known hymn—' Hallelujah, shine the glory '—then much used in religious services. When the owners of the copyright refused permission he wrote ' Hallelujah, 'tis done! ' to supply the want; 1899 S.A. song book.

In the early days of the Army in Philadelphia, in 1880, a reporter of the local *Times* called at the home of Captain Amos Shirley. When the stories of the Army's work had been given the visitor prepared to leave the house. ' But Mrs. Shirley thought that even reporters had souls to be saved,' wrote St. John Ervine in *God's Soldier*, ' and she stopped him with the question, " Now, my brother, how is it with you? Have you given your heart to God? " The startled press man nervously laughed. " I came here to interview you, not to be interviewed," he said, trying to evade her question. But Anna Shirley was of stouter stuff than he imagined, and she eloquently exhorted him to repent, and finally announced that she would pray over him. Visions of being prayed over by one man and five women flashed through the mind of the visitor, and he made a feeble effort to escape by stammering, " I'm afraid it won't do any good." " Well, it certainly won't do any harm," Mrs. Shirley insisted, and in a few moments she had the embarrassed reporter on his knees. The girls had cleared the table, and replaced the dishes with hymn books. Eliza sang . . .

Hallelujah, 'tis done! I believe on the Son . . .

Then Amos Shirley prayed for the conversion of their visitor.'

322. We are out on the ocean sailing (C. Dunbar)

Written by a minister probably in the United States; Ch.M.H.B.

323. We have heard the joyful sound (Priscilla J. Owens (200))

Written for use in a missionary service in the Sunday-school where the author was a worker, and originally sung to the tune ' Vive le roi ' from Meyerbeer's opera *Les Huguenots*. *The Revivalist*, (U.S.A.), 1868; Sankey's *Sacred Songs and Solos*; *Army Bells*.

324. What a wonderful change in my life has been wrought (R. H. McDaniel)

Written shortly after the death of the author's son, in the spring of 1914; *The Musical Salvationist*, August, 1920.

Born in 1850 in the United States of America, Mr. McDaniel was ordained into the Christian ministry at the age of twenty-three.

325. When I can read my title clear (Isaac Watts (3) (verses); William R. Collier (chorus))

The author's *Hymns and Spiritual Songs*, 1707; Ch.M.H.B.; Chorus by a Salvationist of Plympton, Devon.

326. When my heart was so hard (Herbert H. Booth (91))

Salvation Music, Vol. 2; 1899 S.A. song book.

The song is reminiscent of an incident in Bunyan's *The Pilgrim's Progress*:

'Just as Christian came up with the cross, his burden loosed from off his shoulders, and fell from off his back and began to tumble; and so continued to do till it came to the mouth of the sepulchre, where it fell in, and I saw it no more.

'Then was Christian glad and lightsome and said, with a merry heart, "He hath given me rest by His sorrow, and life by His death." Then he stood still awhile to look and wonder; for it was very surprising to him, that the sight of the cross should thus ease him of his burden. . . . Then Christian gave three leaps for joy, and went on singing.'

327. When upon life's billows you are tempest-tossed (Johnson Oatman)

Written in 1897; *Alexander's New Revival Hymns*.

A Methodist minister, Mr. Oatman (1856–1926) spent most of his time in New Jersey. He was also the author of 'There's not a Friend like the lowly Jesus, No, not one ', which within a year of publication had been reprinted in thirty-five different books. He wrote more than five thousand song-poems, seldom receiving more than a dollar for a song. He died at Mount Holly, New Jersey.

Addressing a congregation of business men in Manchester, Canon Peter Green told how it disappointed him that one of his favourites had not been included in a recent hymnal. ' My poetic friends tell me it is doggerel,' he said, ' and my musical friends tell me it is atrocious, but in spite of what they say, I see in it the soundest theology.' He then proceeded to outline, ' When upon life's billows . . . '.

328. When we walk with the Lord (John Henry Sammis)

Hymns Old and New, 1887; 1930 S.A. song book; *The Musical Salvationist*, April, 1940, with music.

Born in New York, Mr. Sammis became a business man in Logansport, Indiana, and for many years took an active interest in Christian work as a layman. Later he gave up his business to take over the duties of Y.M.C.A. secretary, until he became a Presbyterian minister, serving in Indiana, Michigan and Minnesota. From 1909 until his death on June 12, 1919, he was on the faculty of the Los Angeles Bible Institute. He wrote over one hundred gospel songs.

In 1887 Professor D. B. Towner, one-time musical director of the Moody Bible Institute, was singing at a series of meetings being conducted by Mr. Moody at Brockton, Massachusetts. During one of the services a young man arose to give his testimony and said, 'I'm not quite sure—but I am going to *trust*, and I am going to *obey*.' The Professor jotted the words down and sent the story to Mr. Sammis, who turned the idea into a song. The tune was composed by Professor Towner himself.

329. Whene'er we meet, you always say (Richard Jukes (193))

Ch.M.H.B.

Dr. David J. Burrell, Pastor of the Collegiate Church, New York, speaking in 1900 said: 'Just forty years ago a man rose in our Fulton Street prayer meeting, in the presence of a large assemblage of business men, and read these words which he had written during the previous night.' (Here the doctor read the words ' Whene'er we meet . . .')
' At this moment we are all profoundly interested in " the news "; we can scarcely wait for the issues of the daily press. But to one who has really grasped the great verities of our religion, is there any current event to be compared with the tragedy on Golgotha? '

The song is claimed by many people to have had its inspiration in the Irish Revival of 1860.

330. Where are now those doubts that hindered (Ruth Tracy (270))

Written at the request of Commissioner Thomas Coombs, when British Commissioner, who wanted words for a holiness song to the tune ' Where is now the merry party? ' 1930 S.A. song book.

331. Who, when sunk in deep despair (Herbert H. Booth (91))

The War Cry, November 25, 1882; *Salvation Music*, Vol. 2, where the statement is added: ' Written and composed while suffering from a severe attack of rheumatic fever, being the outcome of a far deeper and grander realization. November, 1882.' 1899 S.A. song book.

332. Why should life a weary journey seem? (Emma Johnson)

The Christian Choralist, U.S.A.; *The Musical Salvationist*, October, 1896, an issue entitled ' World-wide favourites '; 1930 S.A. song book.

333. With joy of heart I now can sing (Anonymous)

The Musical Salvationist, June, 1910; 1930 S.A. song book.

334. With stains of sin upon me (Henry Allen)

The Musical Salvationist, October, 1895; 1899 S.A. song book, where the first line reads: ' With loads of sin upon me, a life made black by guilt.'

Son of a waggoner on a rural farm Henry Allen (1865–1943) was born at Gillingham, Kent. For seventeen years, from 1882, he was a Salvationist at New Brompton (now Gillingham) Corps, holding the position of Bandmaster for seven years, and later, as the Junior Soldiers' Sergeant-Major, forming flute and mandolin bands amongst the young people. In addition to being a proficient player on brass instruments of various kinds, he played the clarionet, flutina, concertina, violin and flute.

Each Sunday night in the ' wind-up ' he introduced a new song of his own composition, most of which were of a happy, joyous character and revealed a deep spiritual experience. They included the present song, ' The path is very narrow, but I'll follow ' (chorus 334) and ' My heart with joy is often running over ' (chorus 367).

335. Would you know why I love Jesus (Elisha A. Hoffman (246))

First published in America; *The Musical Salvationist*, May, 1889; 1899 S.A. song book.

336. You may sing of the joys over Jordan (A. Saker-Lynne)

The War Cry, March 29, 1890; 1899 S.A. song book. A number of alterations have been made for the present edition.

A frequent contributor to the early numbers of *The Musical Salvationist*, the author was Bandmaster at Kennington and later at Peckham 2 before becoming an officer.

337. Believe Him! Believe Him! the Holy One is waiting (Albert Orsborn (42))

Written for a Clapton central holiness meeting; 1930 S.A. song book.

This song was written by request. ' This is not to say, without inspiration,' General Orsborn writes. ' Had I waited for inspiration to lay hold on me, most of my songs would never have been written. I have found that inspiration is for the seeker, the ardent lover of the Master, who takes his Bible to his prayer-room, crying, " Speak, Lord, for Thy servant heareth." God constantly sends out His messages, but we must provide the conditions for true reception, especially in that daily background of our private living which determines whether our prayers are acceptable to God.'

338. Blest are the pure in heart (John Keble (verses 1 and 3); William J. Hall (verses 2 and 4))

John Keble's verses are part of a poem of seventeen verses based on Matthew 5: 8, dated October 10, 1819, and first published in the author's *The Christian Year*, 1827; the remaining verses are from *The Mitre Hymn Book*, 1836; 1930 S.A. song book.

Born at Fairford, Gloucestershire, son of the vicar of the nearby parish of Coln St. Aldwyns, John Keble (1792–1866) was elected a Fellow of Oriel, Oxford, when still under nineteen years of age. In 1815 he entered the Anglican Church and in 1836 became the vicar of Hursley, near Winchester, and remained there for the rest of his life. In 1831 he was appointed Professor of Poetry at Oxford. Nearly a hundred of his hymns are in common use today.

Born in London, William J. Hall (1793–1861) became Prebendary of St. Paul's Cathedral in 1826, and Vicar of Tottenham in 1851.

339. Come, with me visit Calvary (John Lawley (56))

The War Cry, January 20, 1893; *The Musical Salvationist*, supplement to Vol. 7 (1892–3); 1899 S.A. song book.

'It was in the days when the National Headquarters was situated at the north end of Blackfriars Bridge, London,' wrote Commissioner Lawley, 'I was walking there from Farringdon Street Station [he was living at Wood Green], and on my way had to pass a large public house at the corner of the turning into Smithfield Market. The sight of the men and women standing in and around in a fuddled, ragged state led me to think of the ability of God to save to the uttermost. As I went on my way I began to sing " To the uttermost He saves " and I sang the chorus right through. When I reached the office I put my thoughts on paper and thus the new song itself was born.'

'That evening', wrote Mrs. General Carpenter in her Life of the Commissioner, 'he was indulging in a pleasure which he always reserved for himself during his brief stays at home, that of putting his boys to bed. He had undressed Bramwell, put on his nightshirt, and as the father knelt with his little son, the last verse came, and with gratitude he wrote it down.'

Mrs. Carpenter also suggested that the germ thought of this song might be found in Lawley's own seeking after the blessing of holiness: 'After a holiness meeting, in which Dowdle had spoken on the changing of Jacob's character, he found Johnny and Ted [Irons] still on their knees.

'" Here, you boys! What seek ye? " he inquired.

'" Full deliverance, and we won't leave the hall till we get it," Johnny replied.

'" God is not far away. It is His will to cleanse you. Surrender yourself entirely. *Stretch out your hand of faith, believe and accept* " ' (see verse 2).

This song was first sang by the author in Edinburgh on January 17, 1893.

340. Eternal Light! Eternal Light! (Thomas Binney)

Originally published in 1826; *The Officer*, January, 1919.

Born of humble parentage at Newcastle upon Tyne, Thomas Binney (1798–1874) became an assistant in a bookseller's shop, where ' his interest in literature was aroused, and the desire created to improve his mind. To that end he diligently studied Latin and Greek, and particularly English composition '. After studying at Wymondley College he took charge of a Congregational Church at Newport, Isle of Wight, where it was said that he was one of the ' most suggestive and inspiring preachers of his time '. The result was that in 1829 he was invited to the pastorate of the famous King's Weigh House Chapel, London, labouring there for over forty years. He was buried in Abney Park Cemetery.

While living in Newport Mr. Binney was sitting at his window, watching the setting sun. He lingered till the stars came out, and was entranced by the picture it presented. While contemplating this peaceful scene the thought came to him that the sky was never free from light—light was eternal. The lines of ' Eternal Light! ' gradually began to take shape in his mind. He closed the window and returned to his room. Before he went to rest the hymn was written.

341. Have you been to Jesus for the cleansing power? (Elisha A. Hoffman (246))

Sankey's *Sacred Songs and Solos*; *Salvation Music*, Vol. 2; 1899 S.A. song book.

342. If you want pardon, if you want peace (George P. Ewens)

The War Cry, June 16, 1881; *Salvation Music*, Vol. 2, set to the secular tune, ' Pretty Louise '; 1899 S.A. song book.

The household was fast asleep when, at two o'clock in the morning, in the year 1880, Ewens had the inspiration for the song, and awakening one of his sons asked him to write down the verses at his dictation.

' George Phippen Ewens, born in Somerset in 1841, was near the end of his thirties when he encountered The Christian Mission. His father, an auctioneer, had become a victim of the drink habit. His dissolute life led to a separation from his wife, who, soon after Phippen's birth, took him and the three other children to live with a sister. Her father—a bank manager and then Mayor of Glastonbury—was one of the last private owners of the famous abbey ruins.

'Phippen found that music greatly interested him. During his seven years' apprenticeship to the printing business, involving twelve working hours a day, he made time to study languages and the then new Pitman's shorthand. He was proud of a teacher's certificate signed by Isaac Pitman and a certificate for advanced Spanish. He married an excellent young woman. . . .

'Coming out of church one Sunday evening [after moving to London], Ewens and his wife were attracted by an open-air meeting in the Westbourne Park district. The missioners came from Hammersmith and belonged to the Movement beginning to be known as The Salvation Army. . . .

'Ewens knew what to expect when William Booth asked him to become an officer. Though he had a family to support, he did not even think of asking what would be his pay! And so bitter was the spite against the Army that he found himself unable to sell his business; he just had to close it down. But Ewens never regretted his decision. . . .

'It was to become editor of this paper [*The War Cry*] that Ewens was called by William Booth. The first issue was prepared by the *Salvationist* editor, G. P. Ewens 'under-studying' him; No. 2—the first issue in 1880—found Ewens in the editor's chair. . . .

'Ewens had long felt that he should not have a settled position while other officers were subject to change, and so, at his request, his editorship of *The War Cry* ended in November, 1886.

'He volunteered for a new Army venture which may not have made such full use of his abilities, but into which he threw himself whole-heartedly. First from Exeter, then from Cullompton, he energetically evangelized the villages of Devon and West Somerset. . . .

'After three and a half years in village work, Major Ewens was brought back to International Headquarters, where he assisted Commissioner Booth-Tucker while the *Life of Catherine Booth* was being written, and also compiled a cable code for the Army's international use.

'Later he was appointed to begin Army work at Gibraltar, and then held further appointments at headquarters, including that of Under Secretary for American and Canadian affairs.

'Throughout the years of his retirement until his promotion to Glory at the age of eighty-five, Ewens continued to bless many by his personal ministry and by his vigorous writing' (*Playboy to Convert* by S. Carvosso Gauntlett).

The deeply spiritual character of the author is revealed by his familiar pen-name, based on his initials, G. P. E.—Grace, Peace, Evermore.

He was the first Salvationist to have had an original song published with both words and music. This was 'The Hallelujah Fountain' in *The War Cry*, October 21, 1882.

343. Just outside the land of promise (Walter H. Windybank)

The Musical Salvationist, January–February, 1949; written after listening to an address on the wanderings of the Israelites in the wilderness.

Born at Stroud, near Petersfield, Hampshire, Major Windybank (1872–1952) was amongst the Army's first converts at Petersfield, when fourteen years of age. A saddle-maker by profession, he became the Junior Soldiers' Sergeant-Major, and an officer in 1892, being commissioned as Lieutenant to Captain (later Lieut.-Colonel) Clifton Bailey. In nearly forty years' active service as a corps officer on the British Field his appointments included Aberdeen Citadel, Hull Ice-house, Norwich Citadel, Leicester Central, Exeter Temple and Wood Green Corps. Upon retirement in 1932 the Major and his wife settled down at Leicester. A large number of his songs have been published in *The Musical Salvationist* and other Army periodicals, and some appear regularly in the ' Star Card ', but this is the first time the Major has contributed to a song book. Some of his songs appeared in *The War Cry* as early as 1893.

344. Sins of years are washed away (Herbert H. Booth (91))

Favourite Songs Supplement; 1899 S.A. song book.

345. Take time to be holy (William D. Longstaff)

Sankey's *Sacred Songs and Solos*; *The Musical Salvationist*, September, 1941.

Written by a Sunderland man (1822–94), son of a ship-owner, in the mid-nineteenth century after listening to an evening sermon on the text, ' Be ye holy; for I am holy ', given by Dr. Griffith John, a missionary home from China. When the Moody-Sankey evangelistic party came to England, Mr. Longstaff became interested in the services held in his home town and brought his song to their notice.

Being a man of independent means he devoted much of his wealth to philanthropic enterprises. He followed the Rev. Arthur Rees when he left the Established Church and formed the Bethesda Free Chapel. Longstaff helped considerably with the financial arrangements. Among his close friends he numbered Dwight L. Moody, Ira D. Sankey and William Booth, who from time to time were guests in his home.

Mr. Longstaff may have been a Salvationist for a time, for a William D. Longstaff, a soldier of the Sunderland Corps, contributed a number of songs to *The War Cry* during the 1880s.

346. There is a dwelling-place above (Richard Mant)

Originally published between 1828 and 1831; 1899 S.A. song book.
Born at Southampton, son of the master of the Grammar School,

Bishop Mant (1776–1848) was educated at Winchester and Trinity College, Oxford, later becoming a Fellow of Oriel. After his ordination in 1802 he became curate to his father; and, after holding various appointments, Rector of St. Botolph's, Bishopsgate, London. In 1820 he became Bishop of Killaloe and in 1823 Bishop of Down and Connor. The Bishop was a prolific writer, his works including *The History of the Church of Ireland, Scripture Narratives* (1831), in which many of his hymns appeared, and *Ancient Hymns from the Roman Breviary, with Original Hymns* (1837). He died at Ballymoney, Co. Antrim, Ireland.

347. Walk in the light: so shalt thou know (Bernard Barton)

The author's *Devotional Verses*, 1827; based upon 1 John 1: 7.

Bernard Barton was born at Carlisle in 1784 and was educated at a Quakers' school in Ipswich. At the age of fourteen he was apprenticed to a shopkeeper in Halstead, Essex, but in 1806 went to Woodbridge, Suffolk, where, a year later, he married the niece of his former master.

The last forty years of his life he spent as a bank clerk in Woodbridge. His death took place in February, 1849, and his simple grave is to be found in the Friends' Burial Ground adjoining the old Meeting House in Woodbridge.

He had many friends who were distinguished in the realm of letters, such as Charles Lamb, Robert Southey, Sir Walter Scott, Lord Byron, Sir John Bowring and Mrs. Hemans.

Mr. Barton published eight volumes of verse during his lifetime, and a collection of his poems and letters was published after his death.

348. Why are you doubting and fearing? (Herbert H. Booth (91))

Written in June, 1883, when the author was twenty-one years of age, and published in *Salvation Music*, Vol. 2, where the order of verses is 4, 3, 1 and 2; 1899 S.A. song book.

349. Yes, there flows a wondrous river (Richard Slater (105))

Written on January 14, 1893, and based on Revelation 22: 1; 1899 S.A. song book.

350. Before Thy face, dear Lord (Herbert H. Booth (91))

The Soldier Soloist, 1892, a collection of special songs and solos sung in meetings conducted by Ballington Booth and published in the United States of America; 1899 S.A. song book.

'I remember the occasion of its first use in public,' wrote Colonel F. G. Hawkes. 'It was in one of the " Two Days with God " meetings at the old Exeter Hall, conducted by the Founder. Originally there were some eight or ten verses. As each verse was sung at the close of the meeting it was commented upon, and people were urged to come forward to the Mercy Seat. It was a solemn occasion.'

Those extra verses included:

> Do I my comrade slight,
> Or envy him his place?
> Do I exaggerate his faults
> Or speak behind his face?
>
> Am I the one to go
> Where all is big and bright?
> Or have I lost the zeal I knew
> To share the hardest fight?

351. Called from above, I rise (Charles Wesley (15))

Short Hymns, 1762; 1878 S.A. song book; based on Acts 22: 16.

352. Centre of our hopes Thou art (Charles Wesley (15))

Hymns and Sacred Poems, 1749; 1930 S.A. song book; one of several hymns written upon the occasion of the author's marriage. Line five of verse one originally read: ' Cemented by love divine.'

353. Come, Holy Ghost, all-quickening fire (Charles Wesley (15))

Hymns and Sacred Poems, 1740; 1878 S.A. song book, where a change of metre called for a slight alteration of the original, and where the first line read: ' Come, Jesus, Lord, with holy fire.'

From among the papers of Commissioner Brengle the following notes were found:

' Years ago the cadets at Clapton were singing—

> My will be swallowed up in Thee . . .
> Called the full strength of trust to prove . . .

and there my heart cried out, " Yes, Lord, let me prove the full strength of trust! "

' Then I was hushed into deep questioning and prayer, for a whisper deep within me asked: " Can you, will you, endure the tests, the trials, that alone can prove the full strength of trust? A feather's weight may test the strength of an infant or an invalid, but heavier and yet heavier weights alone can test the full strength of a man. Will you bear patiently without murmuring or complaining or fainting, the trials I permit to come upon you, which alone can prove the full strength of trust and train it for larger services and yet greater trials? "

' My humbled heart dared not say, " I can ", but only, " By Thy grace I will ". And then we continued to sing:

> My will be swallowed up in Thee . . .

' My whole soul consented to any trial the Lord in His wisdom and love might seem fit to let come upon me. I willed to be wholly the Lord's; to endure, to " bear up and steer right onward " in the face of every tempest that might blow, every overwhelming sea that might threaten to engulf me, every huge Goliath who mocked and vowed he would destroy me. I was not jubilant; my soul was awed into silence but also into strong confidence and a deep rest of quiet faith. . . .

' That far-off moment when we sang those words was to me most solemn and sacred and not to be forgotten. There God set His seal upon my consenting soul for service, for suffering, for sacrifice. From that moment life became a thrilling adventure in fellowship with God, in fellowship and companionship with Jesus. Everything that has come into my life from that moment has, in some way, by God's sanctifying touch and unfailing grace, enriched me.'

354. Come in, my Lord, come in (Bramwell Booth (280))

The War Cry, April 14, 1881; 1899 S.A. song book.

' Most of the songs he wrote expressed his own experience of full salvation. One of the best he scribbled down in Aldersgate Street Station when, trying to board the moving train home to Hadley Wood, he found the door held from the inside by someone obviously not desiring the Salvationist's intrusion. He was left on the platform, with an hour to wait; but to this day Salvationists the world over sing words written in that hour: "Come in, my Lord, come in . . ." (*Knight Errant's Crusade* by S. Carvosso Gauntlett).

355. Come, O my God, the promise seal (Charles Wesley (15))

Short Hymns on Select Passages of Scripture, 1762, and based on Mark 11: 24; Ch.M.H.B.

356. Come, O Thou Traveller unknown (Charles Wesley (15))

Hymns and Sacred Poems, 1742, and based upon the events recorded in Genesis 32: 24–32; Ch.M.H.B.

The words of this hymn were quoted with great effect by Dean Stanley when he unveiled Wesley's memorial in Westminster Abbey.

357. For ever here my rest shall be (Charles Wesley (15))

Hymns and Sacred Poems, 1740, and based on 1 Corinthians 1: 30; Ch.M.H.B.

358. From every stain made clean (Herbert H. Booth (91))

The Musical Salvationist, March, 1888; 1899 S.A. song book.

359. Give me a holy life (Leslie Taylor-Hunt)

The Officer, October, 1928; and *The Musical Salvationist* the same month; 1930 S.A. song book.

' I was led to write these words at the conclusion of a spiritual day conducted by General Bramwell Booth with the cadets in training at Clapton,' wrote the author who was once an officer attaining the rank of Adjutant, and for some time Songster Leader at Clapton Congress Hall. ' The General's words had been used as arrows which penetrated all hearts, not to hurt, but to heal, to strengthen, to uplift, and the sessions throughout the day had been particularly rich in spiritual teaching and power.

' In the final moments of the evening session—it was the covenant service—we sang the chorus, " Give me a heart like Thine ", following which came a period of silent prayer and heart-searching, broken at length by the General's voice quietly inviting all to claim full salvation, and saying, " Remember, it is a gift. It cannot be earned or bought, or acquired in any other way; it is God's precious gift to the seeking soul ".'

360. God of all power and truth and grace (Charles Wesley (15))

Hymns and Sacred Poems, 1742, and based on Ezekiel 36: 23–28 and originally with twenty-eight verses; Ch.M.H.B.

361. He wills that I should holy be (Charles Wesley (15) (verses); Lewis Hartsough (chorus))

Verses in *Short Hymns on Select Passages of Scripture*, 1762, and Ch.M.H.B. The chorus belongs to a song which commences, ' How bright the hope that Calvary brings '.

Born at Ithaca, New York, Mr. Hartsough (1828–72) entered the Methodist Episcopalian ministry in 1851. After holding charges at Utica and elsewhere he was compelled by illness to retire to the Rocky Mountains, where he organized the Utah Mission and became its first superintendent. He wrote many hymns and several tunes and also edited the music edition of *The Revivalist*, 1868. He died at Mount Vernon, Iowa.

362. I am coming to the Cross (William McDonald)

American Baptist Praise Book, 1871; *Hallelujah Hymn Book*; *Revival Music*; 1878 S.A. song book; associated with an American ballad tune, ' Mother kissed me in my dream '.

Born in Belmont, Maine, Mr. McDonald (1820–1901) was a Methodist pastor in Brooklyn, U.S.A. He was the editor of *The*

Christian Witness, and died in Monrovia, California. 'I composed the hymn to aid seekers of heart purity while at the altar,' he wrote. 'As I was sitting in my study one day the line of thought came rushing into my mind, and in a few minutes the hymn was on paper. It was first sung at a camp meeting at Hamilton, Massachusetts, June 22, 1870.'

363. I bring my heart to Jesus, with its fears (Herbert H. Booth (91))

The War Cry, October 16, 1886; 1899 S.A. song book.

It was the singing of verse four (with the original line, 'To His Cross of suffering I would leap ') by officers in the Highbury Nursing Home, London, that presented such a challenge to the soul of the then Major Albert Orsborn that he wrote the words of song No. 473.

364. I bring my sins to Thee (Frances Ridley Havergal (256))

Written at Leamington, and published in *The Sunday Magazine*, June, 1870; *Revival Music*; 1878 S.A. song book. The verses were originally under the heading of 'Lord, to whom shall we go?' (John 6: 68).

365. I bring Thee, dear Jesus, my all (Frederick Booth-Tucker (verses))

The Musical Salvationist, December, 1890, where the final lines of the original were typical of the writer:

> A soldier I'd be every inch,
> E'er loyal and true to the core;
> From battle-front ne'er would I flinch,
> Henceforth given up for the war.

1899 S.A. song book.

Known throughout India as Fakir Singh, Commissioner Booth-Tucker was born at Monghyr, Bengal, India, on March 21, 1853. His father was in the Bengal Civil Service and his mother was a daughter of the Count de Lautour, General in the Grenadier Guards, whose ancestors had been forced from France during the Revolution. During the Indian Mutiny, when Frederick was five years of age, the family settled in England, leaving the parents behind to face the danger in India.

When thirteen years old, Frederick Tucker went to Cheltenham College, where he remained until he was twenty. He played in the cricket eleven and became a prominent member of the college football team.

From the first he was intended for the Indian Civil Service, but during some Moody and Sankey campaign meetings he attended at the Agricultural Hall, London, he realized he had been specially called to serve God. For some time, however, he studied law in London and then, in 1876, joined the Civil Service in the Punjab, his first appointment being Assistant-Commissioner at Amritsar.

In India, Tucker received another challenge. The fighting religion spoken of in a copy of *The War Cry* appealed to him tremendously. He secured leave of absence, visited London, offered himself to William Booth, and eventually returned to India as an officer to pioneer Army work. Adopting the dress and habits of the people, he and his comrades preached the gospel and begged for their sustenance.

In Calcutta he was imprisoned for causing disorder but because of the honoured name which he bore a wave of indignation swept across the land, which resulted in his liberation.

In 1888 he married the Founder's second daughter, Emma, taking the name of Booth-Tucker. He had three periods of command in India, served for some time at International Headquarters, and took charge of Army work in the United States of America, where Mrs. Booth-Tucker was killed in a railway accident. He married Lieut.-Colonel Minnie Reid in 1906. King George V conferred on the Commissioner the Kaisar-i-Hind Gold Medal for his conspicuous public service in India.

After serving as a travelling Commissioner and for some time as the editor of *The Officer*, the Commissioner was promoted to Glory on Wednesday, July 17, 1929.

366. I hear Thy welcome voice (Lewis Hartsough (361))

A monthly paper entitled *A Guide to Holiness*, 1873; *Hallelujah Hymn Book*; *Revival Music*; 1878 S.A. song book; written while Mr. Hartsough was conducting evangelistic services at Epworth, Iowa, in 1872.

367. I thirst, Thou wounded Lamb of God (Johann and Anna Nitschmann (verses I and 2); Nicolaus L. von Zinzendorf (77) (verses 3 and 4); *translated by* John Wesley (3))

Taken from four German hymns which appeared in the Herrnhut *Gesang Buch*, 1735; *Sacred Hymns and Poems*, 1740; Ch.M.H.B.

Daughter of a cartwright and born at Kunewald, near Fulneck, Moravia, Anna Nitschmann (1715–60) became companion in Herrnhut to Zinzendorf's daughter, with whom she came to England in 1737. In 1740 she went to Pennsylvania with her father, and next year joined Zinzendorf and his daughter in work among the Indians. Later she married the Count.

Anna's brother Johann (1712–83) became Bishop of the Brethren's

Unity in 1758, superintended the work in England and Ireland, before moving to Volga, Russia, where he died.

368. I want a principle within (Charles Wesley (15))

Hymns and Sacred Poems, 1749; Ch.M.H.B.

In the Methodist Conference of 1844 young Samuel Bradburn tried to puzzle Mr. Wesley by asking him, ' Can a man fall from sanctification without losing his justification?' Mr. Wesley took up his hymn book and lined out the last verse of this song: ' O may the least omission pain . . . '

369. I want, dear Lord, a heart that's true and clean (George Jackson)

All the World, January, 1897; 1930 S.A. song book.

Born in 1866, Ensign George Jackson, of New Zealand, was a frequent contributor to the early numbers of *The Musical Salvationist*. He died, the victim of consumption, at the age of twenty-seven.

' Ensign Jackson, a very successful and popular officer, had had a splendid training and education, which he used to the best advantage for God and the Kingdom, and was also an excellent musician. His last work in the musical line was the production of the New Zealand " Band Journals ", upon the eighth of which he was engaged when he died. One of his regrets when dying was that he was leaving " Roll over me " unfinished. He had a considerable knowledge of photography, and made most of the slides for the Maori and junior lanterns, and was also engaged upon making some experiments in the zinco-process in connection with the illustrations for the New Zealand *War Cry* and *Young Soldier*. His promotion to Glory has left a gap in the ranks of our force there which it will be impossible to fill ' (*The Officer*, January, 1894).

After the funeral one of his brothers, who had repeatedly resisted all pleading to become a follower of Christ, was going through the Ensign's papers when he came upon two of the verses and part of the third verse of this song:

> I want, dear Lord, a soul on fire for Thee,
> A soul baptized with heavenly energy . . .

Thus the song ended, unfinished, but the effect upon the brother was such that he claimed salvation on the spot and later completed the song himself.

' From a literary standpoint the verses are not of high merit and the sentiment is of course familiar,' said the Rev. F. Luke Wiseman, the former President of the Methodist Conference. ' But experience has shown that this hymn had great power in evangelistic services, as I have many times witnessed. It was included in the Wesleyan evangelistic hymn book, *The Crusader's Hymnal.*'

370. Jesus, lead me up the mountain (William Pearson (73))

The Musical Salvationist, February, 1910.

371. Jesus, save me through and through (William Pearson (73))

The War Cry, August 4, 1881; 1899 S.A. song book.

372. Jesus, Saviour, I am waiting (Ballington Booth)

The War Cry, September 22, 1881, having been used three days before during a Council of War in the Exeter Hall, London, to a tune by an American composer; 1899 S.A. song book.

Born at Brighouse on July, 28, 1857, second son of the Founder, Ballington Booth became a very popular officer, successfully holding a number of responsible positions.

'Ballington was beloved by all,' one writer has said of him. 'While in command of the training home at Clapton he wept over the little slips of the men, laughed with them, and fought and lived with them when they left for the Field. If he visited a corps he had no ambition to be made a hero in the drawing-room of society but preferred to eat and sleep with the officers in their humble quarters. On the platform he could play with an audience as a Paderewski can with an instrument. His anecdotes and solos (to an accompaniment on an English concertina) won him a way into the hearts of all. He was, in short, a combination of the warm sympathy of his mother and the magnetic personality of his father.'

At the age of twenty-seven he took command of Army work in Australia and later with his wife, Maud Charlesworth, daughter of a clergyman of the Church of England, in America. Unfortunately, owing to difficulties with the Founder over being instructed to farewell, after a successful command of eight years, Ballington and his wife seceded from the Army and formed 'The American Volunteers', Ballington becoming its General. A collection of his songs, *The Soldier Soloist*, was published in New York. He died in the U.S.A. on October 5, 1940.

373. Jesus, Shepherd of the sheep (Charles Wesley (15))

From *Hymns and Sacred Poems*, 1749, and entitled, 'After a recovery'; 1899 S.A. song book.

374. Jesus, Thy boundless love to me (Paulus Gerhardt (81); translated by John Wesley (3))

Cruger's *Praxis*, 1653; translation in *Hymns and Sacred Poems*, 1739, and Ch.M.H.B.

Wesley's version is freely condensed from a German hymn which the author is said to have based upon a meditation and prayer in John Arndt's *Paradiesgartlein*, 1612, and includes but nine of the original sixteen verses.

In his *Plain Account of Christian Perfection* Wesley says: ' In the beginning of the year 1738, as I was returning from Savannah, the cry of my heart was—

> O grant that nothing in my soul
> May dwell but Thy pure love alone—

a prayer abundantly answered on the memorable May 24th of that year, when, in the Society Meeting in Aldersgate Street, about a quarter before nine, during the reading of Luther's *Preface to the Epistle to the Romans*, I felt my heart strangely warmed.

' I felt I did trust in Christ, Christ alone for salvation, and assurance was given me that He had taken away my sins, even mine, and saved me from the law of sin and death.'

375. Jesus, Thy fulness give (William Pearson (73))

The War Cry, February 6, 1892; 1899 S.A. song book.

376. Jesus, Thy purity bestow (William Pearson (73))

The War Cry, November 7, 1891; 1899 S.A. song book.

377. Lord, I believe a rest remains (Charles Wesley (15))

Hymns and Sacred Poems, 1740; Ch.M.H.B.; based upon Hebrews 4: 9. Originally there were twenty-seven verses.

378. Lord, I come to Thee beseeching (Ruth Tracy (270))

1899 S.A. song book.

Written for General Bramwell Booth, when Chief of the Staff, who wanted verses to the tune ' None of self'. They had to be ' practical and definite and calculated to lead the singer step by step to a full consecration '. The writing called for a half-night of prayer, and some very deep heart searchings.

379. Lord, I pray that I may know Thee (Ruth Tracy (270))

Written when asked for a song to the tune ' I surrender all ' for the 1930 S.A. song book. Some years before Brigadier Tracy had listened to Commissioner Adelaide Cox speaking in a woman's social officers' meeting on *knowing* the Lord, and had at that time unsuccessfully attempted to put the idea into a song.

380. Lord Jesus, I long to be perfectly whole (James Nicholson)

Written by an American Methodist minister; *Hallelujah Hymn Book*; *Revival Music*; 1878 S.A. song book. Originally the first verse commenced: 'Dear Jesus, I long to be perfectly whole.'

381. Lord Jesus, my heart has been hard and unclean (George Scott Railton (292) (verses); James Nicholson (380) (chorus))

Verses in *The Salvation Soldier's Song Book* (U.S.A.) 1883, and 1899 S.A. song book; chorus in *Hallelujah Hymn Book* and *Revival Music*; verses and chorus in 1930 S.A. song book.

382. Lord, through the Blood of the Lamb that was slain (Herbert H. Booth (91))

The War Cry, March 27, 1886; *Songs of Peace and War*; 1899 S.A. song book.

Written for a 'Two Days with God' series of meetings in the Exeter Hall, London, at the request of William Booth who often used it to open his Sunday morning holiness meetings. Almost every line of the song served him as a text on which to make impressive and heart-searching observations. The author was twenty-four years of age at the time.

383. Love divine, all loves excelling (Charles Wesley (15))

The author's *Hymns for Those that Seek and Those that have Redemption in the Blood of Jesus Christ*, 1747; Ch.M.H.B.; based on Ephesians 3: 19.

The opening lines were probably an echo from current literature of the song of Venus in the last act of Dryden's *King Arthur*:

> Fairest isle, all isles excelling,
> Seat of pleasures and of loves,
> Venus here will choose her dwelling
> And forsake her Cyprian Groves.

Love divine! This is a recurring motif running through the songs of Charles Wesley, so that we have such phrases as 'Glorious love', 'Perfect love', 'Unexampled love', 'Redeeming love', 'Unbounded love', and 'Heart-renewing love'.

In 1747, the year this hymn was published, Charles Wesley wrote to his beloved Sally Gwynne (his future wife) from Holyhead, on his way to Dublin, 'This, this is the one thing needful—not a friend—not health—not life itself, but the pure, perfect love of Christ Jesus.'

384. Love divine, from Jesus flowing (Elizabeth MacKenzie)

The War Cry, November 26, 1887; 1899 S.A. song book.

As Captain Elizabeth Rumsby, the author wrote this song while in charge of the Hendon Corps before being married to Staff-Captain George MacKenzie, the aide-de-camp to the Divisional Commander. She had also commanded the corps at Battersea and Woolwich. After rising in rank and becoming Chief Secretary to Mr. Herbert Booth, the Territorial Commander for Canada, Colonel MacKenzie became a minister in Stratford in Ontario, where he served for twenty years before retiring in 1937. Mrs. MacKenzie died in London, Ontario, in 1943 at the age of ninety.

385. My God! I know, I feel Thee mine (Charles Wesley (15))

Hymns and Sacred Poems, 1740; Ch.M.H.B.

386. O Christ of pure and perfect love (William Booth (119))

The War Cry, April 18, 1896; 1899 S.A. song book.

387. O come and dwell in me (Charles Wesley (15) (verses))

The author's *Short Hymns on Select Passages of Scripture*, 1762; Ch.M.H.B.; based on (verse 1) 2 Corinthians 3: 17, (verse 2) 2 Corinthians 5: 17, and (verses 3 and 4) Hebrews 11: 5. Chorus: 1899 S.B.

388. O disclose Thy lovely face! (Charles Wesley (15))

Hymns and Sacred Poems, 1740, verses taken from two separate hymns; Ch.M.H.B.

389. O for a closer walk with God (William Cowper (25))

Written in 1769 and published in Conyer's *Collection of Psalms and Hymns*, 1772; Ch.M.H.B.; based on Genesis 5: 24.

A tablet in the Church of Holy Trinity, Ripon, is inscribed to the memory of Susannah Powley, only daughter of Mrs. Unwin, the friend of Cowper. In December, 1769, Mrs. Unwin was very seriously ill, and in a letter to another friend Cowper wrote of his distress concerning one whom he called ' the chief of blessing I have met with in my journey'. 'Her illness', he continued, ' has been a great trial to me. Oh! that it may have a sanctified effect, that I may rejoice to surrender up to the Lord my dearest comforts the moment He shall require them. Oh, for no will but the will of my Heavenly Father!' Then he thanked his friend for some verses sent to him and enclosed some of his own in return—the words of ' O for a closer walk with God '.

' I began to compose them yesterday morning [December 9, 1769]

128

before daybreak,' wrote Cowper, ' but fell asleep at the end of the first two verses; when I waked again the third and fourth verses were whispered to my heart in a way which I have often experienced.'

390. O for a heart that is whiter than snow (Eliza Edmunds Hewitt (319))

First published in the U.S.A. about 1892; *The Musical Salvationist*, April, 1905; 1930 S.A. song book.

Mrs. Hewitt is credited with more than two thousand songs.

391. O for a heart to praise my God (Charles Wesley (15))

Hymns and Sacred Poems, 1742; Ch.M.H.B.; based on Psalm 51: 10.

392. O for a humbler walk with God! (Edward Harland)

A Church Psalter and Hymnal, 1855; 1930 S.A. song book.

Born at Ashbourne, Derbyshire, Mr. Edward Harland (1810–90) was ordained deacon in 1833. After serving as curate of Newborough and Swindon he was appointed, in 1851, Vicar of Colwich, Staffs, and became Chaplain to the Earl of Harrowby. In 1873 he was appointed Prebendary of Lichfield Cathedral.

393. O glorious hope of perfect love! (Charles Wesley (15))

Hymns and Sacred Poems, 1742, and Ch.M.H.B., where the last verse read: ' Now, O my Joshua bring me in.' The original nineteen verses were based on the idea of the division of Canaan into lots among the various tribes of Israel.

' The characteristic longing of Charles Wesley was for love,' wrote Dr. J. Ernest Rattenbury. ' Even when he overstressed suffering, it was love that he was really seeking. Scattered all over his works are " Hymns for Love ".'

394. O God of light, O God of love (Arthur S. Booth-Clibborn)

The War Cry, April 13, 1895; 1930 S.A. song book; written on the Continent during times of great persecution.

As a young member of the Society of Friends, Mr. Booth-Clibborn offered his services for the Army's work in France in 1881, and after ably assisting the Maréchale, the eldest daughter of the Founder, in her work in France and Switzerland, married her on February 8, 1887.

Unfortunately, he disagreed with the Founder on certain points of doctrine and constitution and as Commissioner Booth-Clibborn, with the Maréchale, left the Army in January, 1902.

' Religiously fanatical as Commissioner Booth-Clibborn was,' read a tribute, ' he was nevertheless an extraordinary evangelist; a man with a burning call to men to repent and do their first works, and to come out from the world of strife and fashion and politics and money-making and live the simple Christ-life. A man of immense physical stature, his head covered with a shock of fine brown hair, with dazzling eyes and voice strong and musical, he went through France and Switzerland like a prophet resurrected from medieval times. He sang like a bird in the heavens and played upon the emotions of Latin and Teuton congregations with commanding skill. He was a winner of souls. When he preached a note of wrath reverberated in his denunciations of sin. He laboured incessantly, translated and wrote books, composed hymns and devised campaigns of evangelistic conquest ' (*General Booth and The Salvation Army*, by A. M. Nicol). He was promoted to Glory early in 1938.

395. O Jesus, Saviour, Christ divine (William Booth (119))

The War Cry, May 23, 1896; *The Officer*, June, 1896; 1899 S.A. song book; written especially for use with the tune ' Come on, my partners ', which the Founder tried to popularize.

396. O joyful sound of gospel grace (Charles Wesley (15))

Hymns and Sacred Poems, 1742; Ch.M.H.B.

397. O Lamb of God, Thou wonderful Sin-bearer (Catherine Booth-Clibborn)

The Musical Salvationist, June, 1888; 1899 S.A. song book.

Eldest daughter and third child of the Founder and Mrs. Booth, Catherine was born at Gateshead, September 18, 1858, and pioneered the work of the Army on its first overseas battleground: France and Switzerland. Whilst in France she received the designation of ' the Maréchale ', by which she was affectionately called for the rest of her life.

' Like her noble father she cared only for one thing—souls— bringing them to Christ, urging them to love God, goodness, truth and mercy. The dogmatic never appealed to her. She revelled in preaching to the " demi-mondes " of Paris. Her heaven on earth was in pouring forth words of tender sympathy in a theatre, or music-hall, or café, to the derelicts of humanity, and telling them that it is all cant and superstition and dogmatism that makes the world out to be full of sin, or religion to be merely something for the grave and eternity. Her idea of Christ is that He is the Son of man, and unless He was so He could not have brought healing to the broken hearts of men. For this view of the Divine she contended with infidels, anarchists, and the most sensual and the most aesthetic in the land which she loved and to which she devoted the best years of her life. For this she suffered many things.

She endured imprisonment in Neuchâtel; was mobbed and robbed and threatened with violence and things worse than death. ' With this gospel she broke down the walls of prejudice, won an " entree " to the haunts of the vilest as well as to the confidence of Catholic priests, who could not be expected to endorse such a waste of sanctified affection upon an organization which sadly lacked, in their estimation, divine authority ' (*General Booth and The Salvation Army*, by A. M. Nicol).

On February 8, 1887, she was married to Arthur S. Booth-Clibborn (see No. 394). Even after the Booth-Clibborns resigned their commission in January, 1902, the Maréchale retained her character as an earnest evangelical preacher, and drew large crowds to her meetings which she conducted until shortly before she died on May 9, 1955.

398. O Lord, I come just now to Thee (Fred W. Fry (248))

Salvation Music, Vol. 2; 1899 S.A. song book.

399. O Love divine, how sweet Thou art! (Charles Wesley (15))

Lampe's *Hymns on the Great Festivals*, 1746; Wesley's *Hymns and Sacred Poems*, 1749; Ch.M.H.B.; one of the three of Wesley's hymns that Handel set to music. For these words he composed the tune ' Wentworth ', the manuscript of which is in the library of Cambridge University.

400. O Love, revealed on earth in Christ (Catherine Baird)

The Musical Salvationist, March–April, 1950, where it was written for an original tune by Colonel Bramwell Coles. ' I began to write it in my mind many years before it was published,' states the author. ' But during the war, which I believed could never occur, it was nearly completed through my personal reflections on the incompatibility of war with the teachings of Jesus. I did not finish it, however, until Colonel Coles asked for words to his music.' The verses were revised by the author for the song book in order to make the original idea more clear.

Colonel Catherine Baird, of Scottish descent on her father's side and Manx descent on her mother's side, was born in Sydney, Australia, in 1895. As an officer she served in South Africa and the U.S.A. Central Territory. From the editorship of *The Young Soldier* in Chicago she was appointed editor of the International *Young Soldier,* to which later were added the duties as editor of *The Warrior,* becoming Literary Secretary at International Headquarters in 1953.

The Colonel is the author of a number of books, including *The Sword of God, Of Such is the Kingdom, The Banner of Love* and *Evidence of the Unseen.* Songs from her pen have appeared in many Army periodicals, and a number with musical setting in *The Musical Salvationist.*

401. O spotless Lamb, I come to Thee (Catherine Booth-Clibborn (397))

The War Cry, October 28, 1882; *Salvation Music,* Vol. 2; 1899 S.A. song book.

402. O that in me the mind of Christ (Edward H. Joy (161))

The Musical Salvationist, December, 1935; based upon Philippians 2: 5–11. The author composed the music with which the words were published.

403. O Thou God of full salvation (Lilian Watkins)

The War Cry, June, 1895; 1899 S.A. song book. The third verse was written a few months after the rest, at a time of great sorrow in the author's home; 'cheer us while we bear the cross' was a very real cry from the heart.

Lilian Bowyer, born in Bristol, November, 1879, into an Army family, was converted at an Easter Sunday morning knee-drill when just over seven years of age. In November, 1897, she entered training from Cardiff Stuart Hall Corps, and after holding field and divisional appointments proceeded to India in 1912. She married Staff-Captain (later Major) George Watkins in 1922. They continued to serve in India until 1928, and later in West Africa where the Major was Training Principal.

Mrs. Watkins always loved music and singing and at about eight years of age began writing Army songs herself. As she grew older she used her songs as solos, a number of which were published in *The Musical Salvationist.* She was promoted to Glory from Canada in 1964.

404. O Thou to whose all-searching sight (Nicolaus L. von Zinzendorf (77); *translated by* John Wesley (3))

The original verses, in German, were written in September, 1721. Wesley's translation appeared in *Psalms and Hymns,* 1738; Ch.M.H.B.

405. O when shall my soul find her rest (Bramwell Booth (280))

The War Cry, May 15, 1880, and written in the midnight hour waiting at a railway station. 1899 song book.

Speaking at the Congress Hall, Clapton, in 1951, Mrs. Bramwell Booth recalled the first Army holiness meeting she attended in the

Whitechapel hall. ' My spirit was restless,' she said. ' That morning the song " O when shall my soul find her rest " was sung for the first time. Mr. Bramwell had written the words on the Saturday night. The line " For Thou art almighty to keep! " brought light to my soul.'

406. Saviour from sin, I wait to prove (Charles Wesley (15))

Hymns and Sacred Poems, 1742; Ch.M.H.B.; with song No. 216, is part of a poem of thirty-six verses entitled ' Groaning for Redemption '.

The word ' peculiar ' in the fourth verse comes from the Latin *peculium*, the private property belonging to a child or a slave. It also occurs in 1 Peter 2: 9—' Ye are . . . a peculiar people ' and, translated by Weymouth, ' a people belonging specially to God '. See also song No. 98, verse 5.

The morning after the Founder's last operation he quoted the words of ' Saviour from sin, I wait to prove ' in a calm and triumphant voice. ' My dear Saviour,' he murmured softly, ' my dear Saviour, all unworthy as I am, " Thine only may I live and die " ' (Commissioner Lucy Booth-Hellberg in *The Officer*, November-December, 1953, p. 413).

407. Saviour, I want Thy love to know (Harry Anderson)

The Musical Salvationist, April, 1887; 1930 S.A. song book.

Auxiliary H. Anderson was a contributor to the early numbers of *The Musical Salvationist*, where he supplied the music to his own words. He belonged to Belfast and his father, a Methodist, was acquainted with Commissioner John Carleton, who came from Ligoniel, near Belfast.

408. Say but the word, Thy servant shall be healèd (Albert Orsborn (42))

Published on the song sheet used in the meetings in the Royal Albert Hall, London, on February 21, 1952, and described by the General as ' one of those inspirations that come singing into the soul between home and the office '.

409. Send out Thy light and Thy truth, Lord (Ruth Tracy (270))

The Musical Salvationist, September, 1906; 1930 S.A. song book; inspired by an address given by Commissioner Thomas Coombs and written at the express wish of Commissioner James Hay.

410. Spotless Lamb, O wilt Thou make me (Barbara Stoddart (120))

1899 S.A. song book.

411. Tell me what to do to be pure (Samuel H. Hodges (verses); E. R. Latta (chorus))

Sankey's *Sacred Songs and Solos* (chorus only) from a song commencing ' Blessed be the fountain of Blood '; 1899 S.A. song book.

Once a lawyer in the United States, Major Samuel Hodges wrote this song while travelling with the Founder, singing solos in his meetings. A firm believer in the doctrine of holiness, he had frequently discussed with the Founder and the Army Mother the struggles and anguish of soul experienced by many of the converts and soldiers. Their doubts and fears, lack of faith in the doctrine, and the possibility of living here with a heart pure and clean were a cause of much concern. ' In the Whitechapel days ', wrote the author's son, himself an officer in the United States, ' it was customary for the Founder, Mr. Bramwell Booth, George Railton and my father to lunch together. On one of these occasions the Founder stated that he was going to speak on " heart purity " at his next weekly holiness meeting in the Exeter Hall in the Strand and, turning to my father, asked him if he had a solo suitable for that subject. When the reply given was in the negative the Founder immediately suggested that my father should write one. Being a man of much prayer, my father sought the Lord's help and soon the inspiration was forthcoming and the song composed.'

Samuel Hodges later became a Quaker minister and died in August, 1922.

412. There are wants my heart is telling (Herbert H. Booth (91))

Songs of Peace and War; 1930 S.A. song book; based on Amos 7: 8; 8: 2.

413. There is a holy hill of God (William D. Pennick)

1930 S.A. song book; based on Psalm 24: 3–5.

Son of Band Sergeant Shepherd Drake Pennick of the Clapton Congress Hall, London, and born on January 1, 1884, Lieut.-Commissioner Pennick became an officer from the Congress Hall in 1903 and married Lilly, daughter of Colonel John Dean, in 1908. During his more than forty years' service as an officer he held appointments in North China, Belgium, and in North India where he was the Territorial Commander. In addition to writing his songs, four of which are included in our song book, the Commissioner was the author of *Feasts worth Fasting for*. He was promoted to Glory on July 8, 1944. During his last hours he had been able to say, ' In the forty years of my officership I have never slacked. I spent the last five months of it on campaign amongst the non-Christian people. I am going out with my flag flying!'

The Commissioner gave his own account of this song: 'The story which lies behind its writing is one of a seeking after holiness. Strange to tell, although the song speaks so clearly of faith as the ground of reward in this seeking, the writer was still only a seeker. There had been fasting, prayer, Bible study, the reading of the best writers on the subject, but not being mixed with faith, none of these were of profit. But "light is sown for the righteous", and they that hunger after it shall be filled. So it proved, for not long after the song was written William Meadows Taylor's book, *The Model Preacher*, brought the word which made clear the place of stumbling.

'In this most helpful book Taylor gives his testimony. In substance it is as follows: "For four and a half years I sought the blessing of a clean heart. Hundreds of times I knelt, renouncing everything I knew to be wrong and consecrating myself to God. But within twenty-four hours I found myself back again in the same old experience. At last I saw that all along I had been making one great mistake. My renunciation was right, my consecration was right, but each time I came I put a good resolution in the place of faith."

' "What a fool you are!" exclaimed the writer of this song when he had read the statement. "This is just what you have been doing all along." Moving from his chair to his knees, he raised the book in his hands and prayed this very brief prayer—"Lord, I believe!" '

414. Thou hidden love of God, whose height (Gerhard Tersteegen; *translated by* John Wesley (3))

The original was published in Tersteegen's *Geistliches Blumengärtkein*, 1729. The translation made in Savannah, Georgia, in 1736, appeared in Wesley's *Psalms and Hymns*, 1738; Ch.M.H.B.

Born at Mörs, Westphalia, Gerhard (1697–1769), son of a godly tradesman who died soon after his son's birth, became very proficient in Latin and Greek during his early training at the local grammar school, but was compelled by impoverished circumstances to go into business instead of the university.

At the age of fifteen Gerhard was apprenticed in Mülheim, to a trade which he heartily disliked and to a brother-in-law who was utterly incapable of understanding him. He was only a little over sixteen when he received a very realistic appreciation of his unreadiness to meet his Maker. Giving himself to earnest prayer he devoted himself unreservedly to God. To further his decision he abandoned the idea of a mercantile life and chose the easier occupation of a silk-weaver, so that he could have more leisure for contemplation and prayer.

Notwithstanding his singular devotedness of life he passed through a state of soul-darkness, but when the clouds dispersed signed with his own blood a covenant of personal dedication of himself to the service of God.

At the age of twenty-eight he began to exhort in prayer meetings; people came to consult him from many European countries; and if he went away for a rest people would watch for him by the wayside and would carry him off to some place where a congregation would soon gather to hear him preach. He set up a dispensary for the poor in his own house, compounding the medicines himself. He translated some of the writings of the Mystics so that he could help to spread them amongst the people, and left over a hundred hymns. In spite of increasing weakness he maintained his labours of love till he died, at Mülheim.

415. We have not known Thee as we ought (Thomas Benson Pollock)

Hymns Ancient and Modern, Supplemental Hymns, 1889.

Born at Strathallan, Isle of Man, Mr. Pollock (1836–96) graduated in 1859 at Trinity College, Dublin, where he gained the Vice-Chancellor's prize for English verse. At first he decided to study medicine but in 1861 took Holy Orders and became Curate at St. Luke's Church, Leek, Staffs. After serving as Curate at St. Thomas's Church, Stamford Hill, London, he joined his brother in 1865 and became the Curate of St. Alban's Church, Bordesley, Birmingham. In this very poor area the brothers built up a live church, maintaining three assistant clergy, six lay readers and four sisters. After thirty years he succeeded his brother as vicar. In 1870 he published *Metrical Litanies for Special Services and General Use.*

416. What are now those burning longings (Lorelle Damon)

A pamphlet of the author's compositions entitled *Special Songs of Praise and Glory,* 1891, where the fourth verse was the first; 1899 S.A. song book.

Sister of Commissioner Alexander M. Damon, Miss Damon was blind from infancy, the optic nerve being paralysed through, it is thought, being taken into strong sunlight too soon after birth. She was educated at the Perkins Institute in Boston and continued her studies under the tuition of her mother who had been a school teacher. In 1934 her brother received a letter from a pastor in California which verified the authorship of this song: ' In those old days my wife and I were very much attached to your little sister Lorelle. We regarded her then, and have thought of her since, as a real saint of God. Of all Army " specials " to visit our corps she was our favourite. Her sweet smile, and sweet voice, never failed to stir the hearts of her listeners. Especially in song, as you know, she was wonderfully gifted. By the way, I wonder whether you know that a song which has been largely published was your sister's own composition? I refer to that which begins,

> Where are now the golden fancies
> That were mine in days of yore?

In one of the last conversations we had together, Lorelle mentioned the matter.'

417. What is our calling's glorious hope (Charles Wesley (15))

Hymns and Sacred Poems, 1742; Ch.M.H.B.; based upon Titus 2: 14.

418. What now is my object and aim? (Charles Wesley (15))

Short Hymns on Select Passages of Scripture, 1762; Ch.M.H.B.; verses 1 and 2 are based on Psalm 39: 7; verses 3 and 4 on Psalm 42: 2.

419. When shall these conflicts cease (Frederick Booth-Tucker (365))

It was written on board the S.S. *Normannia* in the Atlantic Ocean and first published in *The War Cry*, June 14, 1890; 1899 S.A. song book.

420. Why should I be a slave to sin (William Baugh)

1899 S.A. song book.

One of a large family which had to be clothed and fed on nine shillings a week, William Baugh began work at ten years of age as a cow-minder in his native village of Pitton, near Salisbury. Methodist campaigners influenced his young life and he professed conversion. Moving to Barnsley, he met The Salvation Army, became a soldier and later an officer.

After commanding the corps at Hartlepool, Sheffield and New Radford, he was appointed to Whitechapel, the Army's No. 1 corps, at a time when the 'Skeleton Army' ruined indoor and outdoor meetings alike and persecuted the soldiers and where Commissioner Charles Jeffries was one of his converts. Following Whitechapel, Baugh opened the Regent Hall Corps, where he saw as many as a hundred people surrender to God in one night and where he enrolled five hundred new soldiers. Later he served in Canada and England as a Divisional Commander, then as 'Spiritual Special', often assisting in the Founder's campaigns and, before retirement as a Brigadier in 1914, as Provincial Young People's Secretary for South London. He was promoted to Glory from Penge on July 9, 1942. His son Charles was the Chief of the Staff from 1943–46.

When Baugh was the Captain in charge at the Regent Hall Corps the daughter of a peer came to the Penitent-form for full salvation.

'She was afraid to get out of Romans 7 into Romans 8,' said the Captain. 'Do you think you can get a fuller salvation than you have now?' he asked her. 'Oh, yes!' she replied. 'Obtain it then,' the Captain advised, 'but I think you will feel there is still more to get.' This song comprises the answers the Captain gave to her questions. She gained the victory and became an earnest Christian worker.

421. With my faint, weary soul to be made fully whole (W. H. Burrell)

Written by an American minister and published in *Songs of Joy and Gladness* where the first line commenced: 'With my sin-wounded soul . . .'; 1878 S.A. song book.

422. With my heart so full of sadness (Herbert H. Booth (91))

The Salvation Songster, 1885; 1899 S.A. song book.

423. With panting heart that dares to seek (Robert Johnson)

Written specially for the Sheffield Council of War conducted by the Founder in June, 1884; 1899 S.A. song book.

A Scotsman marked by strong, impulsive emotions, a capable violinist, possessed of a good voice and an attractive manner as a singer, Robert Johnson loved social gatherings and dancing saloons. After conversion in the Army he became an officer in Scotland before being transferred to the Training Home in London where he became a valued member of its famous singing brigade. Chorus 261, 'Down at the Saviour's feet', is from another of his many songs.

424. Ye longing souls, lift up your heads (Charles Wesley (15))

Hymns and Sacred Poems, 1742, and Ch.M.H.B., where it commenced: 'Prisoners of hope, lift up your heads.'

In Charles Wesley's account of his spiritual experience he makes use of the phrase, 'I now found myself at peace with God and rejoiced in hope of loving Christ'—an expression which, writes J. Ernest Rattenbury, 'meant deliverance from sin, absolution, reconciliation and assurance of forgiveness—in a word, a liberation from the legal tyranny which had so harassed him, but it also meant "hope", the "hope of loving Christ". An understanding of the significance of these words gives us the only key which can interpret hundreds of the hymns of Charles Wesley. He had been delivered from the prison of the law of sin and death ("My chains fell off") to become the prisoner of hope'.

In Salvation Army phraseology he was converted, he had passed from death unto life, but it was just the beginning of his spiritual growth—there lay before him the hope of an ever-developing experience.

425. A charge to keep I have (Charles Wesley (15))

Wesley's *Short Hymns on Select Passages of Scripture*, 1762; Ch.M.H.B.; based on Leviticus 8: 35.

426. All I have, by Thy Blood Thou dost claim (Richard Slater (105) (verses); Herbert H. Booth (91) (chorus))

Chorus in *Favourite Songs Supplement*; complete song in the 1899 S.A. song book.

Lieut.-Colonel Slater wrote: ' The words of the chorus and the melody of the song were written by Herbert Booth in 1887 but, as in several other instances, owing to pressure of work, he could not find time to write the verses. I, therefore, was instructed to supply what was lacking. The verses were written on November 7, 1887.'

427. All to Jesus I surrender (Judson Van de Venter)

First published in 1896; *Alexander's New Revival Hymns*; 1930 S.A. song book.

Born on a farm near Dundee, Michigan, U.S.A., on December 5, 1855, Van de Venter graduated from Hillsdale College, visited the great art galleries of Europe in 1885 to study painting and upon returning to the United States of America taught art.

Whilst singing in the choir during a revival campaign in Sharon, Pennsylvania, he felt the call to evangelistic work. He toured America and England where, in partnership with W. S. Weeden, he conducted campaigns. These two men became partners in song-writing as well as in soul-winning, Mr. Weeden supplying the musical settings. The author's closing years were spent in Tampa, Florida, where he died on July 17, 1939.

428. And is it so? A gift from me (Richard Slater (105))

Written on March 16-17, 1888, and published in *The Musical Salvationist*, May, 1888; 1899 S.A. song book.

429. Behold, the servant of the Lord! (Charles Wesley (15))

First published in 1744 and then, the following year, republished at the end of *A Farther Appeal to Men of Reason and Religion*; Ch.M.H.B.

430. Beneath the Cross of Jesus (Elizabeth Cecilia Clephane)

The Family Treasury; *The Musical Salvationist*, June, 1916; 1930 S.A. song book; written shortly before the author's death.

Third daughter of Andrew Clephane, Sheriff of Fife, Elizabeth (1830–69) was born in Edinburgh. Her mother was a member of the Douglas family, of which the Earls of Home are the heads. After the death of their father the daughters lived first at Ormiston, East Lothian, and then at Bridgend, Melrose.

Elizabeth was gentle and retiring in disposition and generous of nature, but was of indifferent health, the result of a chill caught in childhood. The sisters were very interested in the poor of their neighbourhood, spending all they could spare on charity. They gave up even their carriage and horses so that they might devote more money to this purpose. They were members of the Free Church of Scotland.

Mr. Sankey composed the original tune (Tune Book No. 696) for the words in the house of Dr. Barnardo, in Bow Road, London, which later became an Army boys' home.

The following morning at eight o'clock the usual mission service was held in the Bow Road Hall, the preacher being the Rev. W. Hay Aitken, the well-known missioner. A very large congregation attended. It was arranged that Mr. Sankey should sing a solo before the sermon, and he chose to sing ' Beneath the Cross of Jesus ' to the tune composed the previous day. The effect was startling. When the solo was finished Mr. Aitken said that he had intended to speak on the subject of Christian work, but the new hymn had made such an impression upon him and upon his hearers that he had decided to preach upon ' The Cross of Jesus '. The powerful sermon was used to bring many to a knowledge of God and His salvation.

Miss Clephane was also the author of:

> There were ninety and nine that safely lay,
> In the shelter of the fold.

431. Blessèd Saviour, now behold me (William Baugh (420))

The War Cry, November 20, 1886; *The Musical Salvationist*, January, 1891; 1899 S.A. song book.

'About the year 1887,' wrote Lieut.-Colonel Slater, ' while the Music Department was still located at Clapton Congress Hall, a male cadet came to me one day, saying, " I have a tune I think would be of use to you ". It was our custom in the department to make inquiries in all quarters for likely tunes as well as words for Army use, especially for insertion in *The Musical Salvationist*, so that cadets, among other folk, would often come to sing over to us tunes they thought of value for our purposes. We would take them down in shorthand fashion and the results were treasured for future consideration.

'It was so in the present case. The singer had been a sailor, and in Australia, on one of his voyages, he had got to know a tune which had gained his fancy and which he hoped might gain favour. The title of the song was "Minnie, darling, come and wander". In a musical scrap book which I kept in the department I put, for preservation, the copy of the tune that I took down from the cadet. I thought well of the melody, and planned to seek suitable words for it.

'A similar scrap book was also kept for likely sets of words which were cut from Army publications. From time to time these scrap books were gone through in an endeavour to find possible conjunctions of words and tunes.

'One day a copy of a Canadian *War Cry* came to hand. Its song page was examined and we found the set of words by Brigadier Baugh, who was then stationed in Canada. The words were cut out and placed in the scrap book as likely to be of service.

'Later, I was going over the stock of materials in the department and came across the tune from Australia and the words from Canada, and found that they agreed in an admirable way for a song. They were then and there united "in holy matrimony", and have lived together ever since in happy union. The words had already appeared in the International *War Cry* but had failed to gain my attention.'

The song, originally set to the tune 'I will guide thee', had been written in 1886 just before the Brigadier was appointed to Canada, while stationed at Stockport.

432. Brightly beams our Father's mercy (Philip P. Bliss (78))

The Charm, 1871; 1899 S.A. song book.

The imagery employed in this song is said to be based upon a type of lighthouse used on some rock-bound shores in the U.S.A. There were two lights—the great far-stretching beams of the upper lighthouse, which shone twenty or thirty miles out across the water and the lower lights of much less radiance and radius.

When miles out at sea the sailors could see the warning beams of the higher lights, but as they came closer in shore these were of little use because of the great height at which they stood. Then the vessel came within the range of the smaller lights placed on the rocks below.

One dark stormy night, when the waves rolled like mountains and not a star was to be seen, a boat, rocking and plunging, neared Cleveland Harbour.

'Are you sure this is Cleveland?' asked the Captain, seeing only one light from the lighthouse.

'Quite sure, sir,' replied the pilot.

'Where are the lower lights?'

'Gone out, sir,' was the reply.

'Can you make the harbour, then?'

'We must, or perish, sir!'

The old pilot missed the channel and the boat crashed on the rocks and many lives were lost.

'Brethren,' said Mr. Moody after relating the story, 'the Master will take care of the great lighthouse; let us keep the lower lights burning.'

433. Come, Saviour Jesus, from above (Antoinette Bourignon; translated by John Wesley (3))

Hymns and Sacred Poems, 1739; Ch.M.H.B.

Born at Lisle, France, Antoinette Bourignon (1616–80) became a religious mystic and worked in France, Holland, England and Scotland, and published a large number of religious works. As a girl she was worldly and fond of dress and dancing, and as the daughter of a wealthy family she had opportunity of participating in the gay life of the period. She was awakened to a sense of sin, however, by the influence of a Huguenot preacher.

She was betrothed to a wealthy nobleman but after her conversion feared that her soul would be imperilled by such a union with a man of the world. Her family insisted on the marriage and she was tempted to yield, but praying for guidance she believed she heard a voice saying: 'Forsake all earthly things. Separate thyself from the lure of the creature. Deny thyself.'

The wedding was to take place on Easter Sunday, 1640. The night before, in her own room, she gathered together her jewels, cut off her beautiful hair and laid it by them, then wrote the verses of 'Come, Saviour Jesus, from above' which she placed with the jewels and hair.

She then left the house quietly, taking with her only one penny with which to buy bread for the day. Again she thought she heard a voice, 'What, is thy faith in a penny?' She threw away the coin, saying 'No, Lord, my faith is in Thee alone'.

John Wesley made the translation in 1736 when he was suffering reproach and calumny in America.

The Founder used the words as the opening song at the wedding of Bramwell Booth and Florence Soper and stated they were not only being united in marriage, but were making their wedding the occasion of a rededication of themselves to God's service.

434. Come, Thou burning Spirit, come (Charles Fry (31))

Salvation Music, Vol. 2, set to the tune of 'Mother kissed me in my dream'; 1899 S.A. song book.

435. Dear Lord, I do surrender (W. Walker)

Written by a Salvationist bandsman and published in 1899 S.A. song book.

436. Father, I know that all my life (Anna L. Waring)

Written at Clifton, Bristol, in 1846, and published in the author's *Hymns and Meditations*, 1850; *The Musical Salvationist*, October, 1904; 1930 S.A. song book.

Born at Plas-y-Velin, Neath, Glamorganshire, Miss Waring (1820–1910) was brought up in the Society of Friends. However, drawn by a desire to participate in the Sacraments, she was received into the Church of England, being baptized and confirmed at St. Martin's, Winnall, Winchester.

'A gentle spirit, yet of merry, quiet humour', she began to write early in life, some of her early contributions appearing in *The Sunday Magazine*. In her later years she was attracted to the Discharged Prisoner's Aid Society and became a constant visitor to the Bristol prison.

She studied Hebrew that she might be able to read the Old Testament in the original.

437. I ask Thee for the daily strength (Anna L. Waring)

The second half of No. 436.

438. God of almighty love (Charles Wesley (15))

Hymns and Sacred Poems, 1749; 1930 S.A. song book, where the words appeared in three eight-line verses. In the original, the final lines were:

> My feeble mind transform
> And, perfectly renewed,
> Into a saint exalt a worm,
> A worm exalt to God!

439. Have Thine own way, Lord, have Thine own way
   (Adelaide A. Pollard)

Alexander's Hymns, No. 3.

Born in Iowa, U.S.A., Miss Pollard (1863-1934), a Bible teacher and writer of both prose and poetry, spent several years in England and Africa. Back in America she continued her Christian work until, at a railroad station in New York City, *en route* to fill an engagement in Philadelphia, she was taken violently ill. A week later she died.

During a particularly trying period Miss Pollard attended a prayer meeting where she heard an elderly woman pray: 'But it's all right,

Lord; it doesn't matter what You bring into our lives; *just have Your own way with us!* ' The sentence spoke to Miss Pollard's heart as a message from the Lord. That night she wrote ' Have Thine own way, Lord ', which George Stebbins later set to music.

440. How can I better serve Thee, Lord (Bramwell Coles)

Written at the request of General Orsborn for use at the ' Day with God ' meetings, held at the Central Hall, Westminster, in 1947 and published in *The Musical Salvationist*, November–December, 1947.

Born on February 22, 1887, in Cambridge, where his father was the Commanding Officer, Bramwell Coles had the usual educational facilities which fell to the lot of corps officers' children who had to move from town to town with their parents. Ultimately the family lived in London and Bramwell became a member of the Chalk Farm Band and a junior clerk at International Headquarters. For two consecutive years he won third prize in an International Music Competition and in 1909 had the joy of hearing, amidst much excitement at the Congress Hall, Commissioner John Carleton announce that he had been awarded the first prize for his ' Chalk Farm ' march.

' He possesses ', wrote Lieut.-Colonel Slater at the time, ' the most coveted of gifts—from a musician's point of view—the gift of melodic invention.' Later his selection 'Atonement' secured for him a lasting place in the front rank of Army composers.

In 1914 Bramwell Coles entered training for officership and, following a period as the Assistant Sergeant-Major of the Training College, served for a time on the British Field before being transferred to the staff of the International *War Cry*, and later to the Music Editorial Department. Then came eleven years on the staff of the Canadian *War Cry* at Toronto before his return to London, in 1936, to succeed Colonel Frederick G. Hawkes as Head of the Music Editorial Department, a position he held until he retired in May, 1952. His numerous contributions to the Band Journal and to *The Musical Salvationist* have given him a place in the Army music world second to none. One of his last important tasks as Head of the Music Editorial Department was to succeed Commissioner William Dalziel as chairman of the Song Book Revision Council which was engaged in the preparing of the 1953 song book. He was also responsible for preparing *The Salvation Army Tune Book Supplement*.

As a Captain he married Lieutenant Agnes Le Butt in 1917, and six of their children are officers.

Colonel Coles was promoted to Glory on August 9, 1960.

441. I bring to Thee my heart to fill (Herbert H. Booth (91) (verses); W. H. Williams (chorus))

The Musical Salvationist, November, 1887; 1899 S.A. song book.

442. I heard a Voice so gently calling (Agnes Heathcote (312))

The Musical Salvationist, January, 1890; 1930 song book.

Commissioner Lawley, in his diary, described his visit to Calvary with the Founder: 'Feelings indescribable. Hallowed hill. It was here that my pardon was bought; my salvation was sealed; the gates of the skies were opened, and my debt to the uttermost was paid. I stood and sang:

> The Son of God was left alone to die;
> 'Twas all for me . . .

'I also sang:

> I'll follow Thee, of life the Giver . . .'

443. If so poor a soul as I (Charles Wesley (15))

Hymns on the Lord's Supper; Ch.M.H.B. Our present song is verses three, four and five of the original, which began

> Father, Son and Holy Ghost,
> One in Three and Three in One . . .

Our first verse began 'If so poor a worm as I'.

444. I'm set apart for Jesus (William Pearson (73))

The War Cry, November 6, 1886; 1899 S.A. song book.

445. Immortal Love, for ever full (John Greenleaf Whittier)

An extract from a poem of thirty-eight verses, entitled 'Our Master', which, the author stated, 'presents my view of Christ as the special manifestation of the love of God to humanity'. *The Panorama, and other Poems*, 1856.

Born at East Haverhill, Massachusetts, John Whittier (1807–92), a Quaker, was the second child of John and Abigail Whittier. The name 'Greenleaf' was that of the poet's paternal grandmother, of Huguenot stock. The future New England poet came from the yeoman class, his ancestors being hard-working, God-fearing men. His early education was meagre, but his interest in literature was fostered by his reading a copy of Burns' poems and he was later acclaimed as 'America's greatest lyrical and most distinctively religious poet'.

A journalist by choice, he commenced his career as the editor of *The American Manufacturer*, a weekly semi-political paper. He dedicated his powers to the cause of the abolition of slavery, a purpose which never wavered until the day of emancipation dawned at the conclusion of the Civil War. The hymns he wrote are mostly extracts from some of his longer poems. He received his M.A. and D.L. degrees from Harvard and he passed away at Hampton Falls, New Hampshire.

446. In full and glad surrender (Frances Ridley Havergal (256) (verses))

Verses one and two are from a lengthy poem entitled ' From Glory unto Glory ', written at Winterdyne on December 23, 1873, as the author was contemplating the near approach of New Year's Day, and published in the author's *Under the Surface*; *Hallelujah Hymn Book*; *Revival Music*.

Mr. Shaw, of Winterdyne, at whose house the poem was penned, said, ' I well remember Frances bringing it and reading it, saying, " There! I could not have written this before." And as she stood in the twilight, the sunny radiance of her countenance was sealing her words, " The fullness of His blessing encompasseth our way " [from another verse of the original poem].'

The last verse is from the author's *My King*, and was written in 1876; 1878 S.A. song book.

447. Jesus, all-atoning Lamb (Charles Wesley (15))

Hymns and Sacred Poems, 1748; Ch.M.H.B.

448. Jesus calls me, I am going (Lewis Hartsough (361))

Revival Music (verses only); 1878 S.A. song book (with chorus).

449. Jesus, I my cross have taken (Henry Francis Lyte (11) (verses); Jas. L. Elginburg (chorus)

The verses were published in *Sacred Poetry*, 1824, and in the author's *Poems, Chiefly Religious*, 1833; complete song in Ch.M.H.B.

Thought to have been written as a memorial to his wife's courage and fortitude at a time when she had to choose between her home and freedom to serve the Lord Jesus in the Methodist communion. As a young woman, Anne Maxwell, brought up in a Church of England minister's home, received spiritual enlightenment and inspiration from her contacts with the Methodists, and as a result felt constrained to join them in worship. Her father made it clear that if she did so she must be prepared to leave home and family. This did not deter her for it was a matter of real conviction, and at tremendous cost she ' took up her cross ' and literally ' left all to follow her Lord and Master '. Later she married Mr. Lyte, then a curate in the Church of England.

450. Jesus, precious Saviour, Thou hast saved my soul (Harry Davis)

The War Cry, January 10, 1880, written on the top of a London horse omnibus.

Both words and music were published anonymously in *The Musical Salvationist*, April, 1895, the music being arranged by Lieut.-Colonel Slater. The music of the chorus was repeated for the words:

Anything for Jesus, I will dare and not fear;
Anything for Jesus, I will gladly dare—

giving the title of the tune: 'Anything for Jesus.' 1899 S.A. song book. Harry Davis, a packing-case maker, was one of the first soldiers of the Whitechapel Corps, before transferring to Stepney and finally to Balham Congress Hall. Early in life he found he had a capacity for song-writing, 'Jesus, precious Saviour', being his first published attempt. He would probably never have been so prolific a writer but for the encouragement he received at the outset from Mr. Bramwell Booth, who upon the appearance of this song said that the man who wrote so good a thing could do even better. Davis kept on writing until his songs numbered between three and four hundred. He was promoted to Glory early in 1919.

451. Jesus, Saviour, Thou art mine (Bramwell Booth (280))

The Christian Mission Magazine, April, 1878; 1899 S.A. song book.

452. King of love so condescending (William D. Pennick (413))

The Musical Salvationist, December, 1919; 1930 S.A. song book.

'In Southern India there is a vast network of waterways—lakes, rivers, canals and inlets from the sea,' wrote the author. 'Some of these waterways are extremely narrow, even tunnelling through the hills. "King of love" was written in Ceylon in circumstances reminding one of narrowed waters. The heart cried out for some new blessing of song—something beautiful that would help and inspire the souls of men. And so was given "King of love", a simple prayer of adoration and consecration.'

453. Let me hear Thy voice now speaking (Herbert H. Booth (91))

Written in 1884 to an American sentimental song tune, 'Let me kiss him for his mother', and published in *Favourite Songs Supplement*; 1899 S.A. song book.

454. Let me love Thee, Thou art claiming (Herbert H. Booth (91))

Songs of Peace and War; 1899 S.A. song book.

455. Lord, I make a full surrender (*attributed to* Lowell L. Mason)

The Christian Mission Magazine, March, 1875; 1878 S.A. song book.
Lowell Mason, of the U.S.A., is known to us chiefly by his tunes, several of which are in the Army tune book.

456. Lord, in the strength of grace (Charles Wesley (15))

Short Hymns on Select Passages of Scripture, 1762; Ch.M.H.B.; based on 1 Chronicles 29: 5.

457. Lord, Thou art questioning: Lovest thou Me? (Ruth Tracy (270))

The Musical Salvationist, May, 1898; 1930 S.A. song book.
' I was asked by Commissioner Thomas Coombs during one of his Self-Denial campaigns to write a song dealing with Christ's question to Peter, "Lovest thou Me?",' wrote Brigadier Tracy. 'The words came with freedom, except three lines of the chorus. Up and down the room we paced—Wilhelmina Schoch (later Mrs. Lieut.-Colonel Malan) and I who were billeted together. We hummed the tune, "Moment by moment", trying to catch the line which hovered somewhere just out of reach. I shall always be grateful for Wilhelmina's help that day. The line that finally came, "Ask what Thou wilt my devotion to test", was more hers than mine, and we agreed that it was the only right and possible one.' Later the song was adapted to the tune ' The glory song '.

Commissioner Booth-Tucker, speaking at the memorial service of his beloved wife, the Consul, who was taken from him so tragically, said: ' We have a song where the chorus runs thus [original setting]:

> Thou knowest all things, my heart Thou canst read;
> Master, Thou knowest I love Thee indeed.
> Ask what Thou wilt my devotion to test,
> I will surrender my dearest and best.

I remember whenever that song was sung in my meetings sending up a secret prayer, "Don't ask one thing, dear Lord! Take me if You like, but don't take her!" And now the Lord has taken her. My heart is, indeed, crushed with sorrow, but I do not rebel.'

458. Make me a captive, Lord (George Matheson)

Written in 1890 at Row, Dumbartonshire, published the same year in the author's *Sacred Songs*, and based on Ephesians 3: 1; included by General Orsborn on a number of occasions in the *Supplementary Songs* which he has used for officers' councils.

One of Scotland's outstanding preachers and devotional writers,

Dr. Matheson (1842–1906), born in Glasgow, son of a merchant, though from infancy suffering from defective eyesight, had a distinguished scholastic career at Glasgow Academy and University. When he graduated at the age of nineteen he was totally blind. In 1866 he became the assistant minister to Dr. J. R. Macduff at Sandyford Church, Glasgow, and two years later became the minister of the parish of Innellan, on the Firth of the Clyde. During his eighteen years' incumbency he was invited to preach before Queen Victoria at Balmoral.

In 1879 he received his D.D. degree from the Edinburgh University; at the age of forty-four he was invited to St. Bernard's Parish Church, Edinburgh; and he received the degree of LL.D. from the Aberdeen University in 1902. During retirement he produced some of his wonderful devotional books. He died at North Berwick.

459. Master, I own Thy lawful claim (Charles Wesley (15))

Hymns and Sacred Poems, 1749; 1930 S.A. song book; based on Luke 9: 23.

460. Mine to rise when Thou dost call me (Susie Swift)

All the World, April, 1887; 1899 S.A. song book.

Daughter of a banker in Amenia, New York, Susie Swift, with her sister Elizabeth (Mrs. Colonel Brengle), was brought up amid surroundings that included an old-fashioned, comfortable farmhouse, rolling meadow lands, a view of distant mountains, a river for bathing and fishing, woods, flowers and ferns. She traced her ancestors back for 250 years, on her mother's side, to the Paines of Boston who arrived in America in 1624 (four years after the *Mayflower*), and on her father's side, to the Swifts, who landed on American soil in 1630.

Following Susie's graduation from Vassar College, the two sisters, with a college chum, embarked upon a sight-seeing and pleasure tour of Europe. In Glasgow, Scotland, they met The Salvation Army for the first time. Susie and the college chum, eager for any new thrill, insisted on going to one of the meetings, but Elizabeth refused to accompany them, convinced that ' the better type ' of people didn't go there. The two girls knelt at the Penitent-form, and from that moment Susie lost interest in everything except the Army.

Going to London, the three American girls sought out The Salvation Army Headquarters and were introduced to a cultivated, sincere young man named Percy Clibborn. They learned more of the Army and Elizabeth Swift was led into the Light.

One girl had to return home, but the two Swifts continued their stay in London and interested themselves in the work of the Army. Elizabeth spent her days at the Clapton Training Garrison, where Miss

Emma Booth immediately put her to work teaching the less educated girl cadets. Susie was assigned to help edit *All the World*.

In May, 1885, the two sisters returned to America as Army zealots. They held meetings, visited and prayed with the poor and talked with their fashionable friends about their souls. At the end of the summer Susie returned to London to resume her work on *All the World* and became an officer. In later life, however, she joined the Roman Catholic Church, subsequently attaining the position of Mother Superior of a convent.

461. My body, soul and spirit (Mary D. James (verses))

Philip Phillips's *Hallowed Songs* (U.S.A.), 1873, where it is stated to be taken from *Notes of Joy*; *Hallelujah Hymn Book*; *Revival Music*; 1878 S.A. song book. The author was an American who wrote a number of songs between 1870 and 1890.

462. My life must be Christ's broken bread (Albert Orsborn (42))

The War Cry, May 3, 1947.

General Orsborn had been visiting Berlin, where he had met the German officers in council in the war-damaged temple. He writes: ' I was burdened with a sense of my own inadequacy to match the occasion. . . . I cried to God to help me in my spirit, and to let His Spirit work within us all, to bring us together, to bridge what seemed to me to be, in all reason, an impassable gulf. . . . But God revealed to me that not only that day, but always, we have no hope of being a blessing to other souls unless our lives become part of the Saviour's sacramental consecration. I thought of our Lord's cry as He entered the deep waters, " For their sakes I sanctify Myself." Before I left Berlin this song had begun to form itself in my mind. As I travelled toward Holland, along the straight but monotonous autobahn, line by line the song was given to me, the last verse coming in the early morning following my return home.'

463. My mind upon Thee, Lord, is stayed (Herbert H. Booth (91))

The Musical Salvationist, August, 1886; 1899 S.A. song book.

464. Not my own, but saved by Jesus (Daniel W. Whittle (158))

Sankey's *Sacred Songs and Solos*; 1899 S.A. song book.

465. O blessèd Saviour, is Thy love (Joseph Stennett)

Hymns in Commemoration of the Sufferings of our Blessed Saviour, Jesus Christ, 1697; 1930 S.A. song book.

Born at Abingdon, Berks, Dr. Stennett (1663–1713), said to be the earliest English Baptist hymn-writer whose hymns are now in common use, came of a family renowned for intellect and piety. He received some education at the public grammar school at Wallingford and pursued his studies in philosophy, divinity and oriental languages. At the age of twenty-two he went to London, where for five years he engaged in teaching. In 1688 he married Susanna, the daughter of George Gill, a French merchant.

In 1690 he was ordained as pastor of the congregation in Devonshire Square, London, a group of Seventh-day Baptists (or Baptist Sabbatarians) whom he continued to serve until his death.

466. O God, what offering shall I give (Joachim Lange; *translated by* John Wesley (3))

Wesley's free translation of the original German hymn was published in *Hymns and Sacred Poems*, 1739; Ch.M.H.B.

Born at Gardelegen, Saxony, Germany, son of the senior magistrate of the town, Dr. Lange (1670–1744) was trained in the University of Leipzig before becoming a tutor and rector in Berlin and then Professor of Theology at Halle, where he died.

467. O Lord, Thy heavenly grace impart (John F. Oberlin; *translated by* Lucy Wilson)

Memories of John Frederic Oberlin, 1829, by Lucy Wilson (1802–63), wife of the Rev. Daniel Wilson, Vicar of Islington; 1899 S.A. song book.

The words are part of the account of a service in Waldbach Church on June 11, 1820. When the minister had finished his sermon he read the verses of this hymn and said, ' My dear friends, may these be the feelings of our hearts, and as such let us sing them.'

Born at Strasburg, Oberlin (1740–1826), whose father held office in the Gymnasium of that city and ' employed his leisure in the instruction and pious training of his nine children ', was ordained in 1760 and for seven years was engaged in teaching.

While still a young man he became the pastor of Ban de la Roche, Alsace. He found the district a stronghold of evil and backwardness, but soon made roads, built bridges and began to tame savage natures by patient cultivation. He cut down obstinate brush, he felled trees and made the forbidden hills produce fodder for the beasts that had been starving in their stalls. He preached on Sundays; on weekdays he built schools, repaired his church and made his ramshackle home habitable. He scarcely left the district for sixty years and he saved that part of the country, at least, from the revolution that was soon to shake all France. He literally made the wilderness to blossom as the rose.

468. O Love, who formedst me to wear (Johann Scheffler; translated by Catherine Winkworth (7))

The author's *Heilige Seelenlust*, 1657; Miss Winkworth's translation in her *Lyra Germanica*, Second Series, 1858; 1930 S.A. song book.

Born in Breslau, Silesia, Johann Scheffler (1624–77) studied medicine in the university of his native town and at Strasburg, and graduated as Ph.D. and M.D. at Padua. His father, a Polish nobleman, had been forced to leave his native country on account of his staunch Lutheranism, but his son, Johann, whilst in Holland, became acquainted with the writings of the mystics. He withdrew from public worship and Holy Communion and 'exchanged the outspoken force of Luther and Gerhardt for the sentimental introspective manner of Silesian Mysticism'.

In 1649 he was appointed court physician to Duke Sylvius Nimrod, but resigned his post in 1652 to return to Breslau, where he became acquainted with the Jesuits and the writings of the Roman Catholic mystics. In 1653 he entered the Roman Catholic Church and joined the order of St. Francis.

He commenced writing hymns and poetry very early, some of his verses being published when he was but sixteen years of age. He also used the pen-name, Angelus Silesius. Most of his hymns were penned before he entered the Roman Catholic Church and were used chiefly by the Lutherans, whilst Zinzendorf included a large number of them in his 1727 hymn book.

When the Rev. Dick Sheppard was ordained in St. Paul's Cathedral, London, his fingers were clutching a half-sheet of paper in the pocket of his cassock. It was a letter from Archbishop Lang: 'Don't worry any more, dear old boy. You have prepared yourself as carefully as you can. Now lean back on a Father's love, and say over and over again in St. Paul's Cathedral just these words:

> O Love, I give myself to Thee,
> Thine ever, only Thine to be.'

Said Kenneth L. Parry: 'It is good to think of that adorable rebel Dick Sheppard clutching the hymn of a Papist, given to him by an Anglican Prelate.'

469. O Master, let me walk with Thee (Washington Gladden)

Sunday Afternoon, March, 1879. Dr. Gladden had undertaken to furnish each month a short contribution in verse for the devotional section—'The Still Hour'—of this magazine, and it was in this connection that the poem first appeared. There was no thought at the time that it would ever be used for singing, but Dr. Charles H. Richards, a friend of the author, saw possibilities in the poem and published two of the three eight-line verses in his *Songs of Praise*, 1880. 1930 S.A. song book.

Born at Pottsgrove, Pennsylvania, Dr. Gladden (1836–1918) spent his early years on a farm there. He studied at Oswego Academy before going on to Williams College where he graduated in 1859. He then took a theological course, was ordained for the Congregational ministry in 1860, and held pastorates in a number of American cities. For some four years he was the editor of the *New York Independent* and whilst at Springfield edited a magazine called *Sunday Afternoon*. He died at Columbus, Ohio, after serving there as pastor for thirty-two years.

470. Precious Jesus, O to love Thee! (*verses attributed to* Francis Bottome (122); Louise M. Rouse (chorus))

Hallelujah Hymn Book; Revival Music; 1878 S.A. song book; with a chorus which commenced:

> Jesus! Jesus! precious Jesus!
> Thou art all in all to me . . .

The present chorus belongs to song No. 504.

On August 6, 1878, eighty evangelists of The Christian Mission were invited to attend a great War Congress in London. There was to be an entire change of policy. The Christian Mission was to become an Army and the Founder's immediate task was to carry the judgment and ensure the loyalty of his assistants. On the Tuesday afternoon, as Superintendent of the Mission, William Booth delivered an address—the presentation of the constitution of The Salvation Army. The meeting was not the easiest to handle for the new constitution was not acceptable to everyone, but one of the contributory helps was the introduction of two songs which have become a part of the Organization: 'Precious Jesus, O to love Thee!' with the chorus 'Glory, glory, Jesus saves me', and 'Jesus calls me, I am going'. 'These simple words of affirmation and prayer were sung until those men and women felt that nothing mattered except to follow the Saviour in His quest for lost souls' (*Commissioner Lawley* by Mrs. General Carpenter).

471. Redeemed from guilt, redeemed from fears (Henry Francis Lyte (11))

The Spirit of the Psalms, 1834; 1930 S.A. song book.

While living at Sway Cottage, Lymington, Hampshire, Lyte

undertook what was probably his most ambitious literary work—*The Spirit of the Psalms*. In the preface he explained that his was not a literal translation of the Psalms but an attempt to give their spirit in verse. Altogether the book contains 320 metrical versions of which 270 are by the author and include ' Pleasant are Thy courts above ' and ' Praise, my soul, the King of Heaven '.

472. Saviour, I long to be (Anonymous)

1899 S.A. song book.

473. Saviour, if my feet have faltered (Albert Orsborn (42))

The Beauty of Jesus, 1947.

General Orsborn hears more about this than any of his other songs, and suggests that this may be because it carries upon it ' the marks of the Valley of Humiliation '. The setting of the song is 1922, when the author was Divisional Commander for South London. It marks a painful experience when ' I learned that when the Spirit grieves He leaves '.

An accident had resulted in his being an inmate of the Officers' Nursing Home at Highbury, London, where, one Sunday morning, alone in a small room with heart and mind far from being at peace, he heard the other officers at prayers in a room below singing:

> Nothing from His altar I would keep,
> To His Cross of suffering I would leap . . .
> (Song 363, original setting.)

As they sang his spirit was moved and he joined quietly in the singing. The resultant submission to the Holy Spirit led to the writing of this song, which was first used at an officers' meeting at West Croydon.

474. Saviour, my all I'm bringing to Thee (Alice Edwards)

The Musical Salvationist, July, 1893; 1899 S.A. song book.

Born in Battersea, London, in October, 1878, Alice Purdue made her first contacts with the Army in Notting Hill. She was converted as a child of twelve and later became a soldier of the corps. In July, 1895, she received the call for officership and entered the Training Home on December 3, the next year. In 1899 she married Major Robert Edwards, an officer on the British Field who had been a Household Trooper, and who after many years in corps work was transferred to the Public Relations Department in 1925 and retired from active service in 1932. The Major was promoted to Glory in December, 1945, and Mrs. Edwards followed him on October 22, 1958.

Mrs. Edwards had decided to make music her profession and to this end received the groundwork of her training from a very clever musician, who, she said, 'had come down in the world through drink'. He taught her theory, harmony and the pianoforte. Later she received more advanced lessons from an Italian Professor, adding mandolin lessons to the curriculum. While a soldier at Notting Hill she would accompany Lieut.-Colonel Slater's musical party as the pianist.

'The inspiration of the song was the act of my surrender to God's will,' wrote Mrs. Edwards. 'My life was a very happy one, full of bright prospects. I had mapped out plans for my future and had chosen my career for which I had been working very hard. I loved God and tried to serve Him in my own way and intended to do so whilst still following out my life's purpose. Thus it came as a shock to me when, one Sunday morning, God laid His hand on me and, through the medium of the then Staff-Captain (afterward Colonel) Bettridge, called me to consecrate my all to His service. I was unwilling to submit to God's will. Why should God step in at that moment and frustrate all my plans? Why should this cross suddenly cast a dark shadow over my happiness? Why? . . . My soul rebelled against what I felt to be God's unreasonable demands. For a long time I knelt at the Mercy Seat yet received no liberty or peace, and finally rose to my feet with my heart full of darkness, disappointment and bitterness.

'In my own little room I "won through". What a fight I had! It seemed to my small mind that I was sacrificing all for nothing; yet I surrendered, and said, "Lord, with my all I part." I experienced no thrill, or feeling of joy in my soul, but there came into my heart a sense of rest, and peace, and assurance, and thus that morning I stepped out upon the path which has led me through many years of happy useful service for God. Those very words which marked my submission to God's will I afterward put into poetry and then added the music.'

475. Saviour, Thy dying love (S. Dryden Phelps (308))

Written in 1862 and published two years later in *Gospel Hymns*; 1930 S.A. song book.

476. Take my life, and let it be (Frances Ridley Havergal (256))

Written at Areley House, London, on February 4, 1874, and published in the author's *Loyal Responses*, 1878; 1899 S.A. song book.

'I went for a visit of five days,' wrote Miss Havergal. 'There were ten persons at the house, some unconverted and long prayed for, some converted, but not rejoicing Christians. He gave me the prayer, "Lord, give me *all* in the house!" And He just did. Before I left the house every one had got a blessing. The last night of my visit, after I had retired, the governess asked me to go to the two daughters. They were crying . . . both of them trusted and rejoiced; it was nearly midnight. I was too happy to sleep and passed most of the night in praise and renewal of my own consecration; and these couplets formed themselves and chimed in my heart one after another till they finished with " Ever, only, all for Thee ".'

477. The love of Christ doth me constrain (Johann J. Winckler; translated by John Wesley (3))

Porst's *Gesang-Buch*, 1708. The translation in *Hymns and Sacred Poems*, 1739; *The Christian Mission Hymn Book*, with two earlier verses commencing ' Shall I, for fear of feeble men '.

Son of the Town Clerk of Luckau in Sachse-Altenburg, Germany, Johann Winckler (1670–1722) studied at Leipzig where he came under the influence of the Pietist movement. He became a preacher to St. George's Hospital, Magdeburg, in 1692, and later a chaplain in the army, accompanying the troops to Italy and Holland. He visited England in 1697 and on returning to Germany was appointed Diaconus of Magdeburg Cathedral. He encountered much opposition owing to the standards for holy living which he preached. The earlier verses suggest that he wrote the hymn to encourage his own heart.

478. The Saviour of men came to seek and to save (Albert Orsborn (42))

The Musical Salvationist, April, 1925; 1930 S.A. song book.

' Commissioner James Hay wrote me asking if I had ever considered " The old rustic bridge " melody for a set of words,' recalls the General, 'and, if not, would I write some verses to it. After a long time I did so. The simple chorus took a lot of time and trouble. I turned phrases again and again trying and discarding words until, at last, I was satisfied. The song was first used in officers' councils held at Swanwick.

479. Throw out the life-line across the dark wave (Edward S. Ufford)

Sankey's *New Hymns and Solos*; 1899 S.A. song book.

Born at Newark, New Jersey, U.S.A., Edward Ufford (1851–1930) was, as a child, keenly interested in the sea and ships. He carved sailing boats with no little ingenuity from blocks of wood. His greatest delight was to talk with sailors and fishermen, asking them all manner of questions. Lifeboat stories absorbed his interest. He became a Baptist minister at Springfield, Massachusetts, U.S.A., where his old love for nautical matters stood him in good stead.

Not many miles from the shore where he stood on summer days lay an old wreck embedded in the sand. ' My imagination strove to picture what the storm did on that fateful night when it tossed the craft ashore,' he would say when telling the story. ' While my heart was thus yearning for an effective interposition, a thought came to me. " Why not hold an open-air meeting in the village next Sunday afternoon, and warn all who might pass of their danger ? " This was in the fall of 1886. I carried my small organ out into the square and began to sing. There soon gathered a group of listeners. On returning home, the imagery of the sea came before me again. I pictured the storm, and a shipwrecked sailor drifting out beyond human reach, where he might sink. Taking a sheet of paper I wrote the four verses of the hymn in fifteen minutes. Then sitting down to my little instrument, I played a melody without mental effort and the song was born.'

Mr. Sankey used the song in the revival meetings led by Mr. Moody and its popularity inspired the author to set out on an evangelistic tour of the world. He carried with him a set of the latest gear used by the U.S. naval authorities, to form a striking background to his appeal. He carried two ' life-lines ' which had been used in actual life-saving work, and had been instrumental in rescuing many lives from shipwrecks. Mr. Ufford would explain in some detail the use of these lines and then draw his spiritual analogies from them and apply religious truths which were so strikingly obvious.

480. Touch me with Thy healing hand, Lord (Hugh Sladen)

The Musical Salvationist, April, 1920; 1930 S.A. song book.

Grandson of the eighth Earl of Cavan, an active worker with Moody and Sankey when they visited the British Isles in 1870, and sixth son of Colonel Joseph Sladen, Royal Artillery, and Lady Sarah Sladen of Ripple Court, Deal, Kent, Commissioner Sladen became a Salvationist in his teens, his mother also being a soldier of the Deal Corps.

Before becoming an officer in 1898, the Commissioner served at the Trade Headquarters in Clerkenwell Road, London, and as the Young People's Sergeant-Major at the New Southgate Corps. In 1904 he was appointed to the Young People's Department and in 1913, under the direction of General Bramwell Booth, he inaugurated the Life-Saving Scout Organization. Two years after his marriage with Captain Motee Booth-Tucker he became a Divisional Commander and later Chief Secretary for the Northern Territory of Great Britain. In 1931 the Commissioner was made a Freeman of the City of London.

In 1939 he was appointed to Finland as Territorial Commander and later to organize the Army's European Relief Department, when teams of workers were trained and supplied for projects in Holland, Belgium, France, Germany, Austria and Czechoslovakia. For two years prior to his retirement the Commissioner was head of the Public Relations Bureau at International Headquarters.

One Sunday morning in 1919 in his home at Newport, Mon., where he was the Divisional Commander, the author wrote this song at a time when great outpourings of the Holy Spirit's power was being witnessed in the valleys among the mining communities. Wrote the Commissioner: 'Both Mrs. Sladen and I had seen so many people in meetings seeking for blessing, expecting victory, and yet being greatly disappointed because they did not find that for which they were seeking. The cause was an unwillingness to submit to the will of God. Only by a complete surrender and submission to the touch and power of God, through the workings of His Holy Spirit, can the life be melted and moulded according to His divine plan. It was thus hoped that the words and music of this intercessory prayer-song would help those who were ready to place their all, their whole lives, at the disposal of their Lord and Master, and thus able to expect a victorious experience.'

The Commissioner was born on December 9, 1878, and promoted to Glory on May 6, 1962.

481. Unto Thee, O Saviour-King (Charles Coller)

1930 S.A. song book.

Born in Woodford, Essex, in March, 1863, Charles Coller early showed signs of his poetical and musical ability. As a boy he won a prize for a poetical acrostic on the word 'temperance'. He met the Army in 1883. Before entering the Household Troops Band, he was a bandsman at Regent Hall, and later, as an officer, a member of the International Staff Band. From 1893 he was attached, in one position or another, to Salvationist Publishing and Supplies, Ltd., but his natural poetical and musical talents were not stifled thereby. He had a very definite religious experience, and was always ready to bear testimony to the wealth of blessing a full salvation carries with it.

In April, 1895, under the title 'The three bidders', there appeared his first song to be published in *The Musical Salvationist*. For more than forty years, until his promotion to Glory as a Major on March 21, 1935, he kept up his writing. His songs show originality, both in words and in music. He covered a very wide field in his song-making, from the mood of great seriousness to those of joy, courage, aggression and martial faith and daring.

One of Charles Coller's great moments was when he led the massed singers at the composer's festival in the Clapton Congress Hall in February, 1928, in the singing of his own composition, 'Jesus said: I am the Resurrection', in the presence of the Duke and Duchess of York, later King George VI and Queen Elizabeth.

482. Vain, delusive world, adieu (Charles Wesley (15))

First and second verses in *Hymns and Sacred Poems*, 1742, and the Ch.M.H.B. The third verse was written by request for the 1930 S.A.

song book by Lieutenant (now Brigadier) Gladys Taylor (see song No. 879).

The alterations from the original were probably made by the Fry family to suit the tune 'When the swallows homeward fly', to which it was usually sung in meetings. The story of its introduction in Army meetings is thus described by Fred Fry: '.On one occasion we (the Fry family) were with the General and he seemed very much depressed. He told Father he would want him to sing something presently. We had Wesley's hymn book with us, and I turned up "Vain, delusive world, adieu" and suggested it would suit the tune "When the swallows homeward fly". We sang it, and as the audience joined in the chorus—"Only Jesus will I know, Jesus crucified"—his depression vanished and his usual cheerfulness returned.'

483. Welcome, welcome, dear Redeemer (William Mason)

Evangelical Magazine, 1794; Ch.M.H.B.

Born at Rotherhithe, William Mason (1719-91) was an associate of Whitefield and Romaine. He succeeded Toplady as editor of the *Gospel Magazine* in 1777.

484. What shall we offer to our Lord (Augustus G. Spangenberg; translated by John Wesley (3))

Herrnhut Hymn Book, 1737; Wesley's translation in his *Hymns and Sacred Poems*, 1742, and 1930 S.A. song book; written for Count Zinzendorf's birthday of May 26, 1734.

Son of a Lutheran minister, Spangenberg (1704-92) was born at Klettenberg, Hanover. In 1722 he commenced to study law in the University of Jena but soon changed to theology. In 1727 he commenced a lifelong friendship with Count Zinzendorf and eight years later removed to the Moravian Settlement at Herrnhut where he became assistant minister. He visited the Churches of the Moravian Brethren in North America, the West Indies and England. He founded the first English Moravian Settlement at Smith House, Yorks, in 1742. Two years later he was ordained Moravian Bishop for North America. Much of his time was subsequently spent in missionary labours in America, but upon the death of Zinzendorf his presence was needed at Herrnhut, where he became the Chief Adviser of the Brethren. He died at Berthelsdorf.

485. When from sin's dark hold Thy love had won me (Will. J. Brand (52))

Written especially for General Orsborn's 'Day of Renewal' at the Westminster Central Hall on October 19, 1949, and afterward published in *The Musical Salvationist*, July/August, 1951.

486. All glory to Jesus be given (Annie Wittenmeyer)

Sankey's *Sacred Songs and Solos*; 1878 S.A. song book.
The author was an American.

487. At peace with God! How great the blessing (Richard Slater (105))

Written on July 25, 1887, to a Scandinavian air and published in *The Musical Salvationist*, July, 1888; 1930 S.A. song book.

488. Blessèd Lamb of Calvary (George S. Smith (67))

The Musical Salvationist, September, 1887; 1899 S.A. song book.

As Bandmaster of the Kingswood (Bristol) Band, the author seldom missed a Sunday night meeting. On one occasion, however, his wife particularly desired to attend the meeting and the Bandmaster, not too happily, stayed at home to look after the two small children, one of them a baby in arms. That evening were born the words and music of this popular song.

489. Deep were the scarlet stains of sin (Olive Holbrook)

Written to a secular melody to be sung by the now Commissioner Dorothy Muirhead, when on the staff of the International Training College. The words were included in the supplementary song book for field officers' councils, 1948.

Daughter of Army officers, Olive Gill sought the Saviour for herself at an early age and was soon assisting her parents ' in the fight ', even finding opportunity for ' specialing ' as the ' girl preacher ', mostly in the north of England. She entered the Training College in 1915 while her parents were stationed in Halifax, and after fulfilling three corps appointments returned to the Training College as a brigade officer, remaining there until her marriage to Captain (now Commissioner) Theo. Holbrook in April, 1921. Following various appointments, including training and divisional work, the Commissioner became Chief Secretary for the Central America and West Indies Territory in 1946, then Territorial Commander for Rhodesia, and for Western India in 1954, then International Secretary for Asia and Africa in 1960.

Mrs. Holbrook has, in addition to contributing verse, written many articles for Army papers, and at one period wrote regularly under the name of ' Greta Friend '.

490. From the heart of Jesus flowing (Charles Coller (481))

Slightly altered from *The Musical Salvationist*, April, 1914, where the words were set to music of Pinsuti; 1930 S.A. song book, where the first line read, ' Even as a river flowing '.

491. Full salvation, full salvation (Francis Bottome (122))

Written in 1871 and published in 1873; 1878 S.A. song book.

492. I love Thee every hour, Thou loving One (Bramwell Booth (280))

Written on September 26, 1880, and published in *The War Cry*, October 2, 1880; 1899 S.A. song book. Two of the original verses have been omitted.

493. I sought for love and strength and light (Alfred Humphrey)

The Musical Salvationist, March, 1914.

Born at Kingston on Thames, Alfred Humphrey grew up under godly influences and was converted at an early age. He met The Salvation Army when he was a Bible class leader and local preacher. He felt called to serve God in the Army and one morning he signed the Articles of War, in the afternoon he purchased his first uniform and was sworn in as a soldier the same evening.

After serving as Bandmaster and Treasurer of his home corps for two years, Alfred entered the Battersea training garrison in 1889 and six weeks later was commissioned as a sergeant to the Grecian training centre. One day Commissioner T. Henry Howard promoted him to the rank of Lieutenant and told him to attend the officers' councils then being held. The new Lieutenant found a shop which sold braid of the right shade, borrowed a darning-needle and thread to affix his insignia and took his place with the officers. After serving at Stratford and Camberwell he opened from Woolwich the work at Plumstead by holding a series of tent meetings. Within three months he had established a thoroughly organized corps. He was then appointed to Tottenham where he opened the citadel and enrolled three hundred soldiers in the space of three months. Later commands included Islington, where over a thousand people knelt at the Mercy Seat during a period of twelve months, and the Regent Hall. Divisional and national work followed until his retirement as a Colonel. He was promoted to Glory from Winton on February 20, 1933.

494. I stand all bewildered with wonder (W. F. Crafts)

Written by an American minister; published in *Songs of Joy and Gladness* (U.S.A.); *Hallelujah Hymn Book*; *Revival Music*; 1878 S.A. song book; now, in Army circles, always associated with the secular tune 'The gallant hussar'.

495. Jesus, my Lord, through Thy triumph I claim (William Booth (119))

All the World, October, 1901; introduced by the Founder at a Clapton Staff Council, and published in *The Musical Salvationist*, August, 1915; 1930 S.A. song book.

Commissioner Wycliffe Booth tells how, as children, the family of General and Mrs. Bramwell Booth found pleasure in editing and issuing a small children's paper for private circulation. This was a personal contribution by their grandfather, the Founder.

496. Lord, I am Thine, I rest my soul in Thee (Samuel Trevor Francis)

A version slightly different from 1930 S.A. song book.

Son of an artist and born in Cheshunt, Herts, in 1835, Mr. Francis was a London merchant whose numerous songs appeared in various religious newspapers and periodicals. He joined the Brethren assembly at Kennington, London, and for many years practised open-air preaching in the City. He visited many foreign countries, accompanying R. C. Morgan, the first editor of *The Christian*, on some of these journeys. The author died in 1925.

497. Loved with everlasting love (George Wade Robinson)

Hymns of Consecration and Faith, 1890.

Born at Cork, Eire, Mr. Robinson (1838–77) was educated at Trinity College, Dublin, and New College, London. As a Congregational minister he served at Dublin, St. John's Wood, Dudley and Brighton and Southampton. He published two volumes of hymns.

498. Now I feel the sacred fire (Anonymous)

Good News in Songs (U.S.A.); 1930 S.A. song book.

499. O Christ, in Thee my soul hath found (B. E.)

Sankey's *Sacred Songs and Solos*; 1899 S.A. song book.

James Gilmour of Mongolia considered it one of his favourite hymns, as did Henry Drummond, who used it much at his meetings for university students in the Oddfellows Hall, Edinburgh, 1885–89.

500. O the bitter shame and sorrow (Theodore Monod)

Written in English during a series of consecration meetings which the author attended at Broadlands, Hants, the seat of Lord Mount-Temple, in July, 1874, and published on the back of a programme printed in connection with another series of meetings held at Oxford in October of the same year; *Revival Music;* 1878 S.A. song book.

Son of a pastor of the French Reformed Church, Theodore Monod (1836–1921) was educated at Allegheny, U.S.A., before becoming a minister of the same church in 1860, where he was held in high esteem as a pastor, preacher and lecturer. He died in Paris. Many of his French hymns appeared in *Cantiques Populaires* of the McAll Mission in Paris.

501. Once I thought I walked with Jesus (F. A. Blackmer)

The Musical Salvationist, April, 1890; 1899 S.A. song book.

The author was probably an American. The song was introduced by a Canadian officer at 'A Day with God' meeting conducted by the Founder in the Rotunda, Liverpool (*The War Cry*, November 10, 1888).

502. One with my Lord! 'tis glorious to know (Herbert H. Booth (91))

Slightly altered from *Favourite Song Supplement*; 1899 S.A. song book.

503. Only Thee, my soul's Redeemer (Fanny Crosby (17))

Revival Music; 1878 S.A. song book.

The singing of this song by Commissioner James Dowdle at Penrith in 1882 awakened in the heart of the future Colonel Joseph Pugmire, then but a boy, a longing for the joys of full salvation, with the result that two years later he entered the training college and began a life of service that was instrumental in winning thousands of souls to the Saviour.

504. Precious Saviour, Thou dost save me (Louise M. Rouse)

Published in America, the author's homeland, in *Songs of Joy and Gladness*; 1878 S.A. song book.

When nineteen-year-old Ballington Booth went to lead a meeting in Barking he reported: ' One brother said, " Oh! if this ain't Heaven, what'll Heaven be?" Another brother said, "I must jump" . . . and he jumped all round. So we sang, cried, laughed, shouted, and after twenty-three had given their all to the Master, trusting Him to keep them from sinning, as He had pardoned their sin we closed singing, "Glory, glory, Jesus saves me"' (*The Christian Mission Magazine*, October, 1878).

505. Quickened with our immortal Head (Charles Wesley (15))

Short Hymns on Select Passages of Scripture, 1762; 1930 S.A. song book; and based on 2 Timothy 1: 7.

506. Saviour, teach me day by day (Jane E. Leeson)

Hymns and Scenes of Childhood, 1842; 1930 S.A. song book.

Some of the hymns of Miss Leeson (1807–82) of London were produced at public services as 'prophetical utterances' and were delivered slowly, with short pauses as anyone would ordinarily make in reading. For many years the author was a well-known figure in the Catholic Apostolic Church, to whose hymn book she contributed nine hymns and translations. She also published several books of hymns especially for children, and late in life entered the Roman communion.

507. Show me Thy face, one transient gleam (Anonymous)

Sankey's *Sacred Songs and Solos*, taken from *Stockwell Gems*; *Supplementary Songs*, compiled by Commissioner Wm. R. Dalziel for use in officers' councils.

508. The conflict is over, the tempest is past (Francis Bottome (122))

Hallowed Songs (U.S.A.), 1873; *Revival Music*; 1878 S.A. song book.

509. Thee will I love, my strength, my tower (Johann Scheffler (468); *translated by* John Wesley (3))

Scheffler's *Heilige Seelenlust*, Book 1, 1657. Wesley's translation was published in *Hymns and Sacred Poems*, 1739, and was headed 'Gratitude for our Conversion'; Ch.M.H.B.

The theme appears to be Psalm 18: 1, 2, but, although the words suggest autobiography, Scheffler had in mind 'The Confessions of St. Augustine' which include: 'Too late did I love Thee, O Fairness— so ancient, and yet so new! . . . For behold Thou wert within and I without, and there did I seek Thee; I unlovely, rushed heedlessly among the things of beauty Thou madest. Thou wert with me, but I was not with Thee.'

510. When Jesus from Calvary called me (Will. J. Brand (52))

Written at the invitation of the Song Book Revision Council to be used with the Welsh tune 'Crugybar'.

511. Break Thou the bread of life (Mary Artemisia Lathbury (verse 1); Alexander Groves (verses 2 and 3))

The first verse was written specially for the Chautauqua Literary and Scientific Circle as a study song to be used at every session of its 1877 encampment. Verses 2 and 3 appeared in *W.M. Magazine*, September, 1913. *The Musical Salvationist*, March, 1944.

Mary Lathbury (1841–1913), born in Manchester, New York, daughter of a Methodist minister, was an artist, poet and writer. When the Chautauqua movement was originated and held its encampment on the shores of Lake Chautauqua (New York) in 1873, she became private secretary to its founder, Bishop John Vincent, who said of her: 'She lived in the spiritual world, was in constant communion with Heaven, knew the deepest, sweetest feelings of a spirit that had looked into the very face of the invisible God.'

Alexander Groves was born in 1843 and died in 1909.

512. Come, Holy Ghost, our hearts inspire (Charles Wesley (15))

Hymns and Sacred Poems, 1740; Ch.M.H.B.

513. Holy Bible, book divine (John Burton, Sen.)

The Evangelical Magazine, June, 1805, and signed 'J. B. Nottingham'; Ch.M.H.B.

A Baptist Sunday-school teacher, Mr. Burton (1773–1822) was born in Nottingham and died in Leicester, and published *Hymns for Sunday-schools* which contained ninety-six of his own compositions.

514. How firm a foundation, ye saints of the Lord (George Keith)

Part of a hymn in Rippon's *Selection of Hymns from the Best Authors*, 1787; 1930 S.A. song book.

George Keith, publisher and bookseller of Gracechurch Street, London, is said to have been the son-in-law of Dr. Gill, and as his clerk he composed hymns founded on the discourses of his father-in-law while he was preaching them. Duffield, however, in his *English Hymns*, says that the author was the son-in-law of Dr. Rippon, a London Baptist pastor, and as his clerk led the singing in the congregation for a number of years.

Sung to the tune, 'Adeste Fideles', the words have been popular in America and are said to have been sung at the funerals of at least three Presidents.

515. Lamp of our feet, whereby we trace (Bernard Barton 347))

Written in 1827; *The Reliquary*, 1836, with eleven verses; 1930 S.A. song book.

Mr. Barton, 'with all his distinctive notions as a Quaker about "Inward Light", had a deep reverence for the written word and childlike trust in the certainty of its guidance; and expresses his love for inspired truth and his faith in its lessons in the hymn founded on Psalm 119: 105'.

516. Lord, Thy word abideth (Henry Williams Baker (35))

Written expressly for the 1861 edition of *Hymns Ancient and Modern*.

517. Set forth within the sacred word (Will. J. Brand (52))

'Early in 1948, whilst presiding over a festival at Woolwich Town Hall,' writes the author, 'Commissioner Wm. R. Dalziel requested a song in a well-known metre, written on the subject of "adorning the doctrine", which was to be his theme at his forthcoming officers' councils.

'I wrote two songs in 6–8 measure and the Commissioner chose two verses from each.'

518. The Spirit breathes upon the word (William Cowper (25))

Olney Hymns, 1779.

Cowper possibly makes a reference to his own conversion which was brought about through the direct revelation of the Spirit of God. In July, 1764, he found a Bible lying on a bench in the garden. Opening it, he began to turn the pages in order to get some special comfort in the depression which had settled upon him. Light came to his darkened spirit as he read Romans 3: 25. 'In a moment', he says, 'I believed and I received the gospel.'

519. Awake, our souls; away, our fears! (Isaac Watts (3))

Book 1 of the author's *Hymns and Spiritual Songs*, 1709, and entitled 'The Christian Race'; John Wesley's *Charlestown Collection*, 1737; 1899 S.A. song book; based upon Isaiah 40: 28–31.

520. He giveth more grace as our burdens grow greater (Annie Johnson Flint)

First printed on a small hand press and given to the public, but later obtainable in the 'Casterline Card' series No. 5510; *The Officer*, May, 1928.

Born in Vineland, New Jersey, Annie Johnson, having lost both parents before she was six years of age, was adopted by a childless couple named Flint. Whilst still in her teens Annie became afflicted with arthritis and was soon unable even to walk. She had wanted to be a composer and concert pianist, but when illness deprived her of her piano-playing she resorted to writing poetry, a pursuit she considered merely a compensation for being unable to pursue her music, until she realized that her calling was of God. She set several of her poems to music and in later life, being unable to open her hands, wrote many of them on the typewriter, using but her knuckles. She died at Clifton Springs in 1932.

521. My Maker and my King (Anne Steele)

The author's *Poems on Subjects Chiefly Devotional*, 1760, over the signature ' Theodosia '; 1899 S.A. song book.

Anne Steele (1716–78), daughter of a timber merchant and unpaid pastor of the Baptist Church at Broughton, Hampshire, suffered from delicate health which was aggravated by the death of her betrothed on the morning fixed for their wedding.

Her biographer states that she ' spent her life in quiet retirement, suffering the mysterious will of God alone, or in a retreat to which but few kindred spirits had access. . . . But her hymns, the fruit of hallowed affliction, live to bring forth the " peaceable fruits of righteousness " in the souls of other chastened Christians '.

522. To God be the glory, a Saviour is mine (Charles Coller (481))

The Musical Salvationist, May, 1923; 1930 S.A. song book.

523. All scenes alike engaging prove (Jeanne de la Mothe Guyon; *translated by* William Cowper (25))

1878 S.A. song book.

For Madame Guyon (1648–1717) suffering and affliction seemed to be her lot in life. Her mother-in-law treated her with unkindness; her favourite son was taken from her at the age of four years; at the age of twenty-two she herself was prostrated by smallpox which permanently destroyed her beauty, and at twenty-eight she was left a widow. These trials, however, deepened her religious experience and she became a prominent advocate of quietism. Her ardent championing of this system, together with the books she wrote, brought her into difficulties with the Roman Catholic authorities, and she was committed to a convent in 1688. Seven years later she was imprisoned in the Castle of Vincennes, and in 1698 in the Bastille, before being banished to Blois. A number of her hymns were written in prison.

The original opening verse was:

> O Thou, by long experience tried,
> Near whom no grief can long abide;
> My Love! how full of sweet content
> I pass my years of banishment!

524. Come ye yourselves apart and rest awhile (Edward H. Bickersteth (219))

Hymns Ancient and Modern; The Fellowship Hymn Book; based upon Mark 6: 30–34.

525. Compared with Christ, in all beside (Augustus M. Toplady (227) (verses))

The Gospel Magazine, February, 1772, and taken from a much longer poem. 1930 S.A. song book. The chorus is from song No. 499.

526. Dear Lord and Father of mankind (John Greenleaf Whittier (445))

The Musical Salvationist, July/August, 1948; taken from an 1872 poem of seventeen verses entitled ' The Brewing of Soma ' and headed: ' " These libations mixed with milk have been prepared for Indra; offer Soma to the drinker of Soma ", Vashista, translated by Max Müller.'

In India, from remote ages, the barks, leaves and juices of certain plants have been smoked and drunk by religious ascetics, in the belief that such concoctions ministered to their predisposition to quiet contemplation and religious fervour, and could animate their gods to great achievements. Travelling Hindu saints carry such drugs about with them, and the drowsy intoxication which they effect accounts for some of their wild dreams and fanatical emotions. Soma is one of such plants. Between two or three thousand years before Christ, in Vedic times, it used to be gathered by moonlight on certain Indian mountains. After the leaves had been stripped, the plants were taken to the place of sacrifice, where the priests crushed the stalks between stones and allowed the juice to collect. When the decoction was ready it was offered as a libation to the gods and drunk by the Brahmins. It was highly esteemed and, indeed, held in great reverence (Frederick John Gillman in *The Story of our Hymns*).

Whittier, a student of the lore of mysticism, in graphic language described in his poem the brewing of the soma so that being able to picture the mystic rites, the priests intoxicated by the drink and the worshippers elated with their false transports of joy, we can realize the stupidity of it all. Then the Quaker poet modernized the whole scene and pointed an accusing finger at modern life and worship:

> And yet the past comes round again,
>   And new doth old fulfil;
> In sensual transports wild as vain
> We brew in many a Christian fane
>   The heathen Soma still!
>
> As in that child-world's early year,
>   Age after age has striven
> By music, incense, vigils drear,
> And trance, to bring the skies more near
>   Or lift men up to Heaven!

Then follows the twelfth stanza, our first verse.

527. From every stormy wind that blows (Hugh Stowell)

The Winter's Wreath, 1828, an illustrated annual; *Pleasures of Religion with other Poems*, 1832; 1930 S.A. song book.

Canon Stowell (1799–1865), son of the rector of Ballaugh, near Ramsey, Isle of Man, was ordained in 1823, serving as curate at Shepscombe, Gloucestershire, and at Holy Trinity, Huddersfield. In 1828 he was appointed curate-in-charge of St. Stephen's, Salford. In a few weeks there was no standing room in the church and three years later Christ Church, Salford, was built, largely through his efforts. He remained there until his death. Whether Hon. Canon of Chester Cathedral, Bishop's Chaplain or Rural Dean of Eccles, he was ever a powerful champion of evangelical truth, and a lover of children. He was a powerful orator. His first words would be halting, but when he was warmed to his subject the rush of rhetoric fairly swept his hearers off their feet.

These words were sung by eight American missionaries and two children when, by order of the Nana Sahib, they were put to death in Cawnpore in 1857.

528. He walks with God who speaks to God in prayer (Anonymous)

1930 S.A. song book.

529. How wonderful it is to walk with God (Theodore H. Kitching)

The War Cry, February 6, 1915; but not used in congregational singing until the funeral of the author; 1930 S.A. song book.

Late one January night in 1915 Commissioner Kitching was leaning over a gate by the side of a quiet road in the Barnet district of London during a break in one of the customary walks with a younger friend, Major (later Colonel) Edward Joy. Quiet, yes, but for the thud of guns in France, the uncanny trembling of the ground and the soft voices of two men.

The day before, January 18th, the Commissioner had attended meetings conducted by General Bramwell Booth in the Central Hall, Westminster. During the afternoon gathering Commissioner Mildred Duff had given an address in which she had said: 'What a wonderful thing it is that my small mind and spirit, with all the difficulties, and the worries, and the disappointments, can really walk with God. It is a miracle!'

'Listen what came to me after those meetings yesterday,' said the Commissioner. Then he began to repeat:

How wonderful it is to walk with God
Along the road that holy men have trod;
How wonderful it is to hear Him say:
Fear not, have faith, 'tis I who lead the way!

Commissioner Theodore Hopkins Kitching came of Quaker stock and was born in 1866 at the Quaker school at Ackworth, Yorkshire, where his father was a master. The Commissioner became an officer from Southport in 1888, his early service consisting of training work in London and secretarial duties in France and Belgium. From then all his appointments were connected with International Headquarters. He served as Secretary to the Founder and later to General Bramwell Booth, and in 1921 became Editor-in-Chief, the year he was appointed a Commander of the British Empire in recognition of services during the war years.

In 1892 he married Lieutenant Jane Cranshaw. Their four children became officers—Wilfred (the present General), Louise (Mrs. Commissioner Edgar Grinsted), Theodore (Lieut.-Colonel) and William (Adjutant, promoted to Glory in 1949).

Commissioner Kitching was promoted to Glory from a railway station in Paris on February 10, 1930. The full story of his life is told in *T. H. K.* by Lieut.-Commissioner Arch R. Wiggins.

530. I am Thine, O Lord; I have heard Thy voice (Fanny Crosby (17))

Joyful Lays, a collection of songs by Dr. Robert Lowry and W. H. Doane; 1899 S.A. song book.

'Sometimes the words to a melody come to me faster than I can remember them,' wrote the author. 'One evening, for instance, Mr. Sankey played a sweet air. I excused myself and went to my room to compose the words to "O my Redeemer". In this same way I also wrote "I am Thine, O Lord" to a melody by Mr. Doane.'

531. In the secret of Thy presence (Albert Orsborn (42))

The Musical Salvationist, November, 1923; 1930 S.A. song book.

'When I was the Divisional Commander at Norwich,' writes General Orsborn, 'Commissioner Rich, then the British Chief Secretary, asked me for a new song for the annual corps officers' councils to be conducted by Mrs. Bramwell Booth at Clapton. I tried hard to " woo the muse ", but failed to find the least inspiration.

'My wife and I reached London and attended the introductory meeting, but still no song. . . . About 5.30 a.m. I woke with a very real sense of a Presence quite near me. Then slowly, but easily, these verses and the chorus came into my mind. All I had to do was to catch the inspiration and write down the words, which, of course, I did —by candlelight.'

This took place in the home of Lieut.-Colonel and Mrs. Handel Boot, at Leyton.

The song was ready for the meetings that day.

532. Jesus, tender Lover of my soul (Edward H. Joy (161) (verses); Arthur S. Arnott (chorus)

The Musical Salvationist, August, 1920; 1930 S.A. song book.

Colonel Joy used to say that it took four people to bring this song to popularity:

1. The unknown writer of a non-Army melody.
2. Colonel Arnott who wrote the words of the chorus.
3. Colonel Joy who supplied the verses.
4. The anonymous member of the 1920 Music Department who contributed *The Musical Salvationist* arrangement.

'At a Sunday-school anniversary I heard a song which unfortunately I have not been able to trace,' wrote Colonel Arnott about his chorus. 'On arrival at my home I altered the melody and wrote the words.' Colonel Joy heard them sung in Melbourne, and with them in mind travelled to London. He wrote the verses whilst meditating upon the subject, ' Christ, the Gardener of the Soul ', for a cadets' spiritual day.

Colonel Arnott was born in Newcastle, N.S.W., Australia, on June 17, 1870, and one Sunday afternoon twenty-three years later stood listening to a Salvation Army open-air meeting in St. Leonard's Park, North Sydney. That evening he knelt at the Penitent-form and commenced nearly fifty years' service for his Master. His full story has been written by Adelaide Ah Kow in *Arthur S. Arnott*.

For nearly forty years he conducted the annual young people's demonstration held during the congress in Melbourne, and it was for this event that many of his most popular songs were composed, among which are ' I'd rather be a little thing climbing up '; ' The birds up in the tree-tops '; ' Some day I'll see His blessed face '.

He retired from active service in May, 1935, and was promoted to Glory on May 1, 1941.

533. Master, speak! Thy servant heareth (Frances Ridley Havergal (256))

Written on Sunday, May 19, 1867, at Weston-super-Mare, and published in *The Ministry of Song*; 1930 S.A. song book. Verses 1, 6, 8 and 9 have been retained out of the original nine.

534. 'Mid all the traffic of the ways (John Oxenham)

Written in 1916 on Dartmoor in a small chapel ' in the heart of the rolling moor with its great grey tors'. A Fleet Street journalist during the First World War, knowing the strain of hectic days and then nights of Zeppelin raids, the author felt a real need for rest and quietness; hence his visit to Dartmoor and his discovery of a little ' shrine of quietness'. In *My Lady of the Moor* he has described it as ' a little holy place, nesting like a veritable angel's nest among the hills in this great corner of the moor. . . . Here was an abode of peace, a veritable House of God'.

William Arthur Dunkerley (the author's real name), born in Manchester on November 12, 1852, was educated at Old Trafford School and the Victoria University, Manchester. ' John Oxenham' is taken from a character in *Westward Ho !*, a book given to the author by his Sunday-school teacher. His father was in the wholesale provision business with branches in France, Germany, Belgium and America. In due course ' John' spent several years in France as agent for the family business, and later worked in America in the same capacity until 1881, when the American side of the business failed.

On his return home he undertook the publishing of the English edition of *The Detroit Free Press* in co-operation with Robert Barr. Oxenham's first novel, *God's Prisoner*, was published in 1898, and in 1913 *Bees in Amber*, his first book of verse, appeared.

His daughter, in her book about her father, tells of the death of a relative who left a large debt: ' He [her father] shouldered the burden, though it meant interest at 5 per cent being paid promptly every quarter. He knew the debt had been honestly incurred . . . he knew the creditor would be ruined if it were not paid. So he undertook the task . . . a mill-stone round his neck for twenty years.' He died in January, 1941.

535. Nearer, my God, to Thee (Sarah Adams)

Written in November, 1840, at Loughton, Essex, and published in *Hymns and Anthems*, 1841, by the Rev. William Johnson Fox for his South Place Unitarian Chapel, Finsbury Pavement, London; Ch.M.H.B.; based on Genesis 28: 10–22.

Sarah Fuller Flower (1805–48), born at Harlow, Essex, daughter
of an editor proprietor, early took to writing and acting and became an
art critic ' of no mean eminence '. Mendelssohn knew and admired
both Sarah and her sister Eliza; Robert Browning was Sarah's close
friend, and she was the inspiration of his poem ' Pauline '.

In 1829, nine years after the family moved to Dalston, the girls
became motherless. The father also died and the two sisters were
placed under the guardianship of the Rev. William Johnson Fox,
journalist, reformer and philanthropist, and in his later years Member
of Parliament for Oldham.

Sarah wrote poems and articles for Mr. Fox's *Monthly Repository*,
and in 1834 married a fellow contributor, William Bridges Adams,
engineer and inventor—the man who devised the ' fish-plate ' still used
for joining the rails of our railways.

In 1846, Eliza, the elder sister, stricken with consumption, died at
Hurstpierpoint. Sarah had nursed her with loving devotion and being
of a delicate constitution her health was enfeebled and two years later
died herself of the same disease at 1 Adam Street, Charing Cross. On
the family vault at Harlow is recorded: ' She wrote many noble
sacred poems, but her life was the noblest and best, worthy of her
parents and her sister.'

536. O Love that wilt not let me go (George Matheson (458))

The Musical Salvationist, October, 1922.

' My hymn was composed in the Manse of Innellan on the evening
of June 6, 1882,' wrote Dr. Matheson. ' I was at that time alone. It
was the day of my sister's marriage, and the rest of the family were
staying over-night in Glasgow. Something had happened to me which
was known only to myself, and which caused me the most severe
mental suffering. The hymn was the fruit of that suffering. It was the
quickest bit of work I ever did in my life. I had the impression rather
of having it dictated to me by some inward voice than of working it
out myself. I am quite sure that the whole work was complete in five
minutes, and equally sure that it never received at my hands any
retouching or correction.' The Hymnal Committee of the Church of
Scotland desired the change of one word. I had written originally
" climbed the rainbow ", they objected to the word " climbed " and I
put the word " trace ".

537. Prayer is the soul's sincere desire (James Montgomery (14))

Written in 1818 at the request of the Rev. Edward Bickersteth for
use in connection with his *Treatise on Prayer*. In the same year it also

appeared on a broadsheet for the use of the nonconformist Sunday-schools of Sheffield, and later in *The Christian Psalmist* under the title 'What is prayer?'

The author received more testimonies to the benefit derived from this hymn than about any other that he wrote.

538. Spirit of eternal love (Albert Orsborn (42))

The Musical Salvationist, December, 1923; 1930 S.A. song book.

Written for a Clapton holiness meeting. The Training Principal, Commissioner Thomas McKie, suggested the Irish melody 'Sweet Belle Mahone' as a suitable tune for a song. Thinking around this, 'the song', writes the General, 'came and I caught it ere it fled'.

539. Still, still with Thee, when purple morning breaketh (Harriet Beecher Stowe)

Plymouth Collection, 1855; *The Musical Salvationist*, June, 1922.

Author of *Uncle Tom's Cabin*, Harriet Beecher (1812–96), 'a woman of singularly sincere religious feeling', was born in Litchfield, Connecticut, U.S.A. At the age of fifteen she was teaching in her sister's school at Hartford, and in 1833 married the Rev. Calvin Stowe, Professor of Languages and Biblical Literature. She was sister of the Rev. Henry Ward Beecher.

540. Sweet hour of prayer, sweet hour of prayer (William Walford)

New York Observer; Ch.M.H.B.

The author was a blind minister who would announce his text and give his complete sermon from memory. He could also quote large passages from the Psalms and the Prophecies and from most of the New Testament.

In 1842, while chatting with the Rev. Thomas Salmon, a fellow clergyman in Warwickshire, William Walford recited all the verses of 'Sweet hour of prayer' as his friend wrote them down. A short time afterward Salmon, while on a visit to the United States of America, published the poem in the *New York Observer*.

541. Sweet the moments, rich in blessing (Walter W. Shirley (314))

A recast of a hymn by James Allen (1734–1804) which was included in the *Kendal Hymn Book*, and first appeared in its present form in 1770 in a collection of hymns by the Countess of Huntingdon; Ch.M.H.B.

The Rev. James Allen was born, and died, in Gayle, Yorkshire. He studied at Cambridge and became an itinerant preacher, 'roving from one Christian denomination to another'. Finally, for a number of years, he ministered to a small Independent congregation.

542. Take Thou my hand and guide me (Julie von Hausmann; translated by F. S. Cooper)

The words of Miss Julie von Hausmann (born in Riga, Latvia, 1826, and died in Estonia, 1901) first appeared in *Maiblumen* in 1862, and were probably written in the German language; the present English setting was published in *Consecration Melodies* by J. Wakefield McGill, and in *The Musical Salvationist*, August, 1912, after the International Staff Band had used it at the conclusion of every meeting held during its tour of Germany.

543. Talk with me, Lord, Thyself reveal (Charles Wesley (15))

Hymns and Sacred Poems, 1740; Ch.M.H.B.
Another verse originally preceded our first verse; it read:

> Saviour, who ready art to hear,
> (Readier than I to pray)
> Answer my scarcely uttered prayer
> And meet me on the way.

Many modern hymnals follow the alteration made by John Wesley in his 1780 hymn book: 'Talk with us, Lord, Thyself reveal.'
Verse 2 is based on Eve's tribute to her husband as imagined by John Milton in *Paradise Lost*:

> With thee conversing, I forget all time,
> All seasons and their change; all please alike.

544. Thou Shepherd of Israel, and mine (Charles Wesley (15))

Short Hymns on Select Passages of Scripture, 1762; Ch.M.H.B.; based on the Song of Solomon 1: 7.
Verse 2, line 3, originally read—'Where saints in an ecstasy gaze'.
Bernard L. Manning quotes this song as an illustration of the mystical quality of Wesley's verses, and says, 'Wesley is at the height of his inspiration; nothing short of inspiration keeps the daring emotion sane and reverent and orthodox.' J. E. Rattenbury believes ' this hymn is beyond analysis, at least for me; to pull it to pieces would be sacrilege '.
Shortly before William Booth's mother died she asked her loved ones gathered around her bedside to sing the verses beginning ' Thou Shepherd of Israel '—they belong to one of her favourite songs.

545. What a friend we have in Jesus (Joseph Scriven)

Horace L. Hastings's *Social Hymns*, (1865); 1878 S.A. song book.

Joseph Scriven (1820–86) left his birthplace, Dublin, at the age of twenty-five and settled in Canada. His life was marked by tragic sadness and he was subject, as a result, to melancholia.

On the eve of the day upon which he was to have been married, the one whom he had chosen as his life's partner was accidentally drowned. After his bereavement he consecrated his life to Christ's service amongst the poor and needy: among other ways, by sawing wood for poor widows and sick people who were unable to pay for this service.

Whilst in delirium as a result of an attack of typhoid he, too, was accidentally drowned. Over his grave, on the shores of Lake Rice, stands a white granite monument twelve feet high on which are engraved three verses of this song.

The idea of erecting the monument over the author's grave is said to have originated with Colonel Robert Sandall, when editor of the Canadian *War Cry*. The Army, in fact, made the first contribution to the scheme, the Peterborough (Canada) Band supplying the music at the service.

It was not known that Joseph Scriven could write poetry until a friend came across the words of this song in manuscript during the author's last illness. He had written them thirty-one years before for his mother in the hope they would bring her some solace when she was passing through a time of sorrow.

The War Cry reported Commissioner John J. Allan speaking to the members of the 1946 High Council on Mother's Day: ' None present will soon forget Commissioner John Allan telling of his mother, who as a young girl of seventeen years of age, at a time of crisis [she was on Trent Bridge, Nottingham, contemplating suicide] heard a small company of Salvationists singing " What a Friend we have in Jesus ". This Friend became her Friend. Poorly equipped educationally, but mightily equipped by the Holy Spirit, she was sent forth by the Founder as an officer. Beaten for Christ's sake, and rescued by the one who became her life partner, her last words to her boy continue as a motivating power in his life.'

546. What various hindrances we meet (William Cowper (25))

Olney Hymns, 1779. Our present final verse was added for inclusion in *Hymns Ancient and Modern*, and it may have been written by Sir Henry W. Baker; Ch.M.H.B.

547. At even, ere the sun was set (Henry Twells)

Written at the invitation of Sir Henry Baker as an evening hymn for the Appendix of *Hymns Ancient and Modern*, 1868; 1930 S.A. song book.

Born at Ashted, Birmingham, Canon Twells (1823–1900) was about ten years of age when his father gave him a small printing press upon which he produced each month *The Ashted Gazette*, with limited circulation among his family and friends. After receiving his education at the King Edward the Sixth Grammar School, and then at St. Peter's College, Cambridge, where he graduated, he was ordained in 1849. Five years later he was appointed master of St. Andrew's House School at Wells, where he remained until he was elected to the Godolphin School, Hammersmith, in 1856. Referring to these days and this hymn, he wrote: ' I wrote it one afternoon while the boys were under examination (paper work) and I was supposed to be seeing " all fair ". . . . Copies have been kindly sent me in Greek, Latin, German, French, Welsh and Irish. I like to think that it may have brought souls nearer Christ, and if so I heartily thank God for it.'

In 1870, feeling the strain of schoolwork, he became Rector of Baldock, Herts, then at Waltham-on-the-Wolds, near Melton Mowbray. In 1873–74 he was Select Preacher at Cambridge, Rural Dean in 1875, and during May of the same year he was married to Miss Ellen Jane Thompson, daughter of Rev. Matthew C. Thompson, Vicar of Alderminster, near Stratford-on-Avon.

In 1884 Henry Twells was made honorary canon of Peterborough, but ill health led him to resign his living and to retire to Bournemouth, where he built and partly endowed out of his own means the Church of St. Augustine, serving it as Priest-in-charge until his death.

In the church, placed there by a grateful congregation in memory of their beloved pastor, are two stained-glass windows representing Christ the Teacher and Christ the Healer. In one the Saviour is surrounded by a crowd of rapt listeners; in the other by a number of folk seeking the help of the Great Physician. Inscribed under them are two verses of 'At even, ere the sun was set '.

548. Blessèd and glorious King (— Mundell)

1899 S.A. song book.

Brother Mundell has been described as a Salvationist solicitor. According to *The War Cry* of September 23, 1893, ' solicitor Captain Mundell ' defended the case of Cadet Amy Elliott, of the Chelsea Garrison, who had been in Wandsworth Gaol for five days for an unproved offence of singing in the street.

549. Blessèd Jesus, save our children (Emma Booth-Tucker (301))

Slightly altered from the 1899 S.A. song book.

' The Consul wrote the song when her family were quite young and it was inspired by a deep desire and prayerful longings for us children,' wrote Mrs. Commissioner Sladen, the eldest daughter of the author. 'My mother was passionately fond of children and a great believer in the power of a young life consecrated to the service of Christ.'

550. Eternal Father, strong to save (William Whiting)

Hymns Ancient and Modern 1861; 1899 S.A. song book.

William Whiting (1825–78), born in Kensington, London, was Master at Winchester College Chorister's School. He wrote these verses in 1860 and revised them in 1869 and again in 1874. In addition to the author's revisions it was also amended by the compilers of *Hymns Ancient and Modern*.

One of the most impressive occasions upon which the song was used was in May, 1914, when the *Empress of Ireland* sank with its terrible death-roll of Canadian Salvationists, including Commissioner and Mrs. David Rees, Colonel and Mrs. Sydney Maidment and the larger part of the Canadian Staff Band. Regarding the following Sunday afternoon *The Bandsman and Songster* reported: ' There was a poignant episode outside the Canadian Pacific offices in Cockspur Street, London. The Regent Hall Band passed over Trafalgar Square and into Cockspur Street. The band started the familiar hymn, "Eternal Father, strong to save", and the crowd of watchers who had been listlessly waiting for news turned as one man. Hats came off in one deferential motion and the sobbing appeal of the refrain—

> O hear us when we cry to Thee
> For those in peril on the sea—

so moved sorrowing women that many of them sank down on the kerb and wept, while men with convulsively heaving shoulders hid their faces in their hands.'

551. Holy Father, in Thy mercy (Isabella S. Stevenson)

Isabella Stevenson (1843–90), a devout member of the Church of England, was born in Cheltenham, the daughter of a military officer.

' Holy Father, in Thy mercy ', which came into more general use during the two world wars, when the verses brought some measure of comfort to many who were anxiously thinking of loved ones in the midst of great danger, was written in Cheltenham in 1869 on the day the author's invalid brother set sail for South Africa. A copy of the hymn, which had been privately printed, was used by an officer of H.M.S. *Bacchante* during 1881–82. Prince George (afterward George V) and his brother, who were on board and were sailing round the world, sent a copy home to their mother. The Royal Family sang it whilst their boys were on their cruise.

552. I have a Saviour; He's pleading in Glory (Samuel Clough)

Revival Music; 1878 S.A. song book.

Mr. Clough, an Irishman, is said to have been a clergyman of the established church who later joined the Plymouth Brethren.

'On our first visit to Ireland, in 1874,' wrote Ira D. Sankey, 'we came across these words in a printed pamphlet. It was the second hymn to which I wrote music and it was much used in our meetings in London.'

Hugh Redwood, in *God in the Shadows*, tells how, when a young reporter in Bristol, he went to an Army meeting and heard a young Salvationist, Jenny Jewell, sing this song as a solo. The words, the singing and the power of God's Spirit were such that ere the song was finished he was kneeling at the Penitent-form.

553. Jesus, give thy Blood-washed Army (William Pearson (73))

The War Cry, June 5, 1886; 1899 S.A. song book. Written in connection with the International Congress of 1886.

554. Jesus, hear Thy soldiers crying (William Pearson (73))

The War Cry, September 22, 1888; 1899 S.A. song book.

555. Lord, give me more soul-saving love (William Pearson (73))

1930 S.A. song book. Written at a time when new corps were being opened almost every week.

556. O Thou God of every nation (William Pearson (73))

One of the many songs written for the opening of the Clapton Congress Hall, appearing in *The War Cry*, May 11, 1882; 1899 S.A. song book. An extra verse used on that occasion read:

> Lord, we give to Thee this building,
> Let Thy light within it shine,
> Let Thy glory be its gilding,
> Seal it now for ever Thine.
> Now and ever,
> Praise and glory shall be Thine.

Lieut.-Colonel Slater said of this song: 'It comes nearest of all others to supplying the Army with a song of a national anthem type. . . . It is truly Army in its terms, language and sentiments.

'Of all the occasions upon which this song has been used the most tender probably was when, at the conclusion of a staff council held in London, in November, 1889, a delegation of officers journeyed to Clacton-on-Sea to visit the Army Mother, then on her death-bed.

179

Representing all departments of Army work, the nineteen Salvationists paid their respects to one whom they loved and revered, and there they renewed their vows of fidelity to God and the Army. As they knelt around the bed the delegation, amidst tears, sang Pearson's

> O Thou God of every nation,
> We now for Thy blessing call.'

The official record of the High Council which elected General Albert Orsborn reads: ' Within a few minutes the sound of the singing of Colonel Pearson's song, "O Thou God of every nation", with its last verse, "Bless our General . . . Bless our Army!", was heard from the Council Chamber.'

557. Revive Thy work, O Lord (Albert Midlane (147))

The British Messenger, October, 1858; Mr. Midlane's *The Evangelist's Hymnbook* in 1860; 1930 S.A. song book; based on Habakkuk 3: 2.

558. Saviour, we know Thou art (Charles Wesley (15))

The author's *Hymns on the Acts of the Apostles* (left in manuscript); 1930 S.A. song book; based on Acts 2: 47.

559. Thou Son of God, whose flaming eyes (Charles Wesley (15))

Wesley's *Hymns for the Use of Families*, 1767; Ch.M.H.B.

It was originally an evening hymn as seen from the first verse as in *Wesley's Hymns*:

> Thou Son of God, whose flaming eyes
> Our inmost thoughts perceive,
> Accept the evening sacrifice,
> Which now to Thee we give.

560. Thy voice hath spoken, souls have heard (Mary H. Maxwell (266))

Hymns of Consecration and Faith, compiled by the Rev. J. Mountain; 1930 S.A. song book.

561. As pants the hart for cooling streams (Nahum Tate and Nicholas Brady (16))

A New Version of the Psalms of David by Tate and Brady, 1696; 1930 S.A. song book; a paraphrase of Psalm 42.

The original Hebrew word for ' pant ' has reference to the peculiar cry of the thirsty animal and is used only in one other place in the Bible—Joel 1: 20, where it is translated, ' cry '.

This Psalm (42) was written before David had attained to his actual kingdom. He was fleeing before his enemies, and the very words of his plaintive song (42: 6) show us that he was far from altar and priests and sacrifice. He had been like a deer chased by the hounds, and the thought of the tabernacle, with its quiet and its refreshment, is like that of water to the hunted stag. It is in much the same spirit that he is mentioned as longing for a draught from the well ' beside the gate '.

562. Behold the throne of grace (John Newton (41))

Book 1 of *Olney Hymns*; based on 1 Kings 3: 5, and probably written for the weekly prayer meetings held in the Great House, Olney; 1930 S.A. song book.

563. Come, my soul, thy suit prepare (John Newton (41))

Book 1 of *Olney Hymns*; Ch.M.H.B.; based on 1 Kings 3: 5.

For years Spurgeon used to have a verse or two sung before the great prayer in his public services.

564. Day by day the manna fell (Josiah Conder)

The Congregational Hymn Book, 1836; *The Musical Salvationist*, April, 1914; based on Luke 11: 3.

Born at Aldersgate, London, Mr. Conder (1789–1855), son of an engraver and publisher, at the age of fifteen became his father's assistant and ten years later edited his own paper. In addition to being a voluminous writer and a lay preacher, in 1836 he produced the first *Congregational Hymn Book*, contributing fifty-six of his own works.

565. Equip me for the war (Charles Wesley (15))

Hymns on God's Everlasting Love, 1741; Ch.M.H.B.; written during the course of a heated doctrinal controversy carried on by the Wesleys, Whitefield, Toplady and others.

Dr. Henry Bett, M.A., points out that for the last verse Wesley drew upon the noble passage, ' For Thou lovest all the things that are, and abhorrest nothing which Thou hast made: for never wouldest Thou have made any thing, if Thou hadst hated it ' (Wisdom of Solomon 11: 24).

566. Firm in Thy strong control (Anonymous)

1930 S.A. song book.

567. For Thee, dear Lord, my spirit longs (Percy W. Urquhart)

Published anonymously in *The Musical Salvationist*, July, 1889; 1899 S.A. song book.

In the winter of 1889, when the author was the Lieutenant at Birmingham XI, the police were determined to stop the Army's work in the open air; five officers were already serving terms of imprisonment, among whom was the Lieutenant's Commanding Officer. The Lieutenant stood firm, however, and on the Sunday after the corps had been deprived of its leader, he rallied his soldiers round him and, in spite of threats, attacks and much opposition, bravely carried on.

At home that night, feeling very worried because the police had taken his name and with the prospect of a summons hanging over his head, he sought to divert his mind by writing a song.

The tune used for 'Must Jesus bear the Cross alone', and frequently sung in officers' meetings by a young woman who was stationed at a difficult corps near by, had impressed itself upon his mind. To that melody he wrote the words which expressed his devotion and trust at the time of testing.

Though not called upon to suffer imprisonment (he was placed on probation by the magistrate) his consecration held good through ten years of fighting as an officer, and since then as a soldier at Upper Norwood and East Dulwich until his promotion to Glory.

568. Give me a restful mind (Frederick G. Hawkes)

The Musical Salvationist, October, 1946, under the title 'My petition', since when all third lines have been shortened by one syllable so that the song could be used to short metre tunes.

Born in the Essex village of Good Easter in 1869, Colonel Hawkes moved to Mashbury at the age of five. After conversion at fourteen he became a Salvationist at Chelmsford in March, 1887, later joining the corps band. He replied to a request published in *The War Cry*, March 12, 1887, for volunteers to join a travelling musical combination, afterward to become world famous as the Household Troops Band. He was accepted, became the solo euphonium player, and toured the British Isles and the Continent. Whilst a trooper his first composition —words and music—was published, 'Never a step to the rear'.

On October 14, 1892, Frederick Hawkes was appointed to the Musical Editorial Department, where for more than twenty years he assisted Lieut.-Colonel Slater until he succeeded him as the head of the department.

During Colonel Hawkes's term of office he introduced *International Music Album* series (1919), the *Second Series* (now *Triumph*) (1922) and *Festival Series Band Journals* (1923), *Songs for Male Voices*, *The Salvation Soloist*, the present *Band Tune Book*, containing 541 tunes; in addition to which he was for a number of years the Bandmaster at Penge.

At the time of his retirement (in 1936) the Colonel had to his credit more than a hundred vocal pieces and a quantity of band music which included more than a hundred marches and two hundred selections. Amongst his outstanding band items are the selections ' Eventide ', ' Songs of Joy, No. 2 ' and ' Songs of Praise, No. 2 '; the marches ' The Vesper Hymn ' and ' Spanish Chant '; and a number of arrangements from the Great Masters.

In addition to the Colonel's writing of music he is also the author of a number of technical publications which include *Studies in Time and Tempo*; *A Handbook of Conducting*; *The Slide Trombone*; *Musical Caligraphy*; and *Studies in Band Training*.

Colonel Hawkes was promoted to Glory on November 24, 1959.

569. Give us a day of wonders (John Lawley (56))

The Musical Salvationist, December, 1893; and entitled ' Opening of a new barracks '; 1899 S.A. song book.

Commissioner John Lawley is thought to have written the song while accompanying Commissioner Henry Howard to the opening of the new building at Rochdale, where the words were first sung.

570. God of my life, to Thee I call (William Cowper (25))

Olney Hymns, 1779; 1930 S.A. song book.

571. Gracious Saviour, Thou hast drawn me (Anonymous)

1930 S.A. song book.

572. Guide me, O Thou great Jehovah (William Williams)

Written in Welsh and published in the author's first book of hymns, *Alleluia*, which was completed in six parts and printed at Bristol, 1745–47; Ch.M.H.B.

The first verse in the English translation is probably by the Rev. Peter Williams of Carmarthen and was published in *Hymns on Various Subjects*, 1771. Our second and third verses were translated either by William Williams himself, or by his son the Rev. John Williams, afterward first Principal of Trevecca College.

The author, known as the ' Sweet Singer of Wales ', was born at Cefn-y-Coed, near Llandovery, Carmarthenshire, in 1717. When his father, who had been turned out of his church and had been obliged to worship in a cave at daybreak, died, William was left to the prayerful care of his mother and educated for the medical profession.

Hearing of strange happenings in the neighbouring village of Talgarth, the young medical student made his way there one Sunday morning, anticipating fun. After a perfunctory and lifeless church service, the congregation lingered in the churchyard. Suddenly a figure with flashing eyes and an arresting face mounted a tombstone, opened his Bible and began to preach. The speaker (young Howell Harris, who had been influenced by the preaching of John Wesley) was a very Boanerges for energy and denunciation of sin. The Spirit of God moved the people and many souls yielded to the Saviour, among whom was William himself.

Before he was twenty-three Williams was ordained a deacon by the Bishop of St. Davids and began his ministry at Llanwrtyd, but later became an itinerate preacher in the Welsh Calvinistic Church. For almost fifty years he travelled unceasingly, his sermons having a powerful effect upon his countrymen until he died at Pentycelyn, near Llandovery, in January, 1791.

Wrote Commissioner Wm. Elwin Oliphant: ' Paul Gerhardt sang, by his impressive German, all Germany into piety, and William Williams, by his imagery of nature and his love of the Cross, sang all Wales into religion. Both men moved in troublous times, and social upheavals were at their height and threatened to overwhelm their countries; instead of despairing they preached salvation, and instead of rousing they took down the golden lyre of David and sang their countries into faith.'

573. Here, Lord, assembled in Thy name (Edward Boaden)

Methodist Free Church Hymns, 1889; 1930 S.A. song book; written in connection with the Temperance Movement, whose pledge the author had signed in 1838.

Edward Boaden (1827–1913) was born at Helston, Cornwall, and, although educated for the law, entered the ministry of the United Methodist Free Church at Gosport in 1849, became President in 1871, and the first President of the United Methodist Church in 1907.

574. I do not ask Thee, Lord (Fannie Jolliffe)

1899 S.A. song book.

Fannie Pegg, as Mrs. Commissioner Jolliffe was known before her marriage in 1895, was born on September 18, 1862, converted at an Army Penitent-form set up in a disused railway carriage at Leamington, received her officer's commission in 1886, and was one of the few officers to hold the rank of Staff-Lieutenant.

As a single officer she served in training work at garrisons in Northampton, Bath, Oxford, Battersea and Leamington, in special service in charge of a revival brigade of Lieutenants from the training garrison, and eventually in charge of the Sheffield 1 Corps, where the Albert Hall had to be used on Sunday evenings to accommodate the immense crowds.

When, in 1891, Captain Pegg received orders to leave London and take the revival brigade to the Sheffield Division, she did not look forward to the change from garrison work and the separation it involved from her old Captain (later Colonel Mary Tait), and wrote this song to strengthen her heart.

575. I want that adorning divine (Charlotte Elliott (217) (verses))

Christian Remembrances pocket book (about 1846), where each of the nine verses is based on a passage of Scripture; 1930 S.A. song book. The original version has been altered to bring the song into a suitable metre for congregational use.

576. Jesus, I fain would find (Charles Wesley (15))

Short Hymns on Select Passages of Scripture, 1762; Ch.M.H.B.; based on Revelation 3: 19.

577. Jesus, my strength, my hope (Charles Wesley (15))

Hymns and Sacred Poems, 1742; Ch.M.H.B.

578. Jesus, my truth, my way (Charles Wesley (15))

Hymns and Sacred Poems, 1749; 1930 S.A. song book; originally in seven eight-line verses.

579. Jesus, Saviour, pilot me (Edward Hopper)

Sailors' Magazine (New York), 1871; *Spiritual Songs*, 1878; *The Musical Salvationist*, February, 1911; 1930 S.A. song book. The chorus we have usually associated with the verses has been omitted in the present song book as it was no part of the original song.

The author was born in New York City in 1818 of a mother of Huguenot descent and a father, Mansfield Hopper, a prosperous merchant. He graduated from the University of the City of New York, and in 1842 from Union Theological Seminary of the same city.

Following eleven years as a preacher he returned to New York where, in the Church of Sea and Land, until his death he worked among seafaring men. In 1871 he received his D.D. degree from Lafayette College. He died in 1888.

580. Jesus, the gift divine I know (Charles Wesley (15))

Short Hymns on Select Passages of Scripture, 1762; 1930 S.A. song book; based upon John 4: 10–14.

581.   Jesus, Thou joy of loving hearts (*attributed to* Bernard of Clairvaux (45); *translated by* Ray Palmer)

The Sabbath Hymn Book, Andover, Mass., 1858; 1930 S.A. song book; a very free paraphrase of the *Jesu dulcis memoria*.

Dr. Palmer (1808–87), Congregational minister and son of a judge, was born in Little Compton, Rhode Island, U.S.A. He spent his early days in Boston as clerk in a dry goods store (drapers' assistant), before graduating at Yale in 1830, immediately after which he wrote his first hymn, ' My faith looks up to Thee '. For the latter part of his nearly fifty years' service he was Secretary of the American Congregational Union.

His rule was never to receive any compensation for his hymns, merely making a condition that the phraseology of the hymns should not be altered by editors.

582.   Jesus, we look to Thee (Charles Wesley (15))

Hymns and Sacred Poems, 1749; 1899 S.A. song book.

Dr. H. Betts, in writing on the language of Wesley's hymns, and referring to verse 4 says: ' " Comfort " today has the general sense of consolation, but the Latin *confortare* means first of all " to make strong ". . . . I cannot help feeling that it is the sense of strength, rather than consolation, imparted by the manifested presence of our Lord that is meant.'

583.   Jesus, where'er Thy people meet (William Cowper (25))

Olney Hymns, 1779.

' We are going to remove our prayer meeting to the great room in the Great House,' wrote John Newton in April, 1769. ' It is a noble place with a parlour behind it, and holds 130 people conveniently.' ' Jesus, where'er Thy people meet ', based on Exodus 20: 24, was one of two hymns written for the occasion. A special reference to the occasion is found in an omitted verse:

> Dear Shepherd of Thy chosen few,
> Thy former mercies here renew;
> Here to our waiting hearts proclaim
> The sweetness of Thy saving name.

584.   Just where I am, O let me be (Fred P. Morris)

Alexander's Hymns, No. 3; *Songs for the British Commissioner's Councils*, 1947.

585.   Lead, kindly Light, amid the encircling gloom (John Henry Newman (12))

British Magazine, March, 1834; two years later in *Lyra Apostolica*; 1899 S.A. song book.

John Henry Newman (1801–90), later to become Cardinal in the Church of Rome, penned these words on June 16, 1833, in an orange boat which lay becalmed in the Straits of Bonifacio. Newman was returning to England after a visit to the South of Europe, where for health reasons he had been staying at Castro Giovanni. An incumbent of St. Mary's Church, Oxford, he was more troubled in spirit than in body and was approaching a crisis in his spiritual and religious life.

As the boat lay tossing on the waves Newman gave himself up to meditation. He recalled the story of the Israelites in the wilderness being led in the ' encircling gloom ' by a pillar of fire—and a new hymn was born.

586. Lord, for a mighty revival we plead (Harry Dav is (450))

The War Cry, March 18, 1893; 1899 S.A. song book.

587. Lord, here today my great need I am feeling (William H. Woulds)

The Musical Salvationist, June, 1928.

Major Woulds was attracted to the Army by a village open-air meeting in 1890. Converted at Holloway 1 Corps and trained for five months in the Woolwich Garrison, in 1892 he commenced forty-two years of faithful and devoted service as a corps officer in the British Isles. He was promoted to Glory in September, 1940.

The chorus was written while he was in command of the Bedford Congress Hall Corps, cycling home one morning after visiting the hospital where his Deputy Bandmaster had been pronounced incurable. The verses were added shortly afterward, and are based on Matthew 8: 3. At first the Major used the words to the tune ' Come with thy sin ', but while he was stationed at Ilford, his Bandmaster, Lieut.-Colonel Arthur Bristow, provided the music with which the words are now associated.

The Musician, April 2, 1949, refers to a group of Arab Christians endeavouring, with the help of a concertina, to teach a company of men this song at the foot of Mount Carmel, and also of the great impression this same song made when sung by a party of Salvationists at an Easter service at the tomb where tradition holds Christ was buried.

588. Lord, speak to me, that I may speak (Frances Ridley Havergal (256))

Parlane's Musical Leaflets; the author's *Under the Surface*, 1874; *The War Cry*, November 11, 1893; 1930 S.A. song book; written at Winterdyne on April 28, 1872, and based on Romans 14: 7.

589.   O God, if still the holy place (Albert Orsborn (42))

The Local Officer, October, 1907; 1930 S.A. song book.

'This little song was written when I was a Captain in my first corps, Chelmsford,' writes General Orsborn. 'It disappeared for several years and seemed to have perished. . . . A natural outpouring of the soul, this song is, of course, a prayer, and was written during my own private devotions.'

590.   O Jesus, Saviour, hear my cry (T. C. Marshall (281))

The War Cry, October 8, 1887; *The Musical Salvationist*, August, 1891; 1899 S.A. song book.

591.   Saviour, lead me, lest I stray (Frank M. Davis)

Sankey's *Sacred Songs and Solos*; *The Musical Salvationist*, June, 1889; 1899 S.A. song book.

The author was born in Indiana, U.S.A., in 1839, and died in 1896.

592.   Saviour of light, I look just now to Thee (Robert Hoggard)

The Musical Salvationist, June, 1930.

Commissioner Hoggard was a Beverley barge boy 'rapidly coming under the influence and evil companionship of other lads, when happy, song-loving Salvationists crossed his path'.

'When are you going into the Work?' demanded the Founder of Robert, a young convert visiting Hull about 1879.

'When you are ready to receive me, General,' came the prompt reply; and the next night Robert Hoggard visited the village of Barton as a 'special'. Within a few days he received instructions from Commissioner Railton to proceed to Bristol Circus as Lieutenant to Captain (later Commissioner) Isaac Unsworth.

Thus a future Commissioner commenced a career that eventually took him to Korea, South Africa, New Zealand and Canada, and as a visitor to many more lands.

While in charge of the Grecian (Hoxton) Corps he was married to Captain Annie Johns; he retired from active service early in 1932, and in August, 1935, was promoted to Glory from Hadleigh, Essex.

During his command of the Canada—West Territory, and while preparing to receive General Edward J. Higgins, who had arranged to conduct the congress, the Commissioner was taken ill and had to be removed to hospital. His disappointment weighed heavily upon his spirit; but out of darkness came the recurring line:

Saviour of light, I look just now to Thee.

One day while in a very low condition, he found the verse beginning: 'Another touch, I ask another still' forming in his mind. Before leaving the hospital he had completed the whole song, which was soon being sung throughout the territory under his command.

593. There shall be showers of blessing (Daniel W. Whittle (158))

Sankey's *Sacred Songs and Solos*, set to music by James McGranahan. When Philip Bliss (see No. 78) was killed in a train accident at Ashtabula, Ohio, in 1876, McGranahan hurried to the scene and met Major Whittle, the evangelist with whom Bliss had been working. McGranahan introduced himself to Whittle and there, beside the wrecked train and charred bodies, these two men formed a friendship which was to continue through eleven years of joint evangelistic endeavour.

594. Thou Lamb of God, whose precious Blood (Harry Davis (450))

The War Cry, June 16, 1888; 1899 S.A. song book.

595. Unto Thee will I cry (Albert Orsborn (42))

The Musical Salvationist, July/August, 1946.
' Unto Thee will I cry ' was written in New Zealand for the use of the Auckland Congress Hall Band and set to a secular tune. Afterward it was rewritten with music by Lieut.-Colonel Ernest Rance. To quote the author: ' The song was originally born of personal battles on the heights and in the depths—otherwise it could not have been written.'

596. We the people of Thy host (Emma Booth-Tucker (301))

The Musical Salvationist, April, 1911; 1930 S.A. song book; composed for a council of American officers held in New York, for which the first line read, ' We the prophets of Thy host '.

597. When our heads are bowed with woe (Henry Hart Milman)

Bishop Heber's *Hymns*, 1827; 1899 S.A. song book; based on the story of the raising of the widow of Nain's son. The final line of each verse originally read, ' Gracious Son of Mary, hear '.
The youngest son of the Court Physician to George III, Dr. Milman (1791–1868) was born in London, educated at Eton and Oxford. He took Holy Orders in 1816 and became Dean of St. Paul's Cathedral in 1849.

Writer of prose works, valuable in the realm of history, and three religious dramas, the Dean turned his attention to hymn-writing through an invitation by Bishop Heber to contribute to a new hymnal he was publishing, and which appeared in 1827.

Dean Milman died at Sunninghill, near Ascot, and was buried in St. Paul's Cathedral. His best-known hymn was probably ' Ride on, ride on in majesty! '

A recent writer in *Choir* said of the Dean, ' He was indeed a blend of scholar and mystic who had caught the spirit of his Master whom he served so well.'

598. When shall I come unto the healing waters? (Albert Orsborn (42))

The Beauty of Jesus, 1947; written in New Zealand, the words were inspired by seeing and drinking healing waters springing from a hillside.

599. While here before Thy Cross I kneel (William H. Hutchins)

The War Cry, September 2, 1893; *The Musical Salvationist*, May, 1894; 1899 S.A. song book.

In 1936 the author wrote to Lieut.-Commissioner Arch R. Wiggins: ' I went to reside in Luton in 1889 and for three years was a bandsman at the Citadel Corps. It was during that period that I composed this song. After leaving Luton, about forty-four years ago I returned to my native town of Dunstable and to the Methodist Church in which I had been a Sunday-school scholar. For more than forty years I have been a local preacher and I was, for a number of years, the leader of a mission band. At sixty-six years of age I am still happy to be in the pulpit, animated by the words and spirit of my song, " Lord, fill my craving heart ".

' I remember quite well how one day I experienced a wonderful vision of Jesus on the Cross. My soul was stirred and I caught somewhat of His Spirit. But I wanted to be *filled* with His Spirit. I wanted to be more like Him. I felt an intense longing, indeed, a passion, for souls; and it was while under the influence of the Holy Spirit that the words came to be written.'

600. Be it my only wisdom here (Charles Wesley (15))

Short Hymns on Select Passages of Scripture, 1762; Ch.M.H.B.; based on Job 28: 28.

601. Blest be the tie that binds (John Fawcett)

Hymns Adapted to the Circumstances of Public Worship, 1782.

Born at Lidget Green, near Bradford, Dr. Fawcett (1740–1817) was converted at the age of sixteen under the ministry of George Whitefield. At first Fawcett was a Methodist, but in 1765 he became Baptist minister at Wainsgate, near Hebden Bridge, Yorks, where he ministered until his death.

He wrote several prose works and in 1782 published 166 'Hymns adapted to the Circumstances of Public Worship and Devotion', the majority of which had been written to sing after his sermons.

He received his Doctorate of Divinity from Brown University, U.S.A., in 1811.

In 1772 Dr. Fawcett accepted a call to follow Dr. Gill, the celebrated expositor, who was pastor at Carter's Lane, London. The farewell sermon was preached and household goods were loaded on to the wagons which were to take them up to the city. But the love and affection of the country people he had served was very deep and pleadings and tears spoke forcibly. Dr. Fawcett and his wife looked at each other and read each other's heart. The wagons were unloaded and, although it meant considerable financial sacrifice, never again did they consider leaving the country folk whom they loved so much. It was to commemorate this event that the author wrote these words.

602. Fountain of life and all my joy (Charles Wesley (15))

Hymns and Sacred Poems, 1742; Ch.M.H.B.; written on one of the author's birthdays.

The Rev. Luke Wiseman, in his *Life of Charles Wesley*, pointed out the contrast between this song of praise and the author's Birthday Ode of five years before:

' Take an interval of five years and listen to the birthday song in the first and in the last. " December 18, 1736, I began my twenty-seventh year in a murmuring, discontented spirit, reading over and over the third of Job."

' The passage which he read was this: " Opened Job his mouth, and cursed his day . . . and said, Let the day perish wherein I was born . . . " And so on through all that terrific and blood-curdling chapter. Then contrast his birthday hymn which he published in 1742 with its evident challenge to that dismal day. This is not mere recovery from sickness; it is life from the dead.'

603. Happy the home when God is there (Henry Ware)

Hymns and Poetry for the Use of Juvenile Schools and Families, 1846, published by Mrs. Mayo, a worker in an infants' school in London who, in an earlier (1838) collection of hymns, said it was difficult for children to attend school when once they began to work in factories (at that time about nine years of age). Ch.M.H.B.

Henry Ware (1793–1843), son of a Unitarian minister and a professor at Harvard, was born at Hingham, Massachusetts. After having graduated at Harvard he became the minister of the Second Church, Boston, and later was elected Parkman Professor of Pulpit Eloquence and Pastoral Theology at Harvard. His collected works were published after his death.

604. Help us to help each other, Lord (Charles Wesley (15))

Hymns and Sacred Poems, 1742; written for a ' meeting of friends ', when they gathered together in holy fellowship and friendship; Ch.M.H.B. with the original first verse:

> Try us, O God, and search the ground
> Of every sinful heart;
> Whate'er of sin in us is found,
> O bid it all depart!

605. Home is home, however lowly (Arthur S. Arnott (532))

The War Cry, February 28, 1925; 1930 S.A. song book.

' Home is home, however lowly ' owes its being to a request made by a home league local officer of a Melbourne corps for a song suitable for use in a home league demonstration. When first published the song had a chorus—

> Gathered round the family altar
> Kindred spirits kneel to pray,
> Here we raise our Ebenezer
> At the closing of the day.

606. I need Thee every hour (Annie S. Hawks (verses); Robert Lowry (231) (chorus))

Written in April, 1872, the song was published in Dr. Robert Lowry's *Royal Diadem*, 1873, although it had first appeared in a small collection of gospel songs prepared for the National Baptist Sunday-school Association which met at Cincinnati in November, 1872; *Revival Music*; 1878 S.A. song book.

Mrs. Hawks (1835–1918), who contributed to various popular Sunday-school hymn books, was a member of Hanson Place Baptist Church in Brooklyn, U.S.A.

' I remember well the morning when,' wrote Mrs. Hawks, ' in the midst of the daily cares of my home, then in a distant city, I was so filled with a sense of the nearness of the Master that, wondering how one could live without Him, either in joy or pain, these words, "I need Thee every hour ", were flashed into my mind, the thought at once taking full possession of me. Seating myself by the open window in the balmy air of the bright June day, I caught my pencil, and the words were soon committed to paper, almost as they are being sung now. It was only by accident, as it would seem, that they were set to music a few months later and sung, for the first time, at a large Sunday-school convention held in one of the large western cities of America. . . .

' It was not until long years afterward, when the shadow fell over my way—the shadow of a great loss—that I understood something of the comforting power in the words which I had been permitted to give out to others in my hours of sweet security and peace.'

In *Campaigning in Captivity* by Arch R. Wiggins a backslider tells of his conversion while a prisoner of war at Changi in Malaya:

' The night was pitch dark, and a sailor-friend and myself were walking across a meadow when a chorus reached my ears:

> I need Thee, O I need Thee,
> Every hour I need Thee . . .

We stopped to listen and I found myself joining in the quiet singing. Then a Voice within said: " Yes, and *you* need Him." I discovered that the singing was coming from the Salvation Army " Citadel ". On the next Sunday I went to the meeting and found Jesus again.'

607. O there's joy in every heart (Anonymous)

Robert Bird's *Three Hundred Best Hymns*; 1930 S.A. song book.

608. Thy way, not mine, O Lord (Horatius Bonar (4) (verses); Robert Lowry (231) (chorus))

Hymns of Faith and Hope, 1857; 1899 S.A. song book.

609. Awake, my soul, and with the sun (Thomas Ken)

An appendix of the author's 1695 edition of *A Manual of Prayers* for the use of the scholars of Winchester College. 'Awake, my soul, and with the sun ' had, with an evening and midnight hymn, already appeared in a brochure three years earlier. Ch.M.H.B. The words of the morning hymn were written at Brightstone, Isle of Wight.

Before being published the three hymns were written in block letters on large sheets and hung on the walls of the dormitories, where the boys could see them first thing in the morning and last thing at night.

Born at Berkhamsted, Herts, and educated at Winchester and Oxford, Thomas Ken (1637–1711) was ordained in 1661. In 1679 he received his D.D. degree and was appointed Chaplain to the Princess Mary of Orange at the Hague, but was dismissed for his outspokenness regarding a case of wrongdoing at the court. He became Bishop of Bath and Wells in 1685, and in 1688 was imprisoned in the Tower for refusing to read the Declaration of Indulgence. He was deprived of his see altogether in 1691 for refusing to take the oaths on the succession of William III. The bishop was buried in the churchyard at Frome.

Ken's hymns occupy an important place in the evolution of English hymnody. At the time they were written biblical paraphrases were about the only means of praise in the Church, and Ken's hymns heralded the dawn of singing as we know it today in places of worship. Macaulay's verdict of Ken was that he approached ' as near as human infirmity permits, to the ideal perfection of Christian virtue ', whilst James II pronounced him the most eloquent preacher among the Protestants of his time.

610. Be pleased to keep me, Lord, this day (Charles Wesley (15))

Wesley Hymn Book, 1876, where the first verse commences ' Vouchsafe to keep me, Lord, this day '; 1899 S.A. song book.

611. Forth in Thy name, O Lord, I go (Charles Wesley (15))

Hymns and Sacred Poems, 1749; Ch.M.H.B.

Commissioner T. Henry Howard used to close his garden gate in the morning with the words of the first verse upon his lips, and Commissioner George Railton used to quote the same as he came downstairs from his bed.

612. New every morning is the love (John Keble (338))

Written on September 20, 1822, published in the author's *Christian Year*, 1827, and based on Lamentations 3: 22, 23.

613. Once more the sun is beaming bright (attributed to Ambrose of Milan; translated by John Chandler (39))

The translation of the original Latin hymn *Jam lucis orto sidere* was first published in Chandler's *Hymns of the Church*, 1837; 1930 S.A. song book.

Ambrose, Bishop of Milan from 374 to 397, was born in Gaul about 340. He played an important part in the development of church congregational singing and favoured ' humanly composed ' songs at a time when many thought it the proper thing to sing scriptural words only. He himself wrote many songs and has been called the ' Father of Latin Church Song '.

614. Summoned my labour to renew (Charles Wesley (15))

Hymns and Sacred Poems, 1739; taken from two separate hymns; 1899 S.A. song book.

615. This is the day of light (John Ellerton)

Written in 1867; Dean Howson's *Selection of Hymns compiled for use in Chester Cathedral*, 1868.

John Ellerton (1826–93) was born in London, took his B.A. degree at Cambridge in 1849 and a year later became curate at Eastbourne. During over forty years' service in the Church of England he was a curate at Brighton, Vicar of Crewe, Rector of Hinstock and then of Barnes, London. Following a breakdown and recovery in health he took charge of White Roding, Essex, and was nominated Prebendary of St. Albans but was unable to accept the honour owing to the condition of his health. He died in Torquay.

Mr. Ellerton assisted in the compiling of the *London Mission Hymn Book*, 1885, and in the 1889 edition of *Hymns Ancient and Modern*. In 1888 he published his own *Hymns, Original and Translated*. He refused to protect any of his hymns by copyright, regarding himself as the channel through which God had given them to the Church.

616. Abide with me; fast falls the eventide (Henry Francis Lyte (11))

Remains, by the author's daughter, 1850; Ch.M.H.B.

Mr. Lyte preached his farewell sermon to his beloved parishioners in Brixham one Sunday in September, 1847. Already the 'eventide' of life was drawing in around him—consumption had taken its toll of his constitution.

In his home at Berry Head he rested in the afternoon, and in the early evening strolled through the gardens which overlooked Torbay Harbour with all its grandeur. It had been a beautiful day and the sun was setting over the distant Dartmoor in a blaze of glory, which, most probably, he likened to the setting of his own life. Later that evening he handed to a member of the family the words of 'Abide with me', together with a tune of his own composing.

Hoping that a winter spent in a warmer clime might prolong his life, the family party next morning travelled to London *en route* for Nice, where the author died on Nov. 20th. But he had, in the penning of his immortal words, fulfilled the prayer of his heart as expressed in some lines he had written some time earlier:

> O Thou whose touch can lend
> Life to the dead, Thy quickening grace supply,
> And grant me, swan-like, my last breath to spend
> In song that may not die.

Lord Kitchener ordered 'Abide with me' to be sung at a thanksgiving service in Khartoum; Lord Allenby chose it to be sung at a service commemorating the liberation of Jerusalem in the First World War;

Nurse Cavell found solace in its words as she faced the firing squad; and Shackleton found it inspiring as he crossed the trackless Antarctic.

617. Father of love and power (George Rawson)

Worship Song, edited by W. Garrett Horder; *Congregational Hymnary*.

George Rawson (1807–89) was born in Park Square, Leeds. A solicitor by profession, and a member of the Congregational Church, he published his first songs under the signature, 'A Leeds Layman'. He assisted in the preparation of the *Leeds Hymn Book*, 1853, intended for use in the Congregational Church, and *Psalms and Hymns for the Use of the Baptist Denomination*, 1858. The year 1877 saw the publication of his own *Hymns, Verses and Chants* and 1885 *Songs of Spiritual Thought*.

Mr. Rawson retired to Clifton, Bristol, where he died.

618. Glory to Thee, my God, this night (Thomas Ken (609))

These verses form the evening hymn referred to under No. 609; *A Manual of Prayer*, 1695; Ch.M.H.B.

619. How do Thy mercies close me round (Charles Wesley (15))

Hymns and Sacred Poems, 1740; Ch.M.H.B. Written for use before retiring to rest at night.

620. My God, how endless is Thy love! (Isaac Watts (3))

The author's *Hymns and Spiritual Songs*, 1709; 1899 S.A. song book; and based on Lamentations 3: 22, 23 and Isaiah 45: 7.

621. Saviour, again to Thy dear name we raise (John Ellerton (615))

Written in 1866 for the Festival of the Malpas, Middlewich and Nantwich Choral Association, on the reverse side of a piece of paper which contained part of his last Sunday's sermon, and later abridged and revised by the author himself for *Hymns Ancient and Modern*, 1868.

622. Sun of my soul, Thou Saviour dear (John Keble (338))

Part of a poem of fourteen verses dated November 25, 1820, and published in the author's *Christian Year*, 1827; Ch.M.H.B. The original manuscript is preserved at Keble College, Oxford. The poem commenced:

> 'Tis gone, that bright and orbèd blaze,
> Fast fading from our wistful gaze . . .

623. The day Thou gavest, Lord, is ended (John Ellerton (615))

Written in 1870 for *A Liturgy for Missionary Meetings*; revised for *Church Hymns* in 1871; chosen by Queen Victoria for use at her Diamond Jubilee Celebrations.

624. And will the Judge descend (Philip Doddridge (5))

Published in 1755 and based on Matthew 25: 41; Ch.M.H.B.

625. Brief is our journey through the years (Catherine Baird (400))

Written, especially for the 1953 song book, ' because to me ', explains the author, ' there is something false in minimizing the beauties of this world and " pretending ", just to keep up our courage, that we do not mind leaving them for the joys of the hereafter '.

626. Day of judgment! Day of wonders! (John Newton (41))

Written on June 26, 1774; published in *The Olney Hymns*, 1779; Ch.M.H.B.; and based on the *Dies Irae* by Thomas of Celano (see No. 630). These words, which took ' the most of two days to finish ', have been translated into a number of languages.

627. Lo! on a narrow neck of land (Charles Wesley (15))

Hymns and Sacred Poems, 1749; 1899 S.A. song book.

Dr. Henry Bett, commenting on the use of the word ' secure ' in the first verse, points out that it is used in its old sense of meaning ' a feeling of security whether warranted or not '. It is because the sinner is ' insensible ' that he can feel ' secure ' in such a dangerous position.

Wesley wrote these verses after he had visited Land's End, a project-ing rock, ' a narrow neck of land, 'twixt two unbounded seas ', in July, 1743. Already in *The Spectator* Joseph Addison had compared the present time to a ' narrow neck of land ' that rises in the midst of an ocean.

628. Sinners, whither would you wander? (Anonymous)

For a considerable time this song was attributed to Commissioner George Railton, but the claim is false since the song appeared in *The Christian Mission Hymn Book* and Railton did not join William Booth until 1873.

629. Sins of years are all numbered (Lucy Booth-Hellberg)

The Musical Salvationist, November, 1890; 1899 S.A. song book.

Lucy Milward Booth, youngest child of the Founder and Mrs.

Booth, was born at 1 Cambridge Lodge Villas, Hackney, London, on April 28, 1868. In seasons of illness in early womanhood she found some relief in giving expression to her love of music, and the desire and ability to create new melodies, as well as verses, to add to the Army's treasury of song.

After having been entrusted with responsible positions while still young she married a highly gifted Swedish officer, Emanuel D. Hellberg. Together they commanded Army work in India, Switzerland and France. Commissioner Booth-Hellberg died in 1909, after which Mrs. Booth-Hellberg continued as a territorial commander, in Denmark, in South America and Norway. She was awarded the Order of the Founder, and on July 18, 1953, was promoted to Glory from Sweden.

During a visit to Clacton-on-Sea where the Army Mother lay dying Lucy sat up with her all night. Calling her daughter to her side, Mrs. Booth said: ' I want you to love backsliders. Tell them that when they come to where I am, with their feet in the River Jordan, when they are about to appear before the Great White Throne, nothing will avail them but the Blood of Jesus.' She then put her hands on her daughter's head and prayed. The next morning Lucy left Clacton for London, travelling on the seven o'clock train. At Colchester her carriage was filled with rough-looking men. The rain was pouring down and tears flowed from the eyes of the sorrowing daughter. As she sat huddled up in the corner she composed the words of ' Sins of years are all numbered '. Upon reaching London she wrote them down and a little later set them to music.

630. That day of wrath, that dreadful day (Thomas of Celano; *translated by* Walter Scott)

The Lay of the Last Minstrel, 1805; 1878 S.A. song book.

In the thirteenth century some young Italians, including Thomas of Celano, devoted themselves to the service of Christ and to live as near as possible in the same manner as the disciples. With this in view they gave away their possessions and set out on foot to teach the people about Jesus. They lived by faith, looking wholly to the Lord to meet their needs. They became known as ' The Grey Friars ' and were wonderfully used by God. They not only preached, they wrote hymns on all the great doctrines of the Christian faith, for they said, ' If the people sing our hymns they will remember our teaching.'

Sir Walter Scott (1771–1832) was born in Edinburgh. Being early afflicted with lameness, the routine of hard study was interrupted by sojourns in different places where he heard many stories, and also gave him opportunity for wide and extensive reading. He was called to the Bar in 1792 and later was appointed sheriff-substitute of Selkirkshire. He is well remembered by his *Waverley Novels*.

In giving a description of the monks in Melrose Abbey in the days of old, Sir Walter Scott used his translation of what W. T. Stead described as ' one of the most terrible and famous of all hymns of the Church—*Dies Irae* (The Dreadful Day), based on Zephaniah 1: 14–16. The Latin hymn is found in the Mass for the Dead from about 1480, and it became part of the religious life of the Middle Ages.

More than one hundred and thirty English translations have been made of this wonderful hymn.

631. The angel of the Lord shall stand (Harry Hill)

Favourite Songs Supplement; 1899 S.A. song book.

When Harry Hill, a police sergeant and a member of the police band at Hull, became a Salvationist he was appointed Bandmaster of Hull Icehouse Corps. His love for the Army, and especially his interest in its musical development, is proved by the fact that, although he had only two years to serve before drawing his pension, he gladly forfeited his place in the police force and became one of the three original members of the Music Editorial Department at International Headquarters, the others being Lieut.-Colonel Richard Slater (in charge) and Fred W. Fry. In addition he became Bandmaster of the Clapton Congress Hall Band. He remained in the Music Editorial Department until 1888 when he was transferred to the Field, taking charge of the Ramsgate Corps.

632. The blast of the trumpet, so loud and so shrill (Anonymous)

Ch.M.H.B.; probably an old Ranter's song.

633. Thou Judge of quick and dead (Charles Wesley (15))

The author's *Hymns for the Watchnight,* 1746; Ch.M.H.B.

634. Time is earnest, passing by (Anonymous)

Originally extending to eight verses, this song appeared anonymously in three publications—two American and one English—in the same year, 1851; Ch.M.H.B.

635. When the harvest is past, and the summer is gone (Samuel Francis Smith)

Spiritual Songs, 1831; 1930 S.A. song book.

Samuel Smith (1808–95), famous as the author of ' My Country 'tis of thee ', the popular American national hymn, was born in Boston, U.S.A., and educated at Harvard. As a Baptist minister he was one of a committee appointed by the American Baptist Churches of New

York to prepare *The Psalmist: A New Collection of Hymns for the Use of the Baptist Churches*, 1843, and from 1843 to 1849 was editor of *The Christian Review*.

636. When thy mortal life is fled (Samuel Francis Smith (635))

Published in America in 1832; Ch.M.H.B.

637. You must have your sins forgiven (Fred W. Fry (248))

Favourite Songs Supplement; 1899 S.A. song book.

When Colonel Richard Adby was a soldier in his home corps, High Wycombe, he frequently sang as a solo:

> I have work enough to do,
>   Ere the sun goes down,
> For myself and kindred, too,
>   Ere the sun goes down.
> Every idle whisper stilling,
> With a purpose firm and willing,
> All my daily tasks fulfilling,
>   Ere the sun goes down.
>
> Ere the sun goes down,
>   I must do my daily duty
> Ere the sun goes down.

In the training home the words were not considered quite suitable for Army warfare and Fred Fry was asked to supply a new set to the same tune so that Cadet Adby could still use his solo.

638. Your garments must be white as snow (Anonymous)

Salvation Music, Vol. 2, and set to an old plantation melody; 1899 S.A. song book.

The song is often attributed to Herbert H. Booth but it does not appear in his own collection, *Songs of Peace and War*.

'I remember', wrote Commissioner Samuel Hurren, ' once conducting a late open-air meeting in the market-place of a provincial town. Twenty-nine penitent men and women came forward and knelt on the cobbles, market baskets and parcels at their side, while we sang, "Prepare me, prepare me, Lord, to stand before Thy Throne". Never shall I forget the awe-some impression made on me as I looked on the seekers and heard the song mingle with the striking of midnight by the old town clock.'

639. Above the waves of earthly strife (Mary Ann Kidder)

William Bradbury's *Fresh Laurels for the Sabbath School*, 1867; *Revival Music*; 1878 S.A. song book.

Mrs. Kidder (1825–1905), born in Boston and who spent her whole life in Massachusetts, was a Baptist who is said to have written a thousand hymns.

640. Beautiful land, so bright, so fair (R. Moorcock)

Miss Moorcock may have been a Scot as her song appears in a very old Scottish book in the Aberdeen Library; Ch.M.H.B.

641. For ever with the Lord! (James Montgomery (14))

The Amethyst, 1835; Ch.M.H.B.; based on 1 Thessalonians 4: 17, and originally in twenty-one four-line verses.

642. Give me the wings of faith to rise (Isaac Watts (3) (verses); Robert Lowry (231) (chorus))

Watts's *Hymns and Spiritual Songs*, 1709; Ch.M.H.B.

643. How dark and dreadful is the place (John Lawley (56))

The War Cry, February 12, 1898; 1930 S.A. song book.

644. How happy every child of grace (Charles Wesley (15))

Funeral Hymns, 1759, published by W. Pine, Wine Street, Bristol; Ch.M.H.B.; based on Romans 4: 7.

645. I have a home that is fairer than day (Ada Garnett)

Published in the Canadian *War Cry*, November 6, 1886, when the author was stationed as Captain at Coaticook, Quebec; 1899 S,A. song book.

The author (1866 or 1867–1931), born in London, Ontario, was an officer in Canada until she married John Nisbett in 1893. She became the mother of six children and was left a widow in 1914. Most of her thirty-six songs appeared anonymously in the Canadian *War Cry*.

'I have a home' was written in 1883, when the author was only sixteen years of age, for the first farewell meeting to be held in the Lindsay (Ontario) Corps. Hattie Yerex (later Adjutant) was leaving to become an officer. Said the author: 'In the early days of The Salvation Army these were heart-stirring occasions. Little wonder that I was anxious to do my little bit. With pencil and paper, and on my knees pleading divine help, I wrote words appropriate for the occasion. I had learned a song from my music teacher entitled "Home in the valley, far from the sea", and I wrote my song to this tune. However, I could not raise the courage to sing it for her, neither did I let her know my feelings, or of my song.'

One of the most tender uses ever made of the song was when, at the funeral of her mother, the Consul's twelve-year-old daughter (later Mrs. Commissioner Hugh Sladen) sang it as a solo.

646. I'm but a stranger here (Thomas Rawson Taylor)

Published in the author's *Memories and Select Remains* by W. S. Matthews, 1836; Ch.M.H.B.

Born at Ossett, near Wakefield, son of a Congregational minister, Mr. Taylor (1807) was engaged in the office of a merchant and then a printer, before entering the Congregational ministry himself. He served at the Howard Street Chapel, Sheffield, for six months, then became classical tutor at Airedale College. Ill health forced him to resign, and he died at the age of twenty-eight. 'I'm but a stranger here' was written during his last illness.

647. Jerusalem, my happy home (Joseph Bromehead)

Published at Doncaster in a supplement to a *Selection of Hymns of Peculiar Metre*, edited by Dr. E. Williams and the Rev. James Boden, 1801; Ch.M.H.B.

Rev. Joseph Bromehead (1748–1826) took his M.A. degree at Oxford about 1771, became Curate of Eckington, Derbyshire, where probably he died. Some people affirm that 'Jerusalem, my happy home' can be traced to a Latin hymn by Cardinal P. Damiani (1553) based upon 'The Meditations of St. Augustine'. A translation into English of the Latin hymn was made by F. B. P. (sixteenth or seventeenth century), said to be Francis Baker, Priest, a prisoner in the Tower of London during the reign of Elizabeth I, when he wrote his poem which is now in the British Museum.

Confirming the authorship of the words of this song, the preface of a 1795 hymn book was signed by Joseph Bromehead in which five contributions, including 'Jerusalem, my happy home', are over the initial 'B'.

648. O soul, consider and be wise (Will. J. Brand (52))

Written especially for this song book.

'There appears to be a dearth of suitable songs on the unhappy subject, "Hell",' writes the author, 'and this song, whilst avoiding the lurid literalism of the last century, endeavours to utter a grave warning note, but ends with hope and invitation.'

649. O think of the home over there (D. W. C. Huntington)

Hallowed Songs by Philip Phillips, U.S.A., 1873, where it is said to be taken from *Fresh Leaves*; *Hallelujah Hymn Book*; *Revival Music*; 1878 S.A. song book.

The Rev. De Witt Clinton Huntington was born in Townshend,

Vt., U.S.A., on April 27, 1830. He graduated at Syracuse University and received his D.D. and LL.D. degrees from Genesee College. He later removed to Lincoln, Nebraska, U.S.A.

Commissioner Charles Péan, who pioneered the Army work on Devil's Island, relates the following:

' By permission of the Administration we conducted meetings inside the enclosures every Sunday. . . . What a joy it was to my comrades and me when for the first time we passed through the bolted doors of the Convict Settlement, to proclaim the gospel message of pardon and deliverance, and to lift the first prayer toward God from this abyss. We dared not sing, still less invite these unfortunates to sing, burdened as they are with an infamous past. But one Sunday after the reading of the Scripture portion, Mrs. Captain Hausdorf, accompanied by her husband's concertina, sang a solo: " O think of the home over there . . . "

' The young woman's trembling voice raised the song of God in the midst of these brutish beings, a song which brought tears to many eyes. We repeated the chorus, and soon a murmur arose in the dormitory. Voices joined in, and a number of men, with bared heads, sang with us, as if in prayer: " Over there, O think of the home over there." This was the first song sung by these convicts.'

650. O when shall I sweep through the gates (Phoebe Palmer)

Sankey's *Sacred Songs and Solos*; *Revival Music*; 1878 S.A. song book; and written by an American Methodist (1807–74).

651. O where shall rest be found (James Montgomery (14))

Written for the Red Hill (Sheffield) Wesleyan Sunday-school anniversary, March 15 and 16, 1818, and based on Hebrews 4: 9–11; 1930 S.A. song book.

652. On the sweet Eden shore, so peaceful and bright (Mary Ann Kidder (639))

Bright Jewels for the Sabbath School, compiled by the Rev. Robert Lowry, William Sherwin and Chester G. Allen, 1869, and published by Biglow and Main, where its use by permission probably infers that it had appeared elsewhere prior to that date. *The Musical Salvationist*, July, 1914, following its success in the songster festival at the 1914 International Congress; 1930 S.A. song book.

653. One sweetly solemn thought (Phoebe Cary)

The Christian Mission Magazine, May, 1875; 1878 S.A. song book.

Miss Cary (1824–71), born near Cincinnati, Ohio, U.S.A., was the daughter of a farmer who went about his work repeating verses from the Hebrew poets. Both Phoebe and her sister Alice inherited his tastes and became poets and hymn-writers. When their mother died the two girls had to manage their father's log-wood home, look after the younger children and help with the care of the livestock. They were self-educated and their early verses which were sent to the editor of the local paper were written under very primitive surroundings.

One Sunday morning in 1852, while Phoebe and Alice were living together in New York, they spent a week-end at the home of a friend. Returning from worship at the Church of the Puritans, where they had listened to a sermon on the uncertainty of life and the need for Christians to be ever ready to be summoned home to the eternal rest, Phoebe withdrew to a ' little third-floor bedroom ' and wrote ' One sweetly solemn thought '.

The author died at Newport, Kentucky.

The song was popularized by Moody and Sankey in their evangelistic campaigns.

654. The homeland! the homeland! (Hugh Reginald Haweis)

Presbyterian New Psalms and Hymns, 1901; *The Musical Salvationist*, January, 1917.

Mr. Haweis (1838–1901), the skilled violinist and gifted author who wrote ' Music is not the business of my life, but it remains its sweetest recreation ', was incumbent of St. James's, Marylebone, from 1866 until his death.

' The homeland! ' was written in 1855, and was sung to Charles H. Spurgeon just before his death.

655. There is a happy land (Andrew Young)

Bateman and Gall's *Sacred Song Book*, 1843, which for a number of years was popular in Sunday-schools in Scotland; 1899 S.A. song book.

Andrew Young (1807–89), F.R.S., F.R.G.S., born in Edinburgh, studied arts and theology at the university in that city. From 1830–40 he was headmaster at the Niddry Street School, Edinburgh, during which period the number of scholars increased from eighty to six hundred. In 1840 he became head English master at Madras College in the University of St. Andrews, a post he held for thirteen years. After retirement he became superintendent for more than thirty years of the Greenside Parish Church Sunday-school, Edinburgh, in which city he died.

In 1838, whilst Mr. Young was spending an evening with friends in Rothesay, the lady of the house entertained her visitors by playing the piano. An Indian melody called ' Happy Land ' charmed Mr. Young very much, and he requested that it should be played over several times.

Such a melody, he remarked, would make a capital children's hymn if wedded to appropriate words. All that night the music rang in his ears, and whilst walking in the garden next morning he wrote 'There is a happy land'—words which, the author said, 'were sung daily in my classes at Niddry Street School'. When James Gall visited the school he was so pleased with the words and music that he harmonized the melody and had the song published.

656. There is a land of pure delight (Isaac Watts (3))

Hymns and Spiritual Songs, 1707; Ch.M.H.B.

It is claimed that Watts wrote these words when he was about twenty years of age, at his home in Southampton, inspired by a view over the River Itchen looking toward the Isle of Wight. The intervening waters suggested the final passage of Bunyan's Christian over the dark river.

W. Brocklehurst in *Hymns and How they were Inspired*, 1944, contests the Southampton origin and suggests a place between Hessle and North Ferriby on the banks of the Humber, from where the visitor can see the beautiful uplands of the Lincolnshire coast. Mr. Brocklehurst states that Isaac Watts visited Hull about 1720 and that whilst 'the view along Southampton Water would be quite familiar to him (Watts), it seems to me that the view on the higher road between Hessle and Ferriby across the Humber would be more likely to call forth the feelings, and ultimately the fine expressions, which we find embodied in this lovely hymn'.

657. There's a beautiful land on high (James Nicholson (380))

Bible Class Magazine, 1867; Ch.M.H.B.

One day a poor girl informed her minister that she was going to Florida: 'George is out there; he has taken a fruit farm. . . . He wants me to go out to him at once; he has the home all ready and waiting. I shall be glad to get away from the drudgery in which I have been living since father and mother died. But best of all I shall see George and taste the happiness we have both been waiting for for so long.'

Rev. James Nicholson, when on a visit to England, heard the story and his thoughts went to the hope of every Christian—the joy that was set before him—of home and reunion, of sorrow stilled, pain healed, tears wiped away, of a country in which those we love will never again know the pangs of parting, and wrote this song about Heaven.

658. There's a crown laid up in Glory (Arthur Bovan)

The War Cry, April 15, 1893; *The Musical Salvationist*, 1910; and September, 1914, to a German melody, introduced at the 1914 International Congress by the male voice party of the German Staff Band and with which the words are now associated.

In 1891 Arthur White Bovan, homeless and friendless in London, whither he had come to seek employment, sought the Army's aid in Queen Victoria Street. He was given shelter and work, and eventually was converted in the hostel at Quaker Street. Despite his having lost a limb through an accident in childhood, he was made a Lieutenant in 1896 and spent the seven years of his officership, until his promotion to Glory as an Adjutant, in March, 1903, in the Men's Social Work.

Refined in mind, fertile in imagination and poetic in fancy, many of his verses appeared in our various periodicals.

Colonel Reginald Bovan is a son of the author.

659. There's a land that is fairer than day (S. Fillmore Bennett)

The Signet Ring, published in the U.S.A. in 1868; *Hallelujah Hymn Book*; *Revival Music*; 1878 S.A. song book.

Born in Eden, New York, Mr. Bennett (1836–98), school-teacher and editor, served during the civil war with the Union Army. At the conclusion of his military service he settled in Elkhorn, Wisconsin, where he became the proprietor of a drug store. He died in Illinois.

On one occasion Joseph P. Webster, one of the leading composers of the town, entered Mr. Bennett's office looking depressed. He was asked what was wrong. ' Oh, it will be all right by and by,' was the curt reply. Instantly these words suggested to Bennett's mind the idea of a hymn, and within a few minutes ' In the sweet by-and-by ' was completed. The manuscript was handed to Mr. Webster and his whole aspect changed. Turning to the desk, he commenced to compose the tune, and thus the song was born.

In *James Gilmour of Mongolia*, R. Lovett tells of the saintly missionary, who had lost his wife, parting with his two boys, who were to return to their homeland for their education.

' We were at Mamma's grave yesterday for the first time since September 21st,' wrote Gilmour. ' We sang " There's a land that is fairer than day " in Chinese, and also a Chinese hymn we have with a chorus which says, " We'll soon go and see them in our heavenly home ". The children and I have no reluctance in speaking of Mamma, and we don't think of her as here or buried, but as in a fine place, happy and well.'

660. 'Tis true there's a beautiful city (Anonymous)

Favourite Songs Supplement; 1930 S.A. song book.

661. To leave the world below (William Pearson (73) (verses); Robert Lowry (231) (chorus))

The War Cry, March 6, 1880; 1899 S.A. song book.

The third line of the original chorus from *The Revivalist*, 1868, reads:
We'll journey together to Zion.

662. We have a house above (Charles Wesley (15) (verses); Philip Phillips (210) (chorus))

Wesley's *Funeral Hymns*, 1774; Ch.M.H.B.

The chorus, added because of the tune to which it is now associated, belongs to a song which appeared in Phillips' *Hallowed Songs*, 1873, and which commenced:

> And may I still get there?
> Still reach the heavenly shore?
> The land for ever bright and fair,
> Where sorrows reign no more?

663. We know there's a bright and a glorious land (Margaret Chalmers Wilson)

Originally commenced 'We know there's a bright and glorious home' and published in *Service of Praise*, 1865, edited by the author's husband, the Rev. James Hood Wilson, D.D.; Ch.M.H.B.

Margaret Hood (1825–1902) was born at Dunbar, Scotland, married her cousin, Dr. Wilson, in 1869, and died while on a visit to Gullane, East Lothian.

664. We speak of the realms of the blest (Elizabeth Mills)

Ch.M.H.B.; written a few weeks before the author's death after reading a commentary on a verse of Psalm 119 which said, 'We speak of Heaven, but oh! to be there!'

Elizabeth King (1805–29) was born in Stoke Newington, married Thomas Mills, M.P., and died at Finsbury Place, London.

'You see that I am still in the land of the dying,' wrote Philip Phillips shortly before his death. 'Why I linger so long is to me a problem. The precious Saviour is more to me than I ever expected when I was well. . . .

'The lines that come most often to me are these:

> We speak of the land of the blest . . .
> But what must it be to be there!

Blessed be God! I shall soon know. What a singing time we will have when we get there!'

665. We're bound for the land of the pure and the holy (William Hunter (50))

Written in 1842 and published in the author's *Minstrel of Zion* (1845); Ch.M.H.B.

Referring to some open-air meetings held in the Mile End Road in 1865, at which hundreds had listened with great attention, William Booth wrote: 'Afterwards the company marched past the brilliantly lit gin-palaces—we had an efficient company of singers, and as we passed along this spacious and crowded thoroughfare, singing, "We're bound for the land of the pure and the holy", the people ran from every direction. Drunkards came forth to hear and to see; some in mockery joined our ranks; some laughed and sneered; some were angry; the great majority looked on in wonder.'

The singing of this song by two officers in Consett attracted Commissioner Isaac Unsworth to the Army. He became an officer from that corps in 1879. This was also the first Army song to be used by Commissioner Hanna Ouchterlony at the opening of our work in Sweden, in December, 1882.

666. When all my labours and trials are o'er (Charles H. Gabriel)

1930 S.A. song book.

'The Glory Song', written in 1900, was prompted by the slogan of a good soul known as 'Old Glory Face'. 'The one safety-valve of his pent-up enthusiasm in praise of his Lord', wrote Mr. Gabriel, 'was the single exclamation—"Glory!"' And it was good to hear him shout it—not in a harsh raucous tone of voice, yet distinctly and with a charm of earnestness that carried the conviction of holy reverence to all who heard it. To hear him pray was to see the gates of Heaven open, and to be drawn nearer to God. His prayer invariably ended with "And that will be glory for me!"''

Charles Homer Gabriel was born in a prairie shanty in Iowa, U.S.A., on August 18, 1856, and attended a school house during the winter months when there was no work to do on the farm. 'I never saw a musical instrument', he wrote, 'until I was about nine years old; and to this day I couldn't tell the name of that one, as nothing like it has ever come under my observation since. . . . The next musical instrument I saw was a melodeon of that day and style. I rode ten miles to see and hear it, and no music since then has sounded to me more divine.' Then the family bought a small reed organ which Charles quickly learned to play, and at fourteen he saw his first piano. At sixteen he began teaching singing and music and at seventeen his first song was published. He never received a single music lesson. He organized a village band whilst still in his teens and wrote his own band arrangements.

After travelling as a teacher of singing-schools and as a conductor of musical conventions, and for some time serving in a church in San Francisco, in 1892 he settled in Chicago, where many of his most famous songs were written. He edited thirty-five gospel song books, eight books of Sunday-school songs, besides books for male voices and women's voices, anthems and cantatas, as well as many books of instruction. He died at Berkeley, California, on September 14, 1932.

667. When we gather at last over Jordan (F. A. Blackmer (501))

Commencing—

> When we enter the portals of Glory,
> And the great host of ransomed we see—

the song was included in *Songs of Joy and Gladness* (U.S.A.), where it is stated to have been taken from *Gospel in Song* and copyrighted in 1884; *The Musical Salvationist*, May, 1889; 1899 S.A. song book.

The words are based on ' The number . . . shall be as the sand of the sea ' (Hosea 1: 10).

668. Who are these arrayed in white (Charles Wesley (15))

Hymns on the Lord's Supper, 1745, and based on Revelation 7: 13; Ch.M.H.B.—' What are these . . . '

' There is a tradition ', wrote J. Ernest Rattenbury, ' that this hymn was Charles Wesley's memorial to his father and mother. If it be true its verses gain a new tender significance.'

669. Will you meet me at the fountain (Philip P. Bliss (78))

1878 S.A. song book.

At the Industrial Exhibition at Chicago, in 1874, it was an everyday occurrence for appointments to be made and kept at the Central Fountain. The author, whose mind had long been trained to spiritualize even the everyday happenings of life, caught up the idea and this song was the outcome.

670. Am I a soldier of the Cross (Isaac Watts (3))

Dr. Watts's *Sermons*, 1721–24, intended to accompany a sermon on 1 Corinthians 16: 13; Ch.M.H.B.

In his sermon he had said: ' The man of courage can despise the threatenings of the great and the scoffs of the witty, conscious of his own integrity and truth. He can face the world with all its terrors and travel onwards without fear in the paths of piety. The righteous man is as bold as a lion.' Then he clinched his argument by quoting the words, 'Am I a soldier of the Cross . . . ? '

This was the first song that Sankey sang for Moody.

In 1878 when William Booth, then Superintendent of The Christian Mission, went to Bradford for the station's first anniversary he began to line out this song in an arresting voice: 'Am I a soldier of the Cross . . .?' Then he stopped and remarked, ' This is not a bad hymn. But why didn't it say:

> I am a soldier of the Cross,
> A follower of the Lamb,
> I will not fear to own His cause,
> Or blush to speak His name? '

Thus he continued making these amendments and adding his comments, until John Lawley, one of the 600 converts, who firmly agreed with this straight-out way of declaring things, shouted 'Amen!'

Mr. Booth turned about and, sweeping the interrupter with penetrating eyes, said, 'I hope you'll make as good a fighter as you are a shouter.' The ultimate outcome of this was the future Commissioner's offering himself for officership.

In *The Christian Mission Hymn Book* and the 1878 S.A. song book the following chorus was added:

> Let us never mind the scoffs nor the frowns of the world,
> For we all have the cross to bear;
> It will only make the crown the brighter to shine,
> When we have the crown to wear.

671. Come, join our Army, to battle we go (William Pearson (73))

The Salvationist, February, 1879, under the title, 'Song of The Salvation Army'.

'I followed Colonel and Mrs. Dowdle and fiddle—as Commanding Officer to Bradford, Yorkshire,' wrote William Pearson. 'In seven weeks our processions really blocked the streets. About that time I composed "The Salvation Army is marching along" to the tune "Ring the bell, watchman". The town hall chimes often played the tune, and God would have me make the song. Both song and tune were sung lustily by the mill-hands; greater crowds were drawn. Pullen's Theatre was packed and many souls were saved.

'These extraordinary happenings moved the mayor to send for me. I went to the town hall, was put into the witness box and asked to desist from holding open-air meetings in the streets. If not I should be summonsed. I went out the same night and every night, but the summons did not come, and the work rolled on gloriously.'

672. Forward! be our watchword (Henry Alford (103))

Written for the tenth festival of the parochial choirs of the Canterbury Diocesan Union on June 6, 1871, and based on Exodus 14: 15. *The Musical Salvationist*, February, 1920.

In response to Rev. J. G. Wood's request that Dean Alford should write a processional hymn for the occasion, a 'very admirable hymn was sent with the Dean's compliments'. It did not quite meet the case so Mr. Wood wrote to the Dean pointing out that the hymn 'while excellent in its way, was not at all adapted to be sung upon the march. Would he kindly go into his Cathedral, walk slowly along the course which the procession would take, and compose another hymn as he did so?'

The Dean seems to have taken the suggestion in good part for later another hymn was received—' Forward! be our watchword '.

Says the son of Mr. Wood in his biography: ' The manuscript reached my father with a humorous little note to the effect that the Dean had written the hymn and put it into its hat and boots; and that my father might add the coat and trousers himself. On looking at the music, he found, accordingly, that only the treble and bass of the music had been supplied by the composer.'

673. Go, labour on, spend and be spent (Horatius Bonar (4))

Songs for the Wilderness, 1843; 1930 S.A. song book.

This was the first of the author's songs not written expressly for the young. It was intended to encourage the faithful workers in the mission for which he was responsible at Leith, Scotland, and dates from 1836, the year before he left for Kelso.

674. God's trumpet is sounding: To arms! is the call (Frederick Booth-Tucker (365) (verses); Fanny Crosby (17) (chorus))

The War Cry, April 22, 1893; *The Musical Salvationist*, September, 1895; 1899 S.A. song book.

675. Hark, how the watchmen cry (Charles Wesley (15) (verses))

One of the nineteen ' Hymns for the Watchnight' published in *Hymns and Sacred Poems*, 1749; 1899 S.A. song book. The original contained eight eight-line verses.

676. I have read of men of faith (Mark Sanders (Blind Mark))

Favourite Songs Supplement. The author's first song to be published; written in 1886 to an American tune, ' Shouting the Battle-cry of Freedom ', which had been suggested by Lieut.-Colonel Slater; 1899 S.A. song book.

Mark Sanders, born on April 28, 1862, son of poor parents, became blind when three days old. At eleven years of age he was sent to a blind school, but rebelled against the confinement and, in conjunction with his companion, devised a plan of escape. Fortunately, the plan was frustrated and the precocious lad continued his education with no little success, he himself becoming a teacher of others.

Mark's love of music was apparent whilst still at school. He made astonishing progress as a pianist, and developed into a skilful player on various instruments as well as becoming an acceptable singer.

His school-days ended in 1881, and later in the year he attended Salvation Army meetings and became converted. By means of the Braille system he read the Scriptures fluently. In 1882 'Blind Mark', as he became known, became an Army 'special', working first in Devon and Cornwall. In 1887 he went to Jamaica and assisted in pioneering Army work in the West Indies.

Both at home and abroad his music and his original way of presenting his message gained him large and appreciative audiences until a considerable time after his marriage in 1897. The latter part of his life was spent in Salt Lake City, U.S.A., where he remained a Salvationist until his promotion to Glory on August 21, 1943. His gravestone bears the inscription, 'Singer-Composer, Pioneer Missionary. Lovingly remembered by West Indian Salvationists.' The stone was donated by the comrades of the Central America and West Indies Territory.

677. In the Army of Jesus we've taken our stand (Fred W. Fry (248))

The Musical Salvationist, July, 1887; 1899 S.A. song book. The final verse has been recast for the present song book.

678. March to the battlefield (Philip P. Bliss (78))

The Junior Hymnal, 1907, edited by Joseph Brown Morgan and Carey Bonner and issued under the auspices of the Christian Endeavour Council. In this setting an extra line appeared in each verse between our first and second lines, also a chorus. 1930 S.A. song book.

679. O soldier, awake, for the strife is at hand (Fanny Crosby (17))

First appearance, probably in *The American Sacred Songster*, by Philip Phillips of New York; *Hallelujah Hymn Book*; *Revival Music*; 1878 S.A. song book; where the first line began, 'O Christian, awake ...'.

680. Onward, Christian soldiers (Sabine Baring-Gould)

Church Times, and later in *The Hymnary* in 1872; *The Musical Salvationist*, International Congress Number, 1904, where the words began:

> On, salvation soldiers,
> Marching on to war.

The Rev. Baring-Gould (1834–1924), who was born at Exeter, spent a number of his early years in Germany and France, and was educated at Clare College, Cambridge.

Ordained in 1861, he held several livings in the Church of England, including Horbury, near Wakefield, Dalton, near Thirsk, and East Mersea, near Colchester. While curate at Horbury, in 1865, he was asked to arrange for the singing for the annual Whit-Monday procession of the Sunday-school scholars of the mission at Horbury Bridge. In haste he wrote ' Onward, Christian soldiers ', and was as surprised as anyone at its subsequent popularity. It was originally sung to ' St. Albans ', a slow melody taken from Haydn's ' Symphony in D ', but in 1871 this tune was superseded by ' St. Gertrude ' by Sir Arthur Sullivan.

In 1881, ' having in the meanwhile succeeded his father in the estate of Lew Trenchard, Devon, he exercised his privilege as squire and patron by presenting himself to the living there as rector '.

A prolific writer, there came from his pen books on travel, history, antiquarian subjects, theology, novels, and a long series of books on the lives of the saints. He also published a collection of country folksongs. It is said that at one time he had more books attached to his name in the British Museum than any other writer of his time.

681. Onward! upward! Christian soldier (Fanny Crosby (17) (verses); Robert Johnson (423) (chorus))

Sankey's *Sacred Songs and Solos*. The signature, ' T. W. V., Notting Hill', when the song appeared in *The War Cry*, August 14, 1880, is obviously a mistake. 1930 S.A. song book.

682. Rescue the perishing, care for the dying (Fanny Crosby (17))

Songs of Devotion, 1870; *Revival Music*; 1878 S.A. song book.

Miss Crosby, after she had returned from a visit to a mission in one of the worst districts in New York, where she had heard about the needs of the lost and perishing, was very much moved by the thought of the suffering and misery in such places and, before she retired to rest, wrote what has been described as a song ' that has become a battle-cry for the great army of Christian workers throughout the world '. Mr. Doane, who had already suggested the subject, wrote the music.

683. Saviour and Lord, we pray to Thee (— Mundell (548))

1899 S.A. song book.

684. Soldier, rouse thee! War is raging (*attributed to* George Scott Railton (292))

The authorship of the song has not been definitely established but Colonel Robert Sandall, in *The History of The Salvation Army*, Vol. 1, page 149, recorded: ' Railton also gave to the Movement some of its most stirring war songs. One of the earliest and best known of these was either written or adapted by him—which it was not clear. It was printed, with music, in the February, 1874, issue of *The Christian Mission Magazine*, headed "A Christian War Song", without any indication as to authorship. It was given prominence in all editions of *Heathen England* as "Our War Song"! . . . Whether written by Railton or not, the spirit of the composition was entirely in keeping with his own; to him the battle for souls was *real* warfare.'

685.   Soldiers fighting round the Cross (Anonymous)

Arranged from a setting in the *Primitive Methodist Hymn Book*, 1860; Ch.M.H.B.

686.   Soldiers of Christ, arise (Charles Wesley (15) (verses))

Hymns and Sacred Poems, 1749; Ch.M.H.B.; part of a sixteen-verse poem, paraphrase of Ephesians 6: 11–18.

' Charles Wesley, like his brother, met with much opposition and persecution.   More than once he was in danger of losing his life; savage bulls were turned loose into his meetings; his clothing was torn from him and many of his converts were seized by the press-gang.   In this great hymn we seem to hear the shout of victory above the tumult.'

687.   Soldiers of our God, arise! (Robert Johnson (423))

Salvation Music (Scotland), 1884; 1899 S.A. song book.

' Written to the melody of the song "Here's to good old whisky, drink it down",' wrote Lieut.- Colonel Salter, ' this is one of the most vigorous and spirited of Army war songs.   Again and again has it roused a meeting to the glow of enthusiasm.   A band in full strength, putting forth its biggest tone, never seems out of place in accompanying the singing of such war-like strains.   Yet how narrowly the song escaped being lost for ever.   I was told by Johnson himself that he sent the song to *The War Cry*—the only medium he had for getting the song into general use—three times before it was accepted.   For what reasons was it turned down?   Perhaps the tune was hardly known sufficiently; perhaps its title was too startling; perhaps in the weekly pile of some 200 songs sent to the paper in those days, it was overlooked, or rather passed into the waste-paper basket unread owing to the pressure of work in the editorial office.   Johnson had a strong faith in his song, however, so he sent up copy after copy, and was at last rewarded by seeing his words published in the official organ.'

688.   Soldiers of the Cross, arise (William Walsham How (223))

Morrell and How's *Psalms and Hymns*, 1864; *Hymns Ancient and Modern*; 1930 S.A. song book.

689. Sound the battle cry! (William Fisk Sherwin)

Bright Jewels, 1869; *Hallelujah Hymn Book*; *Revival Music*; 1899 S.A. song book.

An American Baptist, born at Buckland, Mass., U.S.A., Mr. Sherwin (1826-88) studied under Lowell Mason and became a teacher of vocal music and the musical director of the famed Chautauqua assemblies. He wrote many gospel songs, and was associated with Robert Lowry and others in preparing *Bright Jewels* and other popular Sunday-school hymn books. He died in Boston, Mass.

Recalling the first Army march through Petrograd (now Leningrad), Russia, in 1917, Commissioner Karl Larsson reported: 'In order to make the Sunday afternoon meeting well known our first march was arranged. With flags flying and bearing a large announcement of the meetings, we marched to a place in Nevsky Prospekt. Here other comrades joined us, and we set off to the accompaniment of a concertina, everybody singing with all their hearts—

> Rouse, then, soldiers, rally round the banner! . . .
> Christ is Captain of the mighty throng—

which caused great interest among the people who were promenading in the sunshine. Hundreds followed us and the crowd grew as we continued. The hall was filled, 450 being present.'

This was also the opening song for the world-wide B.B.C. broadcast from the Royal Albert Hall, London, when General Albert Orsborn led the concluding meeting of the young people's councils at which 6,000 young people were present, including 1,300 delegates to the International Salvationist Youth Congress on Sunday, August 20, 1950.

690. Stand up, stand up for Jesus (George Duffield)

Supplement to the *Church Psalmist*, Dr. Beman's book, prepared by the Presbyterian Publication Committee, Philadelphia, in 1859; *Revival Music*; 1899 S.A. song book.

Dr. George Duffield (1818-88) was a United States Presbyterian minister, serving in Brooklyn, Philadelphia and the West. He caught the inspiration for his song from 'Tell them to stand up for Jesus'— the dying message of Rev. Dudley A. Tyng to the noonday prayer meeting of the Young Men's Christian Association during the revival of 1858, usually known as 'The work of God in Philadelphia'. The Sunday before his death he preached to 5,000 men and 'at least one thousand, it is believed, were slain of the Lord'.

'The following Wednesday,' wrote Duffield, 'leaving his study for a moment, Tyng went to the barn floor, where a mule was at work on a horse-power machine, shelling corn. Patting him on the neck, the sleeve of his silk study gown caught in the cogs of the wheel, and his arm was torn out by the roots! His death occurred in a few hours.'

The following Sunday Dr. Duffield preached from Ephesians 6 : 14 and this song was written as the concluding exhortation. The Sunday-school superintendent gave printed copies of the verses to the children.

691. The Son of God goes forth to war (Reginald Heber (131))

Hymns, Written and Adapted to the Weekly Church Service of the Year, 1827; *The Musical Salvationist*, August, 1912. Specially written for St. Stephen's Day, hence the reference in verse 2 to 'the martyr'.

692. To the front! the cry is ringing (Herbert H. Booth (91))

The Musical Salvationist, December, 1887; 1899 S.A. song book.

When very near the end and when racked with pain, the Army Mother turned to the Founder and asked for a song:

> Victory for me,
> Through the Blood of Christ, my Saviour

was chosen. In the midst of the refrain she exclaimed triumphantly: 'I shall have the victory! I shall have the victory!'

693. To the war! to the war! loud and long sounds the cry (M. Stark)

The War Cry, January 31, 1880; 1899 S.A. song book. The tune with which it is associated is 'Toiling on', by Dr. W. H. Doane of the U.S.A.

The author was a soldier of the 112th Corps, Glasgow, now known as Bridgeton.

694. Wanted, hearts baptized with fire (John Lawley (56))

All the World, January, 1892; 1899 S.A. song book.

Two accounts of the origin of these words have been given.

From *The Bandsman and Songster*: 'The Founder's addresses often suggested themes for Lawley's songs. For instance, the General had been stirring up his congregation on the subject of heart religion: "Oh, for hearts that burn with love to God! Oh, for hearts that ache for the sins of the people!" The words were dropped as seeds to Lawley's heart and mind, and one night in his quarters at Clapton God gave him the song that has inspired thousands, "Wanted, hearts baptized with fire". He wrote down the lines as they came but, strange to tell, he was not sure of their merit until he had asked Brigadier Fred Cox's opinion on them.'

Brigadier Pimm Smith, writing in *The Officer's Review*, quoted Commissioner Lawley as saying: 'While musing one day I said to myself, " Dear me, how scarce kind, loving, tender, compassionate hearts are! Here is the poor, dying, hungry, sinning, sorrowful world, away from God, feeding upon husks, and swiftly and surely bound for a dark, deep hell of despair. Who cares? When Jesus saw the multitudes He was moved with compassion, and why are not we?" The answer that echoed through my soul was—lack of hearts! Hence the song, " Wanted, hearts to love the masses ".'

695. We are marching o'er the regions (Herbert H. Booth (91) (verse I and chorus); Richard Slater (105) (verses 2 and 3))

The Musical Salvationist, June, 1887; 1899 S.A. song book.

As frequently happened with other contributors to *The Musical Salvationist* Herbert Booth was unable to proceed to the completion of his song, and Lieut.-Colonel Slater, the editor, wrote the remaining verses.

696. Who is on the Lord's side? (Frances Ridley Havergal (256))

Home Missions, October 13, 1877; the author's *Loyal Responses* the following year; *The Musical Salvationist*, December, 1921; 1930 S.A. song book; written at Leamington and based on 1 Chronicles 12: 18.

697. Who'll fight for the Lord everywhere (George Scott Railton (292))

The song appeared on the special song sheet used at the Salvation Army exhibition staged at the Agricultural Hall, London, in 1896; 1899 S.A. song book; some lines have been altered for this edition.

698. Above the world-wide battlefield through long and warring years (Will. J. Brand (52))

The Musical Salvationist, December, 1948; written for the flag ceremony at the close of the King's Messengers Session (1948) of the International Training College.

699. Amen for the flag to the Army so dear (William Pearson (73))

Salvation Music, Vol. 2, and set to the old English ballad tune, ' The Union Jack of Old England '; 1899 S.A. song book.

700. Army flag! Thy threefold glory (Albert Orsborn (42))

The Musical Salvationist, June, 1932; inspired by the International Congress of 1914.

701. Emblem of a thousand battles (Doris N. Rendell)

Special Songs for Young People's Anniversaries and Festal Occasions, 1940.

Lieut.-Colonel Rendell, who was born in Knottingley, Yorks, and whose officer father accompanied William Booth on many of his journeys in Britain, remembers as a child being taken on the Founder's knee and hearing him say as he kissed her: 'Hurry and grow up, I want *you* to be one of my officers.'

The Colonel was converted after attending a juniors' meeting at Shepherd's Bush in which a child about her own age had given her testimony. During the night the Colonel awakened her mother with the request, 'I want to be saved too!' So mother and daughter knelt together.

From a Government office in Westminster the Colonel entered The International Training Garrison, Clapton, in 1921, before taking appointments in corps, divisional, International Headquarters and social work.

Some seventy songs, which began during a period of illness, have been published in *The Musical Salvationist* and other Army papers.

The Colonel was a member of the Song Book Revision Council which prepared the material for the present song book.

702. 'Neath our standard, we're engaging (Gustavus Grozinsky)

The Musical Salvationist, February, 1893; 1899 S.A. song book.

Lieutenant Grozinsky was born in Moscow, probably about 1862. His father was an advanced politician and, in the days of Czarist Russia, became a marked man. Eventually he was arrested and sentenced to death, a punishment which was commuted to life banishment in Siberia. Some months later he escaped, managed to communicate with his wife and two children, and settled with them in Cronstadt. After a time he moved to England and lived near the Walworth Road, in South London, where, attracted by the music in an open-air meeting, his son Gustavus knelt at the Mercy Seat at the Camberwell Corps.

His first appointment as an officer was to Scotland to assist Captain (later Lieut.-Colonel) Wm. Starling, who had the oversight of the 'Island Section', which included Wick and Thurso on the mainland and the Orkneys and Shetlands, with his quarters at Thurso. After several other appointments in Britain, Gustavus assisted Commissioner Railton in establishing Army work in Germany.

Later he migrated to Canada and became a soldier of the Edmonton Citadel Corps and was promoted to Glory from an Army eventide home early in 1937.

During the winter at Thurso, Grozinsky, with his Captain, was 'snowed in' for some days, with no outside communication and little food and firing. He had a theory that it would be better to go to bed and stay there for the time being:

1. Bed was the warmest place and would thus save fuel.
2. You did not get quite so hungry in bed, so it would save food.
3. There would be less work to do in bed.
4. He could compose better in bed than when moving about.

Thus the Lieutenant went to bed. Downstairs the Captain found things depressing and became so discouraged that he wrote out his resignation, determined that when the snow cleared he would find a more congenial mode of living. Suddenly there appeared in the kitchen doorway the Lieutenant who, to the accompaniment of his stringed instrument, commenced to sing his latest song: 'I'll be true! I'll be true!' The Captain destroyed his letter of resignation and remained true to his calling until his promotion to Glory in 1952.

703. They bid me choose an easier path (Frederick Booth-Tucker (365))

1899 S.A. song book; the author's *One hundred Favourite Songs of The Salvation Army*, New York, 1899; set to the Scottish melody 'We'd better bide a wee', and thought to have been written at the time Ballington Booth and his wife seceded from the Army.

704. Unfurl the Army banner (William D. Pennick (413))

1930 S.A. song book.
Written in Ceylon during the difficult days of the First World War when the author was very conscious of the Spirit of Christ binding together nationals of all countries under the Army flag. 'Truly,' he wrote, ' His banner over us as a people was love!'

705. We meet the foes of all mankind (T. C. Marshall (281))

The Musical Salvationist, December, 1887; 1899 S.A. song book.
This was one of the earliest songs by the author, who wrote: 'Although I don't think I was the first song-writer to use the expression "yellow, red and blue" and "Blood and Fire" in songs, I think I was the first to emphasize them and to make them the basis of songs and choruses.'

706. We'll shout aloud throughout the land (James C. Bateman (177) (verses); W. T. Giffe (314) (chorus))

Salvation Music, Vol. 2; 1930 S.A. song book.
Bandmaster Arthur Frost, writing in *The Musician*, said: 'When the Founder presented the colours to the Icehouse Corps, in the Corn Exchange, Hull, the Commanding Officer at that time was Captain

Isaac Unsworth. Jim Bateman was a soldier, and William Booth was so taken up with him that six weeks afterwards he made him an officer. It was then that he wrote and sang " We'll shout aloud throughout the land ".'

707. Who are these with colours waving (Albert E. Webber)

Written at Bridport and first published in *The War Cry*, July 9, 1887; 1930 S.A. song book.

Arthur Copping, writing in *The Bandsman and Songster* in August, 1930, said: 'Albert Edward Webber is a modest, able, busy, happy man, who lives in close daily grateful communion with God. The Pokesdown Corps knows him as an Honorary Bandmaster and its acting Songster Leader. His neighbours in Boscombe know him as the head of a little firm of house decorators. The entomological world knows him as a lifelong student of British lepidoptera, and as a painstaking collector of butterflies. The Salvation Army world knows him as a writer of beautiful songs, and as a writer endowed with the double gift for melody and words.'

The author was born at Marley, just outside Plymouth, and later became the Bandmaster at Bridport, then at Boscombe. He commenced song-writing about 1887 and is credited with more than 600 songs, probably the most popular of which is ' Can you wonder why it is I love Him so? ' He also supplied some 150 tunes for his various songs. In 1941 he was promoted to Glory.

708. Come, let us use the grace divine (Charles Wesley (15))

Short Hymns on Select Passages of Scripture, 1762, and based on Jeremiah 50: 5; Ch.M.H.B.

The Methodists have for many years made this their consecration hymn and used it as such in the Methodist Covenant Service held at the beginning of each year.

709. I would be Thy holy temple (Brindley Boon)

Written to be sung by the ' Standard Bearers ' cadets during their Dedication Service at the Royal Albert Hall on May 12, 1950, the words appearing in the souvenir programme issued for the Commissioning of the cadets; *The Musician*, May 13, 1950; *The Musical Salvationist*, November, 1950.

The son and grandson of Salvationists, Brindley Boon was born at Willesden Green. He commenced his music studies at six years of age and, although he had an Army background, his early days were spent with the Methodists. At the age of fifteen he was organist of the Cricklewood Methodist Sunday-school. About this time he was invited to give an item at the local Army corps, and shortly afterward he decided to become a Salvationist. He became Songster Leader at the Childs Hill Corps when seventeen and a half years of age.

A request from the Singing Company Leader of the same corps for a song suitable for singing at the forthcoming young people's anniversary resulted in the author's first contribution to *The Musical Salvationist* (October, 1933). The title of the song, 'A Song of Happiness', was significant in view of the fact that the author and the Singing Company Leader were later united in marriage.

Brindley Boon later became the Songster Leader at Chalk Farm; and was employed on the headquarters of the Men's Social Work, where he was a member of the band and leader of the vocal party.

During the Second World War he served in the Royal Air Force and while stationed at Bournemouth as a sergeant assumed temporary leadership of Boscombe Band and Songsters.

He became widely known on the British Field as a pianist, elocutionist and an acceptable speaker. In 1947 he joined the staff of *The Musician* and two years later entered the ' Standard Bearers ' Session at the International Training College.

Following training he was appointed to Sandwich, but later returned to the Editorial Department on I.H.Q., where, in 1955, he became editor of *The Musician*. In 1961 he became Assistant Editor of *The War Cry* in Toronto, Canada. In 1966 he became National Secretary for Bands and Songster Brigades in the British Territory.

Amongst his numerous contributions to *The Musical Salvationist* are ' New Jerusalem ', which was recorded by the Harlesden Songster Brigade, and ' Beautiful Zion '.

Originally ' I would be Thy holy temple ' was written in two eight-line verses with the following chorus:

> I dedicate myself to Thee,
> O Master who hast chosen me;
> My every selfish aim denying
> I give my all, on Thee relying;
> Take Thou my life and use me at Thy will.
> In deep submission I dedicate myself to Thee.

710.   In this hour of dedication (Doris N. Rendell (701))

Written for the Dedication Service held in connection with the Commissioning of cadets of the ' Challengers ' Session at the Royal Albert Hall in 1946.

711.   Jesus, Thou hast won us (Will. J. Brand (52))

Specially written for this song book.

712.   Lord of life and love and power (Doris N. Rendell (701))

The Musical Salvationist, May, 1950; written for a Dedication Service of cadets at the Royal Albert Hall.

713. Redeemed from the bondage of Satan (Leslie Taylor-Hunt (359))

1930 S.A. song book.

The author writes: 'This song was written at the request of General Bramwell Booth and was first used by him at the swearing-in of 500 new soldiers—captures of the Salvation Siege which he conducted in the Ring, Blackfriars, on January 18, 1928. The General appeared in the "ring"—his fists raised in true sparring fashion—as he illustrated to the enthusiastic crowd how to "hit the devil and hit him hard".'

714. When you find the cross is heavy (George Trevillian)

The War Cry, October 21, 1893; *The Musical Salvationist*, December, 1893, specially for the 'swearing-in of recruits'; 1930 S.A. song book. The author was Band Sergeant of the Ealing Corps, London.

715. Hast thou just begun to pray? (Anonymous)

The authorship has been ascribed to Dr. John Ryland but without confirmation; Ch.M.H.B.

716. Help, Lord, to whom for help I fly (Charles Wesley (15))

Hymns and Sacred Poems, 1749; Ch.M.H.B.

717. Ho, my comrades, see the signal (Philip P. Bliss (78))

The Charm, 1871; *Hallelujah Hymn Book*; *Revival Music*; 1878 S.A. song book.

At a moment when despair had taken hold of a party of General Sharman's men who, while defending supplies in October, 1864, during the American War of Emancipation, had been driven into a small fort upon the crest of the hill, one of the officers caught sight of a white signal flag far across the valley, twenty miles away. The signal was acknowledged and soon the message was waved across from mountain to mountain: 'Hold the fort, I'm coming—W. T. Sharman.' Although more than half the men in the fort were killed the rest held out for three hours, until the advance guard of Sharman's army came up and the six thousand men under General French were obliged to retreat.

At a Sunday-school meeting in Rockford, Illinois, in May, 1870, Major Whittle related this story in the presence of Philip Bliss, who was immediately inspired to write this song. The next day the two men held a meeting in the Y.M.C.A. rooms in Chicago. Mr. Bliss wrote the chorus on the blackboard, sang the verses for the first time in public, and invited the audience to join him each time with the refrain.

It has been said that 'no incident of the war illustrates more thrillingly the inspiration imparted by the knowledge of the presence of our Christian Commander; that He is aware of our position and that, doing our utmost He will supplement our weaknesses by speedy reinforcements. The message of Sharman to the soldiers of Altoona thus becomes the message of the "Great Commander of our Salvation" who signals to all who fight life's battle—"Hold the fort!"''

Despite the author's wish expressed not long before his death that he hoped he would not be known to posterity only as the author of this song, for he believed he had written many better songs, on his monument at Rome, Pennsylvania, he is described as the author of 'Hold the Fort'.

718. In the fight, say, does your heart grow weary? (Richard Slater (105))

The Musical Salvationist, December, 1886; 1899 S.A. song book.

'If ever Richard Slater experienced the sensation of fear I never saw it,' wrote Colonel Fred Hawkes. 'He was fearless in attacking wrong and in defending the truth. The warrior-spirit of the man who wrote it is well expressed in the words of the song, "Never mind, go on!"''

719. I've found the secret of success (Ruth Tracy (270))

1930 S.A. song book.

'This song was one of several written at the request of Captain Miriam Booth who, while still a soldier at High Barnet, was beginning to sing solos in her father's—General Bramwell Booth's—meetings,' wrote Brigadier Tracy. 'I think she sang it first at the Clapton Temple in one of his earliest councils for young people. The tune was of the Captain's selection, and the song had to be of a character to help a young warrior. The sentiments are an echo of a song by General Evangeline Booth which we sang much in our cadet days under her leadership: "When darkest storms your path surround." The General said, "Go on!" I say, in effect, "Hold on!" I had in mind, too, the words I often heard the Founder utter to his officers: "Hold on in the dark, in the very face of death. Have courage. Hold on!"

'Just prior to writing the song I had been overwhelmed by the unhappiness of someone loved and trusted by me who had turned back.'

720. Jesus, my King, to Thee I bow (Charles Wesley (15))

Hymns and Sacred Poems, 1742; *The Musical Salvationist*, September. 1916; 1930 S.A. song book.

721. Lord, see me kneeling at Thy feet (Lucy Booth-Hellberg (629))

All the World, September, 1892; 1899 S.A. song book. Its original title was ' Be Thou my Guiding Star ' and the last two lines of the chorus were:

> While sailing out on life's rough sea,
> Be Thou my Guiding Star.

' On April 23, 1892, her [Lucy Booth's] engagement to a Bombay officer [Colonel John Lampard] was announced. He and she were then on furlough in England. The engagement was brief. On the day on which it was published in *The War Cry*, Lampard wrote the General in great distress, announcing that he felt himself unfit to be the husband of so excellent and noble a lady. The letter . . . was published in the issue of *The War Cry* which followed that in which the announcement of the engagement had been made and was accompanied by an official statement. . . . " Colonel Lucy is, we regret to say, very ill. The shock to her system caused by the mysterious and sudden termination of what seemed to her to be a path of true happiness . . . has utterly prostrated her. Since Friday, she has remained in a state of serious collapse." ' (*God's Soldier* by St. John Ervine, pp. 750–1).

Miss Lucy gradually recovered and a later issue of *The War Cry* carried a letter from her to the many comrades who had upheld her by their prayers. This experience was the background of the song.

722. Must Jesus bear the Cross alone (Thomas Shepherd and George Nelson Allen)

The Oberlin Social and Sabbath School Hymn Book, U.S.A., 1844; The American *Plymouth Collection*, 1855, compiled by the Rev. Henry Ward Beecher; 1859 *Congregational Hymn Book* in Britain; Ch.M.H.B. The first verse originally began:

> Must Simon bear Thy Cross alone
> And other saints go free ?

Thomas Shepherd (1665–1739), son of a minister, took Holy Orders himself and officiated at St. Neots, Huntingdonshire, whence he removed to a living in Buckinghamshire. He later seceded from the Church of England and in 1694 became pastor of a Congregational Church at Castle Hill, Northampton. Leaving there in 1698 he ultimately accepted a Church in Bocking, Essex, where he carried on a successful ministry until his death.

George Nelson Allen was born in Mansfield, Mass., U.S.A., in September, 1812, and lived in Oberlin, where he compiled the hymn book in which this song appears and where he was a professor of music. He died in Cincinnati, Ohio, in December, 1877.

Commissioner Samuel Hurren once conducted a Sunday night meeting at the Penge Corps when during the singing of this song eighty-five persons came forward to dedicate themselves to God, several of whom became officers in the Army.

723. My soul, be on thy guard! (George Heath)

Hymns and Poetic Essays Sacred to the Public and Private Worship of the Deity, 1781; 1930 S.A. song book.

The author was the pastor of a Presbyterian Church at Honiton in 1770, and later became a Unitarian minister. He died in 1822.

724. O almighty God of love (Charles Wesley (15))

Slightly altered from *Hymns and Sacred Poems*, 1742; 1930 S.A. song book.

725. O Lord, how often should we be (Albert Orsborn (42))

1930 S.A. song book.

' This song came as the result of a spiritual crisis when I was " sick and wounded " in the old Gore Road (Hackney) Home of Rest,' writes the General. ' It is a heart-cry, written, I confess with tears, at my bedside, when in prayer.'

726. Oft have I heard Thy tender voice (Bramwell Booth (280))

The Musical Salvationist, July, 1889.

' One of my choice memories,' wrote Colonel Edward Joy, 'is having General Bramwell Booth tell me the story of how one night in his younger days he paid an organ-grinder a shilling so that he might get hold correctly of the tune.' This tune, ' It was my first cigar, my boys ', became the melody for ' I bring my all to Thee, dear Lord '.

Although always elsewhere ascribed to General Bramwell Booth, in *The Consul* this song is stated to have been written by the Founder's daughter, Emma Booth-Tucker: 'When travelling on the Continent she met one of our officers. Knowing that he was familiar with the popular tunes of the day, she asked him if he could recommend to her a good one, with some lilt in it, that would be suitable for her meetings. He was a skilful guitarist, with a charming voice, and two of the tunes he gave her inspired her at once to write some words. . . . One of them was to the tune, "It was my last cigar, my boys . . . " '

727. Oft in danger, oft in woe (Henry Kirke White and Frances Fuller-Maitland)

Hymns partly Collected; Ch.M.H.B., where the first line is, ' Oft in sorrow and in woe '.

Mr. White, the son of a butcher, was born in 1785 in Nottingham. After commencing to learn the hosiery business and entering the legal profession, at about the age of seventeen he felt a call to the ministry, and in 1804 entered St. John's College, Cambridge.

Of delicate constitution and frail body, he found excessive study too big a strain and died at Cambridge in October, 1806, after a very brief but distinguished career which inspired Southey, Lord Byron, Josiah Conder and other eminent poets to write commemorative lines.

During his mathematical examination in June, 1806, having completed all the problems early and finding he had to remain in the room for the whole of the time allowed, Kirke White beguiled the time away by scribbling on the back of his examination paper the first ten lines of this song, though the first line was written, ' Much in sorrow, oft in woe '. The paper was put away and the hymn left incomplete until 1812 when Dr. William Bengo Collyer published his *Hymns partly Collected*. In this compilation he included ' Much in sorrow ', to which he had added six now forgotten lines of his own.

In 1827 Mrs. Bertha Fuller-Maitland compiled and published her *Hymns for Private Devotion, Selected and Original*. In this connection she showed Kirke White's fragmentary poem to her daughter Frances Sara (then fourteen years of age and later to marry John Coloquhon), saying that it was a pity that it was incomplete. The daughter thereupon took the poem to her room and presently returned with a complete hymn which duly appeared in her mother's book. Five years later E. Bickersteth included the song in his *Christian Psalmody* where the first line was altered to ' Oft in danger, oft in woe '.

728. Oft our trust has known betrayal (Richard Slater (105) (verses); A. B. Simpson (chorus))

The Musical Salvationist, October, 1896.

Both the *Keswick Hymn Book* and *Songs of Redemption* use the chorus with a different set of verses. The ' Rev. A. B. Simpson, Auxiliary ' contributed a poem to *The War Cry* of January 9, 1897.

729. Peace, doubting heart! my God's I am (Charles Wesley (15))

Hymns and Sacred Poems, 1739. Of the original, verses 1, 4, 6 and 7 were in the Ch.M.H.B. and 1878 S.A. song book (No. 421); verses 1, 2 and 3 were in the 1899 S.A. song book; verses 4, 6 and 7 were in the 1930 S.A. song book (No. 775). The present selection of verses is as for 1899.

730. Precious promise God hath given (Nathaniel Niles)

The Episcopalian, 1874; 1899 S.A. song book.

Born at South Kingston, Rhode Island, U.S.A., in 1835, Mr. Niles, a lawyer of Morriston, New Jersey, wrote these words while travelling on a street car on his way to business. They were jotted down on the margin of his morning newspaper.

731. Sometimes I'm tried with toil and care (Herbert H. Booth (91))

Christmas Number of *Favourite Songs of the Singing, Praying and Speaking Brigade*, 1885; 1899 S.A. song book.

732. Strive, when thou art called of God (Johann J. Winckler (477); *translated by* Catherine Winkworth (7))

The original ' *Ringe recht, wenn Gottes Gnade* ' appeared in *Freylinghausen*, 1714; written on the three favourite Scripture passages of Ursula Maria Zorn of Berlin, and first published at the end of her funeral sermon. The translation appeared in *Lyra Germanica* in 1855; 1930 S.A. song book.

733. Surrounded by a host of foes (Charles Wesley (15))

Hymns and Sacred Poems, 1749; Ch.M.H.B.; based on 1 John 5: 4.

J. Ernest Rattenbury, in *Evangelical Doctrines of Charles Wesley's Hymns*, writes:

' Charles was ever a fighter. Puritan as he was in conduct, in spirit he was a Cavalier. The true man is never better revealed than in his militant hymns; never was he happier than in his great campaigning days, when he marched along, the Captain of soldiers of Christ, who sang marching and fighting songs.'

734. When peace like a river attendeth my way (Horatio G. Spafford)

1899 S.A. song book.

Mr. Spafford (1829–88) was a lawyer of New York State who, after moving to Chicago, lost a great deal of his wealth in the great fire.

In 1874 a large French steamer, *Ville de Havre*, collided in mid-ocean with a sailing vessel and sank within half an hour. On board was Mrs. Spafford with her four children. On being told that the vessel was foundering, she prayed that they might be saved or, if that were not in accordance with God's will, that they might be made ready to die. The children were lost, but Mrs. Spafford was rescued. Ten days later she landed at Cardiff, from where she cabled her husband, a lawyer in Chicago, ' Saved alone '. Two years later Mr. Spafford wrote this song in commemoration of the death of his children.

Wrote Mr. Moody: ' While living in Chicago, Mr. and Mrs.

Spafford became much interested in the Second Coming of Christ, and decided to go to Jerusalem with his wife and one remaining daughter, and there await the coming of the Lord. Mr. Spafford died not long afterwards.' Mrs. Spafford stayed on near Jerusalem, the head of a society of like-minded people.

735. When you feel weakest, dangers surround (Lucy Booth-Hellberg (629))

The Musical Salvationist, January, 1889, where the words were attributed to Commissioner Mildred Duff.

Commissioner Lucy Booth-Hellberg wrote: ' This was the first of the many songs I composed. I was, I think, about seventeen or eighteen years of age, and sick at the time, my chest causing my darling mother some anxiety. The doctor had called at our old home, " Rookwood ", and whilst my mother was speaking to him, I went to the piano and played the tune.

' Later, Commissioner Duff helped me with the rhyming of the words, but the thought contained in them was quite my own, and sprung from the incident I have mentioned. . . . Soon after it was composed the words, " Keep on believing ", hung on the walls of nearly every slum quarters in London.'

A missionary officer home from China recalled a day when he was surrounded by difficulties political and administrative; and he was beginning to ask himself whether he would do better to resign. He turned on the radio, not with the intention of listening to any set programme, but to take his mind off his immediate problems. He turned the knobs around and as he did so there came over the air the second verse of this song. A record was being used in a programme in some other part of the world, but it came as a message from God and as a challenge to his own soul, with the result that his spiritual battle was won.

736. Will you quit the field? Will you ever yield? (Mark Sanders (Blind Mark) (676))

The Musical Salvationist, December, 1888—an international number. Blind Mark's contribution represented Jamaica, where he was then labouring.

This song was sung at the wedding of Commissioner and Mrs. Oliphant in December, 1888, in the Clapton Congress Hall, conducted by the Founder.

737. With steady pace the pilgrim moves (Richard Jukes (193))

Ch.M.H.B.

738. A friend of Jesus! O what bliss (Joe Ludgate)

Commissioner Booth-Tucker's *One Hundred Favourite Songs of The Salvation Army*, New York, 1899; 1930 S.A. song book.

The author assisted Colonel Jack Addie in commencing the Army's work in Canada, at London, Ontario, to which city he had emigrated from England. He later received a commission as Captain and finally became a Major in our ranks. He is reputed to have had a pleasing voice and manner, and to have been the first officer in Canada to use a concertina.

While attending officers' meetings in Toronto his small daughter was taken seriously ill. Both mother and father, whilst despairing of their little one's life, felt that God could, should He see fit, restore her. Their faith was rewarded and the child was restored.

The experience served to enhance the value of the ' friendship ' they already enjoyed with Him whom they loved and served, and Joe Ludgate was moved to write his song.

There was an extra verse between our second and third:

> A Friend to lead me in the dark,
> A Friend who knows the way;
> A Friend to steer my weak, frail bark,
> A Friend my debts to pay.

Later, having removed to the States, as a minister, he became a chaplain to the U.S.A. Army during the First World War and was attached to the staff of Wheaton Military College as spiritual adviser to the students. He passed to his eternal reward in 1947 from Illinois, U.S.A.

739. All things are possible to him (Charles Wesley (15))

Hymns for Those that Wait for Full Redemption; Ch.M.H.B.; and based on Mark 9: 23.

It has been said that line 4, verse 3, ' 'Tis certain, though impossible ', is an echo from a poem by Samuel Wesley, Junior, entitled ' The Cobbler ',

> Thus everything his friend could say,
> The more confirmed him in his way:
> Further convinced by what they tell,
> 'Twas certain, though impossible.

But Dr. Henry Bett, M.A., reminds us that this last phrase is really a quotation from Tertullian, where, in arguing against Marcion about the death and resurrection of Christ, he uses the famous phrase, 'And being buried He rose again; it is certain, because it is impossible '.

740. As the varied way of life we journey (Lily Sampson)

The Musical Salvationist, January, 1948; written to the Swedish

229

tune ' Trust in God ' for the wedding of Captain Renee Nicholson and Major Ivar Sorman of Sweden.

Brigadier Sampson, born in Perth, Western Australia, of officer parents, was converted at the age of fifteen in a meeting conducted by Commissioner Hugh Whatmore at Newton, N.S.W., and entered the training college from Dulwich Hill Corps in 1926. Since then the Major has served in women's social, editorial, young people's, and training work in her homeland; in the Editorial Department at International Headquarters; and in India.

741. Away, my needless fears (Charles Wesley (15))

Hymns and Sacred Poems, 1749; Ch.M.H.B.

742. Begone unbelief (John Newton (41))

Olney Hymns, 1779; Ch.M.H.B.

Wrote W. T. Stead, referring to this song: ' I can remember my mother singing it when I was a boy, barely able to see over the book ledge in the minister's pew, and to this day, whenever I am in doleful dumps, and the stars in their courses appear to be fighting against me, that one doggerel verse comes back to me as clear as a blackbird's note through the morning mist:

His love in time past forbids me to think . . .

The verse as it is, with all its shortcomings, has been a lifebuoy, keeping my head above water when the sea raged and was tempestuous and when all else failed.'

Erik Routley, in *I'll Praise my Maker*, wrote:

' The first verse was written by a sailor to whom the story in Mark 4: 36–41 about the storm on the Lake of Galilee meant more than it could to any landlubber. He had been not only a sailor, but a sailor on the very verge of shipwreck; and on that stormy night in 1748 it must indeed have appeared to him that Christ was in the vessel. It will be noticed, further, that in this verse and in the last line of the second the word " surely " appears; it is as if Newton had found himself two syllables short in his line, but had no hesitation in filling them up with the keyword of his faith. His faith was indeed " sure ". . . .

' The second verse contains a reference to " cisterns " which puzzles many. . . . The passage that is uppermost in Newton's mind must have been Jeremiah 2: 13. . . . Here the " cisterns " are the symbols of the idolatries which Israel has substituted for the living faith of the God of Israel, and which have deluded them into despair. In Newton's hands the word symbolizes the futility of human devices and the despair to which man is reduced if he puts his trust in them. . . . The whole metaphor is rich and striking and in Newton's best scriptural tradition.'

743. Blessèd Lord, in Thee is refuge (Herbert H. Booth (91))

Said to have been written at a time of great spiritual darkness, at a period when the author was sorely tempted to leave the Army, this song was published in *Songs of Peace and War*; 1899 S.A. song book. Brother McConnell of Belfast Citadel states that he heard in the early days of the Army that this song was written by Herbert Booth when Secretary of the Training Home at Clapton. These buildings had cost a tremendous amount of money for such a young organization as the Army was at the time. The money was to be paid in certain instalments which had fallen behind the scheduled time and the creditors were pressing for the money. Herbert Booth prayed about it but the heavens seemed as brass. It was in despair and on his knees that he wrote the two verses of this song. He had made his promise that the money would be paid within a certain time, and to his great joy the money arrived in time, and the last verse was written and added to the song.

Booth-Tucker, in *The Life of Catherine Booth*, gave the following account of the closing scene at her funeral before the coffin was lowered into the grave: ' Kneeling, at the conclusion of his address, by the coffin side, the General imprinted upon its lid a farewell kiss, while tears of the children fell upon it fast, and the loved one—nay, only the dissolved " earthly house of this tabernacle "—was lowered sadly into its last resting-place, the congregation singing softly a verse which had been a special favourite with Mrs. Booth . . .

> Blessèd Lord, in Thee is refuge,
> Safety for my trembling soul . . . '

W. T. Stead, writing in *Hymns that have Helped*, said of this song: ' It would be impossible in any collection of hymns to ignore the hymnology of The Salvation Army. No religious denomination, no organization of any kind, has done so much to develop the verse-writing instinct latent in most men. Of the bards of the Army Mr. Herbert Booth is conspicuous as the author of this hymn which is worthily and deservedly popular.'

744. But can it be that I should prove (Charles Wesley (15))

Hymns and Sacred Poems, 1749; Ch.M.H.B. Song 775 is also a part of the same original hymn, and is taken from the first part of the setting.

745. Captain of Israel's host, and Guide (Charles Wesley (15))

Short Hymns on Select Passages of Scripture, 1762; Ch.M.H.B.; based on Exodus 13: 21.

746. Commit thou all thy griefs (Paulus Gerhardt (81); *translated by* John Wesley (3))

The original version appeared in the Frankfurt edition of J. Cruger's *Praxis Pietatis Melica* in 1656; Wesley's translation in *Hymns and Sacred Poems*, 1739, and 1899 S.A. song book.

The following song is a part of the same original hymn, and the whole is based on Psalm 37: 5, 6.

747. Give to the winds thy fears

A continuation of song No. 746.

Ch.M.H.B.

748. Father of Jesus Christ, my Lord (Charles Wesley (15))

Hymns and Sacred Poems, 1742, where there were twenty-nine verses; Ch.M.H.B.; based on Romans 4: 13–16.

Said Bernard L. Manning: ' Here we have a favourite device of Wesley's. He likes to use a word which refers us to a passage of Scripture, but to change and often strengthen its meaning. Faith " laughs " at impossibilities. Wesley has taken the notion of laughing from the story of Sarah's incredulity about Isaac's birth.

' Originally it was Sarah who laughed in scornful unbelief. Wesley baptizes Sarah's laughter, and in his scheme of things it is faith, not unfaith, which laughs. The point is very small but characteristic.'

749. Father of Jesus Christ the Just (Charles Wesley (15))

Hymns for those that Seek and those that have Redemption in the Blood of Jesus Christ, 1747; 1899 S.A. song book.

750. Fight the good fight with all thy might (John S. B. Monsell)

Hymns of Love and Praise, 1863; *The Musical Salvationist*, September, 1922; 1930 S.A. song book. It was popularized during the time of the Boer War, when ' it became a sort of National Anthem, something after the manner of " O God, our help in ages past " but not to the same extent '.

When H.R.H. the Duke of Windsor was Prince of Wales he contributed to a symposium in a Christmas Number of *The Bandsman and Songster*, and stated that this was his favourite hymn.

Said to have written almost three hundred hymns, Dr. Monsell 1811–75) was born at St. Columb's, Londonderry, son of the Archdeacon and precentor of Christchurch Cathedral. In 1832 he took his B.A. degree at Trinity College, Dublin, and two years later took Holy Orders.

The year 1837 saw the publication of *Hymns and Miscellaneous Poems*, the first of a number of works.

While Rector of St. Nicholas's, Guildford, Surrey, Dr. Monsell took a personal interest in the renovation of his church and used often to visit and superintend the work in an informal way. On one occasion as he was standing in the aisle a large piece of stone fell upon his head. He was carried unconscious to the rectory and never recovered.

751. Give me the faith that Jesus had (William Pearson (73))

The War Cry, April 19, 1884; 1899 S.A. song book.

In a Swedish State Church hymn book the last verse of this song appears as a complete hymn (No. 231). The index of the hymn book gives the name, rank and dates of birth and death of the writer, and of the translator into Swedish, the late Commissioner Emmanuel Booth-Hellberg.

752. Give me the faith which can remove (Charles Wesley (15))

Hymns and Sacred Poems, 1749; Ch.M.H.B.

Referring to the line 'And love them with a zeal like Thine ', J. Ernest Rattenbury writes: ' Most accounts of John Wesley's conversion stop after recording his words about the warmed heart and forgiven sins, and ignore the most important sentence in his Journal: " I began to pray with all my might for those who had in an especial manner despitefully used me and persecuted me." The first thing he did was not to testify, that came after, but to *love* his enemies. The celestial fire that kindled the hearts of the brothers was a flame of sacred love. . . . That more than anything else is the proof that they were really converted.'

753. Happy we who trust in Jesus (Thomas Kelly (97))

Hymns on Various Passages of Scripture, 1806; Ch.M.H.B.

Certain alterations have been carried out at the request of the Song Book Revision Council. The last line of the first verse originally was: ' Happy, though despised and poor '.

754. He leadeth me! O blessèd thought! (Joseph Henry Gilmore)

The Watchman and Reflector; Hallelujah Hymn Book; Revival Music; 1878 S.A. song book.

Born at Boston, U.S.A., Mr. Gilmore (1834–1918), was a Baptist minister who became Professor of Logic in Rochester University, New

York, in 1868. He wrote book reviews and published various types of textbooks as well as composing a number of hymns.

These verses were based on the Twenty-third Psalm and were written at the close of a lecture in the First Baptist Church, Philadelphia, in 1862.

'I had been specially impressed with the blessedness of being led by God,' wrote the author, 'of the mere fact of His leadership, altogether apart from the way in which He leads us and what service He is leading us to. At the close of the service we adjourned to Deacon Watson's house, at which I was staying. . . . During the conversation the blessedness of God's leadership so grew upon me that I took out my pencil and wrote this hymn just as it stands.'

He later handed it to his wife and thought no more about it; but she, without his knowledge, sent it to *The Watchman and Reflector*. Within three years it had found a place among the songs of the Church.

755. Hold Thou my hand! so weak I am, and helpless (Grace J. Frances)

Sankey's *Sacred Songs and Solos*; *The Musical Salvationist*, January, 1940.

Grace J. Frances is one of the many pen names of Fanny J. Crosby, whose biographical particulars will be found under song No. 17.

In *Memories of Eighty Years* Fanny Crosby wrote: 'While the great majority of my hymns seemed to be the result of some passing mood, or of some deep though intangible feeling whose expression demanded the language of poetry, quite a number were called into being in response to a definite event in my own life. "Hold Thou my hand" belongs to this class. For a number of days before I wrote this hymn, all had seemed dark to me.

'That was quite an unusual experience, for I have always been most cheerful; and so in my human weakness I cried in prayer: "Dear Lord, hold Thou my hand!" Almost at once the sweet peace that comes of perfect assurance returned to my heart, and my gratitude for this evidence of answered prayer sang itself in the lines of the hymn.'

756. I am trusting Thee, Lord Jesus (Frances Ridley Havergal (256))

The author's *Loyal Responses*, 1878; 1930 S.A. song book.

Written at Ormont, Dessous, Switzerland, in September, 1874, said to have been the author's 'own favourite' and found in her pocket Bible after her death, these verses expressed the spirit she breathed both in life and death.

Among her last words were: 'Not one thing hath failed; tell them all round. Trust Jesus! It's simply trusting Jesus.'

757. I kneel beside Thy sacred Cross (W. Elwin Oliphant)

The Musical Salvationist, November, 1887; 1899 S.A. song book.

William Elwin Oliphant was a curate at St. Paul's, Onslow Square, when he came under the influence of the Army Mother's preaching. He entered the Army work in 1884 and four years later married Célestine Schoch, a member of a distinguished Netherlands family. In addition to his service in the British Territory, the Commissioner, with his wife, had charge of the Army's work in Holland, Belgium, Sweden, Germany, Italy and Switzerland. On account of the Commissioner's frail health after retirement they lived in Ospedaletti, a little village on the Mediterranean shore, from whence the outbreak of the Second World War caused them to move to San Remo. On February 17, 1941, at the age of eighty, the Commissioner was promoted to Glory, and Mrs. Oliphant followed him in April of the same year. There were no Salvationists present save the German officer, Adjutant Martha Hirschberger, who had cared for their children while they were on active service. She practically had to perform the burial rites, then continued to care for the Oliphants' invalid son until he too passed away.

Commissioner Oliphant was the author of *Oberlin, Savonarola, Gerhard Tersteegen*, and *The Story of German Song*, an authoritative work on the hymnology of that country. He was the possessor of the Order of the British Empire and also of the Order of Oranje Nassau.

'Early in the year 1887', wrote Lieut.-Colonel Slater, ' Commissioner (then Major) Oliphant was stricken down by a most serious illness—lung trouble. At times the doctor had doubts if he would recover. There were personal sorrows, and also unexpected disappointments which swept down like a tempest, partly causing and largely intensifying the jeopardy in which his life lay. It seemed to the sick man that just as the great opportunities of the Army were within his grasp, they were to be dashed to the ground and his life was to end in cruel frustration.

' He occupied a bedroom on the upper floor of the left wing of the Clapton Congress Hall, and there he had to fight a battle between faith and doubt. Under these circumstances the words of this song were written, the record of the conflict and the final victory.

' The Music Department at this time occupied a room at the end of a passage on the left side of the building, leading out into the covered way toward the lecture hall.

' One day a message came to me there, asking me to go and see Major Oliphant in his room. I looked with grief upon the thin, pale form of the stricken man. After a few words of greeting, he said, " I have been wanting to see you. I have a few verses which I thought you might set to music." And from underneath the bedclothes he brought out two sheets of crumpled writing paper, on which were the verses of this song. It was with solemn feeling that I took charge of these pieces of paper, for I thought it likely that they might be about the last to bear any writing from his feeble hand.'

A more complete story of Commissioner Oliphant can be found in *Curate of Onslow Square*.

758. I must have the Saviour with me (Lizzie Edwards)

Alexander's *New Revival Hymns*; 1930 S.A. song book.

' Lizzie Edwards ' was one of the many pen names used by Fanny Crosby (17).

759. I want the faith of God (William Pearson (73))

The War Cry, October 24, 1891; 1899 S.A. song book.

760. I'll go in the strength of the Lord (Edward Turney)

Originally published about 1860; *The Sunday School Hymnary*, 1905; *Hymns Ancient and Modern*; 1930 S.A. song book.

Dr. Turney (1816–72), an American Baptist minister, was born at Easton, Connecticut, and graduated at Madison University, New York. He was successively pastor at Hartford and Granville, Ohio, and professor at Madison University and Fairmont Theological Seminary, Cincinnati. He died at Washington.

761. I'm not ashamed to own my Lord (Isaac Watts (3))

The author's *Hymns and Spiritual Songs*, 1707, and based upon 2 Timothy 1: 12.

In *The Life of Henry Drummond*, George Adam Smith recalled his closing hours. Dr. Barbour had played to him the music of 'Art thou weary, art thou languid ' and other hymn tunes, but with no response. Then he tried ' Martyrdom ', to which Drummond beat time with his hand and joined in the words, ' I'm not ashamed to own my Lord '. When the hymn was done Drummond said, ' There's nothing to beat that, Hugh.'

762. In heavenly love abiding (Anna L. Waring (436))

Hymns and Meditations, 1850; *The Musical Salvationist*, December, 1911.

763. Jesus Christ is now amongst us (Anonymous)

Ch.M.H.B.

Probably a Ranter contribution to Army ' hymnody '.

764. Jesus, Lover of my soul (Charles Wesley (15))

Hymns and Sacred Poems, 1740; Ch.M.H.B.; the first line is based upon 'Thou sparest all: for they are Thine, O Lord, Thou lover of souls' (Wisdom of Solomon 11: 26). The words were written soon after the great spiritual awakening which came to the author in 1738.

765. Leader of faithful souls and Guide (Charles Wesley (15))

Hymns for those that Seek and those that have Redemption in the Blood of Jesus Christ, 1747; Ch.M.H.B.

766. Leave God to order all thy ways (Georg Christian Neumark; *translated by* Catherine Winkworth (7))

The author's *Musikalisch-poetischer Lustwald*, 1657; the translation appeared in *Lyra Germanica*, 1855, and 1930 S.A. song book.

The son of a clothier, Neumark (1621–81) was born at Lagensalza, Thuringia, and educated at the Gymnasia of Schleusingen and Gotha. On his way to attend the University of Konigsberg he was robbed by highwaymen on the Gardelegen Heath and stripped of all his possessions but his prayer-book and a little money that was sewn into his clothing. The university now being out of the question he tried to find employment, but sought in vain in town after town.

At last, in Kiel, he succeeded in enlisting the interest of a fellow Thuringian who was the chief pastor and who found for him a tutorship in the family of a judge. This most unexpected relief was the immediate occasion of his writing these words.

Neumark remained in Kiel till he had saved enough to enable him to matriculate at Konigsberg (1643). There he studied law and poetry. Later he was appointed Court poet, librarian and registrar to the administration of Duke Wilhelm II of Saxe-Weimar, and financial custodian of the ducal archives. In 1681 Neumark became blind.

767. Let thy heart be at rest (Catherine Baird (400))

The Musical Salvationist, June, 1939; the words are adapted from John 14 and especially written to the music of 'Brahms' Lullaby'.

768. Lord, it belongs not to my care (Richard Baxter)

Part of a longer composition given in *Poetical Fragments*, dated, 'London, at the door of eternity: Rich. Baxter, August 7, 1681.' 1930 S.A. song book.

Born at Rowton, Salop, in 1615, Richard Baxter was educated at Wroxeter and Ludlow. When eighteen years of age he was persuaded to make trial of court life, but after a month at Whitehall, he returned home.

In 1639 Richard Floey, a Stourbridge ironmaster, refounded and endowed the Grammar School at Dudley; Baxter was installed as master and ordained by the Bishop of Worcester. Twelve months later he went as curate to Bridgnorth, where he spent two years before proceeding to Kidderminster. For a time he was a chaplain to one of Cromwell's regiments, but ill health made an enforced rest necessary. During this period he wrote his famous *The Saints' Everlasting Rest*.

On regaining his health he returned to Kidderminster, remaining there until 1660 when he removed to London. At the restoration he became a Chaplain to King Charles II and was offered the Bishopric of Hereford, which he refused.

On the passing of the Act of Uniformity, in 1662, he was one of the two thousand Nonconformists—the 'ejected' ministers—and he retired to Acton. The Act of Indulgence, in 1672, permitted him to return to London where he again commenced to preach. In 1685, after the accession of James II, he was brought, for alleged sedition, before the notorious Judge Jeffreys who treated him in a brutal manner. Condemned to pay 500 marks, and to be imprisoned until the fine was paid, he lay in the King's Bench Prison for nearly eighteen months, and was released only on the mediation of Lord Powis.

When greeted by Judge Jeffreys with the remark, ' Richard, I see the rogue in thy face ', Baxter replied, ' I had not known before that my face was a mirror.'

In spite of his sufferings and persecution ' he knew nothing of low spirits or nervous depression, notwithstanding all his bodily sufferings. His hopes of Heaven and its blessedness were rarely clouded from the beginning to the end of his Christian course '.

Lieut.-Commissioner Gustave Isely wrote: ' If ever a saintly poet lived up to the pious accents of his own hymns, Richard Baxter was that man. His whole career may serve to illuminate the truth in the verses of " Lord, it belongs not to my care ". Champions often become martyrs, though all martyrs do not die at the stake, and some like Baxter, die daily. " Whether I die or live " was in every sense with him an oft-recurring alternative.'

769. Lord Jesus, Thou dost keep Thy child (Jean Sophia Pigott)

1878 S.A. song book. The author (1845–1882) was Irish.

When on the verge of retirement Mrs. General Carpenter published *God's Battle-School*; she recounted therein some of the battles and victories of her earlier years. She concluded with: ' Now I am facing the westering sky . . . the badge of fifty years' active service has been given to me. As I look back through the years to the sweet spring-time of life, and through the summer to the autumn, and now facing the winter—which has a loveliness all of its own—with a heart full of gratitude to God, my testimony is:

> This life of trust, how glad, how sweet;
> My need and Thy great fulness meet,
> And I have all in Thee.'

770. My faith looks up to Thee (Bramwell Booth (280))

The Salvationist, February, 1879; *The Musical Salvationist*, December, 1889; 1930 S.A. song book.

771. My faith looks up to Thee (Ray Palmer (581))

Spiritual Songs for Social Worship, compiled by Lowell Mason and Dr. Hastings in 1833; Ch.M.H.B.

In 1830, at the age of twenty-two, and shortly after graduating from Yale College, Dr. Palmer read a German poem of two verses which pictured a penitent sinner before the Cross. His heart was deeply moved by the sentiments expressed in the poem so that he was led to translate them into English, and then he followed on with four other verses of his own. 'I wrote them with very tender emotion,' he recalled, 'and ended the last line with tears.'

The verses were written in a pocket notebook, and there they remained for the next two years, until he met Lowell Mason in a bookshop in Boston.

'I'm making a new booklet of hymns and tunes,' said Mason. 'Have you any verses I can set to music for the publication?' Palmer remembered the verses in his notebook and tore the page out and handed it to Mason, who put it away in his pocket without even reading it. He did read the verses, however, in the quiet of his own study and was wonderfully impressed by them, so that when he met his friend a few days later, he said to him: 'You may live many years and do many good things, but I think you will be best known to posterity as the author of "My faith looks up to Thee".'

772. My God and Father, while I stray (Charlotte Elliott (217))

The author's *Invalids' Hymn Book*, 1834; Ch.M.H.B. There have been several alterations in the text of the song throughout the years; our version is as given by the author's brother in his *Psalms and Hymns*, 1835, apart from the omission of three verses.

It was one of the favourite hymns of Queen Alexandra and was sung at the private funeral service in Sandringham Church.

773. My hope is built on nothing less (Edward Mote)

Hymns of Praise, A New Selection of Gospel Hymns combining all the Excellencies of our Spiritual Poets, with many Originals, 1836; Ch.M.H.B.

Born in Upper Thames Street, at the back of Queen Victoria Street, London, Edward Mote (1797–1874) as a youth spent his Sundays on the streets in play; he did not know there was a God. Later in life he became the Baptist minister at Horsham, Sussex, a position he held for twenty-six years until he died.

' One morning [in 1834] it came into my mind as I went to labour,' recalled the author, ' to write an hymn on the " Gracious Experience of a Christian ". As I went up Holborn (London) I had the chorus—

> On Christ, the solid Rock, I stand,
> All other ground is sinking sand.

' In the day I had the four verses complete and wrote them off. On the Sabbath following I met Brother King as I came out of Lisle Street meeting, who informed me that his wife was very ill and asked me to call and see her.

' I had an early tea and called afterwards. He said it was the usual custom to sing a hymn, read a portion and engage in prayer before he went to the meeting. He looked for his hymn book but could not find it anywhere. I said I had some verses in my pocket-book; if he liked, we would sing them! We did, and his wife enjoyed them so much that he asked me, as a favour, to leave a copy of them for her. I went home and by the fireside composed the last two verses, wrote the whole off, and took them to Sister King.

'As these verses so met the dying woman's case, my attention to them was arrested. I had a thousand printed for distribution and I sent one to the *Spiritual Magazine*, without my initials, which appeared some time later.'

774. My rest is in Heaven, my rest is not here (Henry Francis Lyte (11))

The author's *Poems, Chiefly Religious*, 1833; Ch.M.H.B.

It was estimated that 5,000 people gathered in Abney Park Cemetery for the funeral of Commissioner James Dowdle, conducted by the Founder on July 28, 1900, and a report of that event says that ' strong men wept ' as the Founder outlined this song.

775. Not all the powers of Hell can fright (Charles Wesley (15))

Hymns and Sacred Poems, 1749, and Ch.M.H.B., where the original first verse was included:

> Are there not in the labourer's day
> Twelve hours, in which he safely may
> His calling's work pursue?
> Though sin and Satan still are near,
> Nor sin nor Satan can I fear,
> With Jesus in my view.

Song 744 is taken from the second part of the same original hymn.

776. Now I have found the ground wherein (Johann Andreas Rothe; *translated by* John Wesley (34))

Count Zinzendorf's *Christ-Catholisches Singeund Bet-Büchlein*, 1727; the translation appeared in *Hymns and Sacred Poems*, 1740, and Ch.M.H.B.

Son of the pastor at Lissa, near Görlitz, in Silesia, the author was born on May 12, 1688, and entered the University of Leipzig twenty years later to study theology. He graduated M.A. and in 1712 was licensed as a general preacher. In 1718 he became tutor to a private family at Leube.

A sermon which he preached at Gross-Hennersdorf brought him to the notice of Count Zinzendorf, who became his friend and patron with the result that in 1722 he was appointed pastor at Berthelsdorf. It is said that 'he was an excellent pastor, uniting in himself ripe scholarship and exemplary piety'.

When Herrnhut, the Moravian settlement, was established, Rothe became pastor there as well.

Later, however, differences arose between Rothe and Count Zinzendorf which led to Rothe's resignation, in 1737, and his accepting a call to Thommendorf as assistant pastor. He took charge of the pastorate in 1742 and died there on July 6, 1758.

He has been described as 'a man of considerable gifts and of unbending integrity, a good theologian, and an earnest, fearless and impressive preacher, beloved by all who came within the sphere of his influence'.

The original hymn is said to have been written by Rothe for Zinzendorf's birthday on May 26, 1728.

Both Commissioner Evan Smith and Brigadier Fred Cox, who served as the Founder's private secretaries, recall occasions when William Booth, unable to sleep at night, would ring for them, and many times, toward the end of his life, they heard this grand old man quoting this song, especially verse four—'Though waves and storms go o'er my head'.

The Founder's eighty-third birthday, the last he spent on earth, was a happy, hallowed and memorable occasion. With his Headquarters officers singing this song around him he reaffirmed his belief in the doctrine of the bleeding Lamb. In between the verses he declared: 'I stood on that foundation nearly seventy years ago. I am on the same foundation tonight; and if God in His mercy spares me till next year I shall be there on my eighty-fourth birthday, and again on my eighty-fifth, and eighty-sixth. And I know where I shall be on my eighty-seventh and eighty-eighth, and eighty-ninth; and should I live to be ninety or a hundred, you will find me on the same foundation.'

777. Peace, perfect peace, in this dark world of sin? (Edward H. Bickersteth (219))

Songs in the House of Pilgrimage; 1930 S.A. song book.

One Sunday morning in August, 1875, the vicar of Harrogate, Canon Gibbon, had preached from Isaiah 26: 3 and referred to the fact that in the Hebrew the words are, ' Peace, Peace ', twice repeated, and happily translated in the Authorized Version as ' perfect peace '.

The sermon by the Canon set working the mind of the Vicar of Christ Church, Hampstead—who could often more easily express himself in verse than in prose, and who was on holiday in Harrogate—so that when, in the afternoon, he visited an aged and dying relative and found him somewhat troubled, he endeavoured to express in verse the spiritual comfort which he desired to convey. Taking a sheet of notepaper he wrote down the song exactly as it now stands, and then read it to the old saint.

Mr. Bickersteth's son later stated that he could remember his father coming in to tea that Sunday afternoon, saying, ' Children, I have written you a hymn', and reading it to them at that meal. His custom at that particular meal on Sundays was to ask each member of his family to repeat a hymn, doing the same himself or reading out some new original composition.

778. Simply trusting every day (Edgar Page Stites (274))

Sankey's *Sacred Songs and Solos*; 1930 S.A. song book.

In Chicago in 1876 a newspaper cutting of this song was handed to Mr. Moody, who asked Mr. Sankey to write a tune for it. He assented on condition that he (Moody) would vouch for the doctrine taught in the words. He promised and the tune was written.

In *Hotchpotch* Commissioner Adelaide Cox gives an interesting account of a drink-sodden woman who came under the influence of the Army through prison visitation. She would like to give herself to the Saviour, she said, but she could never pass a public house without going in for a drink. How true this was was evidenced by the many times she went to prison. At last she was brought to the point where she believed—but her faith was very much mixed with doubt. Upon her release Salvationists met her and helped her, and gave her good advice. Whenever she came to a public house, she would close her eyes and run past the door of the pub singing—

Trusting as the moments fly . . .

The flicker of faith became a bright light and in time the public house had no further attraction; and the old lady became known to all by the name of ' Trusting '.

779. Soldiers who to Christ belong (a Latin hymn *translated by* Isaac Williams)

The author's *Hymns translated from the Parisian Breviary*, 1839; 1930 S.A. song book.

Williams (1802–65) was born at Cymcynfelin, Cardiganshire, son of a barrister of Lincoln's Inn, London. He studied at Harrow and Trinity College, Oxford, where he received the prize for Latin verse (1823). It is said that he was so proficient in Latin that he thought in its language and had to translate his ideas into English. Later he took Holy Orders in the Church of England.

780. Spirit of faith, come down (Charles Wesley (15))

Hymns of Petition and Thanksgiving for the Promise of the Father, 1746; Ch.M.H.B.

781. The cross that He gave may be heavy (Ballington Booth (372))

The Officer, January, 1893; *The Musical Salvationist*, June, 1893; 1899 S.A. song book.

782. The sands of time are sinking (Anne Ross Cousin)

The Christian Treasury, 1857; *The Musical Salvationist*, February, 1934.

Mrs. Cousin (1824–1906) was the daughter of Dr. Cundell of Leith and in 1847 married Rev. W. Cousin, a minister of the Free Church of Scotland, then at Melrose. She published a volume of verse under the title *Emmanuel's Land and Other Pieces* in 1876, written in the Free Church manse at Irvine, where her husband was then the minister.

' The sands of time are sinking ' was originally a poem of nineteen verses based on passages from the writings of Samuel Rutherford who, born in 1600 and minister of Anwoth, Kirkcudbrightshire, when twenty-seven years of age, spent his time, while shut up in prison far away in the north, writing letters to the churches. Many of the thoughts contained in those letters have been embedded in Mrs. Cousin's verses, which she wrote as she sat at work one Saturday evening.

783. Though Thy waves and billows are gone o'er me (Albert Orsborn (42))

A heart cry, inspired by Psalm 42, and written on the train bound for Scotland for the 1951 congress. The General writes, ' One's own sorrows and struggles come through the years into a song of this character.'

784. Though thunders roll and darkened be the sky (John Lawley (56))

The Musical Salvationist, April, 1923; 1930 S.A. song book.

The spirit of resignation and trust which filled the Commissioner's whole being is reflected in these grand verses, which were written during his last illness.

The words are reminiscent of a song which the author penned some time previously, after hearing of the death of the Consul in the U.S.A. It contained these words:

> Though gales may blow and storms of sorrow roll,
> Thy will be done!
> Though angry seas sweep o'er my trembling soul,
> Thy will be done!
> He'll steer my bark towards the harbour light,
> And keep me safe till faith is lost in sight.

785. Though troubles assail (John Newton (41))

Gospel Magazine, January, 1777; *Olney Hymn Book*; Ch.M.H.B.

Written in February, 1775, for the service at the Great House, Olney, and based on Genesis 22: 14.

786. Through the love of God our Saviour (Mary Peters)

The author's *Hymns Intended to Help the Communion of Saints,* 1847; Ch.M.H.B.

Wife of Rev. John McWilliam Peters, the Rector of Quenington, Glos, Mary Peters (1813–56) was the daughter of Richard Bowly of Cirencester. She published *The World's History from the Creation to the Accession of Queen Victoria* in seven volumes. Most of her hymns were written before she was thirty years of age and several of them were contributed to the Plymouth Brethren's *Psalms, Hymns and Spiritual Songs,* 1842.

787. Unto the hills around do I lift up (John Campbell)

Church Hymnal for the Christian Year, dated 1877.

These words form one of the few versions of Psalm 121 which give the correct rendering of the opening verse of the Psalm, that is, that the hills themselves are not the source of our help, they symbolize the futility of expecting help from such sources (see R.V.).

John Douglas Sutherland Campbell, the 9th Duke of Argyle, was born on August 6, 1845. In 1871 he married H.R.H. Princess Louise, daughter of Queen Victoria and, as Marquis of Lorne, was Governor-General of Canada from 1878 to 1883. From 1895 to 1900 he was Member of Parliament for South Manchester. The Duke carried the King's sceptre with the cross at the coronations of both Edward VII and George V, became well known as a writer of both prose and verse, and died on May 2, 1914.

When announcing his death the International *War Cry* (May 9, 1914) recalled:

'In December, 1911, his Grace presided at the opening of a four-storey extension of Spa Road Elevator. . . . At the invitation of the General, the Duke spoke a few words to a thousand men of the City Colony who were assembled in the Bermondsey Town Hall, as well as at the actual opening ceremony in the new wing of the elevator.

'His Grace felicitously described the Spa Road Elevator as the largest institution in the world for the remaking of men, and claimed it as one of the most successful achievements of the Army's Founder.

'At the opening of the Clapton Mothers' Hospital by H.R.H. the Princess Louise, His Grace accompanied his beloved consort and assured Mrs. Booth of his continued and warmest sympathy with the Army. . . .

' " I am glad you still have the good old uniform," he said. " May it always be in the advance of benevolence and civilization wherever it may be found." '

788. What a work the Lord has done (Albert Orsborn (42))

The Field Officer, April, 1909; 1930 S.A. song book.

'It was winter, 1908, at Lowestoft South,' writes the General. 'We had passed from a highly successful summer into a wintry reaction. Everything was " down ", and perhaps the officers shared the depression.

'My Lieutenant, at family prayers, was very much stirred and cried out desperately, almost challengingly, to the Lord: " Thou hast promised ' greater things ', O Lord, wilt Thou show them here, in this corps? " After prayers I penned this little song. Adversity was its mother, but it has proved a comely child.'

789. When we cannot see our way (Thomas Kelly (97))

Hymns Not Before Published, 1815; 1899 S.A. song book.

A newspaper reported the first High Council (1929) thus:

' The Council has been sitting with only two intervals for thirteen hours. They began their stern duty with a brilliant winter sun shining on the snow-clad grounds of the Court; they finished when a pale moon accentuated the deep shadows which wrapped the mansion. It is true that fifty-five Commissioners decided that the General's reign should end, but there was hardly a dry eye in the oak-panelled Council Chamber when the result of the secret ballot was announced. The women who were there shed tears unrestrainedly.

' Mrs. Booth was overcome and turned to the comforting arms of her daughter Mary. Then very softly the President, Commissioner James Hay (New Zealand), said: " We will sing this hymn:

> When we cannot see our way,
> Let us trust and still obey;
> He who bids us forward go,
> Cannot fail the way to show." '

790. A wonderful Saviour is Jesus, my Lord (Fanny Crosby (17))

Sankey's *Sacred Songs and Solos*; especially written for the tune supplied to the author by Wm. J. Kirkpatrick.

791. Be glad in the Lord and rejoice (Mary Elizabeth Servoss)

Sankey's *Sacred Songs and Solos*; *The Musical Salvationist*, 1910.

Miss Servoss was born at Schenectady, New York, on August 22, 1849. Her life was not easy. For eighteen years she was the constant companion of a disabled grandmother, following which period she nursed her mother through a protracted illness and tended her father until he passed away. She was a great admirer of Fanny Crosby and was thus inspired to write a number of songs. After the death of her parents she lived in Edeson, Illinois.

792. Christ now sits on Zion's hill (Anonymous)

The Small Book issued in 1821 by the founder of Primitive Methodism, Hugh Bourne, and is probably his own composition (see No. 155); Ch.M.H.B.

Joseph Ritson, in *The Romance of Primitive Methodism*, refers to this song as being much used by the early-day Primitive Methodists—especially the latter part of it—in seasons of persecution.

793. Come, shout and sing, make Heaven ring (James C. Bateman (177))

The War Cry, October 20, 1881; *Salvation Music*, Vol. 2; 1899 S.A. song book; written to the ballad tune, ' I traced her little footsteps in the snow '.

This song was sung as a solo by Gipsy Smith on May 13, 1882, at the opening of Clapton Congress Hall, where it ' made an immediate hit '.

794. Earthly kingdoms rise and fall (Will. J. Brand (52))

The Musical Salvationist, January, 1946.

In March, 1942, Colonel Bramwell Coles sent the author the trio of one of his new marches, ' Defenders of the Faith '. ' Do you think that the title would stir your thoughts to a set of words?' the Colonel asked. ' It conjures up visions within me of bold knights in armour, with their trusty blades, defending a castle against desperate foemen. But I do not think I can put this or any spiritualization of it into poetry.' Brother Brand completed the words within a few days.

795. God is keeping His soldiers fighting (William Pearson (73))

1899 S.A. song book.

Colonel Edward H. Joy used to say that this song was written in his home when he was a boy.

On May 2, 1887, six Salvationists were sent to Derby Jail to serve seven days' hard labour for holding an open-air meeting in the High Street, Eckington. Nineteen-year-old Lieutenant Mary Fairhurst, a beautiful girl with an intrepid spirit, was among them. Brought up in the Church of England at Sheffield, she had entered the training home when only seventeen years of age.

With Captain Myra Davis, her Commanding Officer, she was put to picking oakum until her fingers bled. On the second night of their imprisonment in the jail, the Derby 2 Band came and played outside, ' God is keeping His soldiers fighting ', and Mary Fairhurst joined in the singing of the chorus. Her spirit was undaunted. The day of release came and mighty crowds gathered to do the Salvationists honour. Later Mary married Captain John Cooper and her four children are officers in the Army today.

On Sunday, May 3, 1942, Derby commemorated the Fifty-fifth Anniversary of the Salvationists' imprisonment and the Central Band marched to the gates of the old jail and there played the same tune their predecessors had played to the captives.

On Thursday, November 15, 1945, as officers released from Second World War internment entered the Clapton Congress Hall for their London welcome, the International Staff Band played the music of this song.

796. Hark, hark, my soul, what warlike songs are swelling (Frederick W. Faber (80); *altered by* George Scott Railton (292))

The original words appeared in Faber's *Oratory Hymns*, 1854; *Hallelujah Hymn Book*; *Revival Music*; 1878 S.A. song book where they commenced:

> Hark, hark, my soul, angelic songs are swelling
> O'er earth's green fields and ocean's wave-beat shore.

The original version has, however, undergone a transformation at the hands of Commissioner Railton. One can hardly imagine a greater contrast than between the two sets of words—from being a soothing and comforting hymn, it has been transformed into a virile, warlike song, challenging the soul to heroic endeavour in the battles of the Lord.

797. Hark! the sounds of singing (Charles Coller (481))

The Musical Salvationist, March, 1915; 1930 S.A. song book.

798. Joy! joy! joy! there is joy in The Salvation Army (William Pearson (73))

The War Cry, July 13, 1882; 1899 S.A. song book; and is an adaptation of a song which was published in William B. Bradbury's *Fresh Laurels*, 1867, and which commenced:

> Joy, joy, joy, there is joy in Heaven with the angels,
> Joy, joy, joy, for the prodigal's return.

When Colonel Albert Jakeway went to Czechoslovakia he discovered that this song was very popular with the local Salvationists. He was a little perplexed, however, because the first word of their translation was a two-syllabled word, and was informed that they had translated the English word ' Joy ' by the Czech word for ' Splendour ', an expression which gives an added force to the joy found in our Organization.

799. Let us sing of His love once again (Francis Bottome (122))

1878 S.A. song book.

800. Make the world with music ring (Charles Coller (481))

The Musical Salvationist, June, 1918, under the name of Colonel William Pearson; 1930 S.A. song book.

Despite the fact that this song has also been attributed to Commissioner John Lawley, Major Coller submitted it, with a number of other songs, in connection with a special song book for the 1914 International Congress. None of his contributions were published but ' Make the world with music ring ' appeared a year or two afterward in a small song book issued for an officers' council.

801. March on, salvation soldiers (James C. Bateman (177))

The Musical Salvationist, February, 1892; 1899 S.A. song book. The author also supplied the tune with which the words are associated.

802. Marching on in the light of God (Robert Johnson (423))

Salvation Music, Vol. 2; 1899 S.A. song book. The author also gave the musical setting.

803. On to the conflict, soldiers, for the right (William Howard Doane)

Published originally in America, it appeared in Great Britain in *Evangelical Echoes*, published by Fullerton and Smith, in 1884; *The Musical Salvationist*, October, 1918; 1930 S.A. song book.

A great friend of Fanny Crosby, setting many of her songs to music, Dr. Doane was born at Preston, Connecticut, February 3, 1832. He was a member of a choir at the age of ten, a good flute player at twelve, and a church organist at fifteen. Although educated for a musical profession he became a manufacturer of wood-turning machinery, taking out many patents for his inventions.

But music, particularly gospel music, retained his deep interest. His first book of Christian songs appeared in 1862, and he is said to have composed more than one thousand three hundred numbers. He received his Doctor of Music degree from the Dennison University.

Superintendent of a large Sunday-school in Cincinnati, Ohio, and a lifelong Baptist, he died in South Orange, New Jersey, December 23, 1915.

804. Ring the bells of Heaven, there is joy today (William O. Cushing)

Hallelujah Hymn Book; Revival Music; 1878 S.A. song book.

Born in Hingham, Massachusetts, the author (1823–1903) entered the ministry in America. When he lost his power of speech he prayed: 'Lord, give me something to do for Thee!' He always felt that his gift for writing hymns for the Sunday-schools was the answer to his prayer.

One day Mr. Cushing received from George F. Root, the American composer, a fascinating tune which he had written for a secular song, 'The Little Octoroon'. It made an instant appeal, and Mr. Cushing longed to use the melody in the Sunday-school. One day the sight of a man kneeling at the altar at the close of an evangelistic service gave him the inspiration for his song. He thought of the bells of Heaven and how they must be ringing in gladness for the sinner's return and, to quote his own words, ' " Ring the bells of Heaven " flowed at once into the waiting melody '.

805. Salvation is our motto (J. Slack)

The Musical Salvationist, January, 1888; 1899 S.A. song book.

Both words and music of this song were composed when the author was an officer serving in South Africa, where he had been transferred from Great Britain in 1886 with his wife, formerly Isabella Roxburgh of Lossiemouth, Scotland. Staff-Captain Slack was on tour in the Cape Western Division and was the guest of South Africa's saintly preacher and writer on holiness, the Rev. Andrew Murray.

806. Shout aloud salvation, and we'll have another song (George Scott Railton (292))

The War Cry, May 26, 1881, with the first line, 'Shout aloud salvation, boys'; 1899 S.A. song book; written to an American song tune.

Lieut.-Colonel Slater, referring to this song, wrote: 'Of the Commissioner's confidence in the ultimate triumph of Jesus, and of the robust, manly, spirit-compelling faith in his ideals (for he was an idealist in religion), how splendidly this song expresses! The last verse breathes the spirit of assured victory.'

807. Strike, O strike for victory (Mary Ann Kidder (639))

Salvation Army Music, 1880; 1930 S.A. song book.

808. We are marching home to Glory (William Pearson (73)) (verses); R. F. Hughes (chorus))

The War Cry, April 10, 1880; 1899 S.A. song book.

The author of the chorus was an American living in the latter part of the nineteenth century.

809. We are marching on with shield and banner bright (Fanny Crosby (17))

Expressly written for Wm. B. Bradbury's *Fresh Laurels for the Sabbath School*, 1867, Bradbury himself supplying the music; *Hallelujah Hymn Book*; *Revival Music*; 1878 S.A. song book.

In verse 2 the opening line read, 'In the Sunday-school our Army we prepare', but in Christian Mission days this had become 'In the Mission hall our army we prepare'.

810. We are sweeping through the land (George Scott Railton (292))

The War Cry, July 11, 1891; *The Musical Salvationist*, March, 1896, set to an original tune by Herbert H. Booth which did not find a permanent place in our collections; 1899 song book.

811. We'll be heroes (Anonymous)

Hallelujah Hymn Book; Revival Music; 1878 S.A. song book.

One day while in India Colonel Walter Shaw was very much impressed by three young Hindu boys standing by an idol-god in the centre of their village singing 'We'll be heroes, we'll be heroes', knowing full well that they would most probably be called to suffer for the stand they were taking that day.

812. We're a band that shall conquer the foe (William Hodgson)

The War Cry, February 7, 1880, when the author was stationed at Whitby; 1899 S.A. song book.

William Hodgson, born on July 20, 1853, 'The Blood-washed Collier', entered Army service from Spennymoor, County Durham, in 1879 and rendered valiant service until his retirement in August, 1911. He, with his wife, then became an active soldier of Walthamstow 2 Corps, London, until his promotion to Glory on June 8, 1926. Lieut.-Commissioner Herbert Hodgson is a son.

'In 1880 The Christian Mission was just merging into The Salvation Army,' wrote Lieut.-Colonel Slater, 'but in many of the districts in which it operated some of the more " chapely " kind of people were not taking very kindly to the change of methods.

'It was at this time that Staff-Captain Hodgson was appointed by the Founder to take charge of the Limehouse Corps in London.

'A leading business man there invited the Captain to luncheon. After the meal he beckoned him into the drawing-room and said, " Now I wish to say a few straight words to you. We don't want The Salvation Army, but if you will be our minister you will have all you require. If you persist in Salvation Army methods you will lose everybody here." A great temptation this was to the young man, quite unused to London ways. However, he did not take long to reply. " Mr. ——," he said, " I have been appointed Captain of this corps by the General, and I intend to continue as long as my leaders see fit to leave me in charge."

' " Then you are a fool and you will lose all your people," angrily retorted the business man.

' Shortly after this the Captain was left with only one or two comrades who remained faithful to him and the Army. Whilst sitting down in his quarters, with no comforts and very little prospect of financial assistance, he was tempted to leave his post and return to his comfortable home. Dropping on his knees, the young Captain took paper and pencil and wrote this song with its inspiring chorus. It was sung to a tune which was very popular at that time. When he farewelled from Limehouse some months later he had the joy of counting one hundred soldiers on his roll.'

813. Ye valiant soldiers of the Cross (Anonymous)

American Sacred Songs, 1868, with the refrain:

Let us never mind the scoffs
Or the frowns of the world,
For we all have a cross to bear.

Revival Music; 1878 S.A. song book, set to a tune no longer used and with the following chorus:

> We're soldiers fighting for our God,
> Let trembling cowards fly;
> We'll stand unshaken, firm and fixed,
> With Christ to live and die.

814. For all the saints who from their labours rest (William Walsham How (223))

Hymns for Saints Days, and Other Hymns by a Layman, 1864; *The Musical Salvationist*, October, 1935.

815. For those we love within the veil (William Charter Piggott)

Songs for Use in Field Officers' Councils, 1948.

Written for a commemoration service in the earlier part of the First World War.

William Charter Piggott (1872–1943), born in Huddersfield, trained in the Headingley College (Methodist), Leeds, entered the Congregational Ministry in 1902, and served at Greville Place, London, Bunyan's Meeting at Bedford, Whitefield's Tabernacle, and from 1917 at Streatham. He was the Chairman of the Congregational Union in 1931. Of his many hymns five were included in *Songs of Praise*.

816. Rejoice for a comrade deceased (Charles Wesley (15))

Funeral Hymns, 1744; Ch.M.H.B.; where it commenced, 'Rejoice for a brother deceased'.

Of the fifteen hymns in the 1744 pamphlet, eight of them are in this metre, a metre which would now be considered rather joyous for the subject of death, but it does reflect the attitude of the Wesleys and of the early-day Methodists and Salvationists toward death, an attitude that finds its expression in the Army phrase, 'promoted to Glory'.

817. Safe in the arms of Jesus (Fanny Crosby (17))

W. H. Doane's *Songs of Devotion for Christian Associations*; *Hallelujah Hymn Book*; 1878 S.A. song book.

'On April 30, 1868,' wrote Miss Crosby, 'Dr. W. H. Doane came into my house and said, "I have exactly forty minutes before my train leaves for Cincinnati. Here is a melody—can you write words for it?" Then followed a space of twenty minutes, during which I was unconscious of all else except the work I was doing. At the end of that time I recited the words, "Safe in the arms of Jesus", to Dr. Doane. He then wrote them down, and had time to catch his train.'

The song has a very touching association with the brutal murder of Bishop Hannington in Africa:

'I grew faint with struggling and was dragged by the legs over the ground,' he recorded in his diary. 'I said, "Lord, I put myself into Thy hands, I look to Thee alone." Then another struggle and I got to my feet, and was thus dashed along. More than once I was violently brought into contact with banana trees, some trying in their haste to force me one way, others the other, and the exertion and struggling strained me in the most agonizing manner. In spite of it all, and feeling I was being dragged away to be murdered [as indeed he was]—I sang—

Safe in the arms of Jesus—

and then I laughed at the very agony of my situation.'

818. Servant of God, well done! (James Montgomery (14))

Originally twelve verses long, 'Servant of God, well done!' was penned to commemorate the labours and death of Rev. Thomas Taylor, a Wesleyan Methodist minister, and published in the author's *Greenland and other Poems*, 1819; 1899 S.A. song book.

Thomas Taylor co-operated with the Wesleys for fifty-five years, refusing attractive offers elsewhere and enduring great hardship. He was chosen as the President of the Conference in 1796. In one of his last sermons, on October 14, 1816, when nearly eighty years of age, he remarked that he would 'wish to die like an old soldier, sword in hand'. The suddenness of his death a few days later is referred to in one of the omitted verses:

His sword was in his hand,
Still warm with recent fight,
Ready that moment, at command,
Through rock and steel to smite.

819. Shall we gather at the river (Robert Lowry (231))

Happy Voices, 1865; Ch.M.H.B.

Sitting in the study one sultry afternoon in 1864, during a terrible epidemic that raged in Brooklyn, Dr. Lowry thought naturally of death. Many friends and acquaintances had been suddenly called from their homes and loved ones, and this song gave expression to the emotions of his heart amidst that season of sorrow and death. The author also wrote the tune associated with the words.

820. Shall we meet beyond the river (Horace Lorenzo Hastings)

The Young Reaper, a Philadelphia Sunday-school paper in which the Rev. Robert Lowry edited the music; Ch.M.H.B.

Born at Blandford, Mass., U.S.A., in 1831, Mr. Hastings commenced writing songs and preaching in his seventeenth year. 'Shall we meet' was written in 1858 in New York. In 1866 the author established *The Christian*, a monthly paper in which many of his songs appeared.

821. Summoned home! the call has sounded (Herbert H. Booth (91))

Songs of Peace and War, 1890, under the title, 'A Soldier's Reward—a Funeral March'; 1899 S.A. song book.

'Mrs. Booth was dying all through the summer of 1890,' wrote Lieut.-Colonel Slater. 'The end was seen to be approaching by the beginning of August. The Commandant (Herbert Booth) saw that it was his painful duty to make some arrangement for the funeral of his beloved mother, particularly with respect to appropriate funeral music for the bands to play. A double Funeral Band Journal was planned, for which the Commandant had promised a march. Anxiety, ceaseless toil, all kinds of unforeseen demands on his time and attention prevented that promise being fulfilled.

'The printer had reached the limit of time for waiting, yet no idea for the funeral march had come. I had to wait on him, finding him weary, perplexed, with one officer and another with important questions interrupting the interview, while we spoke of the wanted march. It seemed hopeless to expect anything worthy of the occasion under these circumstances. At length, as the shadow of night fell upon the room, the Commandant sat at the organ, as a kind of rest from his thoughts, and said as he touched the keys, " What I wanted was a march something like this." He played, the unlocked feelings of his soul rushed forth, and he went forward from bar to bar, while I sat as close to the windows as possible to catch the fast fading light, to put down the music as it proceeded from the organ. In astonishment he found that almost without a change of note what was played and what was put to paper was the author's now celebrated funeral march, " Promoted to Glory ".'

Apparently the words were added after the band journal had gone to press.

822. We shall meet our loved ones there (Fred W. Fry (248) (verses))

The Musical Salvationist, February, 1891; 1899 S.A. song book.

Although this song is attributed to Fred W. Fry, it is actually his adaptation of a negro spiritual used by the coloured Jubilee Singers from Fisk University when they visited Great Britain in 1871.

In *The Life of Catherine Booth* Commissioner Booth-Tucker recalled that over and over again the Army Mother asked that the refrain of this song might be sung as she was racked with pain. Then, he pictured in graphic language the scenes of the funeral service in the Olympia, how the platform was reached, the appointed places taken, and the solemn service proceeded. ' Deeply touching was the moment when the bereaved family, rising to their feet, sang the favourite chorus which had so often comforted the dying sufferer:

" We shall walk through the valley of the shadow of death." '

823. When the roll is called in Heaven (Anonymous)

Salvation Music, Vol. 2; 1899 S.A. song book.

824. When the trumpet of the Lord shall sound, and time shall be no more (James Milton Black)

1899 S.A. song book.

Mr. Black (1856–1938), president of a youth society, met a girl of about fourteen, poorly dressed, sitting on a doorstep of a dilapidated house in his native town of Williamsport, U.S.A. Her ragged clothes and shoes and general appearance told its own story of the ravages of drink. Mr. Black invited the child to attend the Sunday-school. She did for some time, but one evening when the roll was called she failed to respond to her name. Remarking on her absence, the president spoke of the sadness of any not being present when the names were called from the Lamb's Book of Life. The thought moved him to exclaim, ' O God, when my name is called up yonder, may I be there to respond!'

Wanting something especially suitable to sing on this occasion Mr. Black searched the hymn book, but was unable to find just the type of hymn required. On his way home the thought came to him, ' Why not write a hymn yourself?' Within fifteen minutes of reaching home he had completed the words. Then, turning to the piano, he played the tune exactly as it is sung today. ' I have never dared to change a single word or note of the song,' he said later

825. Who, who are these beside the chilly wave (Tullius Clinton O'Kane)

Hallelujah Hymn Book; Revival Music; 1878 S.A. song book.

Mr. O'Kane (1830–1912) was a professor in Ohio Wesleyan University. For some years he had been a travelling salesman for musical instruments, in his spare time writing gospel songs.

826. All have need of God's salvation (William McAlonan (260))

The Musical Salvationist, October, 1890, when the author was associated with the Army's Trade Department at Clerkenwell; 1899 S.A. song book.

827. All round the world the Army chariot rolls (William Pearson (73))

The War Cry, Jan. 5, 1884; 1899 S.A. song book.

828. All the world shall be our conquest (James C. Bateman (177))

The War Cry, December 24, 1887; 1930 S.A. song book.

829. Christ for the world, we sing (Samuel Wolcott)

Songs for the New Life (Chicago, 1869); 1930 S.A. song book.

Born at South Windsor, Connecticut, U.S.A., Dr. Wolcott (1813–86) was educated at Yale College and Andover Theological Seminary. For two years he was a missionary in Syria; then ill health necessitated his return to America, where he was minister of several Congregational churches. Although his hymn-writing commenced late in life he is said to have written over two hundred numbers.

The author attended a meeting on February 7, 1869, of the Young Men's Christian Association of Ohio, whose motto over the pulpit was 'Christ for the world, and the world for Christ'. On his way home he composed the verses based on the motto.

830. From Greenland's icy mountains (Reginald Heber (131))

Evangelical Magazine, 1822; 1899 S.A. song book.

King George III authorized a missionary service and collection in every church in the country for the furthering of the missionary work of the Society for the Propagation of the Gospel. This was to take place on Whit-Sunday, 1819. On the Saturday evening while Dr. Shipley, the Vicar of Wrexham and Dean of St. Asaph, was preparing for the morning service, he asked his son-in-law, Reginald Heber, who was to participate in the day's services, if he could prepare something suitable to be sung.

The family and a few friends were gathered in the vicarage library and were discussing the coming services. Heber retired to a quiet corner and began to write rapidly. Fifteen to twenty minutes had scarcely elapsed before he rejoined the company and read aloud the first three verses of the now world-famous hymn.

An extra verse was added a few minutes later, and the hymn was sung in Wrexham Church the following morning, being set to an old ballad tune, ''Twas when the sea was roaring'.

831. God bless our native land (William Edward Hickson)

Written in 1836 as a new national anthem and published in the *Second-Class Tune Book* (No. 3 of the *Singing Master*); 1930 S.A. song book.

Born in London and later living at Wrotham, Kent, Mr. Hickson (1806-70), a boot manufacturer of Smithfield, retired from business at thirty-seven to devote himself to literary and philanthropic pursuits. Keenly interested in musical culture amongst the ordinary people he published *The Singing Master; containing instructions for teaching Singing in Schools and Families*, as well as *The Use of Singing as part of the Moral Discipline of Schools*. At one time he was a member of the Royal Commission to inquire into the conditions of hand-loom weavers in Great Britain.

832. In Christ there is no East or West (John Oxenham (534))

Bees in Amber, 1913.

Written in 1908 for the missionary pageant, 'The Pageant of Darkness and Light', in connection with the 'Orient in London' Exhibition. John Oxenham planned the scenes and wrote the libretto. The chairman on this occasion was the President of the Board of Trade, Mr. Winston Churchill. The pageant was widely produced during the years 1908-14.

833. Peace in our time, O Lord (John Oxenham (534))

Wide Horizons, 1940; *The Musical Salvationist*, June, 1936, to a dignified musical setting by Eric Ball.

834. Salvation! Shout salvation (Charles Coller (481))

1930 S.A. song book.

835. Tell them in the East and in the West (Arthur S. Arnott (532))

The Musical Salvationist, October, 1920.

'When returning from the 1914 International Congress', wrote Colonel Arnott, 'it was my custom to take my concertina into the dining saloon when the stewards were setting the tables and play a march while they walked round. By and by I found that a catchy melody had revealed itself, which subsequently became the chorus:

Tell them of the Baby in the manger laid . . .

'When the next congress (Australian) loomed up I thought of the melody that came to me on the boat and, looking round for an idea for a verse, saw something that gave me the necessary clue and introduced it at the beginning.'

The clue was, according to the author's own words, the discovery of a piece of music that led off with the idea of starting with C in the stave and coming down to E, and in the following phrase starting with C again and coming down to F.

836. To save the world is our desire (William Pearson (73))

The War Cry, June 15, 1882; 1899 S.A. song book.

837. To save the world the Saviour came (Richard Slater (105) (verses); W. H. Clark (chorus))

The Musical Salvationist, June, 1889; 1930 S.A. song book.

The verses were written at the request of Herbert Booth to have something more in keeping with the Army spirit to take the place of W. H. Clark's words (in an American collection, *The Wells of Salvation*), which began:

> From mountain top and dreary vale,
> From temples old and hoary,
> Proclaim redemption's wondrous tale,
> And give to Jesus Glory.

838. We are witnesses for Jesus (William D. Pennick (413))

The Musical Salvationist, November, 1918; 1930 S.A. song book.

Composed for a quartet of men officers to sing in a meeting conducted by Commissioner Booth-Tucker in the Union Church, Coonoor, Nilgiri Hills, South India, in December, 1916. 'Its application is readily seen,' wrote the Commissioner. ' In the original, what is now verse 2, was verse 1; thus the theme of witnessing began with those already serving " in the lands beyond the sea ". It was just a heart-expression of the work of officers on the mission field.'

The chorus originally commenced:

> Preach the word, O preach the word,
> Make the gospel story heard.

839. We're an Army fighting for a glorious King (William Pearson (73))

1899 S.A. song book.

840. We're the soldiers of the Army of salvation (T. C. Marshall (281))

The Musical Salvationist, December, 1887; 1899 S.A. song book.

Written at Northampton while the author was attached to Herbert Booth's training home staff. Three other members of the staff, accompanied by a few local Salvationists, had been conducting a meeting in a village chapel a few miles away, and were returning in a wagonette singing a song about 'sailing in the old ship of Zion'. Marshall thought the tune eminently suitable for a marching war song and the next day wrote the words.

841. A little ship was on the sea (Dorothy Ann Thrupp)

The Young Soldier, July 1, 1899, where it is stated to be ' No. 44 in *Young Soldier Song Book* '.

Daughter of Joseph Thrupp of Paddington Green, London, Miss Thrupp (1779–1847) wrote a number of hymns and herself edited *Hymns for the Young* about 1830.

842. Around the throne of God in Heaven (Anne Shepherd)

The author's *Hymns adapted to the Comprehension of Young Minds* (about 1838); 1899 S.A. song book.

Born at Cowes, Isle of Wight, the daughter of the Rev. E. H. Houlditch, Rector of Speen, Berkshire, Mrs. Shepherd (1809–57) was also a novelist.

843. Be the matter what it may (Anonymous)

The American Songster, 1868; 1899 S.A. song book.

844. Children of Jerusalem (John Henley)

Sacred Song Book for Children, by C. H. Bateman, in 1843; the next year in John Curwen's *Hymns and Chants*; a number of times in the ' Star Card '; based on Matthew 21: 15.

John Henley was born at Torquay in 1800 and entered the Wesleyan ministry at the age of twenty-four. He died at Weymouth in May, 1842.

845. Children, sing for gladness (Anonymous)

Army Bells.

846. Come to the Saviour, make no delay (George F. Root (229))

Hallelujah Hymn Book; Revival Music; 1878 S.A. song book.

847. Father, lead me day by day (John Page Hopps)

Hymns, Chants and Anthems, 1877; *Army Bells.*

Born in London, Mr. Hopps (1834–1912) was Baptist minister at Hugglestock and Ibstock. In 1856 he became an assistant to the Rev. George Dawson in Birmingham, following which he held pastorates at various Unitarian churches. He was the editor of a number of collections of hymns. He died at Shepperton.

848. Gentle Jesus, meek and mild (Charles Wesley (15))

Hymns and Sacred Poems, 1742, with seven verses; *Hymns for Children*, 1763, with fourteen verses. 1899 S.A. song book, with five verses. We have taken six of the verses and made two songs; this and No. 849.

Among Britishers visited by (the then) Major Harding Young in the Central Internment Camp at Tjimahi, Indonesia, in 1944 was a man of seventy, suffering intensely from cancer. ' His domestic relationships had been very unhappy,' wrote Arch R. Wiggins in *Campaigning in Captivity*, ' and for many years he had been quite indifferent to religion, though in early life he had attended church in a Kentish village. Young often sat up with him all night, talking to him about the love of Christ, but the old man did not respond until just before his death, when he suddenly whispered, "I'd like to pray." He knew no prayer other than that taught him by his mother in the long ago, and he began:

> Gentle Jesus, meek and mild,
> Look upon a little child.

' " It was ", says Lieut.-Colonel Young, " a sight I shall never forget. That skeleton frame torn with pain, and that scarcely audible voice breathing its final prayer. I am certain that he entered into salvation as he slowly uttered the words:

> Fain I would to Thee be brought,
> Gracious Lord, forbid it not . . . "

849. Lamb of God, I look to Thee (Charles Wesley (15))

A continuation of song No. 848.

850. God make my life a little light (Matilda B. Betham-Edwards)

Good Words in 1873; 1930 S.A. song book.

Miss Betham-Edwards (1836–1919) was born at Westerfield, near Ipswich, and died at Hastings. She published a volume of poems in 1885, also some novels. As a journalist the author attended the 1904 International Congress, following which she contributed to *The Independent Review* a very interesting article giving her impressions of the Founder.

851. Great God! and wilt Thou condescend (Ann Gilbert)

The author's *Hymns for Infant Minds*, 1810; 1899 S.A. song book.

Mrs. Gilbert was born on January 30, 1782, in a house opposite Islington Church, in what was then a rural district of London.

When Ann was four the family moved to Lavenham in Suffolk, where they lived until she was fourteen and where, with her sister

Jane, she was taught by her father, Isaac Taylor, and learned his own trade, engraving, at which they worked for many hours a day.

Three years after the family moved to Ongar, where the father became the pastor of the Congregational Chapel, Ann won the prize in a competition (1799) sponsored by an annual called *The Pocket Book*. This encouraged her and her sister Jane in their writing endeavours, and the publishers of *The Pocket Book* invited them to prepare books for children. They also made their own illustrations. ' Twinkle, twinkle little star ' was one of their compositions.

Collaboration ceased when, in 1813, Ann married Rev. Joseph Gilbert, classical and mathematical tutor at the Congregational College, Masborough, Rotherham, and subsequently at Hull and Nottingham.

Ann herself was responsible for *Hymns for Sunday-school Anniversaries*, *Hymns for Infant Schools*, and *The Wedding among the Flowers*.

She died at Nottingham on December 20, 1866.

852. Hushed was the evening hymn (James Drummond Burns)

The author's *The Evening Hymn*, 1856, a collection of thirty-one original hymns and prayers for every evening in the month; *The Musical Salvationist*, September, 1941.

Born in Edinburgh, Mr. Burns (1823–64) was educated in that city, receiving an arts degree from the Edinburgh University. He became the Free Church minister at Dunblane in 1845, but ill health necessitated his resignation three years later. He went abroad in search of health and stayed for a period in Madeira. In 1855 he became the minister of the Presbyterian Church in Hampstead. He died at Mentone but was buried in Highgate Cemetery.

853. I love to hear the story (Emily Huntington Miller)

The Little Corporal, 1867, a magazine of which the author was joint editor in Chicago; *Army Bells*.

The author (1833–1913), daughter of Rev. Thomas Huntington, D.D., was born at Brooklyn., Conn., U.S.A., and received the B.A. degree from Oberlin College In 1860 she married Professor John E. Miller.

' I had had a very serious illness and was slowly recovering,' wrote Mrs. Miller. ' Though too weak to do much literary work, the fact that *The Little Corporal* would be published without my usual contribution was something of a worry to me. I determined, if possible, that this should not happen, so one afternoon, when I felt a little stronger, I took pen and paper and began to write " I love to hear the story ". I remember the words were suggested rapidly and continuously as if I were writing from dictation. In less than fifteen minutes the hymn was written and sent away without any corrections.'

854. I love to hear you tell (William Henry Parker)

Mr. Parker (1845–1929), born at New Basford, Nottingham, a prominent member of the local Baptist church, was particularly interested in writing for the Sunday-school; most of his hymns first appeared on Sunday-school anniversary leaflets; 'I love to hear you tell' was published in 1901.

855. I think, when I read that sweet story of old (Jemima Luke)

The Sunday School Teachers' Magazine, 1841; 1899 S.A. song book.

Although Mrs. Luke (1813–1906), born at Colebrooke Row, Islington, was prevented from being accepted for the Indian mission field by a serious illness, she took a real interest in that work to the end of her life, and for a number of years published the *Foreign Mission Magazine*. In 1843 she was married to Rev. Samuel Luke, a Congregational minister and one of the founders of the Sunday-school Union.

In 1841 the author, then Miss Thompson, went to the Normal Infant School in Gray's Inn Road, London, to obtain some knowledge of the system pertaining there. Among the marching pieces which the teachers had to learn was a Greek air which appealed to her very much. Thinking it would be suitable for a children's hymn she searched but failed to find any words that could be adapted to the tune.

A little later she travelled by stage coach to Taunton. 'It was a beautiful spring morning,' she wrote. 'There was no other passenger inside the coach. On the back of an envelope I wrote in pencil the first two verses in order to teach the tune to the village school supported by my stepmother, and which it was my province to visit.'

Miss Thompson's father superintended the Sunday-school and used to let the children choose their own opening hymn. A few weeks later he was much surprised when they sang a new hymn, 'I think, when I read that sweet story of old', and was more surprised still when he discovered that it was his daughter's composition. He sent the words to *The Sunday School Teachers' Magazine*.

856. If Jesus Christ was sent (Ann Gilbert (851) (verses); Lewis Hartsough (361) (chorus))

Written in 1812 and published in the 1886 edition of *Hymns for Infant Minds*; 1899 S.A. song book.

857. Jesus bids us shine with a clear, pure light (Susan Warner)

Published anonymously in *The Little Corporal*, July, 1868, a monthly magazine published in Chicago and edited by Mrs. Emily Miller (see Song No. 853); *Army Bells*.

Daughter of a lawyer, who faced financial difficulties, and sister of Anna (see Song No. 858), Susan Warner (1819–85) was born at Highland Falls, Orange County, New York. Both sisters became successful novelists and hymn-writers and both were deeply religious.

Under the pen name of Elizabeth Wetherell, Susan wrote *The Wide Wide World*, which was published in 1850 and is said to have gained wider circulation in its day than any other book except *Uncle Tom's Cabin*.

She also taught a Bible class for cadets in the U.S. Military Academy at West Point, where she was buried.

858.　Jesus loves me! This I know (Anna B. Warner)

The Golden Chain, 1861; Ch.M.H.B.

Anna B. Warner (1820–1915), sister of Susan (see Song No. 857), was born in New York and died at Highland Falls, N.Y.

She wrote under the pen name of Amy Lethrop. In 1858 she edited *Hymns of the Church Militant*, and in 1869 published *Wayfaring Hymns, Original and Translated*.

As a Sunday-school teacher it was her custom to write a new hymn for her scholars once a month, setting it to a tune with which they were familiar.

The two gifted sisters collaborated in the writing of a religious novel, *Say and Seal*, a best-seller published in 1859, and this song was written for one of the fictitious characters to sing. In the story, Johnny Fax, a motherless boy, learned about Jesus from his Sunday-school teacher, Mr. Linden. Johnny became very ill and was visited by Mr. Linden, who loved to read to him and to tell him Bible stories and to teach him hymns. Just before the lad's death Mr. Linden taught him to sing 'Jesus loves me! This I know'.

William Bradbury, also an American, saw the words and composed the now equally famous tune in 1861.

859.　Jesus, tender Shepherd, hear me (Mary Duncan)

Written for the author's own children between July and December, 1839, shortly before she died and published by her mother in *Memoirs*, 1841; the following year issued separately in *Hymns for my Children*; 1899 S.A. song book.

The words were set to music by Sir John Stainer, a chorister and afterward the organist of St. Paul's Cathedral, and became the national evening prayer hymn for Scottish boys and girls, much like 'Gentle Jesus, meek and mild' did in England.

Mrs. Duncan was born in Kelso on April 26, 1814, daughter of the parish minister, Rev. Robert Lundie. Her younger sister (see Song

No. 247) became the wife of the Scottish hymn-writer and preacher, Horatius Bonar (see Song No. 4).

Mary went to school in London and early showed some talent for writing verse. In 1836 she married Rev. William Wallace Duncan, minister of Cleish, Kinross-shire, and has been described as ' a rare spirit, amiable, accomplished and beautiful '. Unfortunately, a chill contracted at the end of 1839 developed into a fever and brought her to an early death on January 5, 1840.

860. Jesus wants me for a sunbeam (Nellie Talbot)

The Musical Salvationist, April, 1915.

Miss Talbot, visiting London as a delegate from her Sunday-school, is said to have written these words at the special request of the children of the family with whom she stayed.

Later they were put to music by E. O. Excell of the U.S.A.

861. Jesus, who lived above the sky (Ann Gilbert (851))

Hymns for Infant Minds, 1812, the joint production of Jane and Ann Taylor; 1899 S.A. song book.

862. Now the day is over (Sabine Baring-Gould (680))

Church Times, 1865; *The Musical Salvationist*, September, 1941; written for the author's Sunday-school children at Horbury Bridge, near Wakefield, where he was curate. Based on Proverbs 3: 24.

863. Remember thy Creator while youth is on thy side (Frederick G. Hawkes (568))

The Musical Salvationist, February, 1894—a number entitled ' Songs for Children '; 1899 S.A. song book.

864. Saviour, like a shepherd lead us (Dorothy Ann Thrupp (841))

Published anonymously in a later edition of the author's *Hymns for the Young*, 1836; Carus Wilson's *Children's Friend*; 1899 S.A. song book.

865. Standing by a purpose true (Philip P. Bliss (78))

Sunshine, 1873; *Hallelujah Hymn Book*; *Revival Music*; 1899 S.A. song book; written especially for the author's Sunday-school class in the First Congregational Church at Chicago.

866. Tell me the stories of Jesus (William Henry Parker (854))

Written in 1885; probably first published in an anniversary hymn-sheet for the Sunday-school of the Chelsea Street Baptist Church,

Basford, Nottingham; *Sunday School Hymnary*, 1905; written because of an oft-repeated request by the author's young scholars, ' Teacher, tell us another story.'

867. The wise may bring their learning (Anonymous)

The Book of Praise for Children, 1881; *Congregational Church Hymnal*, 1887; *Army Bells*.

868. There He stood amid a crowd (Kitty Wood)

Captain Wood of Chicago became a missionary in Ceylon, where she married an interpreter to the Supreme Court. She passed away in 1926.

The War Cry, April 17, 1886, written when the author was a cadet in America; *The Musical Salvationist*, June, 1894, and 1899 S.A. song book, with the following chorus by Colonel Hawkes, who wrote the music of the complete song:

> Jesus loves the children, just as much today
> As, when on earth, He stopped them in their play,
> Called them unto Him, and a blessing to each gave;
> Just the same today He wants each little one to save.

869. There's a Friend for little children (Albert Midlane (147))

A children's magazine entitled *Good News for the Little Ones*, December, 1859; 1899 S.A. song book.

Written the previous February, the song originally commenced, ' There's a rest for little children ', but it is said that the author, realizing later that the ' rest ', ' home ', ' robe ', ' song ', ' crown ' and so on were only to be obtained through the ' Friend ', decided to rearrange his verses and place the ' Friend ' first. Sir John Stainer wrote the well-known tune to these words, naming it ' In Memoriam ' to commemorate his little child who had gone to be with the ' Friend ' that the song speaks about.

870. Under the flag we've taken our stand (Ruth Tracy (270))

Army Bells; 1930 S.A. song book.

Written in connection with the Agricultural Hall meetings (1896), and sung by the children as an action song, ' at the request of the young people's department of that day, and with the inspiration of Commissioner Mildred Duff '—with whom the Brigadier was then working on *The Young Soldier*.

871. We bring no glittering treasures (Harriet C. Phillips)

Methodist Episcopalian *Hymns*, 1849; 1899 S.A. song book; written about 1848 for a Sunday-school festival in New York.

The author (1806–84) was born at Sharon, Connecticut, U.S.A., and was for many years a Sunday-school worker.

872. When He cometh (William O. Cushing (804))

Probably appeared first in *Chapel Gems* in the U.S.A.; Wm. B. Bradbury's *Fresh Laurels for the Sabbath School*, 1867; *Army Bells*; based on Malachi 3: 17.

873. When, His salvation bringing (John King)

The Psalmist, 1830; 1899 S.A. song book; probably written for Palm Sunday. Rev. John King, M.A. (1789–1858), was born in Eyton, Wellington, Shropshire, and became the incumbent of Christ Church, Hull.

874. When Jesus looked o'er Galilee (Catherine Baird (400))

The Musical Salvationist, September, 1938. The author says of this song: 'It belongs to those moments of reverie when one tries to see into the mind of our Lord.'

875. Accept my youth, my strength, my prime (Frederick Booth-Tucker (365))

The Musical Salvationist, July, 1894—a special number entitled ' Songs from Many Lands '; 1899 S.A. song book. The Commissioner's contribution represented the Foreign Department, International Headquarters, where he was the Foreign Secretary.

876. Angry words, O let them never (Anonymous)

The American Sacred Songster, 1868; *Hallelujah Hymn Book*; *Revival Music*; 1878 S.A. song book.

877. Be strong in the grace of the Lord (Walter H. Windybank (343))

Written after the Major had seen the necessity for songs in the *Junior's Guide* (' Star Card ') that would fit tunes already published. ' Be strong ' appeared in 1944 and is based on 2 Timothy 2: 1.

878. He who would valiant be (John Bunyan (alt.))

English Hymnal, 1906, to the tune ' Monks Gate ', the Sussex folk-song tune discovered by Vaughan Williams; *Army Songs for Junior Anniversaries*, 1903; *The Musical Salvationist*, November, 1934.

John Bunyan, author of *The Pilgrim's Progress*, was born at Elstow, near Bedford, in 1628. A travelling tinker, he was converted in 1653, and while spending twelve years in Bedford Prison for his preaching of God's word wrote his immortal work. He died on August 31, 1688, and was buried in Bunhill Fields, City Road, London.

Known as 'The Pilgrim Song', the words are taken from the second part of *The Pilgrim's Progress* which pictures Christian's wife and children on their pilgrimage, and the hardships and encouragements they met on the way, with Great-Heart as their conductor. Valiant, after hearing a terrible catalogue of dangers and 'dismal stories', remained unshaken in his resolution.

The original final verse read:

> Hobgoblin nor foul fiend
> Can daunt his spirit;
> He knows he at the end
> Shall life inherit.
> Then fancies fly away;
> He'll not fear what men say;
> He'll labour night and day
> To be a pilgrim.

879. Jesus, with what gladness I can truly sing (Gladys M. Taylor)

1930 S.A. song book.

Brigadier Taylor, born of Salvationist parents, became a corps cadet at Southport when Commissioner Alfred J. Gilliard was Captain and second-in-command of the corps. He suggested that the author should try her hand at song-writing, and the same evening she produced her first set of verses, minus the last line, which the Captain himself encouragingly completed.

In 1927 at Springbourne, Bournemouth, Lieutenant Taylor met with a cycle accident, which called for a time in Highbury Nursing Home instead of taking part in the 'Salvation Siege'. During these days she wrote this song. When Colonel Gerrit Govaars was editing the 1930 edition of the song book and several songs were discarded owing to difficulties of copyright and other reasons, he asked Captain Taylor to write one, whereupon she submitted her 'Siege' song.

The Brigadier, who is a member of the Editorial Department, International Headquarters, has for many years worked among the Primary children at the New Barnet Corps and is a frequent contributor to Army periodicals, particularly *The Young Soldier*, where, under a pen name, she writes for the smaller readers. She is also the compiler of *The Joy Hour* and editor of *The Deliverer*.

880. Just as I am, Thine own to be (Marianne Farningham)

Voices of Praise, 1887; *Army Bells*; said to have been inspired by Miss Charlotte Elliott's hymn, 'Just as I am, without one plea'.

Miss Marianne Hearn (1834–1909), to use the author's real name, was born in Farningham, Kent. Taught to read by her grandmother, and to write by the minister, at the age of six she could read any chapter in the Bible.

She was a member of the Baptist Church and served *The Christian World* and *Sunday School Times* for many years. Most of her hymns, which first appeared in *The Christian World*, were collected in book form.

881. Now, in my early days (John Fawcett (601))

The author's *Hymns adapted to the Circumstances of Public Worship and Private Devotion*, 1782; 1899 S.A. song book; and based on Psalm 119: 9.

882. O Jesus, I have promised (John Ernest Bode)

1869 *Appendix to Psalms and Hymns*, S.P.C.K.; *Army Bells*; 1930 S.A. song book.

Written, probably in 1866, for use at the service at which three of the author's family (two sons and a daughter) were to be confirmed.

Son of Mr. William Bode, some time head of the Foreign Department at the General Post Office, Rev. John Bode, M.A. (1816–74), was born in London, educated at Eton and Oxford, and took Holy Orders in 1841, becoming Rector at Westwell, Oxfordshire, in 1847.

He was appointed Bampton Lecturer in 1855 and when the late Matthew Arnold was elected Professor of Poetry at Oxford, Mr. Bode was only one vote behind. Amongst the books he published was *Hymns from the Gospel of the Day*, 1860. Mr. Bode became Rector of Castle Camps, Cambridgeshire, in 1860, and died there.

883. Plan our life, O gracious Saviour (W. B. Coton)

Coton's *Selection of Community Hymns*, where it is entitled, 'The Youth Movement Hymn'; *Prize and Accepted Settings of the Hymn Tune Association*, 1947, set to an original tune named 'Pontypridd', composed by F. G. Walker; *New Songs for Young People*, May, 1950.

Wilfrid Bayliss, M.I.Mar.E. (1882–1952), who wrote hymns and verse under the name 'W. B. Coton', was born in Portsmouth, the son of an Admiralty inspector and one of a family of eight. As a boy he moved with his family to Pontypridd and grew up under the influence of the great Welsh nonconformist fervour of that time. There he took an extremely active interest in the affairs of his chapel and travelled considerable distances to hear the great preachers of his day. Later his work as a marine engineer took him to Newcastle upon Tyne and Tipton, Staffs, where he became managing director of an engineering firm.

At the age of forty-four a complete breakdown in health and a serious operation preceded about twenty years in hospital, where the writing of new hymns and the encouragement of others to do so became the great object of his life.

884. Rise up, O youth! for mighty winds are stirring (Will. J. Brand (52))

Written in 1938 and published in *The Musical Salvationist* supplement, August, 1940.

885. Saviour, while my heart is tender (John Burton, Jun.)

One hundred Original Hymns for the Young, 1850; *Army Bells*.

John Burton (1803-77), a Congregationalist and born at Stratford, London, followed his father's calling as a cooper and basket-maker. From childhood he is said to have displayed a devout piety which was deepened by a painful illness which for ten years made him a constant sufferer, very often in a helpless condition.

The author, who died at West Ham, London, is usually referred to as John Burton, Jun., to distinguish him from John Burton of Nottingham who wrote Song No. 513.

886. Soldiers of King Jesus (Doris N. Rendell (701))

The Musical Salvationist supplement, February, 1937, where it commenced, 'Knights in shining armour'.

Writing about the song, Lieut.-Colonel Rendell said: 'Here the thought is of a youthful Army, gay and brave, marching with lightness and courage. It is a call to "put on the whole armour", to carry the light of the gospel into dark places, to use the inspiration and enthusiasm and eagerness of youth in the service of the King of kings, catching, too, a sense of our glorious heritage—the present opportunity made possible by the faithful devotion and fearless courage of the saints of the past.'

887. The Lord is King! I own His power (Darley Terry)

The Methodist School Hymnal.

Born at Mirfield, Yorks, Mr. Terry (1848-1934), a printer in Dewsbury, was for many years a member of the Methodist New Connexion Church, which he served in several capacities, particularly in young people's and temperance work. He was a representative of the United Methodist Church on the New Hymn Book Committee, and he 'wrote this hymn whilst a member of the United Methodist School Hymnal Committee and sent it in under a pen name'. He died at Prestatyn.

888. Thou art the Way, none other dare I follow (Arch R. Wiggins)

Written because 'when some are questioning the very existence of God it is good to make a reaffirmation of one's creed'. The first verse appeared in *The Musician*, May 4, 1940, and the complete song in *The Warrior*, August, 1950. Shortly afterward an officer wrote to the editor of *The Warrior*, saying, 'You will be glad to know that during the singing of the second verse on Sunday morning a man came to the Penitent-form.'

First a scholar of the Church of England Sunday-school, then converted in the Methodist Church, Lieut.-Commissioner Wiggins became interested in the Army through an uncle-bandsman at Norland Castle and his parents' Salvationist maid, before becoming a bandsman at Harlesden and one of the first songsters of the corps when the brigade was formed in 1911. In 1914 he entered the International Training College.

As a Lieutenant he was appointed to Devizes to assist Captain (now General) Wilfred Kitching. Other west country corps appointments followed before duties in divisional work. In 1920 the Commissioner was married to Captain Grace Lyons, daughter of Commandant and Mrs. John Lyons, and two years later began his long association with the Editorial Department at International Headquarters, where his responsibilities have included the editorship of *The Life-Saving Scout and Guard* and *The Bandsman and Songster*, which became *The Musician* in 1938.

Five years as Editor-in-chief in Australia preceded his editorship of the International *War Cry* and his appointment as Editor-in-chief at International Headquarters in April, 1952. The Commissioner retired from active service in April, 1959.

Lieut.-Commissioner Wiggins is the author of *Father of Salvation Army Music, Campaigning in Captivity, Knights of the Blizzard, T. H. K.*, and many songs in *The Musical Salvationist*.

889. We have heard our marching orders (Will. J. Brand (52))

Written by request for *Special Songs for Young People's Anniversaries and Festal Occasions*, No. 10 (1948).

890. We're in God's Army and we fight (Catherine Baird (400))

New Songs for Young People, January, 1950.
' I wrote this in an effort to make clear that The Salvation Army is exactly the opposite to the armies of violence,' the Colonel reveals. ' To save, not to destroy is our aim.

'And though we go to battle, it is not with men, but to overthrow by means of God's weapons of love and grace, the evil in the world.'

891. Yield not to temptation, for yielding is sin (Horatio R. Palmer)

National Sunday-school Teacher's Magazine; later in the author's *Songs of Love for the Bible* (1874); *Hallelujah Hymn Book; Revival Music*; 1878 S.A. song book; written in 1868 while the author was studying the theory of music.

Horatio Palmer (1834–1907), who received his Doctorate of Music in 1880 from the Chicago University, was born at Sherburne, New York. Taking up music as his profession, he studied at Berlin and Florence, and became an organist at seventeen. He was appointed Director of the Rushford Academy of Music, New York, in 1857. He was the author of several works on the theory of music, and editor of the music editions of a number of hymnals to which he contributed some of his own tunes. He died at Yonkers, New York.

892. And are we yet alive (Charles Wesley (15))

Hymns and Sacred Poems, 1749; Ch.M.H.B.

' If we read with historical feeling ', wrote Dr. J. Ernest Rattenbury, ' there is something very moving in the hymn with which the Methodist Conference, for nearly 200 years, has opened its proceedings. In early days itinerate preachers underwent great hardship and poverty; their journeyings over the roads of England, the mobs they had to face and the continual peril to their lives, must have given significance to the hymn that they sang—strange as the opening question seems to us today—when after a year's separation they meet together in Conference.'

893. Father, let me dedicate (Lawrence Tuttiett (verses))

The author's *Gems of Thought on the Sunday Special Services*, 1864; 1930 S.A. song book.

Lawrence Tuttiett (1825–97) was born at Cloyton, Devonshire, son of a naval surgeon, and educated at Christ's Hospital and King's College, London. He had intended to follow the medical profession but, turning to the church, was ordained in 1848 and in 1880 received a canonry at St. Ninian's Cathedral, Perth.

Many of his hymns were composed on returning from his visitation of the sick or the burial of the dead, to express the feelings that had been engendered.

894. My times are in Thy hand (William Freeman Lloyd)

Hymns for the Poor of the Flock, 1838, though possible appearing elsewhere three years earlier.

Born at Uley, Gloucestershire, Mr. Lloyd (1791–1853) took a great interest in Sunday-school work and became one of the secretaries of the Sunday-school Union as well as editor of various magazines and periodicals in the interest of the young. He was also associated with the Religious Tract Society. He died at Stanley Hall, Gloucestershire.

895. O God of Bethel, by whose hand (Philip Doddridge (5))

Written, as was the custom of Philip Doddridge, the Nonconformist minister of Northampton, to follow a sermon he preached on 'Jacob's Vow' (Genesis 28: 20–22) on January 16, 1736. There are many variations. 1930 S.A. song book.

'O God of Bethel' was a favourite with David Livingstone whilst wandering in the wilds of Africa, and was sung on April 18, 1874, when his remains were borne to their last resting-place in Westminster.

896. The Lord of earth and sky (Charles Wesley (15))

Hymns and Sacred Poems, 1749; *Hymns for New Year's Day*, 1750; Ch.M.H.B.; a paraphrase of our Lord's parable of the Barren Fig Tree (Luke 13: 6–9).

The verse commencing

> When justice bared the sword,
> To cut the fig-tree down

has been omitted from the present setting.

897. We greet with joy the glad new year (Julia Peacock)

1899 S.A. song book.

The author was a soldier of the Brighton Congress Hall Corps and a frequent contributor to Army periodicals in the 1890s. For *The War Cry* of February 8, 1896, she compiled a page of songs, including two of her own.

898. Christic the Lord is risen again (Michael Weisse; *translated by* Catherine Winkworth (7))

First published in Bohemia, 1531; translation in *Lyra Germanica*, 2nd Series, 1858. John Telford suggests that it may be based upon 'Christ ist erstanden', one of the first German hymns, traced as early as the twelfth century.

While Michael Weisse (1480–1534), born at Neisse, in Silesia, was a monk in Breslau he came under the influence of Luther's writings and joined with the Bohemian Brethren, among whom he rose to a position of influence, becoming a member of their Council and editor of their first hymn book in German. He died at Landskron.

899. Christ the Lord is risen today (Charles Wesley (15))

Hymns and Sacred Poems, 1739, and first sung to a tune called 'Georgia', an adaptation of Handel's 'See the Conquering Hero comes'. Ch.M.H.B. The 'Hallelujahs' were added later.

'Hallelujah', a word so definitely associated with The Salvation Army right around the world, has been associated with Easter morning since the early Christians greeted each other with 'Hallelujah! the Lord is Risen!' to which the reply came, 'He is risen indeed!'

900. Have you heard the angels singing (Cornelie Booth (140))

The Musical Salvationist, July, 1894, a special number entitled 'Songs from Many Lands'; reprinted from the Canadian *War Cry*; 1899 S.A. song book. The author and her husband, Commandant Herbert Booth, were at the time in charge of Army work in the Dominion of Canada.

901. I know that my Redeemer lives (Samuel Medley (172))

George Whitefield's *Psalms and Hymns*, 21st edition, 1775; in 1800 was included in the author's London edition of his *Hymns*; Ch.M.H.B.; the original setting contained nine verses and was based on Job 19: 25.

902. In wondrous love and might arrayed (Julia Peacock (897))

The War Cry, April 4, 1896; 1899 S.A. song book.

903. Let us rejoice, the fight is won (Percy Dearmer)

Songs of Praise; written particularly for a tune which had been published in *The English Hymnal*—a German tune for which the author considered some suitable Easter words should be provided.

Born in London, Dr. Dearmer (1867–1936) was educated at both Westminster School and in Switzerland before entering Christ Church, Oxford. In *Hymns in Christian Worship*, H. A. L. Jefferson wrote of him as 'a man of versatile and brilliant gifts; artist, poet, preacher, writer and social reformer, and a scholarly exponent of liturgical history'. For fifteen years he served as Vicar of St. Mary the Virgin Church, Primrose Hill, London. He was Secretary of the Committee of *The English Hymnal* and editor of *Songs of Praise*. In 1931 he was appointed Canon of Westminster.

904. Look, ye saints! The sight is glorious (Thomas Kelly (97))

The author's *Hymns*, 3rd edition, 1809; Ch.M.H.B.; based on Hebrews 2: 9.

905. Low in the grave He lay (Robert Lowry (231))

Written in 1874; published in *Brightest and Best*, 1875; 1899 S.A. song book.

906. O joyful sound! O glorious hour (Thomas Kelly (97) (verses))

The author's *Hymns*, 1804; altered version in Hall's *Mitre Hymn Book*, 1836; 1899 S.A. song book.

Our version is a somewhat altered form of a song which commenced with an earlier verse:

> Come, see the place where Jesus lay
> And hear angelic watchers say:
> He lives, who once was slain!
> Why seek the living midst the dead?
> Remember how the Saviour said
> That He would rise again.

907. Welcome, happy morning (Venantius Fortunatus; *translated by* John Ellerton (615))

Translation in Borthwick's *Supplementary Hymn and Tune Book*, 1869, the original being part of a long poem on the Resurrection addressed to the author's friend Felix, Bishop of Nantes.

Fortunatus (530–609), a native of Italy, studied at Milan and Ravenna and for a number of years lived a life of pleasure. According to tradition he was miraculously cured of blindness by the oil from the lamp of St. Martin's, Tours, and whilst on a pilgrimage thither he met Queen Radegunda who had founded a nunnery at Poitiers. Through the Queen's influence Fortunatus was led to take Holy Orders, and was later elected Bishop of Poitiers.

908. Holy Spirit, hear us (William Henry Parker (854))

The School Hymnal, 1880; the following year in *Children's Book of Praise*; although, as most of the author's hymns, was probably first printed in sheet form for his own Sunday-school at New Basford, Nottingham.

909. Lord God, the Holy Ghost (James Montgomery (14))

Cotterill's *Selection*, 1819; Ch.M.H.B.

910. O Holy Ghost, on Thee we wait (Will. J. Brand (52))

Written as a song for Whitsuntide with the title, 'A Prayer for the Spirit'.

911. At harvest time our eyes behold (Ruth Tracy (270))

Harvest Festival Songs, 1891; 1930 S.A. song book.
Written after listening to Commissioner Mildred Duff speaking on the words of Jesus in John 12: 24.

912. Come, ye thankful people, come (Henry Alford (103))

The author's *Psalms and Hymns*, 1844; revised by Dean Alford himself in his *Poetical Works*, 1865; *Harvest Festival Songs*, 1891; 1930 S.A. song book.

913. Eternal Source of every joy (Philip Doddridge (5))

Written on January 1, 1736, as a hymn for New Year's Day, based on Psalm 65: 11 and first published in 1755; *Harvest Festival Songs*, 1891, and 1930 S.A. song book included the chorus

> In summer, autumn, winter, spring,
> Salvation heavenly joy doth bring;
> Then praises sing unto our King,
> Whose love is shown in everything.

914. Our thankful hearts need joyful songs (Richard Slater (105))

Written in August, 1898; 1899 S.A. song book.

915. Seeds now we are sowing, and fruit they must bear (Richard Slater (105))

Written on February 12, 1891, and first appeared in *The Musical Salvationist* for July of that year.

916. Sing to the Lord of harvest (John S. B. Monsell (750))

The author's *Hymns of Love and Praise*, 1866; *The Musical Salvationist*, August, 1902; 1930 S.A. song book. The author also provided an original musical setting as a duet for treble and alto voices.

917. Sow in the morn thy seed (James Montgomery (14))

First used at the Sheffield Sunday-school Annual Whitsuntide Festival in 1832; published in the author's *Poet's Portfolio*, 1835, and in his *Original Hymns*, 1853.

In February, 1832, the author was returning to Bath and travelling between Gloucester and Tewkesbury, when he saw a number of women and girls ' dibbling ' in a field, that is, making holes in the soil into which they dropped two or three seeds. As the journey continued his thoughts turned into verse, and (to quote his own words)

'I found them running lines, like furrows, along the field of my imagination'.

918. Sowing in the morning, sowing seeds of kindness (Knowles Shaw)

Fillmore's *Songs of Glory*; in 1887 in John Burnham's *Song Evangel* for the use of the Metropolitan Tabernacle; 1899 S.A. song book.

Knowles Shaw, born in Venice, Ohio, in 1834, was, when about eighteen years of age, playing a violin at a dance when God spoke to him through the last words of his dying father—'Prepare to meet thy God'—spoken to him five years earlier. Shaw left the dance hall never to return, and in due course was ordained as a minister.

919. Sowing the seed by the dawn-light fair (Emily Sullivan Oakey)

Family Treasure, 1861; *Revival Music*; 1878 S.A. song book.

The author (1829–83), born in Albany, New York, was a frail, delicate woman who never knew an hour of real good health. She was educated at the Albany Female Academy and became an author and linguist.

920. This is the field, the world below (Joseph Hinchsliffe)

A tract entitled *Favourite Hymns, Odes and Anthems, as sung at the Methodist Chapels in Sheffield, Rotherham, Doncaster and Nottingham Circuits*, 5th edition, 1797; Ch.M.H.B.

Mr. Hinchsliffe, born in Sheffield in 1760, was a silversmith and cutler and a member of the choir of the Wesleyan Society at Norfolk Street, Sheffield, and later at Dumfries, where he died in 1807.

921. To Thee, O Lord of earth and sky (T. C. Marshall (281))

The War Cry, September 14, 1889; *The Musical Salvationist*, July, 1891; 1899 S.A. song book.

922. To Thee, O Lord, our hearts we raise (William Chatterton Dix)

Written in 1863 and printed the following year in St. Raphael's (Bristol) *Hymns for the Service of the Church*.

Son of a surgeon, William Chatterton Dix (1837–98) was born in Bristol and educated at the Grammar School of that city, being intended for a mercantile career. He did, however, become the manager of a marine insurance company in Glasgow. He was a very earnest Christian and the author of several books.

The 'old boys' of the Bristol Grammar School have erected a memorial to him in the Bristol Cathedral.

923. We plough the fields, and scatter (Matthias Claudius; *translated by* Jane Montgomery Campbell)

Rev. Charles S. Bere's *Garland of Song*, 1861; *Harvest Festival Songs*, 1891; 1930 S.A. song book; part of a poem of seventeen verses in the sketch entitled *Paul Erdmann's Fest*, and is a picture of a north German harvest thanksgiving in a farm-house.

Matthias Claudius (1740–1815), born at Reinfeld, near Lübeck, Holstein, son of a Lutheran pastor, although intended for the Church, came under the influence of a company of free-thinkers and left the study of theology for literature and law. He became editor of *The Wandsbeck Messenger*, and in 1776 was appointed one of the Commissioners of Agriculture and Manufactures of Hesse Darmstadt, later editing one of the official newspapers there. A severe illness revealed his need of a spiritual foundation and he returned to the faith of his childhood. In 1788 he was appointed auditor of the Schleswig-holstein Bank at Altona.

Miss Campbell (1817–78), daughter of the Rev. A. M. Campbell, Vicar of St. James, Paddington, taught singing to the children of her father's parish school, and later, in Bovey Tracey, Devon, gave valuable assistance to the Rev. Charles S. Bere in the compilation of his works.

924. We praise Thee, Lord, with heart and voice (William Pearson (73))

1899 S.A. song book.

925. A child this day is born (Anonymous)

Sandy's *Christmas Carols*, 1833; *The Musical Salvationist*, November, 1947. There are twenty-one verses in the original where the refrain begins ' Novels, Novels, Novels ' (' novels ' meaning news).

William Sandys (1792–1874) was a London solicitor, but was well known also as an antiquarian and took a special interest in music, particularly in folk music.

926. All my heart this night rejoices (Paulus Gerhardt (81); *translated by* Catherine Winkworth (7))

Crüger's *Praxis Pietetis Melica*, 1656; translation in *Lyra Germanica*, part 2, 1858; *The Musical Salvationist*, December, 1938. The original German hymn had fifteen verses.

927. Angels, from the realms of Glory (James Montgomery (14))

Iris, a Sheffield newspaper edited by the author, December 24, 1816; Ch.M.H.B.; the original included an extra verse:

> Sages, leave your contemplations,
>   Brighter visions beam afar;
> Seek the great Desire of Nations,
>   Ye have seen His natal star;
> Come and worship . . .

928. As with gladness men of old (William Chatterton Dix (922))

Rev. A. H. Ward's *Supplement*, 1860; *Hymns of Love and Joy*, a small collection of hymns for private circulation published by the author in 1861; Christmas number of *The Musical Salvationist*, 1902; written while the author, unable through illness to attend the church services on the Feast of the Epiphany, January 6, 1860, lay thinking about the event they would be celebrating in church. Matthew 2: 1–12 seemed to him to be fraught with real practical teaching for ourselves, and the Wise Men, to his mind, were examples to be followed.

929. Away in a manger, no crib for a bed (*attributed to* Martin Luther)

Christmas Carols, Old and New.

Born in 1483 at Eisleben, a village in Saxony, where his father was a miner, Martin Luther grew up amid hardness and poverty. He went to the grammar school in Eisenach and helped his father to pay for his books and school fees by singing from door to door. It was on such an occasion, when thus singing between school hours, that Frau Ursula Cotta, a lady of ample means and noble heart, was struck by his voice and face, and became his lifelong patron. This friendship was young Luther's providential introduction into that higher society, in which he was later to move so freely. From school he passed to the University of Erfurt, where he received his master's degree in 1503, and two years later he entered its monastery as a monk.

Luther is remembered not only for the part he played in the Reformation, but for his being a leading figure in the development of congregational singing in the Church. He is attributed with having written thirty-seven hymns and is also known to have composed a number of tunes. There is a tradition that 'Away in a manger', usually ascribed to Luther, was written for his small son's Christmas celebration in 1520. Luther died on February 18, 1546.

Verse 3 is a later addition and has been ascribed to an American, John T. McFarland, one-time secretary of the Board of Sunday-schools in New York.

930. Christians awake, salute the happy morn (John Byrom)

The author's *Poems* (1773); Ch.M.H.B.

On Christmas morning, 1749, Dr. Byrom playfully presented to his favourite daughter Dolly a neatly folded sheet of notepaper on which was written a forty-eight-line poem entitled ' Christmas Day for Dolly '. The original manuscript is still preserved in the Cheetham Library at Manchester.

Some time later a copy of the poem fell into the hands of John Wainwright, organist of Manchester Old Parish Church, who, seeing the possibilities in the words, set them to the tune with which we are now so familiar. The following Christmas Eve, Wainwright, having practised the new Christmas hymn, took his choristers over to Kersal Cell, the home of Byrom, and as the clock struck twelve they sang ' Christians awake ' for the first time.

John Byrom (1692–1763) was born at Kersal Cell, Manchester, and was educated at King's School, Chester, Merchant Taylor's School, and Trinity College, Cambridge. He took his degree in medicine at Montpellier but, instead of practising as a doctor, earned his livelihood by teaching shorthand. Among his many pupils were Lord Chesterfield, Sir Horace Walpole, and Charles Wesley. Byrom invented the dots for vowels which Sir Isaac Pitman later adopted in his method of shorthand writing, and was the inventor of the two well-known fictitious characters, ' Tweedledum and Tweedledee '. He was ' extremely tall, carried a stick and wore a curious low-polled, slouched hat, from under the long-peaked brim of which his benignant face bent forward a cautiously inquisitive kind of look, as if he were in the habit of prying into everything '.

931. Come, Thou long-expected Jesus (Charles Wesley (15))

Hymns for the Nativity of our Lord, 1744; 1899 S.A. song book.

932. Do you know the song that the angels sang (A. P. Cobb)

Written probably by an American; *The Christian Choir*, edited by Ira D. Sankey and James McGranahan, published in 1884 and 1896; *Christmas Carols Old and New*.

933. Hark the glad sound! the Saviour comes (Philip Doddridge (5))

Translations and Paraphrases of the Church of Scotland, 1745; an abridgement of the original hymn composed on December 28, 1735, and based on our Lord's address in the synagogue (Luke 4: 16–30); 1899 S.A. song book.

934. Hark! the herald angels sing (Charles Wesley (15))

Written and published in *Hymns and Sacred Poems* in 1739; Ch.M.H.B.

According to tradition Charles Wesley, coming out one Christmas morning on his way to church, heard the bells ringing and exclaimed, ' Hark, how all the welkin rings glory to the King of kings '—' Welkin ' being an old word meaning ' the vault of heaven '. Thus it was this remark which later expanded into the well-known Christmas song which originally began with the same words. For many years the words were sung to Handel's ' See the Conquering Hero comes '.

935. It came upon the midnight clear (Edmund Hamilton Sears)

Christmas number of the *Christian Register*, 1850, at Boston, U.S.A.; Christmas number of *The Musical Salvationist*, 1902.

A descendant of Richard Sears who came from John Robinson's congregation in Holland to join the Plymouth Colony in 1630, Dr. Sears (1810–76) was born in Sandisfield, Berkshire, Massachusetts. Educated at Union College, Schenectady, he graduated in 1834 and began to study law, but later took to a theological course at Harvard Divinity School before entering the Unitarian ministry. Nominally of this persuasion he once wrote, ' Though I was educated in the Unitarian denomination, I believe and preach the divinity of Christ.'

936. O come, all ye faithful (*translated by* Frederick Oakeley)

Though sometimes ascribed to St. Bonaventura (1221–74), 'Adeste Fideles' is more probably a Latin hymn of French or German authorship of the seventeenth or eighteenth century. It is found with its tune in a manuscript volume dated 1751, at Stonyhurst, and in a similar manuscript, possibly of earlier date, in the Henry Watson Library, Manchester. Canon Oakeley's translation was made in 1841 for use in the services at St. Margaret's, Cavendish Square, London, and was included in the *People's Hymnal*, 1867, where it began ' Ye faithful approach ye '. *Christmas Carols Old and New*; 1930 S.A. song book.

Frederick Oakeley (1802–80), born at Shrewsbury, son of a former Governor of Madras, was for a period Canon and Prebendary of Lichfield Cathedral. Whilst at St. Margaret's he introduced an ultra-ritualistic service which led to a crisis and the withdrawal of his licence. In 1845 he was received into the Roman Catholic Church. He worked for many years among the poor in Westminster, and in 1852 he was made a Canon of Westminster.

937. O little town of Bethlehem (Phillips Brooks)

English Hymnal, 1906; *Christmas Carols, Old and New*; written for the children of Dr. Brooks's Sunday-school at Holy Trinity Church,

Philadelphia, in 1868, three years after he had spent part of the Christmas week in Bethlehem.

Born at Boston, Mass., U.S.A., Phillips Brooks (1835–93) was educated at Harvard and was ordained in 1859. He became Rector of the Church of the Advent, Philadelphia, and later of Holy Trinity, Philadelphia, and in 1869 took charge of the famous Trinity Church, Boston. Both Harvard and Oxford bestowed a D.D. degree upon him, and in 1891 he became Bishop of Massachusetts.

Six-feet-six in height, Phillips Brooks ' attained national fame as a preacher and writer; he was also a giant in his tenderness of spirit and attractiveness of personality and radiance of countenance '. When a little girl was told that Bishop Brooks had gone to Heaven she replied spontaneously, ' Oh, Mummy, how happy the angels will be.'

938. Once, in royal David's city (Cecil Frances Alexander (22))

The author's *Hymns for little Children*, 1848; *The Musical Savationist*, November, 1920; based on the words of the Creed, ' Who was conceived of the Holy Ghost, born of the Virgin Mary '; 1930 song book. In the original there is a final verse:

> Not in that poor lowly stable,
>   With the oxen standing by,
> We shall see Him; but in Heaven
>   Set at God's right hand on high;
> When like stars His children crowned,
> All in white shall wait around.

939. See, amid the winter's snow (Edward Caswall (45))

The Masque of Mary and Other Poems, 1858; *The Musical Salvationist*, November, 1949.

940. Silent night! Holy night! (Joseph Mohr)

Leipziger Gesangbuch, 1838.

Joseph Mohr (1792–1848) was born at Salzburg, Austria, son of a musketeer in the service of the Archbishop. Joseph studied at the local grammar school and was a member of the choir of St. Peter's Church in the same city. He became a priest at the age of twenty-three and spent the whole of his priesthood with the small Catholic communities in and around Oberndorf, the small Austrian village in the mountains about eighteen miles down the River Salzach from Salzburg.

Franz Gruber, the organist at the neighbouring village of Arnsdorf, wanting something new for Christmas, composed the lovely tune with the aid of his guitar to his friend Mohr's words one evening just before Christmas, 1818. (See *He had no revolver* by F. L. Coutts, pp. 40–42.) Because the church organ was out of order at the time the carol was first sung during a Christmas service to the accompaniment of the guitar. The church was later destroyed by fire, but a memorial church has been erected in which there are two beautiful stained glass windows, one showing Gruber playing his guitar and the other depicting Mohr with pen in hand writing his immortal words.

The organ-builder who came from Zillertal to Arnsdorf to carry out the necessary repairs heard the carol, took it back to his own village and taught it to four sisters named Strasser, young women famed for their renderings of the Tyrolean mountain songs. They introduced it into their concert programmes throughout the Tyrol.

941. The first Nowell the angel did say (Anonymous)

Christmas Carols Old and New.

Probably three hundred years old, ' The First Nowell ' was discovered in 1823 by Davis Gilbert, who included it in his second edition of a book of carols.

The French word ' Noel ' is the equivalent for ' Christmas ', whilst our ' Nowell ' is said to be a contraction of ' Nouvelle ', meaning ' good tidings ', or ' good news '.

942. When wise men came seeking (Richard Slater (105))

A slightly altered version of that written in October, 1892, and published in *All the World*, December of the same year; 1899 S.A. song book.

943. While shepherds watched their flocks by night (Nahum Tate (16))

The Appendix with Hymns to the New Version of the Psalms by Nahum Tate and Nicholas Brady; 1899 S.A. song book.

944. For Thy mercy and Thy grace (Henry Downton)

Church of England Magazine, 1843.

Rev. Henry Downton (1818–85), son of the sub-librarian of Trinity College, Cambridge, was born at Pulverbatch, Shropshire, and was himself educated at Trinity College. He took his M.A. degree in 1843, became perpetual curate of St. John's, Chatham, the same year, and in 1857 the English Chaplain at Geneva. He died at Hopton.

945. Heavenly Father, Thou hast brought us (Hester Periam Hawkins)

Written by Mrs. Hawkins (*née* Lewis) of Bedford, joint editor of *The Home Hymn-book, Manual of Sacred Song for the Family Circle*, 1885,

for the golden wedding celebrations of her father and mother in 1885.
An omitted verse makes a personal reference to this 'family occasion':

> Father, all Thy gifts are precious,
> But we thank Thee most for this,
> That so many years of toiling
> Have been soothed by wedded bliss;
> Since our hearts were first united,
> Life has not been free from care,
> But our burdens were the lighter
> When each bore an equal share.

946. O God, our help in ages past (Isaac Watts (3))

Part 1 of the author's paraphrase of Psalm 90 in his *Psalms of David*,
1719; John Wesley's *Collection of Psalms and Hymns*, 1737, where he
substituted 'O' for 'Our' at the commencement of the first verse;
1899 S.A. song book; written about the year 1714, shortly before the
death of Queen Anne, at a time of great national anxiety.

'In the estimation of our readers this hymn is the second favourite
(to quote *John O'London* in 1925). I should have chosen it myself and
I think it ought to have been the Wembley Hymn. . . . It has peculiarly
English associations, for the Psalm on which it is founded was a burial
hymn in England as early as 1662 and, as Mr. Stead observed, it was
chanted as a dirge at the funeral of John Hampden. In the roll of its
words, which suggest muffled thunder, one seems to hear the foot-
tread of all faith.'

947. Sing we many years of blessing (Will. J. Brand (52))

Written for the jubilee celebrations of the Dartford (Kent) Corps
in the late 1930s. The first line commenced, 'Sing we fifty years of
blessing'.

948. Blest be the dear uniting love (Charles Wesley (15))

Hymns and Sacred Songs, 1742; Ch.M.H.B.

949. God be with you till we meet again (Jeremiah Eames Rankin)

First sung in the Congregational Church, Washington, where the
author ministered for fifteen years; Sankey's *Sacred Songs and Solos*;
The Officer, June, 1895; the Supplement to *The Musical Salvationist*,
1894–95; 1899 S.A. song book.

Dr. Rankin (1828–1904), a Congregational minister born at
Thornton, New Hampshire, U.S.A., and who edited the *Gospel
Temperance Hymnal* and *Gospel Bells*, was for several years President of
Howard University, Washington. He composed this song in 1882 as
a Christian good-bye, on the basis of the etymology of 'good-bye',

which means 'God be with you'. The author sent a copy of the first verse to two music composers, one a comparatively unknown writer, a Mr. Tomer, who was a school-teacher and a clerk in the Treasury Department, the other, Charles Converse, composer of 'What a friend we have in Jesus', with a request that each submit a tune suitable for the words. Dr. Rankin selected Mr. Tomer's melody.

950. Lord of heaven and earth and sea (Frank Samuel Turney)

Written and printed specially as an 'Ode for Dedication Day, March, 1927' for the University Baptist Church, Baltimore, Maryland, U.S.A. The following notice appeared as a sub-heading:

'This song of prayer and thanksgiving, specially written for the occasion, dedicates our beautiful church to its high and holy purpose of divine worship, with a prayer for personal dedication as " living stones " in a spiritual house. A note of praise for the spared lives of honored and beloved brethren and a tribute to the revered memory of Dr. A. C. Dixon, precedes a prayer for the years which are yet to be.'

Son of a London City Missioner, Mr. Turney was born on October 14, 1863, and was brought up in the Baptist Church, but in 1887 became a member of the Dawes Road Congregational Church, Fulham. He occupied the offices of Choir Secretary, Musical Director of the Sunday-school, and Deacon. For a time he was deputy conductor of both the London Sunday-school Choir and the Nonconformist Choir Union Festivals at the Crystal Palace.

An authority on hymnology, Mr. Turney was for fifty years in the employment of the publishers, Morgan and Scott. As a proof-reader he came into intimate friendship with Mr. Sankey on the compilation of *Sacred Songs and Solos*. Later Mr. Turney was connected with the Torry-Alexander Revivalist Mission and toured Australia and the U.S.A. He died on October 27, 1932, and was buried in Fulham Old Cemetery.

951. O God, in whom alone is found (Henry Ware (603))

Lyra Sac. Americana, 1868; 1930 S.A. song book.

952. O Lord, regard Thy people (Albert Orsborn (42))

1930 S.A. song book.

Written at the request of General Bramwell Booth and used at the stone-laying ceremony of the William Booth Memorial Training College, Denmark Hill, London, in May, 1928.

953. O Saviour, now to Thee we raise (Anonymous)

1899 S.A. song book; probably an early Army production for it breathes the spirit of those warlike and adventurous days.

954. This stone to Thee in faith we lay (James Montgomery (14))

Written on October 30, 1822, for the stone-laying ceremony of Christ Church, Attercliffe, Sheffield, and published in the author's newspaper *Iris* on November 5th the same year. 1899 S.A. song book.

955. Thy presence and Thy glories, Lord (Samuel Medley (172))

Written in 1789 with an earlier verse—'Great God! Thy glory and Thy love'; 1930 S.A. song book.

956. Bring your tithes into the storehouse (Barbara Stoddart (120))

The War Cry, October 28, 1893; 1899 S.A. song book.

957. Christ of self denial (William Pearson (73))

The War Cry, September 19, 1891; 1899 S.A. song book; originally began:

> God of Self-Denial, Thou for help dost call,
> Self has given little, Thou hast given all.

958. O Lord of heaven and earth and sea (Christopher Wordsworth)

Third edition of *The Holy Year*, 1863, a collection of original hymns by Wordsworth, written to cover the various church seasons and occasions and to teach doctrine and illustrate the teaching of the Book of Common Prayer.

Nephew of William Wordsworth the poet and son of the Rector of Lambeth (later Master of Trinity College, Cambridge), Christopher Wordsworth (1807-85) was born at the Rectory, Lambeth, London. After a brilliant career at Winchester and Cambridge he took Holy Orders in 1833 and three years later was elected headmaster of Harrow School. He received his Doctorate of Divinity in 1839. Five years later he was appointed Canon of Westminster and Archdeacon in 1865. From 1869 he was Bishop of Lincoln, where he died.

959. This, our week of Self-Denial (Will. J. Brand (52))

Written especially for this song book.

960. Lord, we ask Thy richest blessing (David Thomas)

1899 S.A. song book.

Father of Lieut.-Colonel David Thomas, who was promoted to Glory on May 7, 1924, the author was born on January 17, 1829, and died, one of the oldest soldiers of the Pembroke Dock Corps, on March 19, 1904.

961. O Father, all creating (John Ellerton (615))

Written at the request of the Duke of Westminster for the marriage of his daughter, Lady Elizabeth Harriet Grosvenor, to the Marquis of Ormonde on February 2, 1876. Four years later it was included in *Prebendary Thring's Collection*.

962. O God of love, to Thee we bow (William Vaughan Jenkins)

Composed for the author's own wedding.

William Vaughan Jenkins (1868-1920) was born in Bristol and educated at the Bristol Grammar School, ultimately becoming a chartered accountant. A choir leader, he was also interested in the Adult School Movement and took some active interest in the compiling of *The Fellowship Hymn Book* for that movement.

963. O Guest divine, be with us now (Will. J. Brand (52))

The Musical Salvationist, May, 1945; written for the wedding ceremony of two young officers, friends of the author.

964. O Perfect Love, all human thought transcending (Dorothy Frances Gurney)

Supplement to *Hymns Ancient and Modern*; *The Musical Salvationist*, September, 1936.

Granddaughter of Bishop Blomfield and daughter of the Rector of St. Andrew Undershaft, London, Dorothy Frances Blomfield (1858–1932) was born at Finsbury Circus, London.

'I wrote the hymn for the marriage of my sister, Mrs. Hugh Redmayne,' said the author. 'We were all singing hymns one Sunday evening, and had just finished " O Strength and Stay ", a great favourite with my sister. She remarked how sorry she was that it was unsuitable for a wedding and, turning to me, said, " What is the use of a sister who writes poetry if she cannot write me new words to this tune? " I picked up the hymn book and said, " Well, if nobody will disturb me there, I will go into the library and see what I can do." After about a quarter of an hour I came back with the hymn " O Perfect Love ". It had been no effort to me after the initial idea had come to me of the twofold aspect of perfect union, love and life.' Later Sir J. Barnby made an arrangement to be used as an anthem for the marriage of Princess Louise with the Duke of Fife on July 27, 1889.

Mrs. Gurney was the author also of

> The kiss of the sun for pardon,
> The song of the birds for mirth,
> One is nearer God's heart in a garden
> Than anywhere else on earth.

—and two volumes of poems.

965. Our Jesus freely did appear (John Berridge (verses 1-3))

Gospel Magazine, August, 1775, and signed 'Old Everton'; 1930 S.A. song book.

The author (1716–93), born at Kingston, Northamptonshire, was once described as an 'eccentric but sanctified genius, who, with Wesley and others, worked in the pulpit, with his pen, at home and abroad for the religious renovation of his country'.

In an epitaph for his own tombstone, this eccentric divine gave, in his own characteristic manner, some particulars concerning his life. It read thus:

'Here lie the remains of John Berridge, late Vicar of Everton, and an itinerant servant of Jesus Christ, who loved his Master and His work, and after running on His errands for many years was caught up to wait on Him above. Reader, art thou born again? (No salvation without a new birth.) I was born in sin, February, 1716; remained ignorant of my fallen state till 1730; lived proudly on faith and works for salvation till 1754; was admitted to Everton Vicarage, 1755; fled to Jesus for refuge, 1755; fell asleep in Jesus, January 22, 1793.'

966. Saviour, let Thy sanction rest (Thomas Raffles)

New Congregational Hymn Book, 1859; dated November 3, 1852, and written for the marriage of the Rev. J. F. and Mrs. Guenett; Ch.M.H.B.

Dr. Raffles (1788-1863), son of a London solicitor, was born in Spitalfields, London, and commenced his first pastorate in the Congregational ministry at Hammersmith in 1809. Three years later he commenced his forty-nine years' ministry at St. George Street Church, Liverpool, where for many years he wrote a hymn for his congregation every New Year's Day. These were published in 1868.

967. Spirit divine, Thou loveliest and holy (Bramwell Walker)

Written for the author's own marriage to Captain Marge Bevan in December, 1950, at Northcote, Victoria.

An Australian and son of Brigadier William Walker, who wrote the popular chorus, 'I am coming to the Saviour who can wash away my sin', Bramwell Walker as a Captain was one of the party chosen to represent his territory at the International Youth Congress in 1950.

968. The voice that breathed o'er Eden (John Keble (338))

Written with four other verses by special request for the *Salisbury Hymn Book* and dated July 12, 1857; 1930 S.A. song book.

969. We pray Thee, Lord, Thy blessing send (Theodore H. Kitching (529))

1930 S.A. song book.

The song would appear to have been written expressly by the author for his own family, for it was used at the wedding of each of his children, General Wilfred; Mrs. Commissioner Grinsted (Louie); Lieut.-Colonel Theodore; and Adjutant William.

970. Father, we for our children plead (Thomas Hastings)

1899 S.A. song book.

Son of Dr. Seth Hastings, the author (1784–1872) was born at Washington, Lichfield County, Connecticut, and brought up amid rough frontier life where his opportunities for education were meagre; but at an early age he developed a taste for music, began teaching in 1806, and eventually obtained his Mus. Doc. degree. The last forty years of his life were spent in New York, where he took charge of several church choirs. His aim was always the greater glory of God through better musical worship and, although not a great poet, he achieved considerable success in this direction for it is reputed that at one time the American hymnals contained more hymns by Hastings than by any other American writer.

971. O Father, Friend of all mankind (Catherine Baird (400))

The Musical Salvationist, November, 1949; written ' especially for the Dedication of Children section of the song book, with a view to avoiding anything sentimental, adhering only to the Army's ideals concerning this lovely ceremony of dedication '.

972. When mothers of Salem (William Medlen Hutchings)

William Hutchings (1827–76), a Congregationalist, born at Devonport, was a printer and publisher in London. He wrote ' When mothers of Salem ' for the anniversary service of St. Paul's Chapel Sunday-school, Wigan, in 1850; 1899 S.A. song book.

One of the most moving moments during the Remembrance Service in the Agricultural Hall, Islington, for the Army Mother, in October, 1893, was when a thousand children sang these words while a lantern slide was shown of Jesus blessing the children.

973. And now to Thee we render (James F. Swift)

The final verse of one of the eight hymns published in the author's *Hymns for Home and Sacred Festivals*, 1875; written in 1873 and first sung at the Wesleyan Choral Festival in St. George's Hall, Liverpool, in 1874.

Born in Manchester on December 28, 1847, James Swift, organist at the Cranmer Wesleyan Chapel, Liverpool, and later at St. Andrew's Church in the same city, wrote a number of instrumental pieces under the *nom de plume* of ' Godfrey Marks ', and a number of hymns.

974. Give to Jesus glory (W. H. Clark)

See under Song No. 837.

975. God be in my head (Anonymous)

Sarum Primer, 1558; *Oxford Hymn Book*, 1908; *The Musical Salvationist*, November, 1932.

' This miniature song of praise is taken from a Primer in use at Salisbury Cathedral in the sixteenth century. . . . Many ancient hymns contained prayers for the various members of the body, or lists of special dangers from which protection was sought. They were known as Loricas or Breastplates' (*The Fellowship Hymn Book*, 1933).

976. Jesus, so dear to us (V. Hill)

From a complete hymn in *The Fellowship Hymn Book* and probably written especially for the folk-song melody, ' *Treue Liebe* ', with which it is associated.

977. Let nothing disturb thee (Teresa of Avila)

Said to have been taken from Teresa's bookmark, this benediction appeared in *The Musical Salvationist*, July, 1949.

Teresa was born of noble parents in Old Castile in 1515 and at the age of fourteen was sent to a convent, taking the veil four years later at Avila. In 1562 she founded a house of reformed Carmelites for nuns at Avila and in 1567 a house for friars at Medina del Campo. She suffered much ill health and died at Alva in 1582.

She was the author of several works, and in art she is usually shown with a flaming arrow piercing her heart, an allusion to one of her visions.

978. O Father, let Thy love remain (Hendrik Ghysen; *translated by* William Palstra)

Sixth verse of ' O Thou great Christ, Thou Light Eternal ', which was set to an original melody, ' *Christe qui lux es et dies* ' (Staatsburg), 1535; *The Musical Salvationist*, March, 1949.

Hendrik Ghysen (1660–93), a gold and silversmith in Amsterdam, Holland, was a chanter at the Amstel Church in that same city. In 1686 he made out of seventeen different versions of Psalms one new version which was highly appreciated by the general public.

Son of Salvation Army officer parents, Commissioner William Palstra, who entered the work from Weltevreden, Indonesia, in 1925, was interned during the Japanese occupation of that country. On being repatriated to the Netherlands in 1946 he became the Training Principal. He became the Territorial Commander in 1960 and, after serving as International Secretary for Europe, retired in 1969.

979. Praise God, from whom all blessings flow (Thomas Ken (609))

Known universally as 'The Doxology' this is the final verse of Bishop Ken's three hymns. 'The Morning Hymn' (see No. 609); 'The Evening Hymn' (see No. 618); and 'The Midnight Hymn' which is now omitted from most hymnals.

980. Praise God, I'm saved! (Thomas Leighton)

The Army 'Doxology', set to a secular melody entitled 'The anchor's weighed' and usually sung with actions, appeared in *The Musical Salvationist*, May, 1887, where it was the refrain of an Army song:

> A voice fell softly from on high,
> When I, for sin, was weeping sore;
> Lord, save me, was my heartfelt cry
> As loud I knocked at mercy's door.
> 'Twas Jesus' voice, I heard Him sweetly say:
> My Blood has washed thy many sins away;
> Praise Him, who bled and died on Calvary's tree.

Staff-Captain Leighton, known as 'Tommy the Nailer' because he had been a maker of wrought-iron nails, and Staff-Captain Wm. McKernon travelled the country together. In their unregenerate days, as they tramped, they composed songs to sing in public houses; after conversion they remained together and used their gifts for the advantage of the Army.

981. The Lord bless thee, and keep thee

The words of Numbers 6: 24–26, and published as a benediction in *The Musical Salvationist*, July, 1915.

982. The world for God, the world for God (Evangeline Booth (152))

The Musical Salvationist, January, 1935.

General Evangeline Booth wrote 'The world for God' in 1934 during the few weeks between her farewell tour of the United States and her assuming Army leadership in London. One of the General's first decisions was to call the forces of The Salvation Army in all parts of the world to a spiritual offensive against sin and darkness under the title, 'The World for God'. The thought had found expression in the second verse of the song of which this benediction is the chorus:

> The world for God! The world for God!
>   I call to arms the soldiers of the Blood and Fire,
> Go with the Holy Bible. Its words are peace and life
>   To multitudes who struggle with crime and want and strife!
> Go with your songs of mercy; show Christ in loving kindness;
>   Make known the sufferings of the Cross, the sacrifice of God,
> For behold! on a hill—Calvary, Calvary!

983. This, this is the God we adore (Joseph Hart (151))

The last of seven verses which appeared in 1759 and originally commenced, 'No prophet, nor dreamer of dreams'; based on Deuteronomy 13: 1; Martin Maden's *Psalms and Hymns*, 1763; Ch.M.H.B.

LIST OF AUTHORS, TRANSLATORS AND SOURCES

An asterisk indicates that the song has been translated by the person named.

ADAMS, Sarah, 535
AGNEW, May, 162 (ch.)
ALDERSLEY, Nathan, 48
ALEXANDER, Cecil Frances, 22, 86, 118, 938
ALEXANDER, James W., 81*
ALFORD, Henry, 103, 672, 912
ALLAN, J. D., 236
ALLEN, George Nelson (with Thomas Shepherd), 722
ALLEN, Henry, 334
AMBROSE of Milan, 613
ANDERSON, Harry, 407
ANSTEY, H. G., 154
ARNOTT, Arthur S., 532 (ch.), 605, 835
AUBER, Harriet, 116

B. E., 499
BAIRD, Catherine, 400, 625, 767, 874, 890, 971
BAKER, Henry Williams, 35, 516
BAKEWELL, John, 70
BARING-GOULD, Sabine, 680, 862
BARNARD, Samuel, 6
BARTON, Bernard, 347, 515
BATEMAN, James C., 177, 309, 320, 706, 793, 801, 828
BAUGH, William, 420, 431
BAXTER, Lydia, 49
BAXTER, Richard, 768
BENNARD, George, 82
BENNETT, S. Fillmore, 659
BENSON, Mrs. John T., 274
BERNARD of Clairvaux, 45, 81, 581
BERRIDGE, John, 965
BETHAM-EDWARDS, Matilda B., 850
BEVAN, Emma Frances, 180*
BICKERSTETH, Edward H., 219, 524, 777
BINNEY, Thomas, 340
BLACK, James M., 824
BLACKMER, F. A., 501, 667
BLAKE, Charles, 234
BLISS, Philip P., 78, 135, 175, 199, 233, 250, 255, 321, 432, 669, 678, 717, 865
BOADEN, Edward, 573
BODE, John Ernest, 882
BONAR, Horatius, 4, 221, 222, 237, 262, 608, 673
BONAR, Jane C., 247

BOON, Brindley, 709
BOOTH, Ballington, 372, 781
BOOTH, Bramwell, 280, 354, 405, 451, 492, 726, 770
BOOTH, Cornelie, 140, 900
BOOTH, Evangeline, 152, 982
BOOTH, Herbert H., 91, 106, 164, 166, 171, 206, 228, 249, 269, 305, 326, 331, 344, 348, 350, 358, 363, 382, 412, 422, 426 (ch.), 441, 453, 454, 463, 502, 692, 695, 731, 743, 821
BOOTH, William, 119, 167, 386, 395, 495
BOOTH-CLIBBORN, Arthur S., 394
BOOTH-CLIBBORN, Catherine, 397, 401
BOOTH-HELLBERG, Lucy, 629, 721, 735
BOOTH-TUCKER, Emma, 301, 549, 596
BOOTH-TUCKER, Frederick, 365, 419, 674, 703, 875
BOTTOME, Francis, 122, 296, 470, 491, 508, 799
BOURIGNON, Antoinette, 433
BOURNE, Hugh, 155, 291 (with William Sanders)
BOVAN, Arthur, 658
BOWRING, John, 72
BRADY, Nicholas, 16, 561 (with Nahum Tate)
BRAND, Will. J., 52, 485, 510, 517, 648, 698, 711, 794, 884, 889, 910, 947, 959, 963
BRIDGES, Matthew (with Godfrey Thring), 94
BROMEHEAD, Joseph, 647
BROOKS, Phillips, 937
BROWNE, Simon, 110
BUELL, Hattie, 283
BUNYAN, John, 878
BURNS, James Drummond, 852
BURRELL, W. H., 421
BURTON, Henry, 143
BURTON, John, Jun., 885
BURTON, John, Sen., 513
BYROM, John, 930

CAMPBELL, Etta, 196
CAMPBELL, Jane Montgomery, 923*
CAMPBELL, John, 787
CARTER, R. Kelso, 309 (ch.)
CARY, Phoebe, 653
CASSON, Hodgson, 290

293

INDEX TO THE FIRST LINES OF SONGS

304